MACBETH

ALSO IN THE **NO FEAR SHAKESPEARE GRAPHIC NOVELS** SERIES:

HAMLET
ROMEO AND JULIET

NO FEAR SHAKESPEARE | Graphic Novels

MACBETH

ILLUSTRATED BY KEN HOSHINE

SPARKNOTES

SPARK PUBLISHING
120 FIFTH AVENUE
NEW YORK, NY 10011
WWW.SPARKNOTES.COM

ISBN-13: 978-1-4114-9871-6
ISBN-10: 1-4114-9871-2

LIBRARY OF CONGRESS CATALOGING-IN-PUBLICATION DATA

HOSHINE, KEN, 1977-
    MACBETH / [ILLUSTRATED BY KEN HOSHINE].
        P. CM.—(NO FEAR SHAKESPEARE GRAPHIC NOVELS)
    ADAPTATION OF MACBETH BY WILLIAM SHAKESPEARE.
    ISBN-13: 978-1-4114-9871-6 (PBK.)
    ISBN-10: 1-4114-9871-2 (PBK.)
    1. GRAPHIC NOVELS. I. SHAKESPEARE, WILLIAM, 1564-1616. MACBETH. II. TITLE.
PN6727.H594M33 2008
741.5973—DC22

                                                                    2007044538

PLEASE SUBMIT CHANGES OR REPORT ERRORS TO WWW.SPARKNOTES.COM/ERRORS.

PRINTED AND BOUND IN THE UNITED STATES

10   9   8   7   6   5   4   3   2

FRONTMATTER, BACKMATTER, AND FOLIO FONT BY MATT WIEGLE

ACKNOWLEDGMENTS

I WOULD LIKE TO THANK NINA RASTOGI, GREG JOHNSON, KEVIN BAIER, JOHN CROWTHER, AND THE REST OF THE SPARKNOTES STAFF FOR THEIR EXCEPTIONAL ASSISTANCE AND PATIENCE THROUGHOUT THE ENTIRE PROCESS. I WOULD ALSO LIKE TO THANK MY FRIENDS AND FAMILY FOR THEIR SUPPORT. AND A VERY SPECIAL THANKS TO J, WITHOUT WHOM I COULD NOT HAVE COMPLETED THIS PROJECT.

· CHARACTERS ·

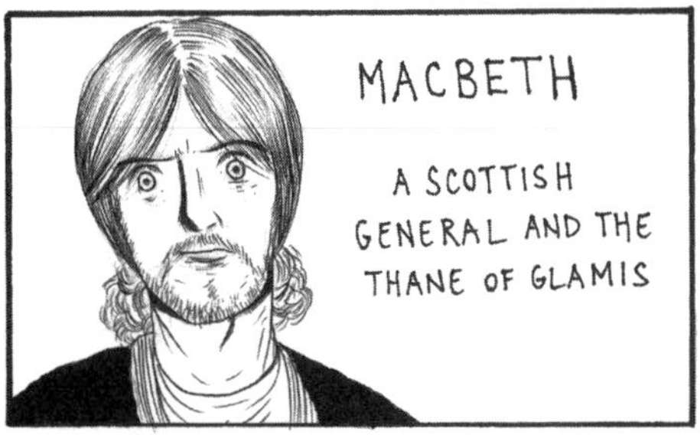
MACBETH
A SCOTTISH GENERAL AND THE THANE OF GLAMIS

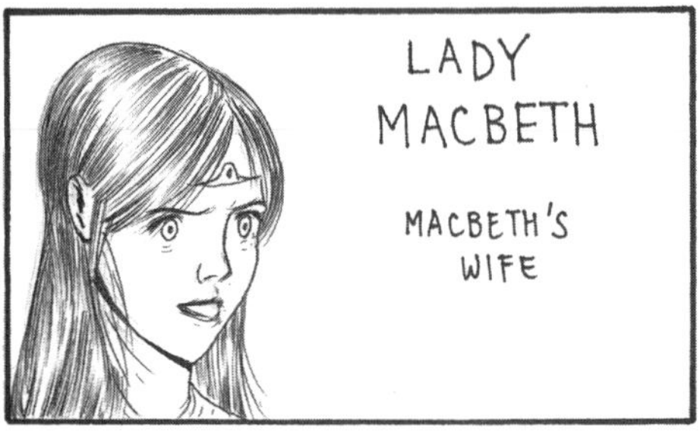
LADY MACBETH
MACBETH'S WIFE

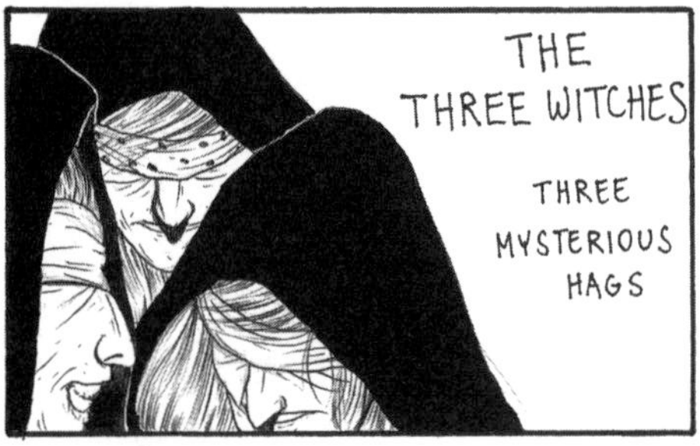
THE THREE WITCHES
THREE MYSTERIOUS HAGS

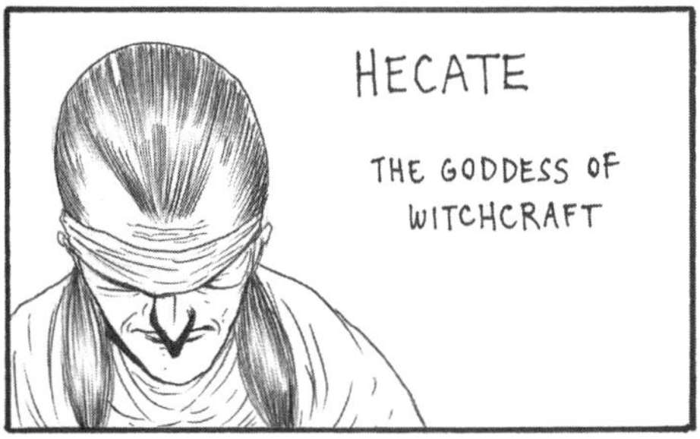
HECATE
THE GODDESS OF WITCHCRAFT

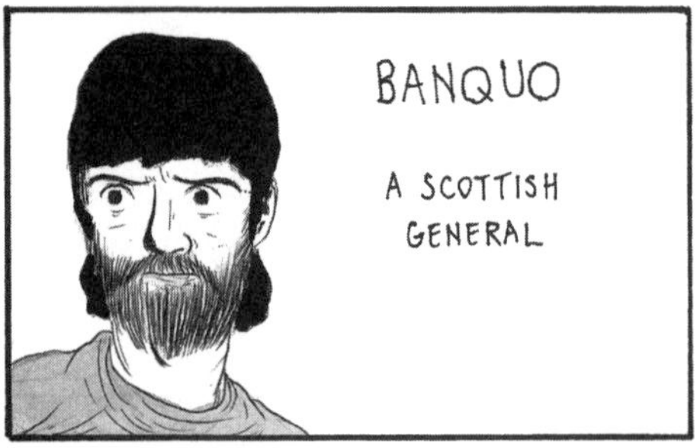
BANQUO
A SCOTTISH GENERAL

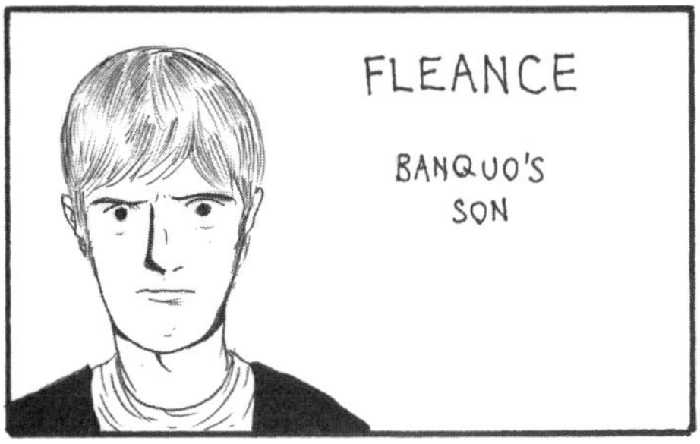
FLEANCE
BANQUO'S SON

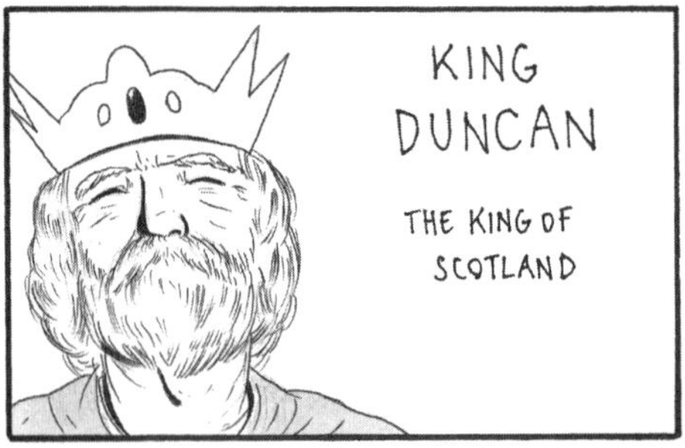
KING DUNCAN
THE KING OF SCOTLAND

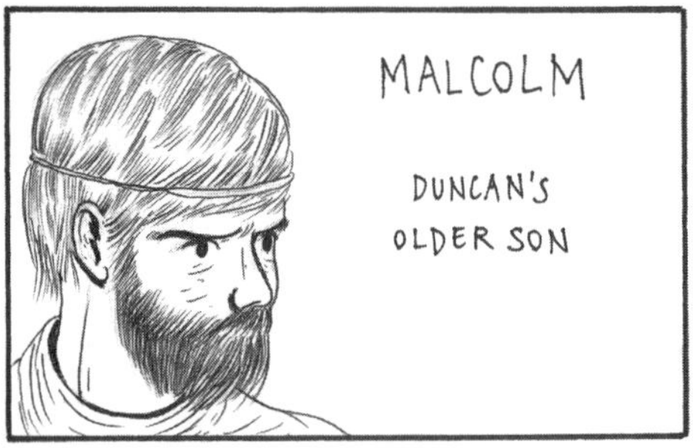
MALCOLM
DUNCAN'S OLDER SON

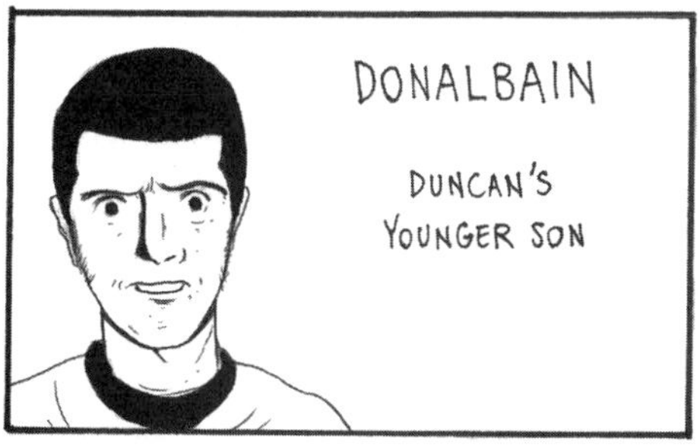
DONALBAIN
DUNCAN'S YOUNGER SON

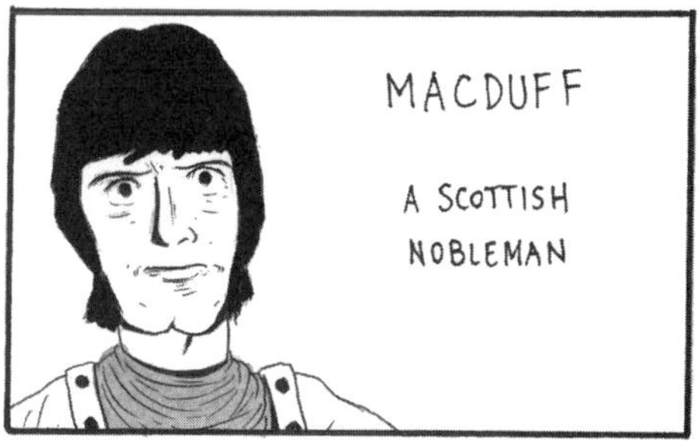
MACDUFF
A SCOTTISH NOBLEMAN

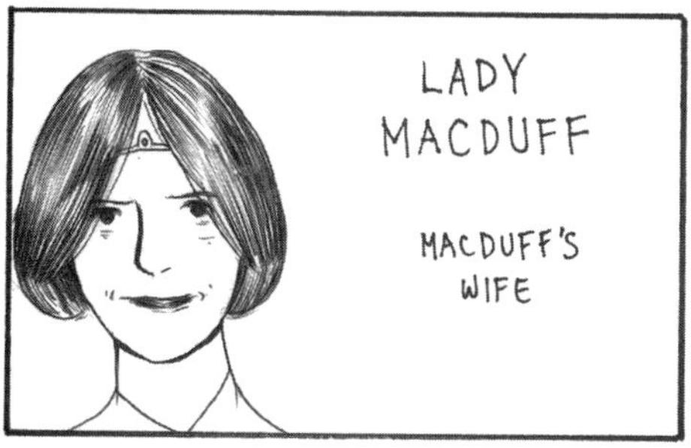
LADY MACDUFF
MACDUFF'S WIFE

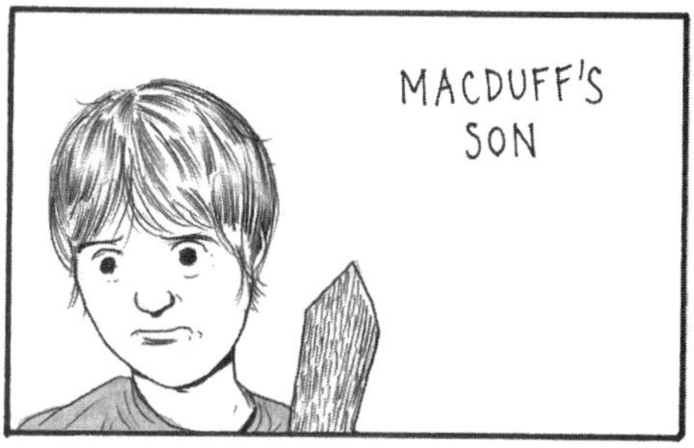
MACDUFF'S SON

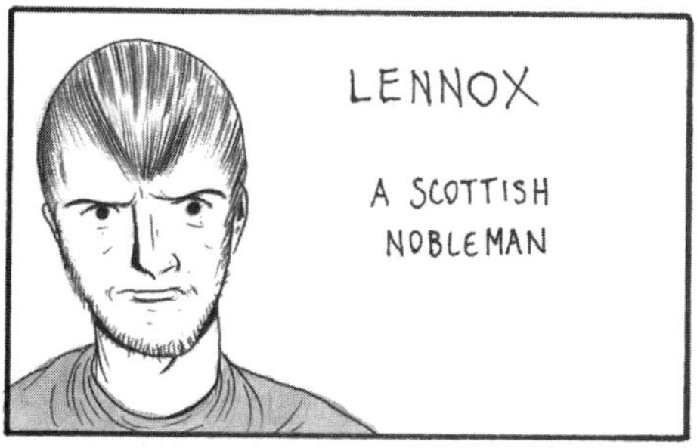
LENNOX
A SCOTTISH NOBLEMAN

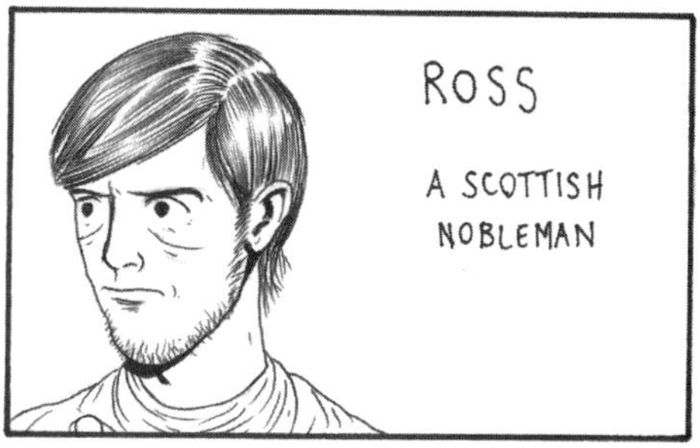
ROSS
A SCOTTISH NOBLEMAN

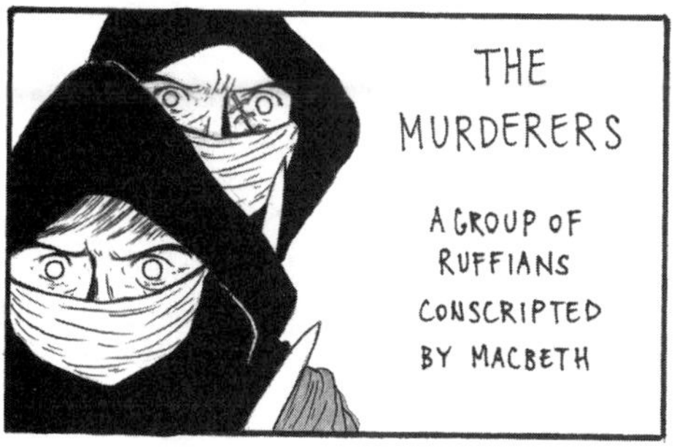
THE MURDERERS
A GROUP OF RUFFIANS CONSCRIPTED BY MACBETH

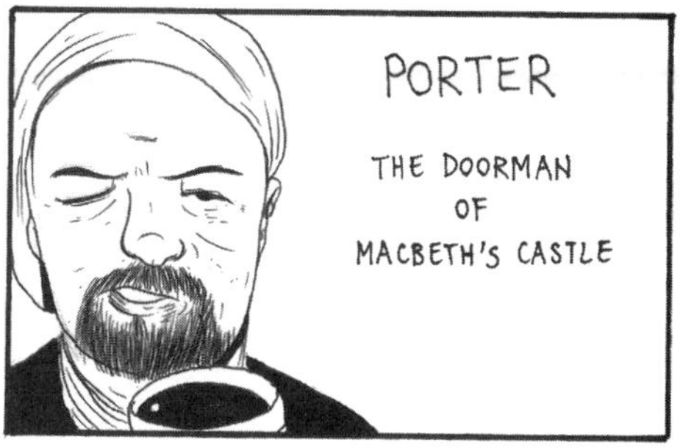
PORTER
THE DOORMAN OF MACBETH'S CASTLE

ACT I

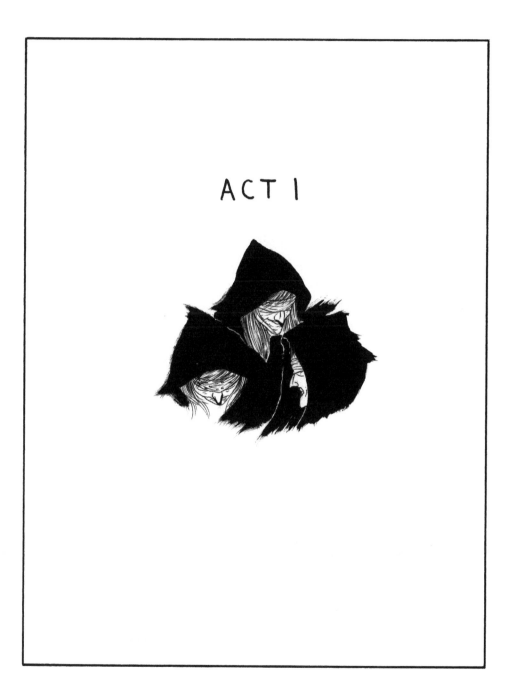

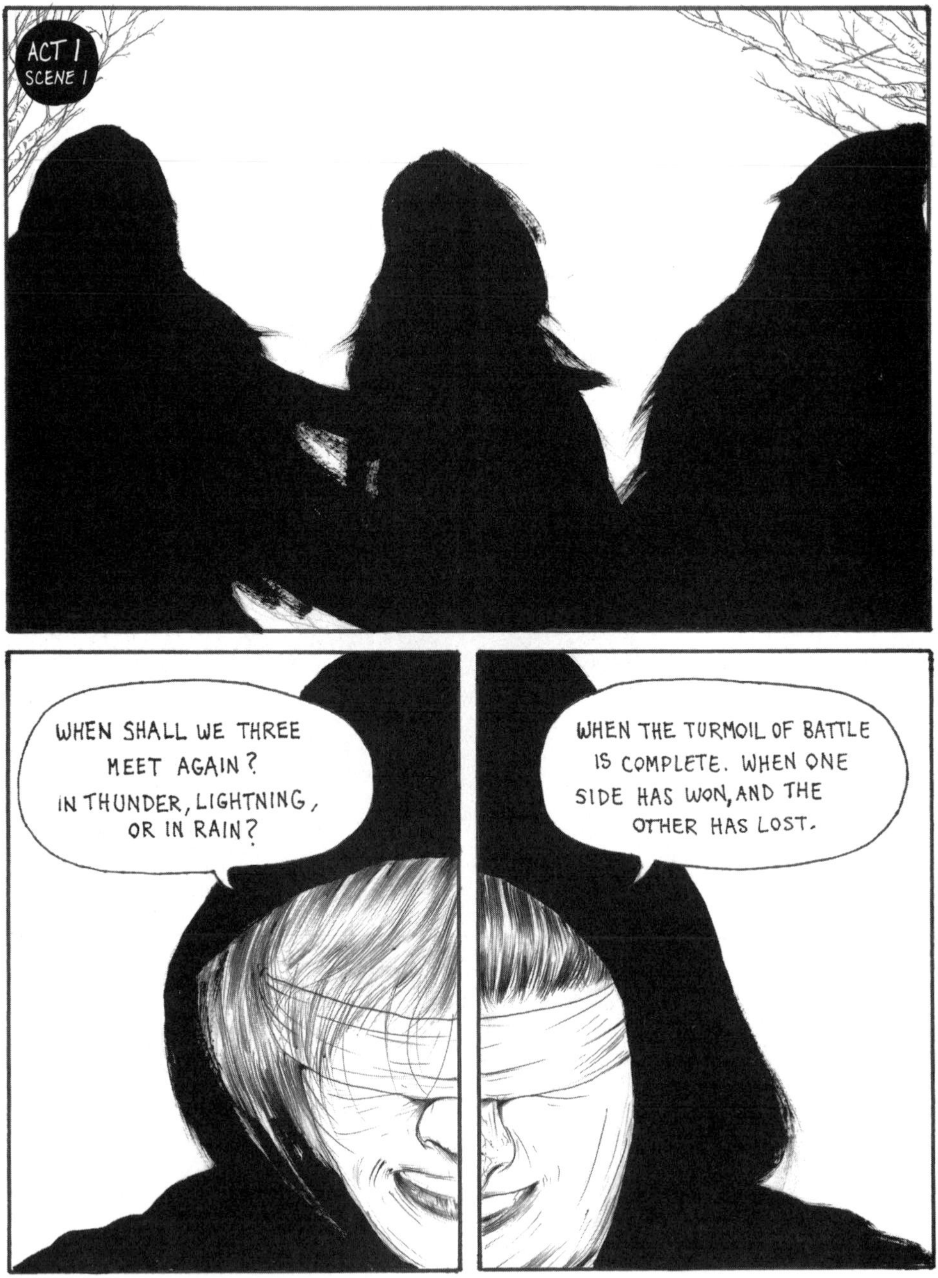
ACT I
SCENE I
WHEN SHALL WE THREE MEET AGAIN? IN THUNDER, LIGHTNING, OR IN RAIN?
WHEN THE TURMOIL OF BATTLE IS COMPLETE. WHEN ONE SIDE HAS WON, AND THE OTHER HAS LOST.

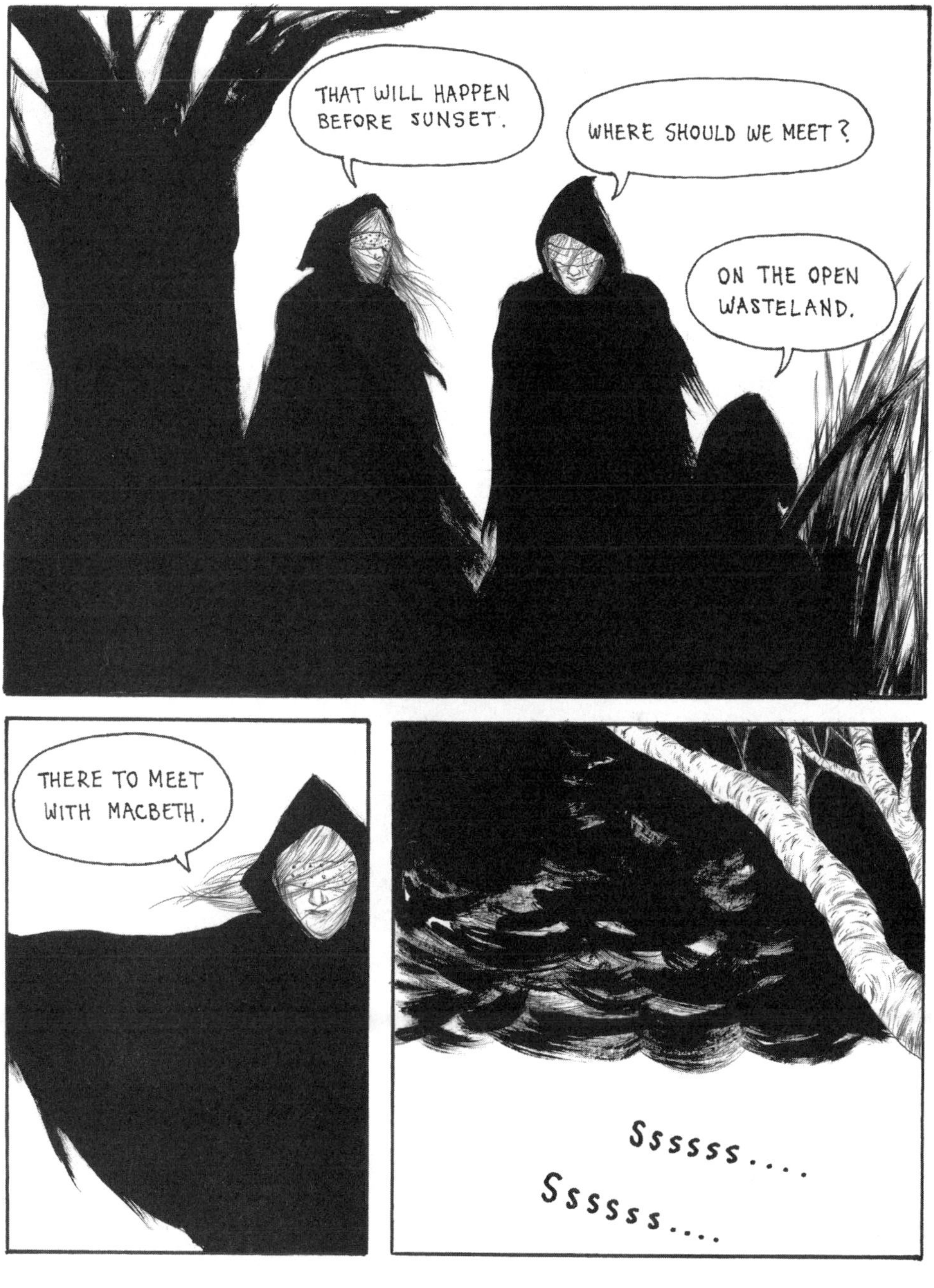
THAT WILL HAPPEN BEFORE SUNSET.
WHERE SHOULD WE MEET?
ON THE OPEN WASTELAND.
THERE TO MEET WITH MACBETH.
Ssssss....
Ssssss....

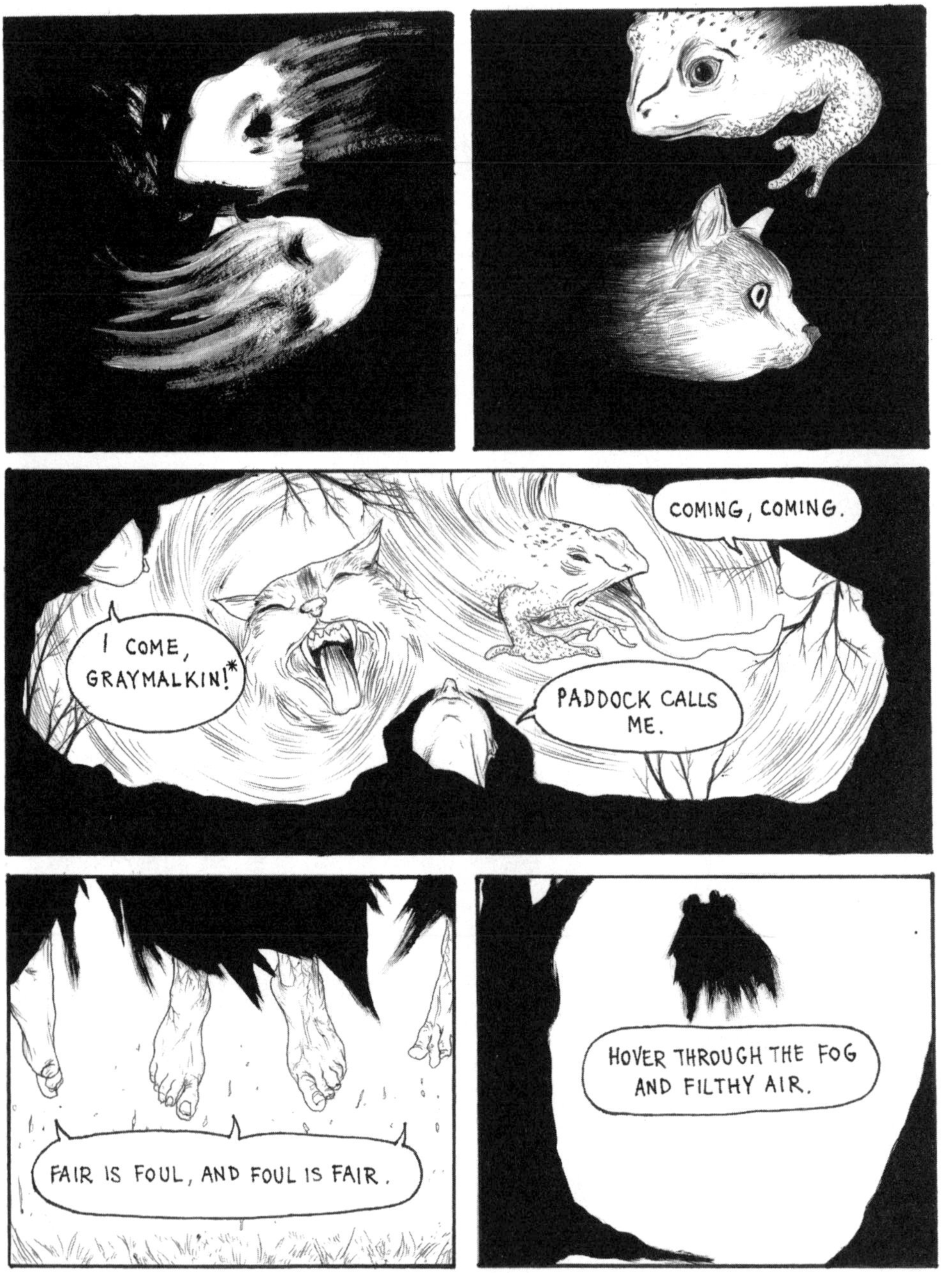
COMING, COMING.
I COME, GRAYMALKIN!*
PADDOCK CALLS ME.
FAIR IS FOUL, AND FOUL IS FAIR.
HOVER THROUGH THE FOG AND FILTHY AIR.

* GRAYMALKIN, PADDOCK = THE NAMES OF THE WITCHES' FAMILIARS, OR SPIRIT HELPERS

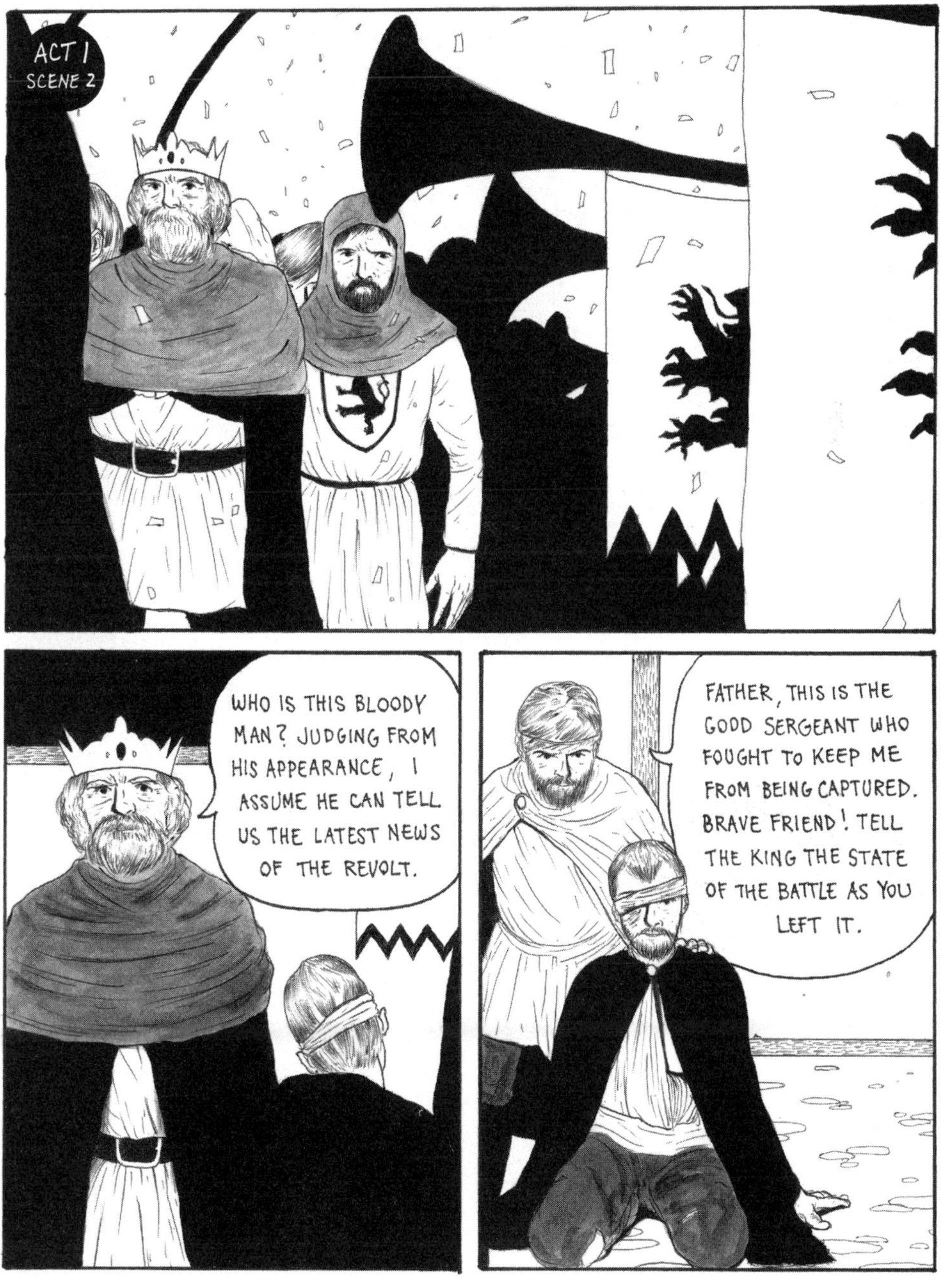
ACT I
SCENE 2
WHO IS THIS BLOODY MAN? JUDGING FROM HIS APPEARANCE, I ASSUME HE CAN TELL US THE LATEST NEWS OF THE REVOLT.
FATHER, THIS IS THE GOOD SERGEANT WHO FOUGHT TO KEEP ME FROM BEING CAPTURED. BRAVE FRIEND! TELL THE KING THE STATE OF THE BATTLE AS YOU LEFT IT.

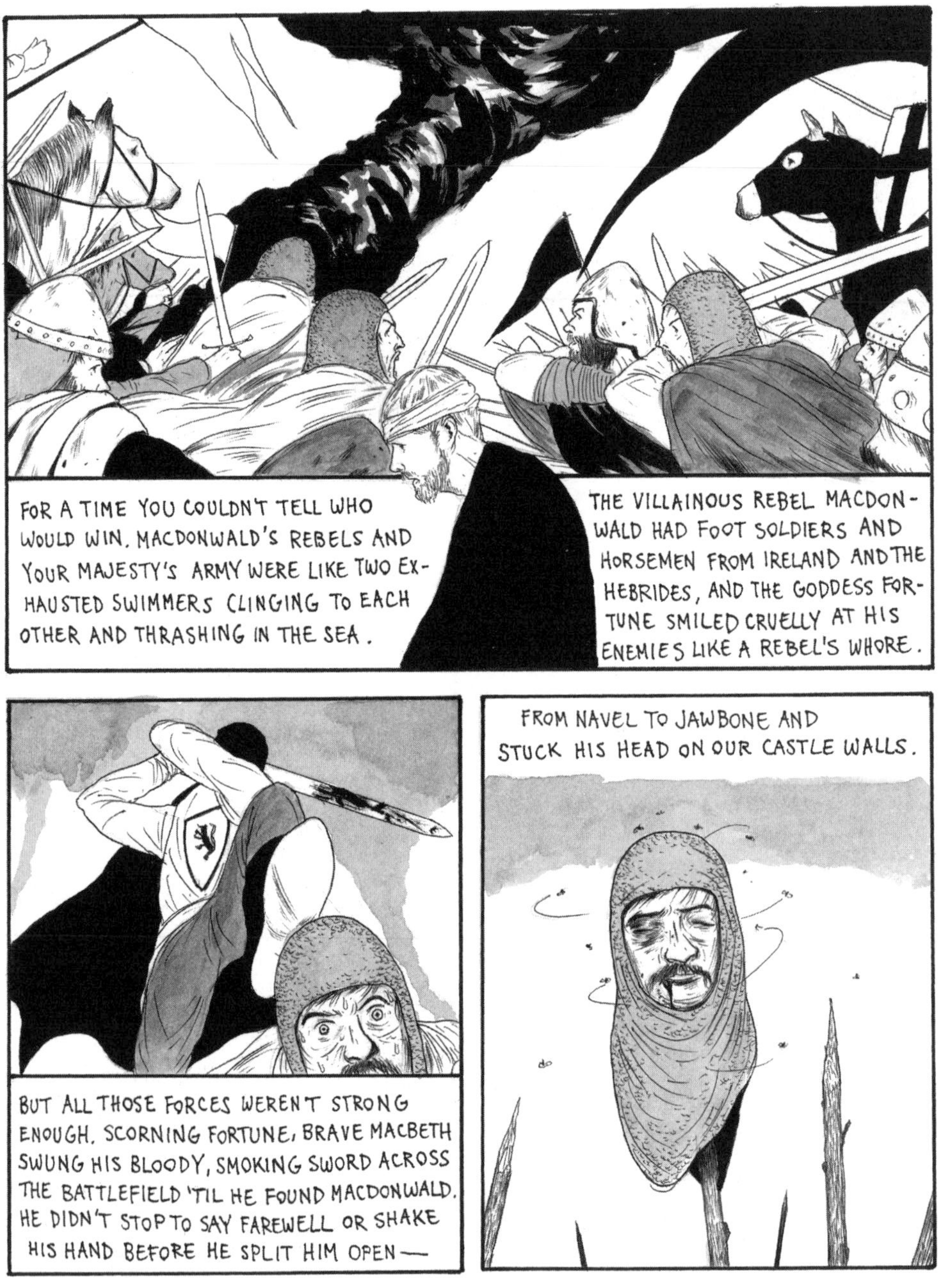
FOR A TIME YOU COULDN'T TELL WHO WOULD WIN. MACDONWALD'S REBELS AND YOUR MAJESTY'S ARMY WERE LIKE TWO EXHAUSTED SWIMMERS CLINGING TO EACH OTHER AND THRASHING IN THE SEA.
THE VILLAINOUS REBEL MACDONWALD HAD FOOT SOLDIERS AND HORSEMEN FROM IRELAND AND THE HEBRIDES, AND THE GODDESS FORTUNE SMILED CRUELLY AT HIS ENEMIES LIKE A REBEL'S WHORE.
BUT ALL THOSE FORCES WEREN'T STRONG ENOUGH. SCORNING FORTUNE, BRAVE MACBETH SWUNG HIS BLOODY, SMOKING SWORD ACROSS THE BATTLEFIELD 'TIL HE FOUND MACDONWALD. HE DIDN'T STOP TO SAY FAREWELL OR SHAKE HIS HAND BEFORE HE SPLIT HIM OPEN—
FROM NAVEL TO JAWBONE AND STUCK HIS HEAD ON OUR CASTLE WALLS.

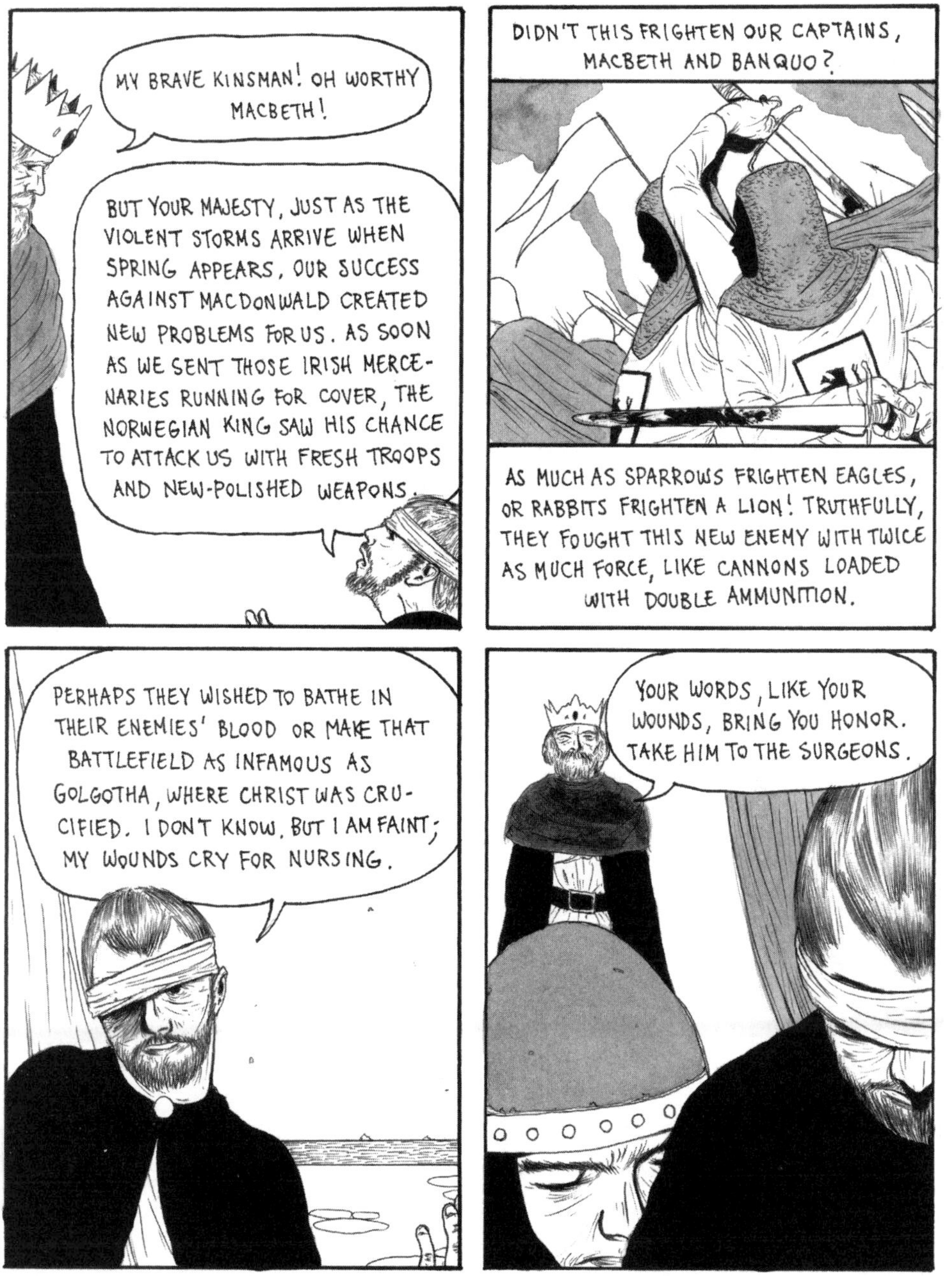
MY BRAVE KINSMAN! OH WORTHY MACBETH!
BUT YOUR MAJESTY, JUST AS THE VIOLENT STORMS ARRIVE WHEN SPRING APPEARS, OUR SUCCESS AGAINST MACDONWALD CREATED NEW PROBLEMS FOR US. AS SOON AS WE SENT THOSE IRISH MERCENARIES RUNNING FOR COVER, THE NORWEGIAN KING SAW HIS CHANCE TO ATTACK US WITH FRESH TROOPS AND NEW-POLISHED WEAPONS.
DIDN'T THIS FRIGHTEN OUR CAPTAINS, MACBETH AND BANQUO?
AS MUCH AS SPARROWS FRIGHTEN EAGLES, OR RABBITS FRIGHTEN A LION! TRUTHFULLY, THEY FOUGHT THIS NEW ENEMY WITH TWICE AS MUCH FORCE, LIKE CANNONS LOADED WITH DOUBLE AMMUNITION.
PERHAPS THEY WISHED TO BATHE IN THEIR ENEMIES' BLOOD OR MAKE THAT BATTLEFIELD AS INFAMOUS AS GOLGOTHA, WHERE CHRIST WAS CRUCIFIED. I DON'T KNOW. BUT I AM FAINT; MY WOUNDS CRY FOR NURSING.
YOUR WORDS, LIKE YOUR WOUNDS, BRING YOU HONOR. TAKE HIM TO THE SURGEONS.

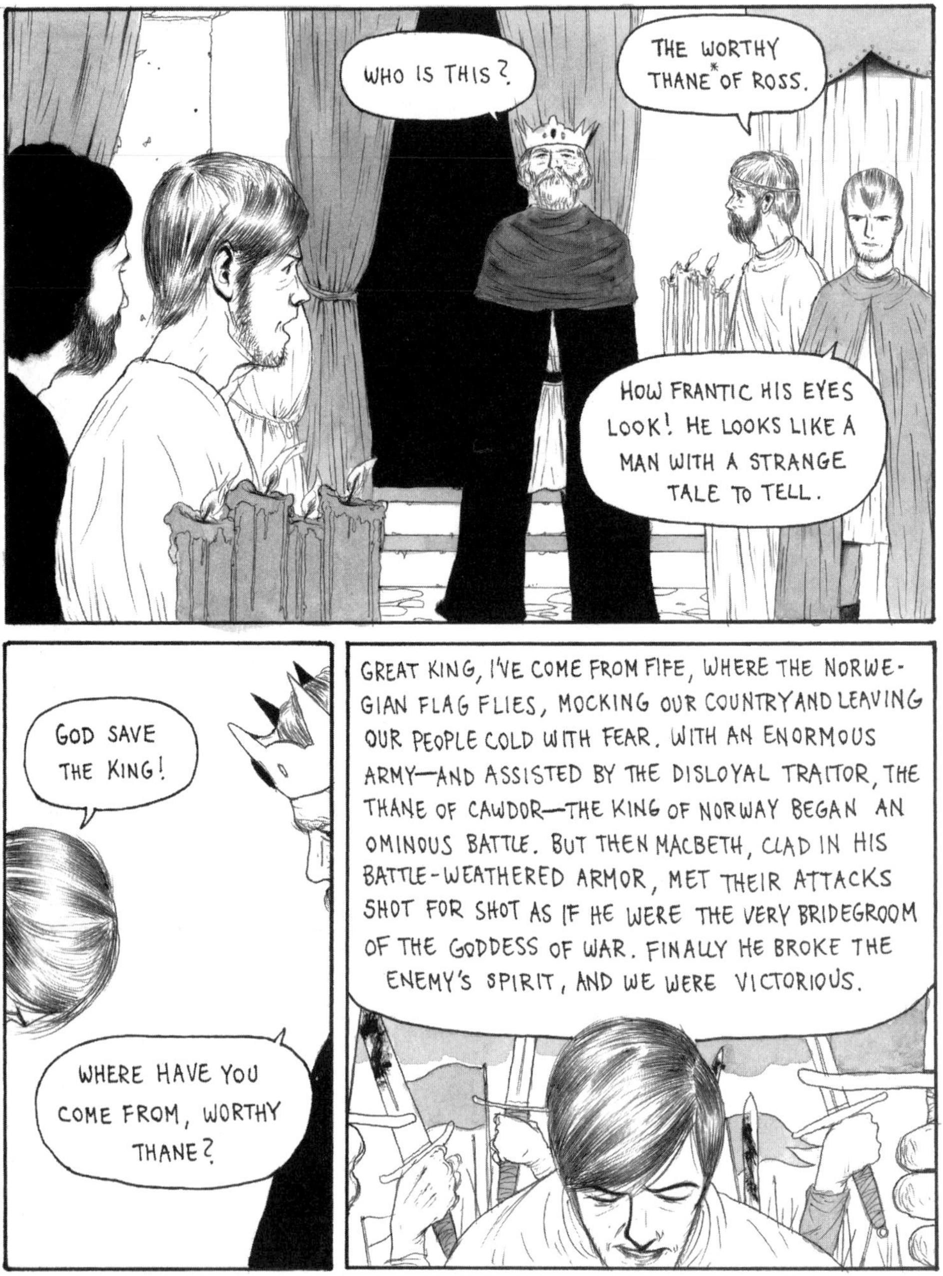
WHO IS THIS?
THE WORTHY THANE* OF ROSS.
HOW FRANTIC HIS EYES LOOK! HE LOOKS LIKE A MAN WITH A STRANGE TALE TO TELL.
GOD SAVE THE KING!
WHERE HAVE YOU COME FROM, WORTHY THANE?
GREAT KING, I'VE COME FROM FIFE, WHERE THE NORWEGIAN FLAG FLIES, MOCKING OUR COUNTRY AND LEAVING OUR PEOPLE COLD WITH FEAR. WITH AN ENORMOUS ARMY—AND ASSISTED BY THE DISLOYAL TRAITOR, THE THANE OF CAWDOR—THE KING OF NORWAY BEGAN AN OMINOUS BATTLE. BUT THEN MACBETH, CLAD IN HIS BATTLE-WEATHERED ARMOR, MET THEIR ATTACKS SHOT FOR SHOT AS IF HE WERE THE VERY BRIDEGROOM OF THE GODDESS OF WAR. FINALLY HE BROKE THE ENEMY'S SPIRIT, AND WE WERE VICTORIOUS.

* THANE = SCOTTISH TITLE OF NOBILITY

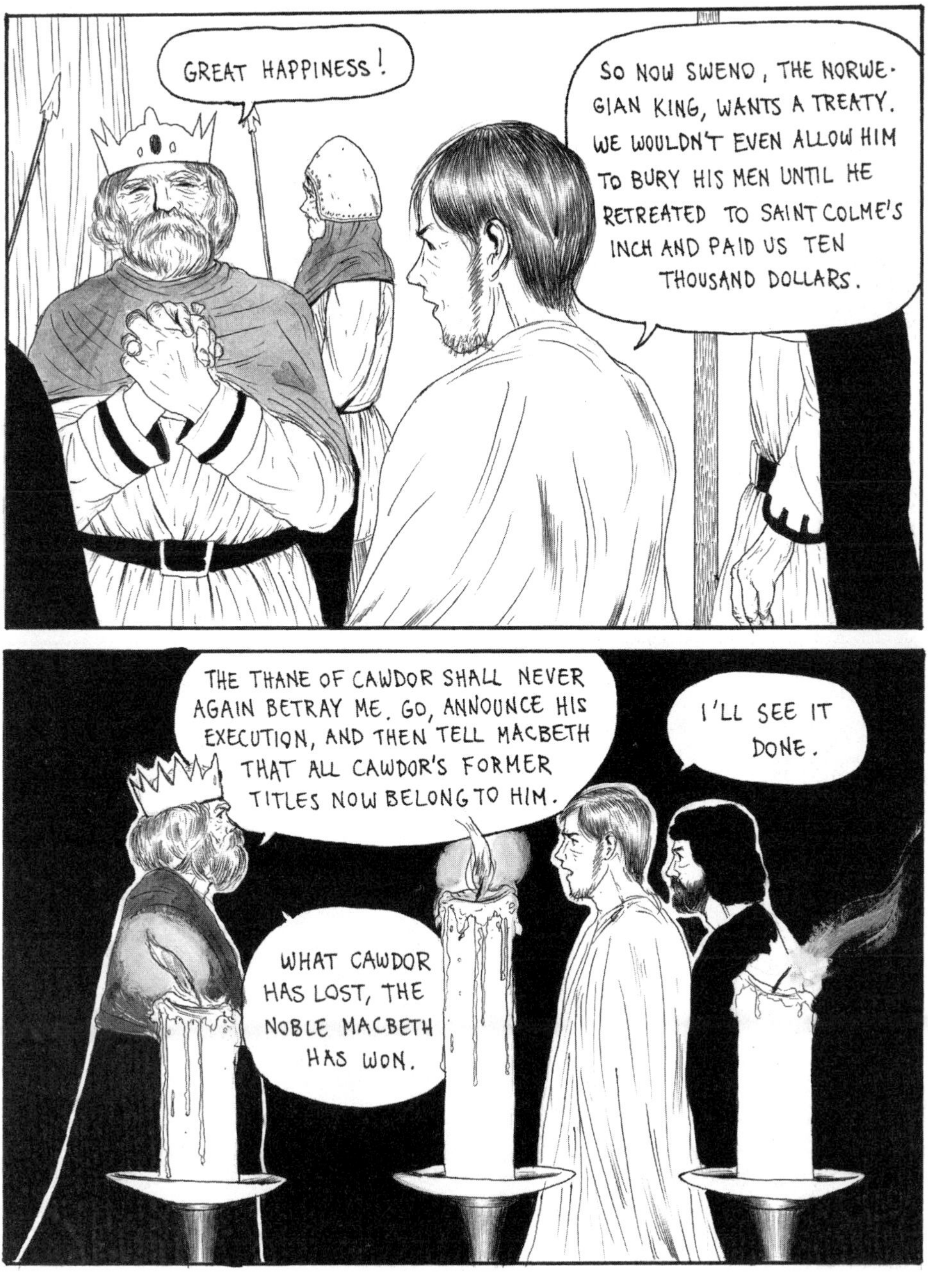
GREAT HAPPINESS!
SO NOW SWENO, THE NORWEGIAN KING, WANTS A TREATY. WE WOULDN'T EVEN ALLOW HIM TO BURY HIS MEN UNTIL HE RETREATED TO SAINT COLME'S INCH AND PAID US TEN THOUSAND DOLLARS.
THE THANE OF CAWDOR SHALL NEVER AGAIN BETRAY ME. GO, ANNOUNCE HIS EXECUTION, AND THEN TELL MACBETH THAT ALL CAWDOR'S FORMER TITLES NOW BELONG TO HIM.
I'LL SEE IT DONE.
WHAT CAWDOR HAS LOST, THE NOBLE MACBETH HAS WON.

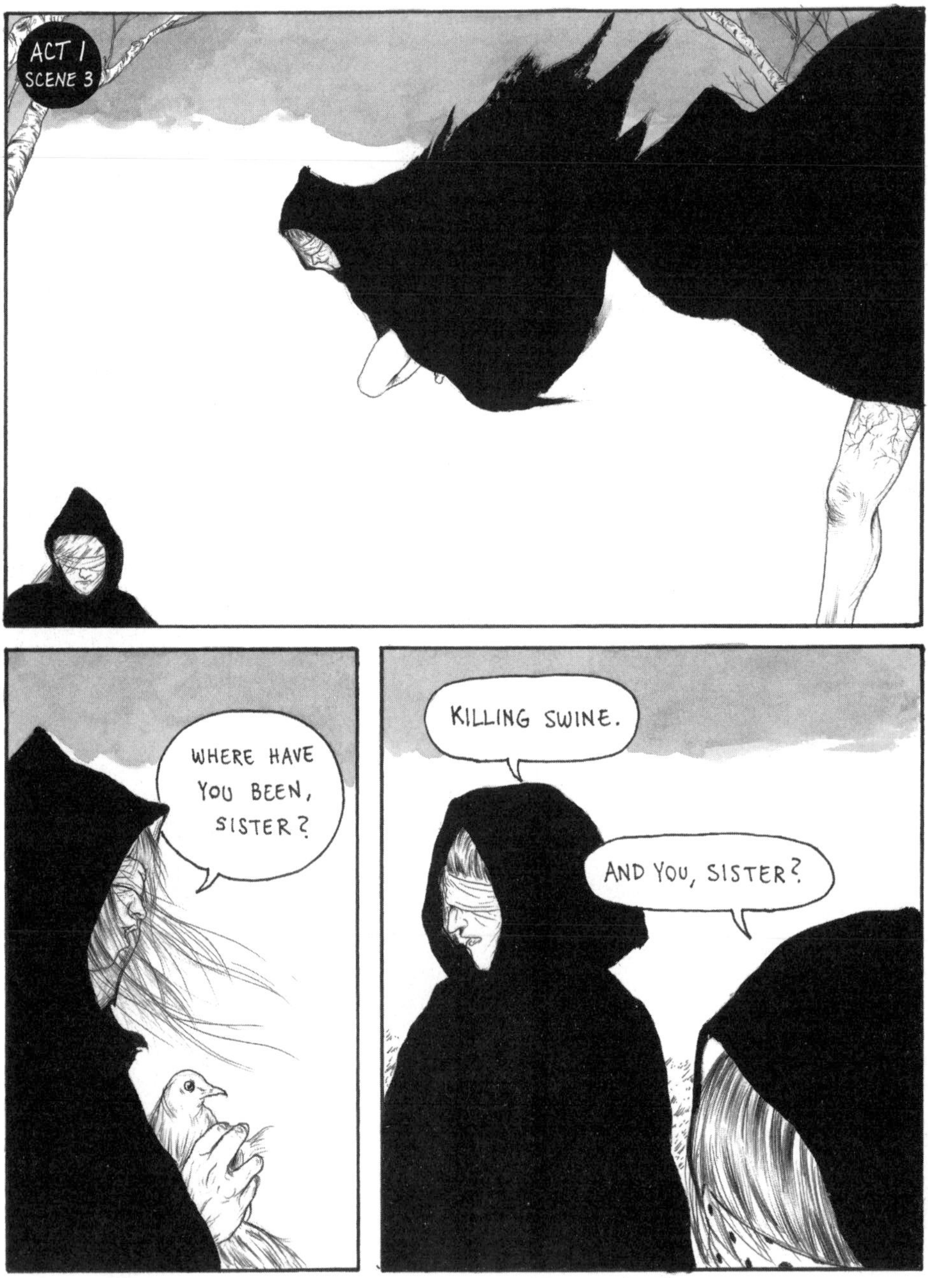
ACT I
SCENE 3
WHERE HAVE YOU BEEN, SISTER?
KILLING SWINE.
AND YOU, SISTER?

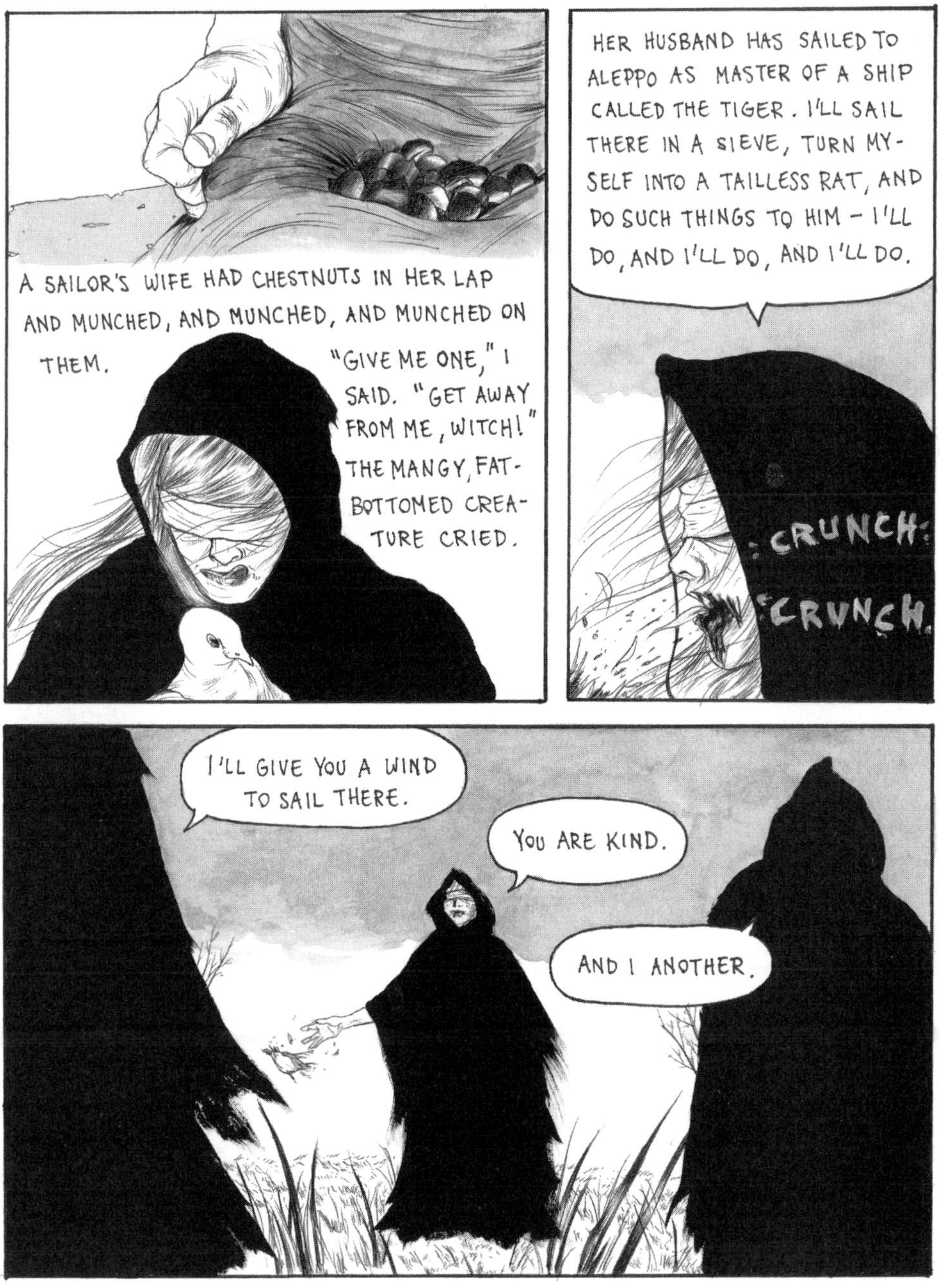

A SAILOR'S WIFE HAD CHESTNUTS IN HER LAP AND MUNCHED, AND MUNCHED, AND MUNCHED ON THEM.
"GIVE ME ONE," I SAID. "GET AWAY FROM ME, WITCH!" THE MANGY, FAT-BOTTOMED CREA-TURE CRIED.
HER HUSBAND HAS SAILED TO ALEPPO AS MASTER OF A SHIP CALLED THE TIGER. I'LL SAIL THERE IN A SIEVE, TURN MY-SELF INTO A TAILLESS RAT, AND DO SUCH THINGS TO HIM – I'LL DO, AND I'LL DO, AND I'LL DO.
CRUNCH
CRUNCH
I'LL GIVE YOU A WIND TO SAIL THERE.
YOU ARE KIND.
AND I ANOTHER.

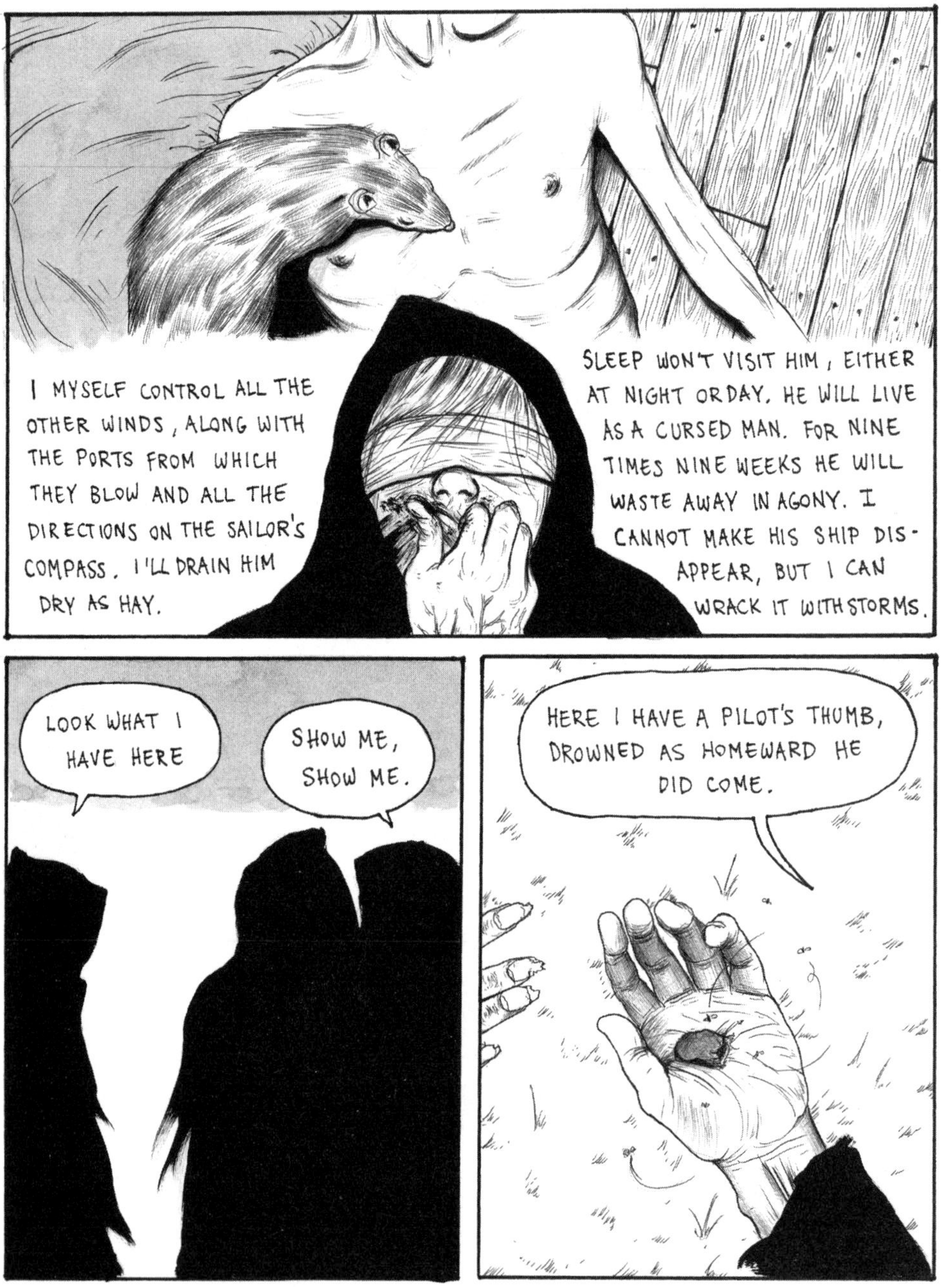
I MYSELF CONTROL ALL THE OTHER WINDS, ALONG WITH THE PORTS FROM WHICH THEY BLOW AND ALL THE DIRECTIONS ON THE SAILOR'S COMPASS. I'LL DRAIN HIM DRY AS HAY.
SLEEP WON'T VISIT HIM, EITHER AT NIGHT OR DAY. HE WILL LIVE AS A CURSED MAN. FOR NINE TIMES NINE WEEKS HE WILL WASTE AWAY IN AGONY. I CANNOT MAKE HIS SHIP DISAPPEAR, BUT I CAN WRACK IT WITH STORMS.
LOOK WHAT I HAVE HERE
SHOW ME, SHOW ME.
HERE I HAVE A PILOT'S THUMB, DROWNED AS HOMEWARD HE DID COME.

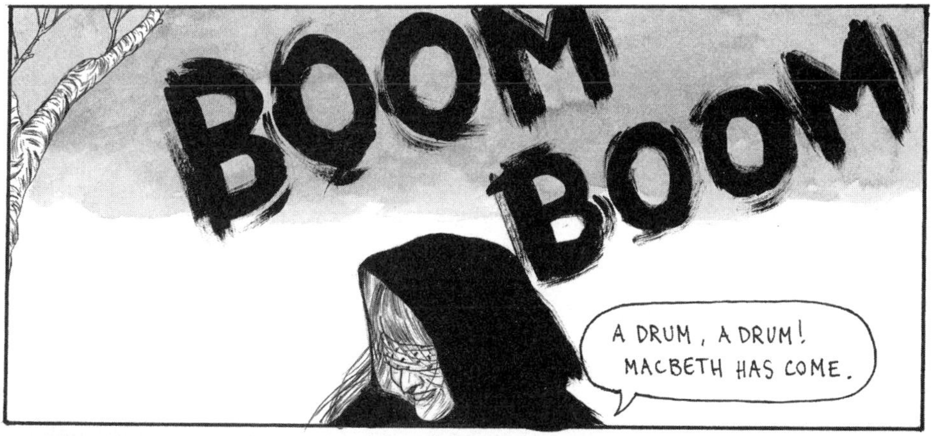
BOOM BOOM
A DRUM, A DRUM! MACBETH HAS COME.

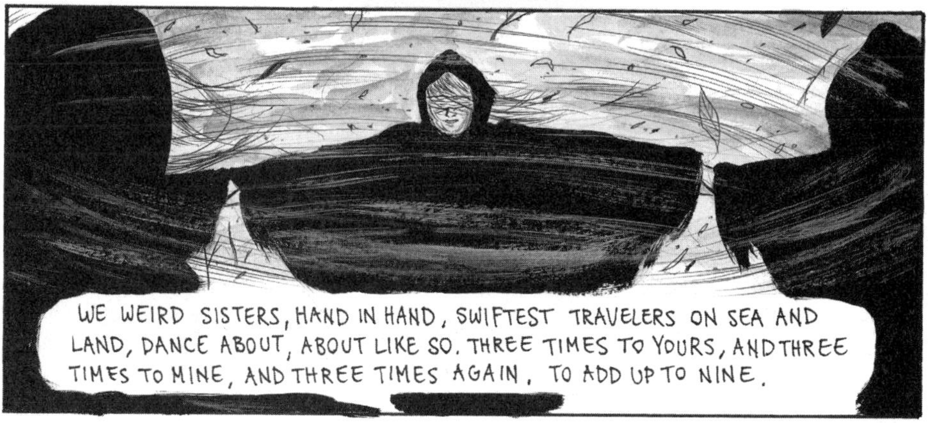
WE WEIRD SISTERS, HAND IN HAND, SWIFTEST TRAVELERS ON SEA AND LAND, DANCE ABOUT, ABOUT LIKE SO. THREE TIMES TO YOURS, AND THREE TIMES TO MINE, AND THREE TIMES AGAIN, TO ADD UP TO NINE.

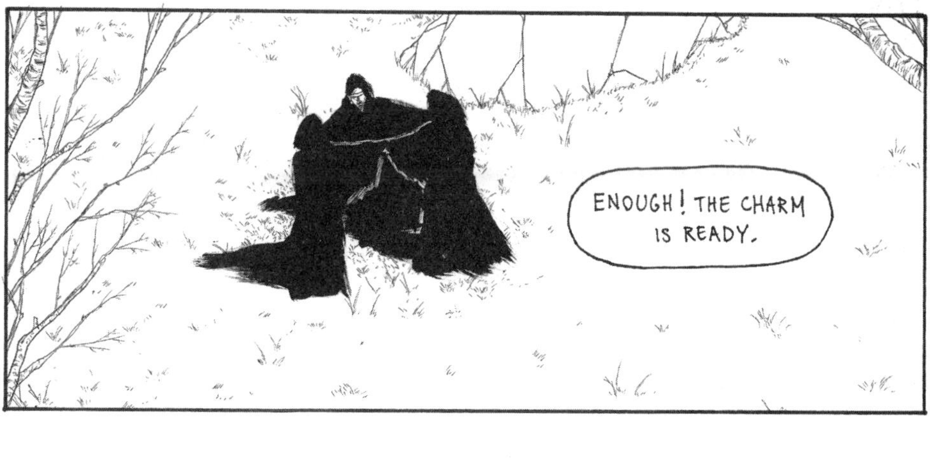
ENOUGH! THE CHARM IS READY.

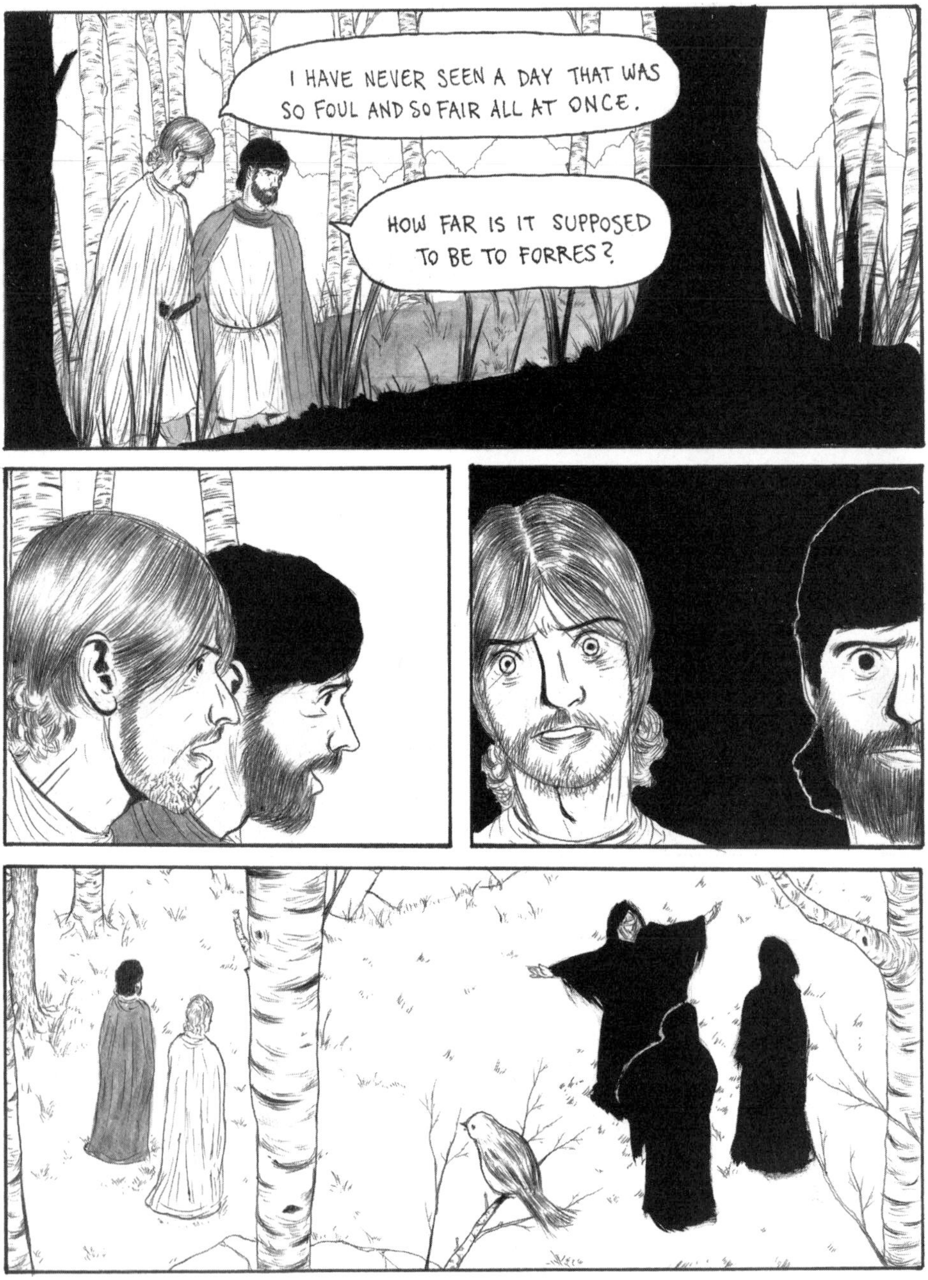
I HAVE NEVER SEEN A DAY THAT WAS SO FOUL AND SO FAIR ALL AT ONCE.
HOW FAR IS IT SUPPOSED TO BE TO FORRES?

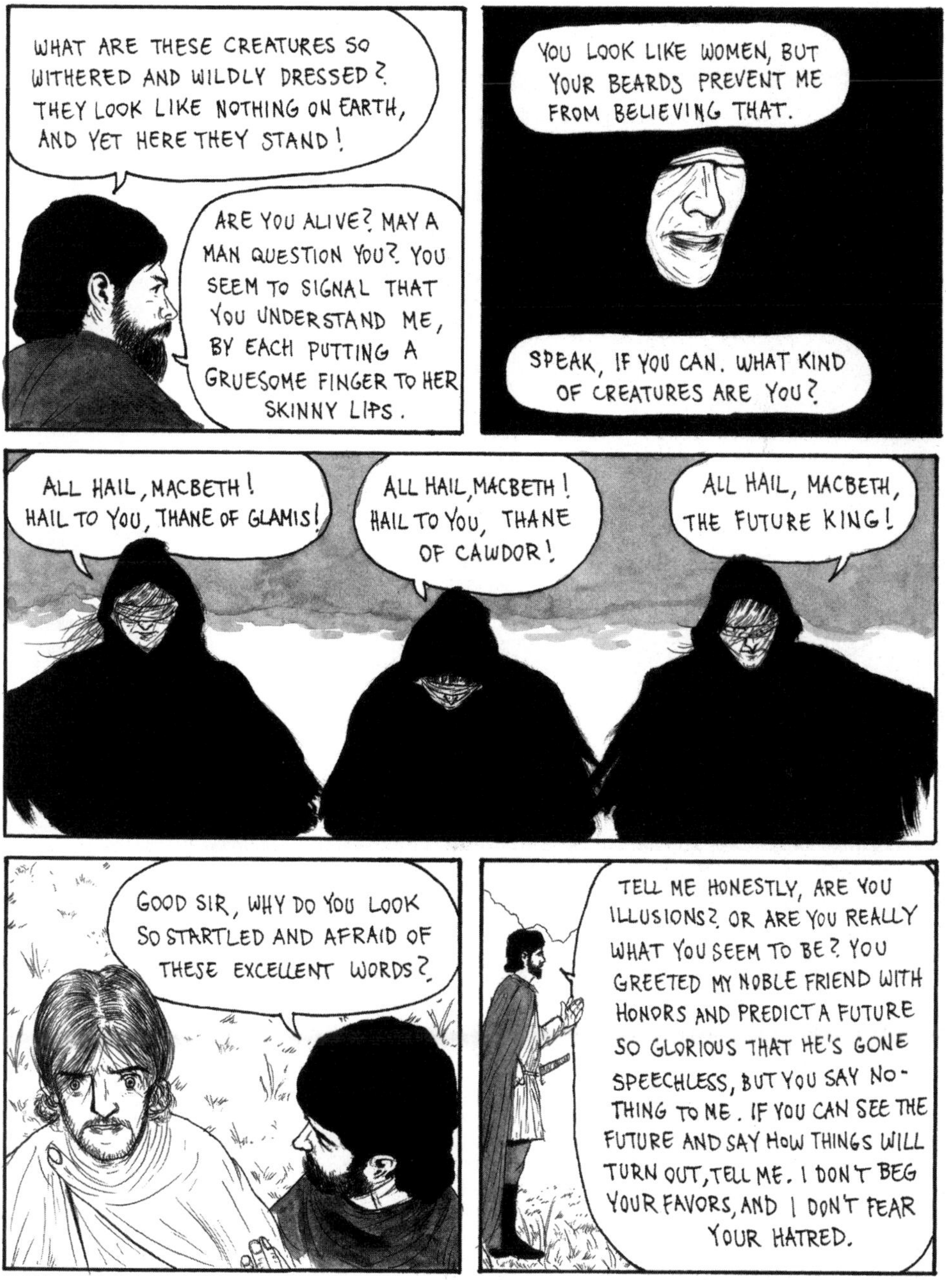
WHAT ARE THESE CREATURES SO WITHERED AND WILDLY DRESSED? THEY LOOK LIKE NOTHING ON EARTH, AND YET HERE THEY STAND!
ARE YOU ALIVE? MAY A MAN QUESTION YOU? YOU SEEM TO SIGNAL THAT YOU UNDERSTAND ME, BY EACH PUTTING A GRUESOME FINGER TO HER SKINNY LIPS.
YOU LOOK LIKE WOMEN, BUT YOUR BEARDS PREVENT ME FROM BELIEVING THAT.
SPEAK, IF YOU CAN. WHAT KIND OF CREATURES ARE YOU?
ALL HAIL, MACBETH! HAIL TO YOU, THANE OF GLAMIS!
ALL HAIL, MACBETH! HAIL TO YOU, THANE OF CAWDOR!
ALL HAIL, MACBETH, THE FUTURE KING!
GOOD SIR, WHY DO YOU LOOK SO STARTLED AND AFRAID OF THESE EXCELLENT WORDS?
TELL ME HONESTLY, ARE YOU ILLUSIONS? OR ARE YOU REALLY WHAT YOU SEEM TO BE? YOU GREETED MY NOBLE FRIEND WITH HONORS AND PREDICT A FUTURE SO GLORIOUS THAT HE'S GONE SPEECHLESS, BUT YOU SAY NOTHING TO ME. IF YOU CAN SEE THE FUTURE AND SAY HOW THINGS WILL TURN OUT, TELL ME. I DON'T BEG YOUR FAVORS, AND I DON'T FEAR YOUR HATRED.

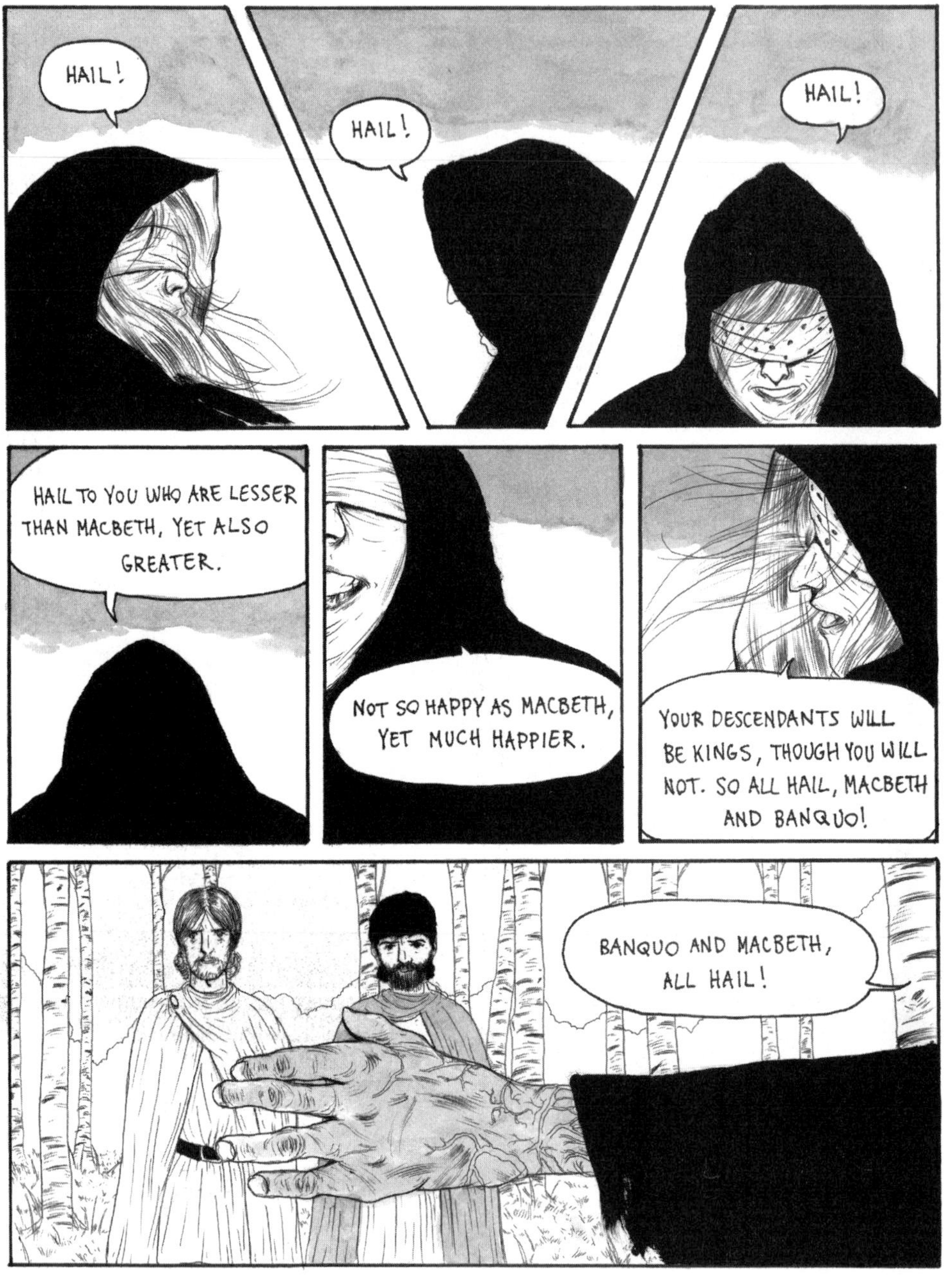
HAIL!
HAIL!
HAIL!
HAIL TO YOU WHO ARE LESSER THAN MACBETH, YET ALSO GREATER.
NOT SO HAPPY AS MACBETH, YET MUCH HAPPIER.
YOUR DESCENDANTS WILL BE KINGS, THOUGH YOU WILL NOT. SO ALL HAIL, MACBETH AND BANQUO!
BANQUO AND MACBETH, ALL HAIL!

WAIT! YOU INCONPLETE SPEAKERS, TELL ME MORE. I KNOW THAT I AM THE THANE OF GLAMIS BECAUSE I INHERITED THE POSITION WHEN MY FATHER, SINEL, DIED. BUT HOW CAN YOU CALL ME THE THANE OF CAWDOR? THE THANE OF CAWDOR LIVES, A RICH AND POWERFUL GENTLEMAN.

AND FOR ME TO BE KING IS AS IMPOSSIBLE AS MY BEING THANE OF CAWDOR. TELL ME WHERE YOU LEARNED THIS STRANGE INTELLIGENCE, AND WHY YOU STOP US AT THIS DESOLATE PLACE WITH THIS PROPHETIC GREETING. SPEAK, I COMMAND YOU.

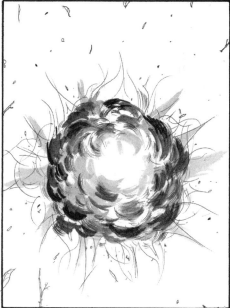

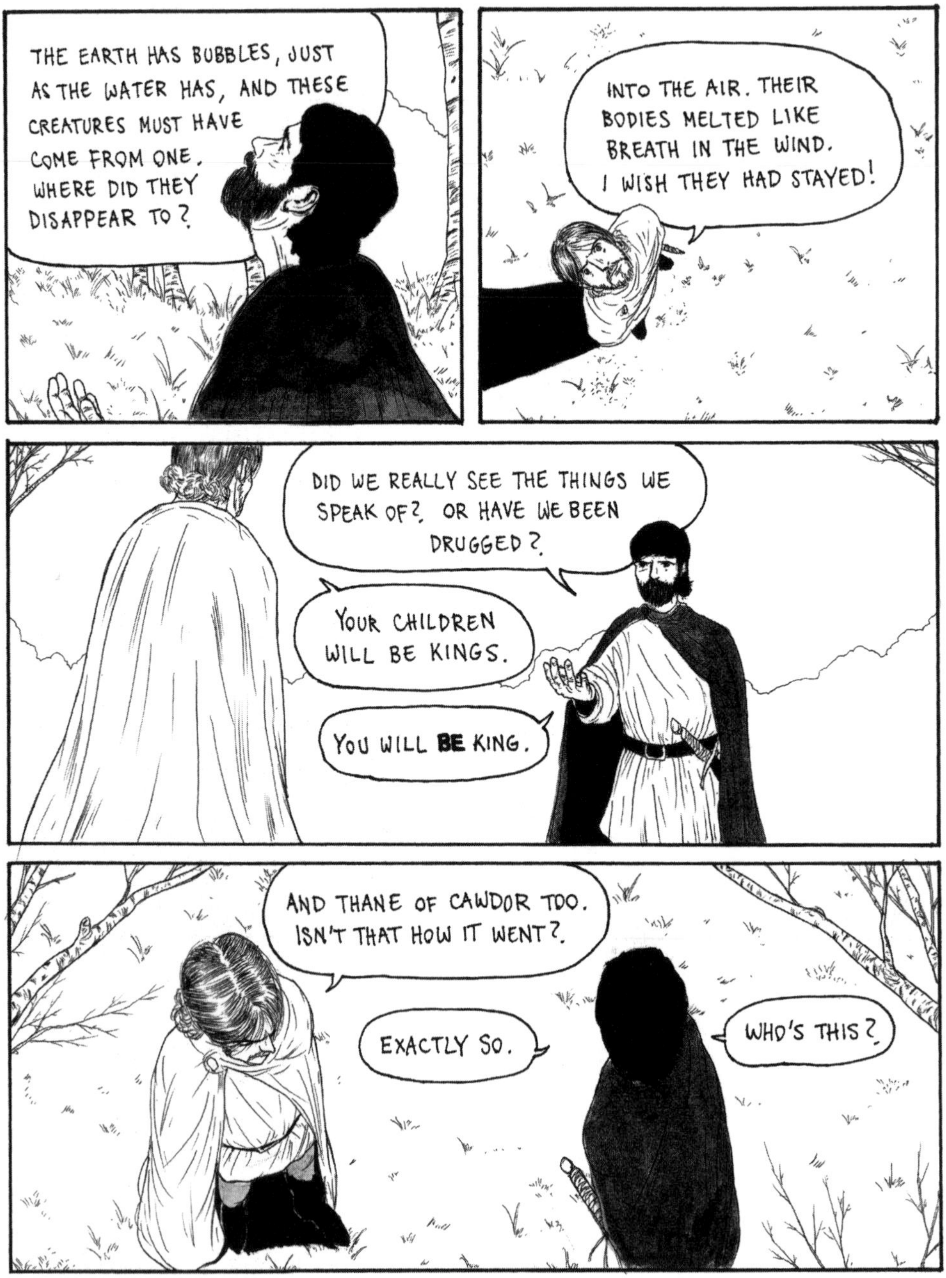
THE EARTH HAS BUBBLES, JUST AS THE WATER HAS, AND THESE CREATURES MUST HAVE COME FROM ONE. WHERE DID THEY DISAPPEAR TO?
INTO THE AIR. THEIR BODIES MELTED LIKE BREATH IN THE WIND. I WISH THEY HAD STAYED!
DID WE REALLY SEE THE THINGS WE SPEAK OF? OR HAVE WE BEEN DRUGGED?
YOUR CHILDREN WILL BE KINGS.
YOU WILL BE KING.
AND THANE OF CAWDOR TOO. ISN'T THAT HOW IT WENT?
EXACTLY SO.
WHO'S THIS?

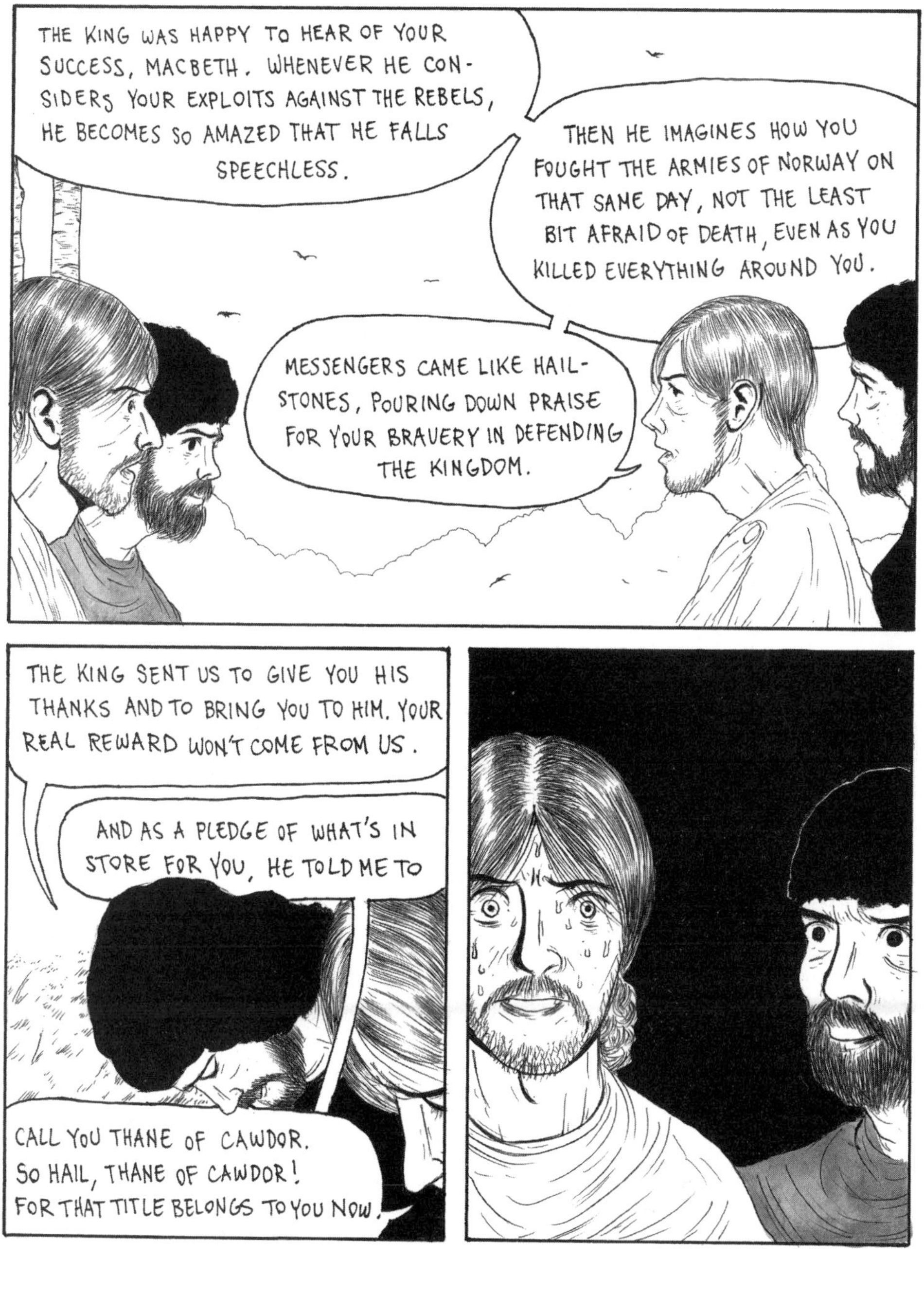
THE KING WAS HAPPY TO HEAR OF YOUR SUCCESS, MACBETH. WHENEVER HE CONSIDERS YOUR EXPLOITS AGAINST THE REBELS, HE BECOMES SO AMAZED THAT HE FALLS SPEECHLESS.
THEN HE IMAGINES HOW YOU FOUGHT THE ARMIES OF NORWAY ON THAT SAME DAY, NOT THE LEAST BIT AFRAID OF DEATH, EVEN AS YOU KILLED EVERYTHING AROUND YOU.
MESSENGERS CAME LIKE HAILSTONES, POURING DOWN PRAISE FOR YOUR BRAVERY IN DEFENDING THE KINGDOM.
THE KING SENT US TO GIVE YOU HIS THANKS AND TO BRING YOU TO HIM. YOUR REAL REWARD WON'T COME FROM US.
AND AS A PLEDGE OF WHAT'S IN STORE FOR YOU, HE TOLD ME TO
CALL YOU THANE OF CAWDOR. SO HAIL, THANE OF CAWDOR! FOR THAT TITLE BELONGS TO YOU NOW.

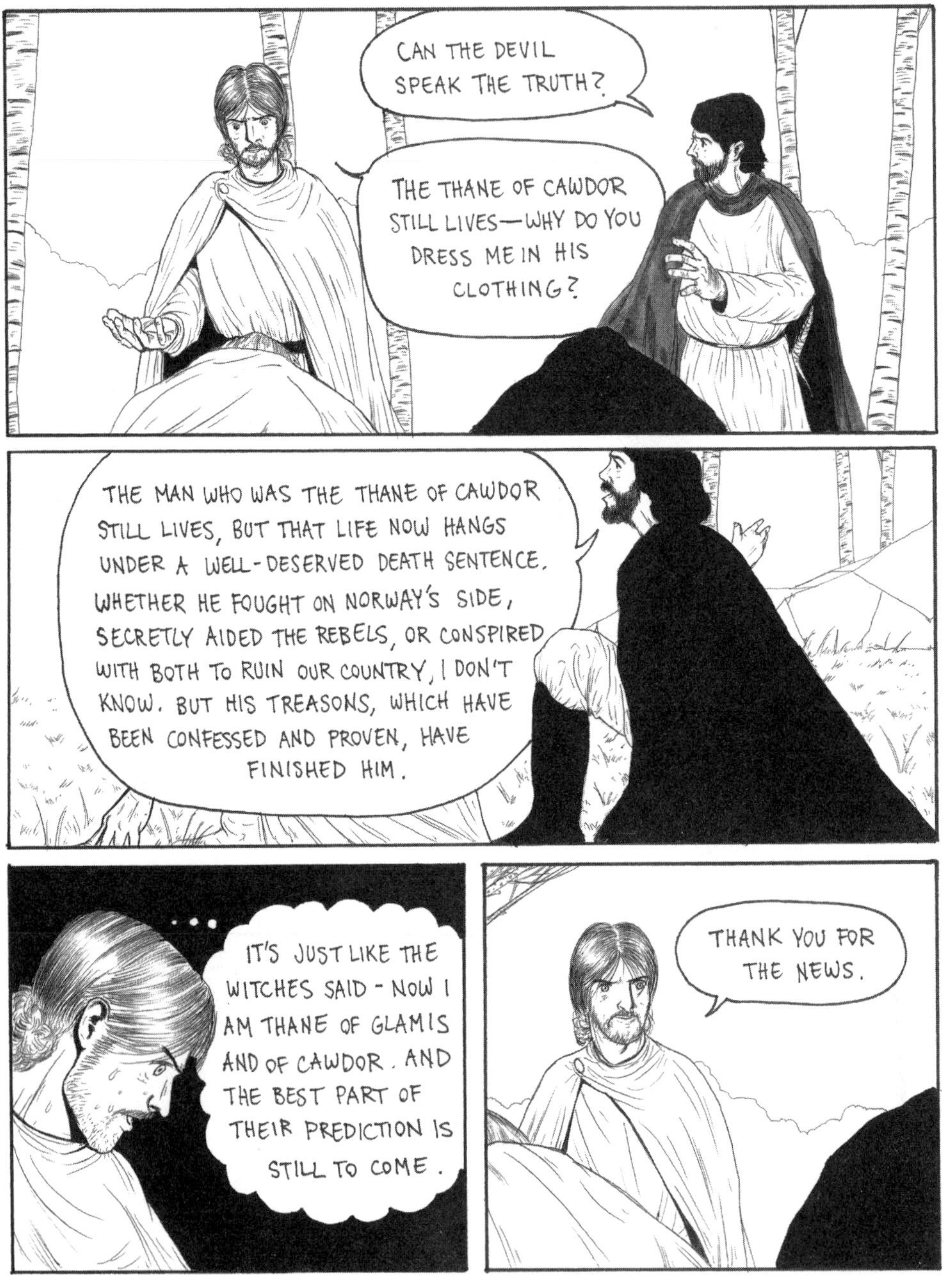
CAN THE DEVIL SPEAK THE TRUTH?
THE THANE OF CAWDOR STILL LIVES—WHY DO YOU DRESS ME IN HIS CLOTHING?
THE MAN WHO WAS THE THANE OF CAWDOR STILL LIVES, BUT THAT LIFE NOW HANGS UNDER A WELL-DESERVED DEATH SENTENCE. WHETHER HE FOUGHT ON NORWAY'S SIDE, SECRETLY AIDED THE REBELS, OR CONSPIRED WITH BOTH TO RUIN OUR COUNTRY, I DON'T KNOW. BUT HIS TREASONS, WHICH HAVE BEEN CONFESSED AND PROVEN, HAVE FINISHED HIM.
IT'S JUST LIKE THE WITCHES SAID - NOW I AM THANE OF GLAMIS AND OF CAWDOR. AND THE BEST PART OF THEIR PREDICTION IS STILL TO COME.
THANK YOU FOR THE NEWS.

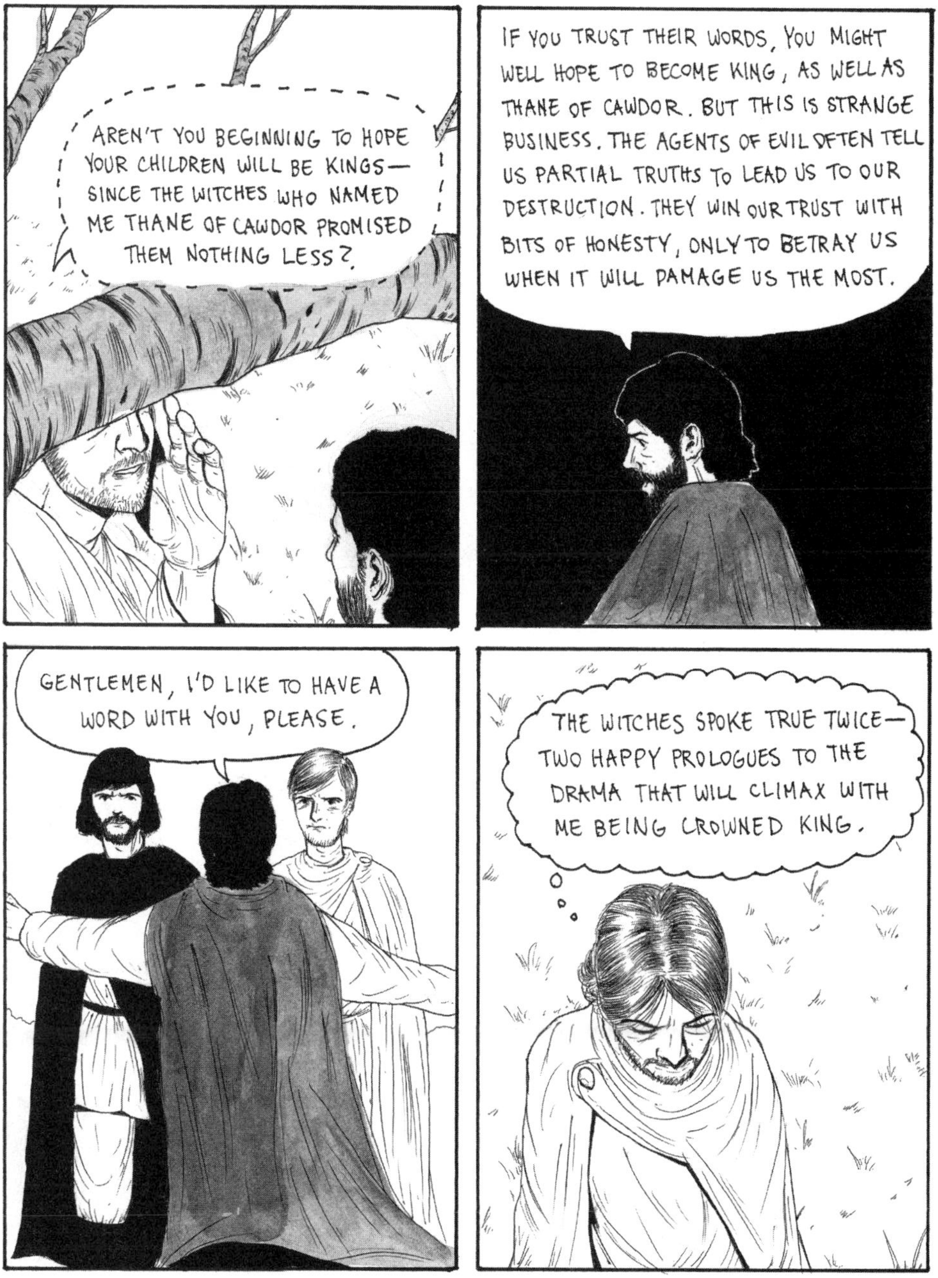
AREN'T YOU BEGINNING TO HOPE YOUR CHILDREN WILL BE KINGS— SINCE THE WITCHES WHO NAMED ME THANE OF CAWDOR PROMISED THEM NOTHING LESS?
IF YOU TRUST THEIR WORDS, YOU MIGHT WELL HOPE TO BECOME KING, AS WELL AS THANE OF CAWDOR. BUT THIS IS STRANGE BUSINESS. THE AGENTS OF EVIL OFTEN TELL US PARTIAL TRUTHS TO LEAD US TO OUR DESTRUCTION. THEY WIN OUR TRUST WITH BITS OF HONESTY, ONLY TO BETRAY US WHEN IT WILL DAMAGE US THE MOST.
GENTLEMEN, I'D LIKE TO HAVE A WORD WITH YOU, PLEASE.
THE WITCHES SPOKE TRUE TWICE— TWO HAPPY PROLOGUES TO THE DRAMA THAT WILL CLIMAX WITH ME BEING CROWNED KING.

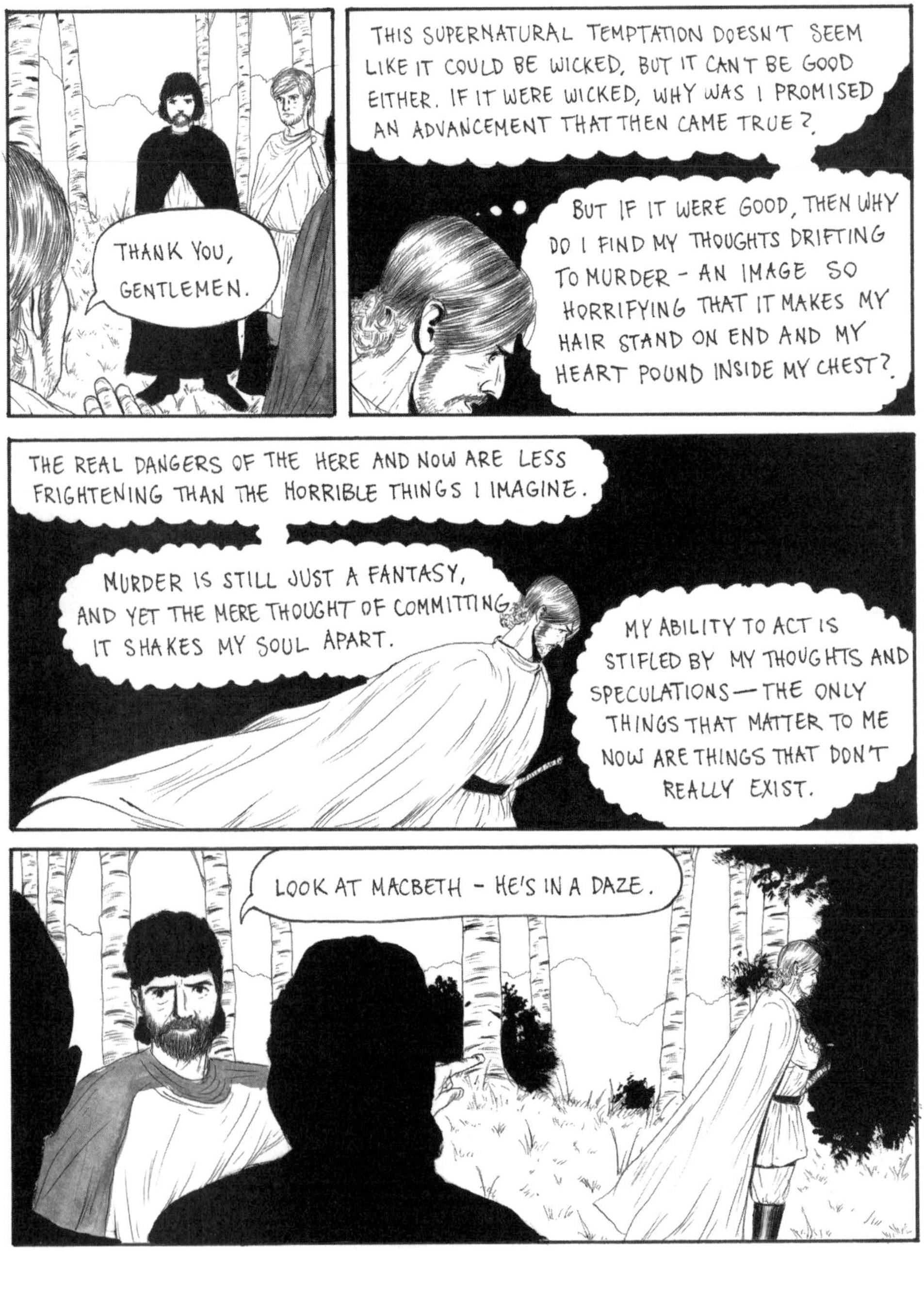
THANK YOU, GENTLEMEN.
THIS SUPERNATURAL TEMPTATION DOESN'T SEEM LIKE IT COULD BE WICKED, BUT IT CAN'T BE GOOD EITHER. IF IT WERE WICKED, WHY WAS I PROMISED AN ADVANCEMENT THAT THEN CAME TRUE?
BUT IF IT WERE GOOD, THEN WHY DO I FIND MY THOUGHTS DRIFTING TO MURDER - AN IMAGE SO HORRIFYING THAT IT MAKES MY HAIR STAND ON END AND MY HEART POUND INSIDE MY CHEST?
THE REAL DANGERS OF THE HERE AND NOW ARE LESS FRIGHTENING THAN THE HORRIBLE THINGS I IMAGINE.
MURDER IS STILL JUST A FANTASY, AND YET THE MERE THOUGHT OF COMMITTING IT SHAKES MY SOUL APART.
MY ABILITY TO ACT IS STIFLED BY MY THOUGHTS AND SPECULATIONS—THE ONLY THINGS THAT MATTER TO ME NOW ARE THINGS THAT DON'T REALLY EXIST.
LOOK AT MACBETH - HE'S IN A DAZE.

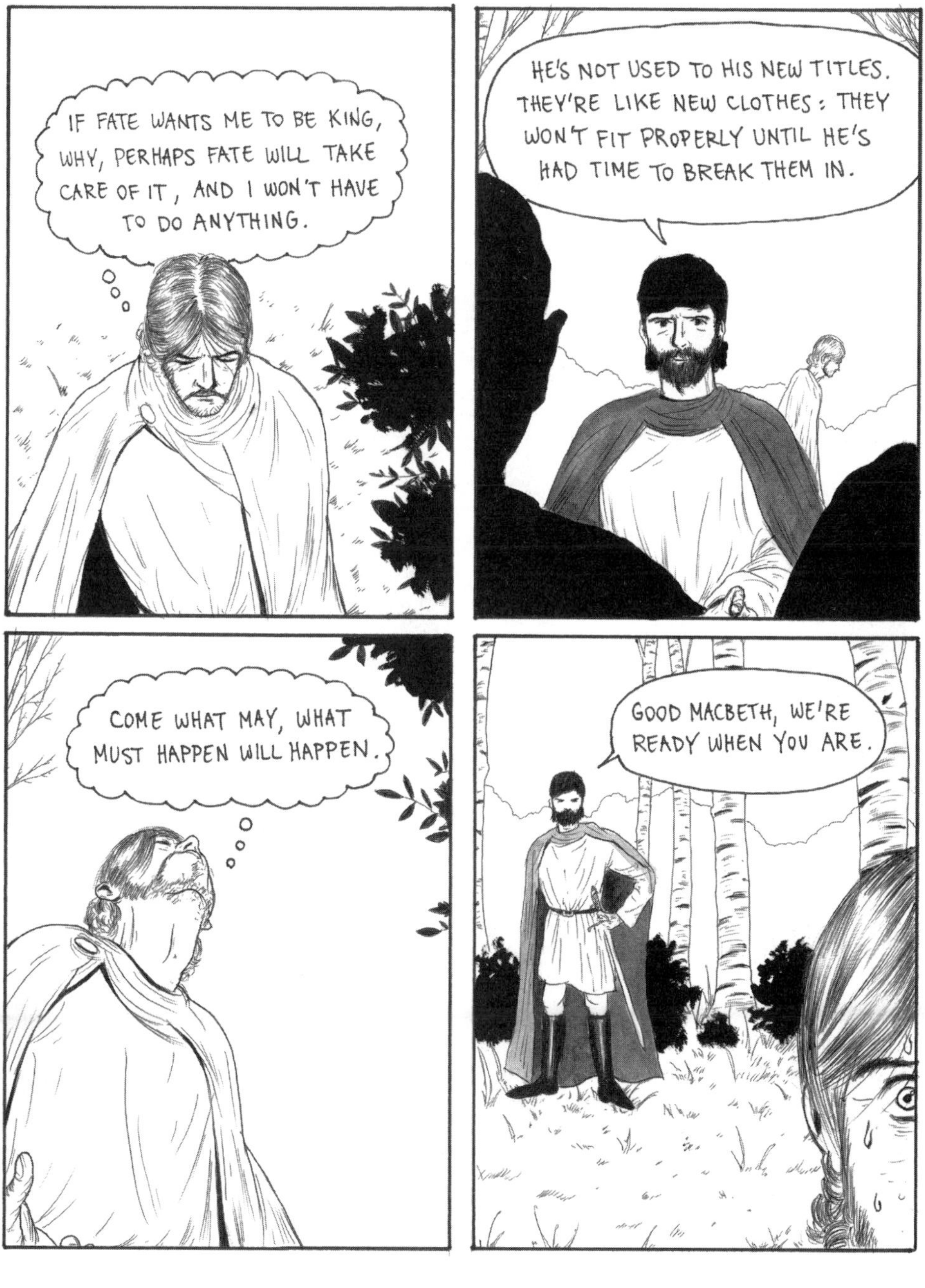
IF FATE WANTS ME TO BE KING, WHY, PERHAPS FATE WILL TAKE CARE OF IT, AND I WON'T HAVE TO DO ANYTHING.
HE'S NOT USED TO HIS NEW TITLES. THEY'RE LIKE NEW CLOTHES: THEY WON'T FIT PROPERLY UNTIL HE'S HAD TIME TO BREAK THEM IN.
COME WHAT MAY, WHAT MUST HAPPEN WILL HAPPEN.
GOOD MACBETH, WE'RE READY WHEN YOU ARE.

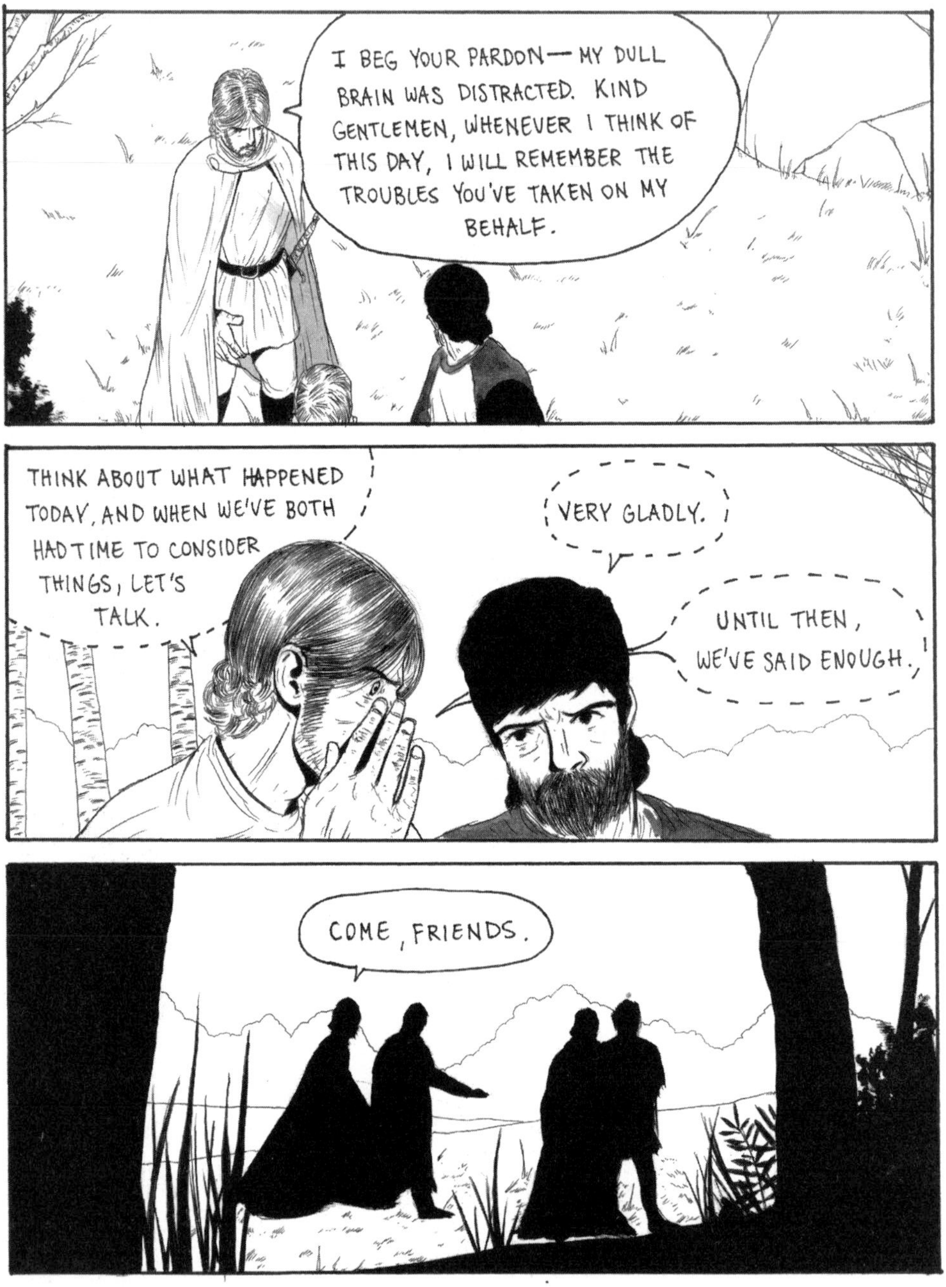
I BEG YOUR PARDON— MY DULL BRAIN WAS DISTRACTED. KIND GENTLEMEN, WHENEVER I THINK OF THIS DAY, I WILL REMEMBER THE TROUBLES YOU'VE TAKEN ON MY BEHALF.
THINK ABOUT WHAT HAPPENED TODAY, AND WHEN WE'VE BOTH HAD TIME TO CONSIDER THINGS, LET'S TALK.
VERY GLADLY.
UNTIL THEN, WE'VE SAID ENOUGH.
COME, FRIENDS.

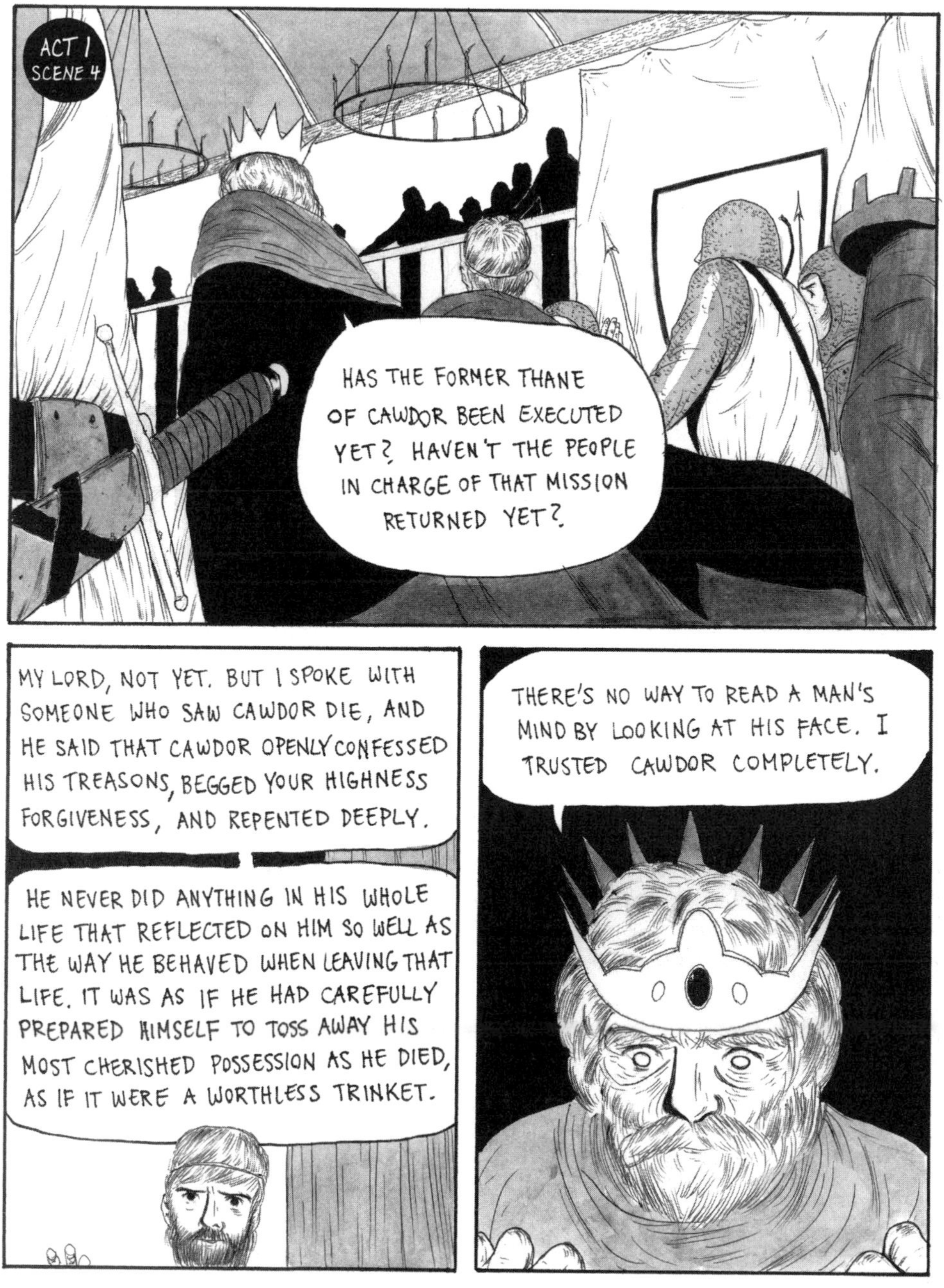
ACT I SCENE 4
HAS THE FORMER THANE OF CAWDOR BEEN EXECUTED YET? HAVEN'T THE PEOPLE IN CHARGE OF THAT MISSION RETURNED YET?
MY LORD, NOT YET. BUT I SPOKE WITH SOMEONE WHO SAW CAWDOR DIE, AND HE SAID THAT CAWDOR OPENLY CONFESSED HIS TREASONS, BEGGED YOUR HIGHNESS FORGIVENESS, AND REPENTED DEEPLY.
HE NEVER DID ANYTHING IN HIS WHOLE LIFE THAT REFLECTED ON HIM SO WELL AS THE WAY HE BEHAVED WHEN LEAVING THAT LIFE. IT WAS AS IF HE HAD CAREFULLY PREPARED HIMSELF TO TOSS AWAY HIS MOST CHERISHED POSSESSION AS HE DIED, AS IF IT WERE A WORTHLESS TRINKET.
THERE'S NO WAY TO READ A MAN'S MIND BY LOOKING AT HIS FACE. I TRUSTED CAWDOR COMPLETELY.

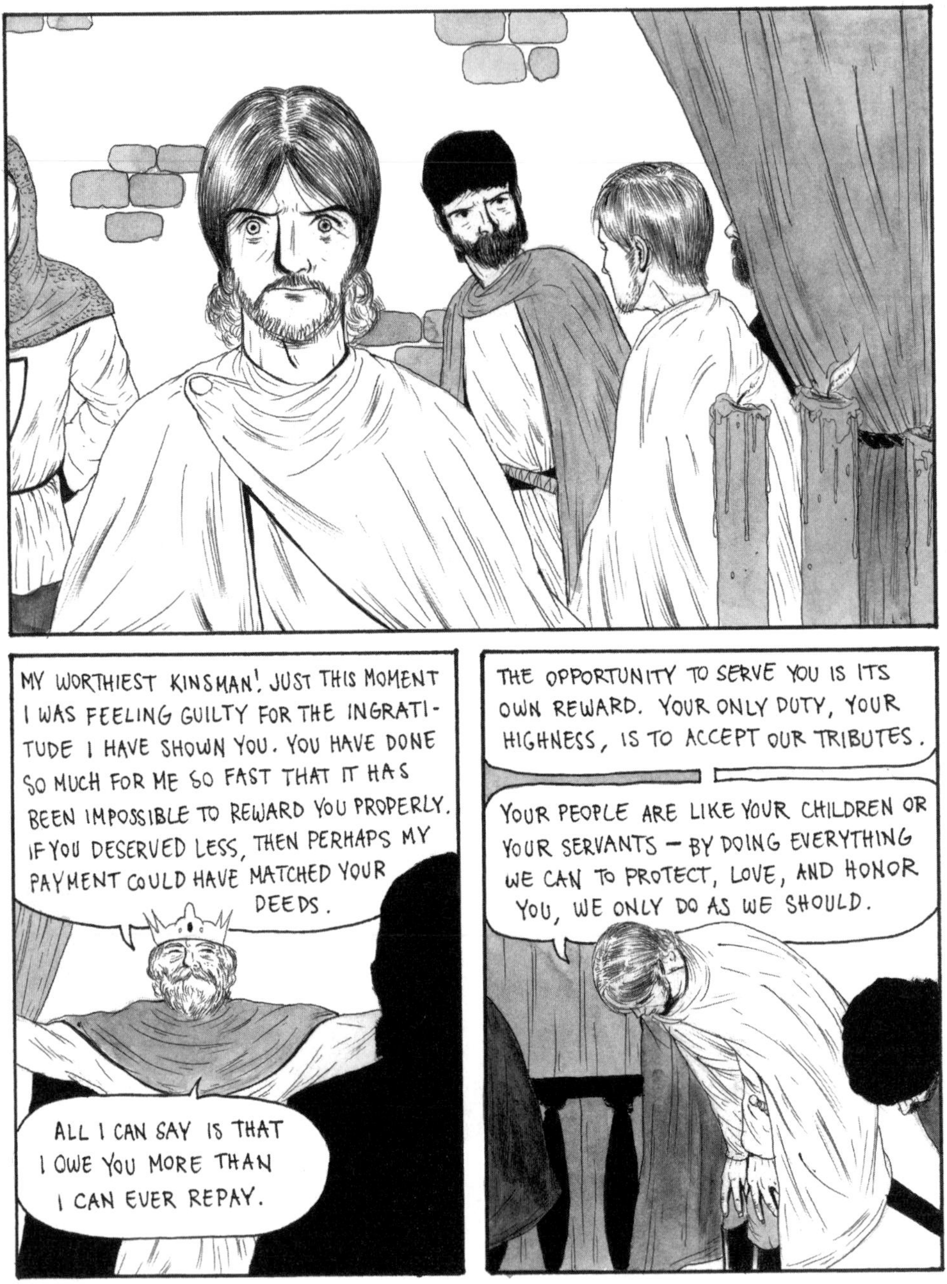
MY WORTHIEST KINSMAN! JUST THIS MOMENT I WAS FEELING GUILTY FOR THE INGRATITUDE I HAVE SHOWN YOU. YOU HAVE DONE SO MUCH FOR ME SO FAST THAT IT HAS BEEN IMPOSSIBLE TO REWARD YOU PROPERLY. IF YOU DESERVED LESS, THEN PERHAPS MY PAYMENT COULD HAVE MATCHED YOUR DEEDS.
ALL I CAN SAY IS THAT I OWE YOU MORE THAN I CAN EVER REPAY.
THE OPPORTUNITY TO SERVE YOU IS ITS OWN REWARD. YOUR ONLY DUTY, YOUR HIGHNESS, IS TO ACCEPT OUR TRIBUTES.
YOUR PEOPLE ARE LIKE YOUR CHILDREN OR YOUR SERVANTS — BY DOING EVERYTHING WE CAN TO PROTECT, LOVE, AND HONOR YOU, WE ONLY DO AS WE SHOULD.

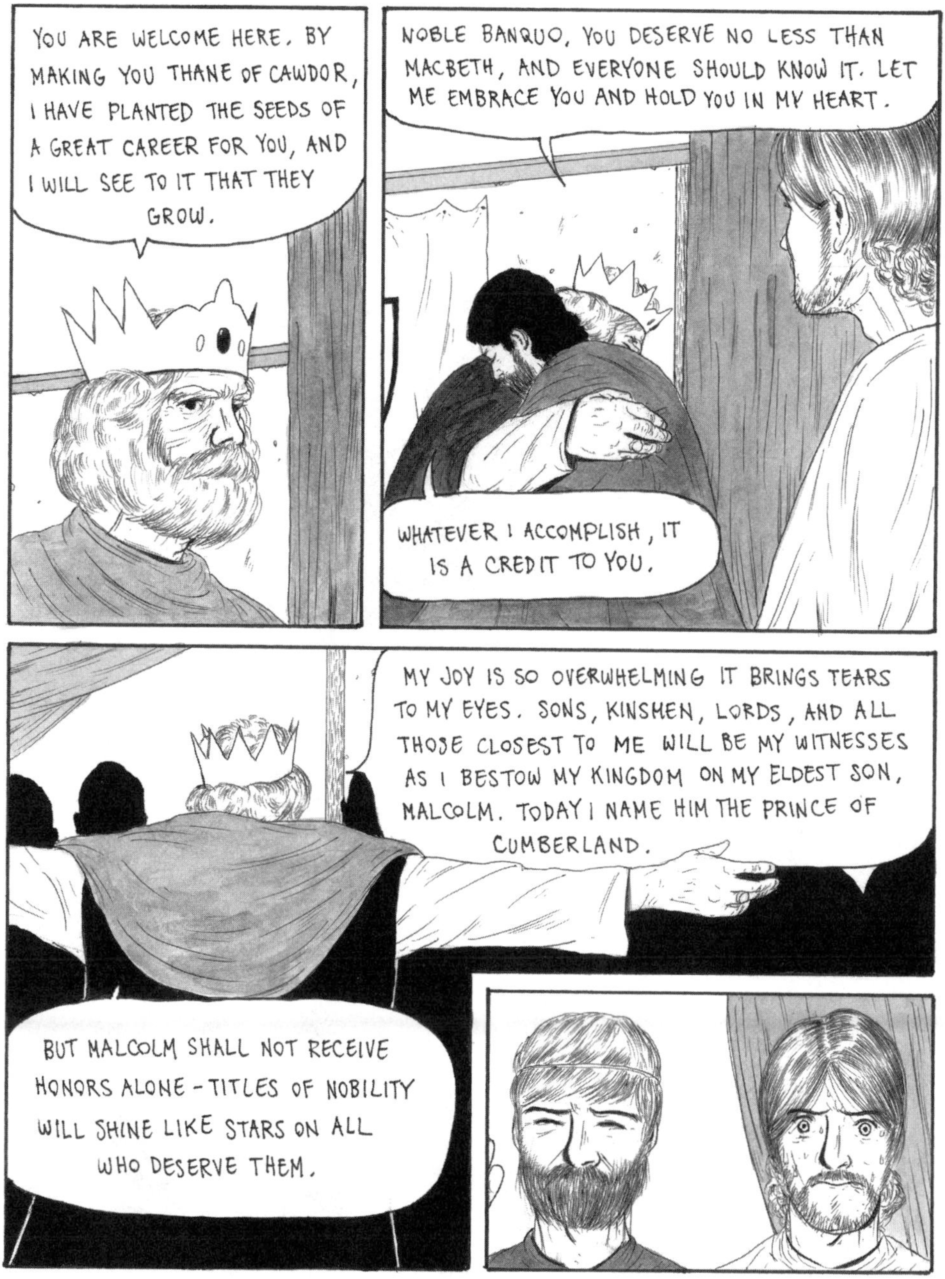
YOU ARE WELCOME HERE. BY MAKING YOU THANE OF CAWDOR, I HAVE PLANTED THE SEEDS OF A GREAT CAREER FOR YOU, AND I WILL SEE TO IT THAT THEY GROW.
NOBLE BANQUO, YOU DESERVE NO LESS THAN MACBETH, AND EVERYONE SHOULD KNOW IT. LET ME EMBRACE YOU AND HOLD YOU IN MY HEART.
WHATEVER I ACCOMPLISH, IT IS A CREDIT TO YOU.
MY JOY IS SO OVERWHELMING IT BRINGS TEARS TO MY EYES. SONS, KINSMEN, LORDS, AND ALL THOSE CLOSEST TO ME WILL BE MY WITNESSES AS I BESTOW MY KINGDOM ON MY ELDEST SON, MALCOLM. TODAY I NAME HIM THE PRINCE OF CUMBERLAND.
BUT MALCOLM SHALL NOT RECEIVE HONORS ALONE - TITLES OF NOBILITY WILL SHINE LIKE STARS ON ALL WHO DESERVE THEM.

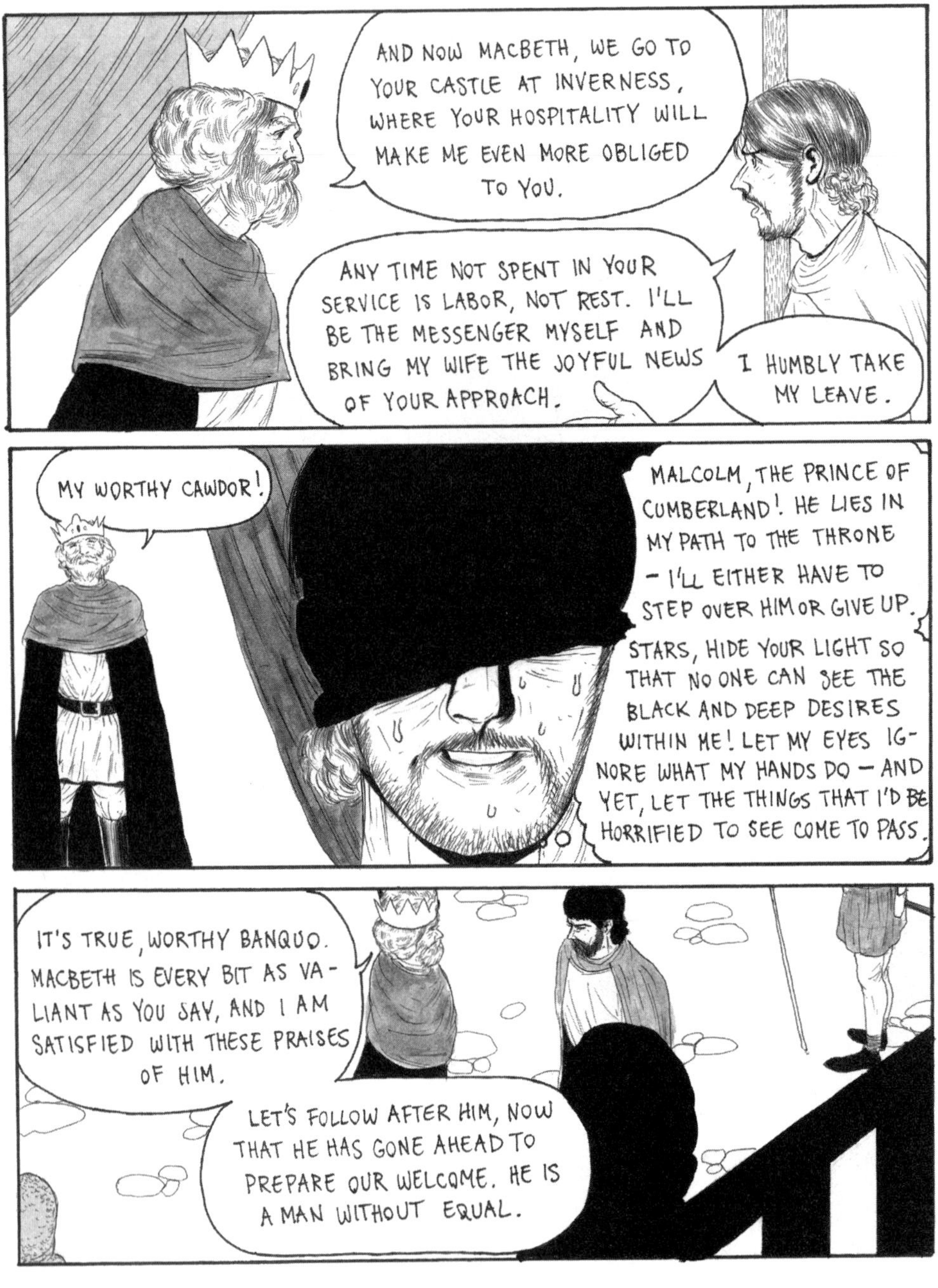
AND NOW MACBETH, WE GO TO YOUR CASTLE AT INVERNESS, WHERE YOUR HOSPITALITY WILL MAKE ME EVEN MORE OBLIGED TO YOU.
ANY TIME NOT SPENT IN YOUR SERVICE IS LABOR, NOT REST. I'LL BE THE MESSENGER MYSELF AND BRING MY WIFE THE JOYFUL NEWS OF YOUR APPROACH.
I HUMBLY TAKE MY LEAVE.
MY WORTHY CAWDOR!
MALCOLM, THE PRINCE OF CUMBERLAND! HE LIES IN MY PATH TO THE THRONE – I'LL EITHER HAVE TO STEP OVER HIM OR GIVE UP.
STARS, HIDE YOUR LIGHT SO THAT NO ONE CAN SEE THE BLACK AND DEEP DESIRES WITHIN ME! LET MY EYES IGNORE WHAT MY HANDS DO – AND YET, LET THE THINGS THAT I'D BE HORRIFIED TO SEE COME TO PASS.
IT'S TRUE, WORTHY BANQUO. MACBETH IS EVERY BIT AS VALIANT AS YOU SAY, AND I AM SATISFIED WITH THESE PRAISES OF HIM.
LET'S FOLLOW AFTER HIM, NOW THAT HE HAS GONE AHEAD TO PREPARE OUR WELCOME. HE IS A MAN WITHOUT EQUAL.

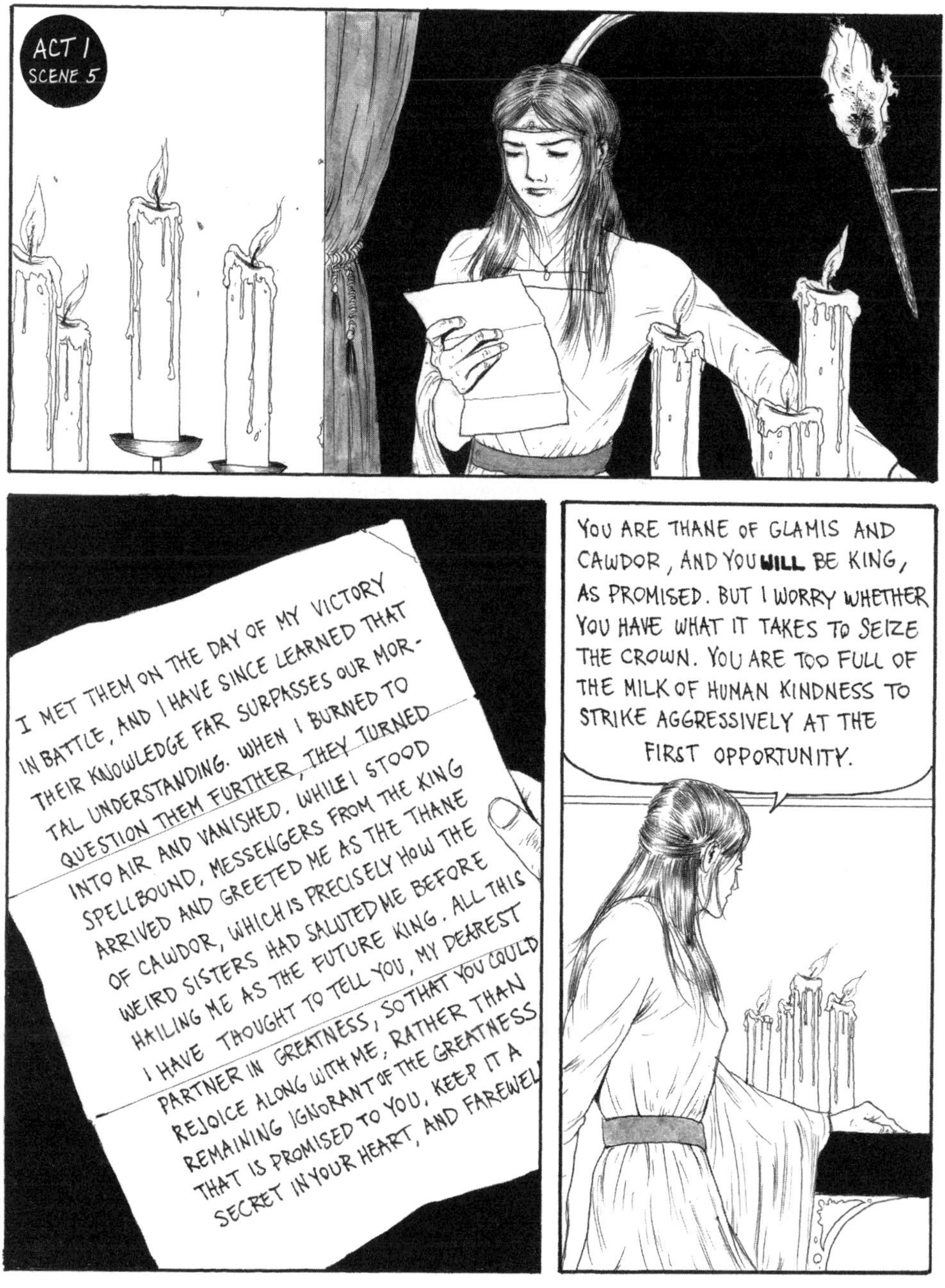
ACT I
SCENE 5
I MET THEM ON THE DAY OF MY VICTORY IN BATTLE, AND I HAVE SINCE LEARNED THAT THEIR KNOWLEDGE FAR SURPASSES OUR MORTAL UNDERSTANDING. WHEN I BURNED TO QUESTION THEM FURTHER, THEY TURNED INTO AIR AND VANISHED. WHILE I STOOD SPELLBOUND, MESSENGERS FROM THE KING ARRIVED AND GREETED ME AS THE THANE OF CAWDOR, WHICH IS PRECISELY HOW THE WEIRD SISTERS HAD SALUTED ME BEFORE HAILING ME AS THE FUTURE KING. ALL THIS I HAVE THOUGHT TO TELL YOU, MY DEAREST PARTNER IN GREATNESS, SO THAT YOU COULD REJOICE ALONG WITH ME, RATHER THAN REMAINING IGNORANT OF THE GREATNESS THAT IS PROMISED TO YOU. KEEP IT A SECRET IN YOUR HEART, AND FAREWELL
YOU ARE THANE OF GLAMIS AND CAWDOR, AND YOU **WILL** BE KING, AS PROMISED. BUT I WORRY WHETHER YOU HAVE WHAT IT TAKES TO SEIZE THE CROWN. YOU ARE TOO FULL OF THE MILK OF HUMAN KINDNESS TO STRIKE AGGRESSIVELY AT THE FIRST OPPORTUNITY.

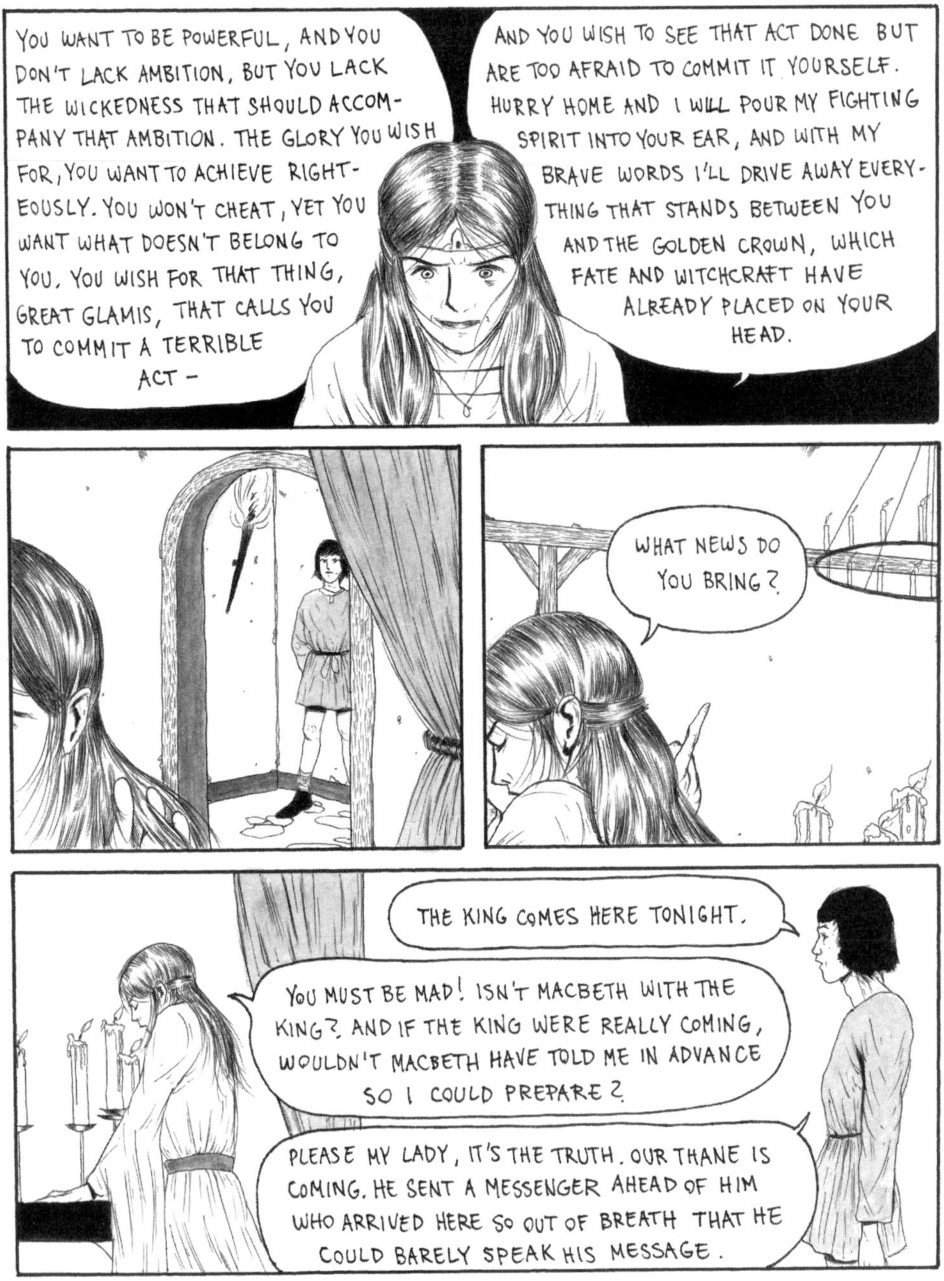
YOU WANT TO BE POWERFUL, AND YOU DON'T LACK AMBITION, BUT YOU LACK THE WICKEDNESS THAT SHOULD ACCOMPANY THAT AMBITION. THE GLORY YOU WISH FOR, YOU WANT TO ACHIEVE RIGHTEOUSLY. YOU WON'T CHEAT, YET YOU WANT WHAT DOESN'T BELONG TO YOU. YOU WISH FOR THAT THING, GREAT GLAMIS, THAT CALLS YOU TO COMMIT A TERRIBLE ACT -
AND YOU WISH TO SEE THAT ACT DONE BUT ARE TOO AFRAID TO COMMIT IT YOURSELF. HURRY HOME AND I WILL POUR MY FIGHTING SPIRIT INTO YOUR EAR, AND WITH MY BRAVE WORDS I'LL DRIVE AWAY EVERYTHING THAT STANDS BETWEEN YOU AND THE GOLDEN CROWN, WHICH FATE AND WITCHCRAFT HAVE ALREADY PLACED ON YOUR HEAD.
WHAT NEWS DO YOU BRING?
THE KING COMES HERE TONIGHT.
YOU MUST BE MAD! ISN'T MACBETH WITH THE KING? AND IF THE KING WERE REALLY COMING, WOULDN'T MACBETH HAVE TOLD ME IN ADVANCE SO I COULD PREPARE?
PLEASE MY LADY, IT'S THE TRUTH. OUR THANE IS COMING. HE SENT A MESSENGER AHEAD OF HIM WHO ARRIVED HERE SO OUT OF BREATH THAT HE COULD BARELY SPEAK HIS MESSAGE.

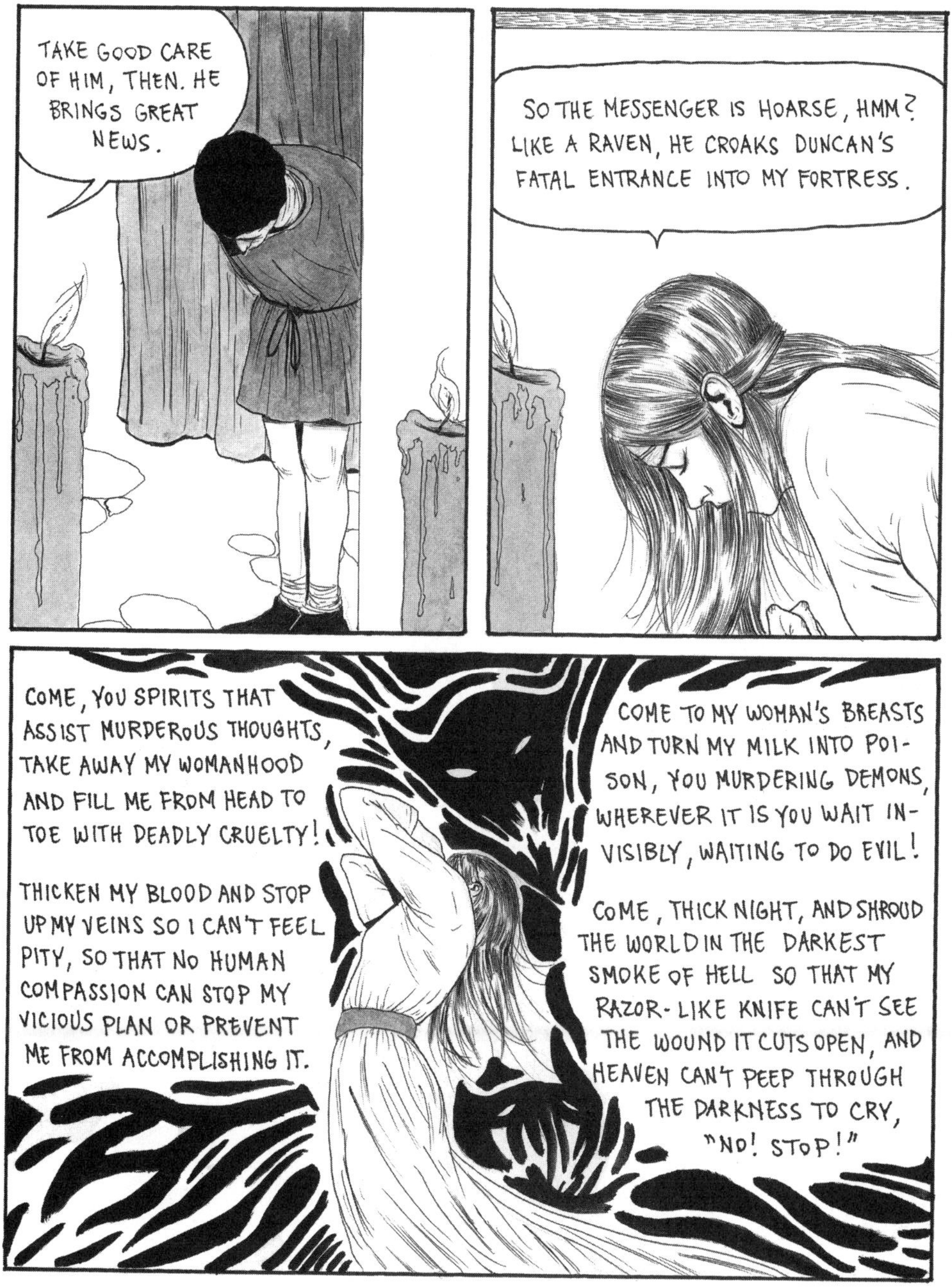
TAKE GOOD CARE OF HIM, THEN. HE BRINGS GREAT NEWS.
SO THE MESSENGER IS HOARSE, HMM? LIKE A RAVEN, HE CROAKS DUNCAN'S FATAL ENTRANCE INTO MY FORTRESS.
COME, YOU SPIRITS THAT ASSIST MURDEROUS THOUGHTS, TAKE AWAY MY WOMANHOOD AND FILL ME FROM HEAD TO TOE WITH DEADLY CRUELTY!
THICKEN MY BLOOD AND STOP UP MY VEINS SO I CAN'T FEEL PITY, SO THAT NO HUMAN COMPASSION CAN STOP MY VICIOUS PLAN OR PREVENT ME FROM ACCOMPLISHING IT.
COME TO MY WOMAN'S BREASTS AND TURN MY MILK INTO POI-SON, YOU MURDERING DEMONS, WHEREVER IT IS YOU WAIT IN-VISIBLY, WAITING TO DO EVIL!
COME, THICK NIGHT, AND SHROUD THE WORLD IN THE DARKEST SMOKE OF HELL SO THAT MY RAZOR-LIKE KNIFE CAN'T SEE THE WOUND IT CUTS OPEN, AND HEAVEN CAN'T PEEP THROUGH THE DARKNESS TO CRY, "NO! STOP!"

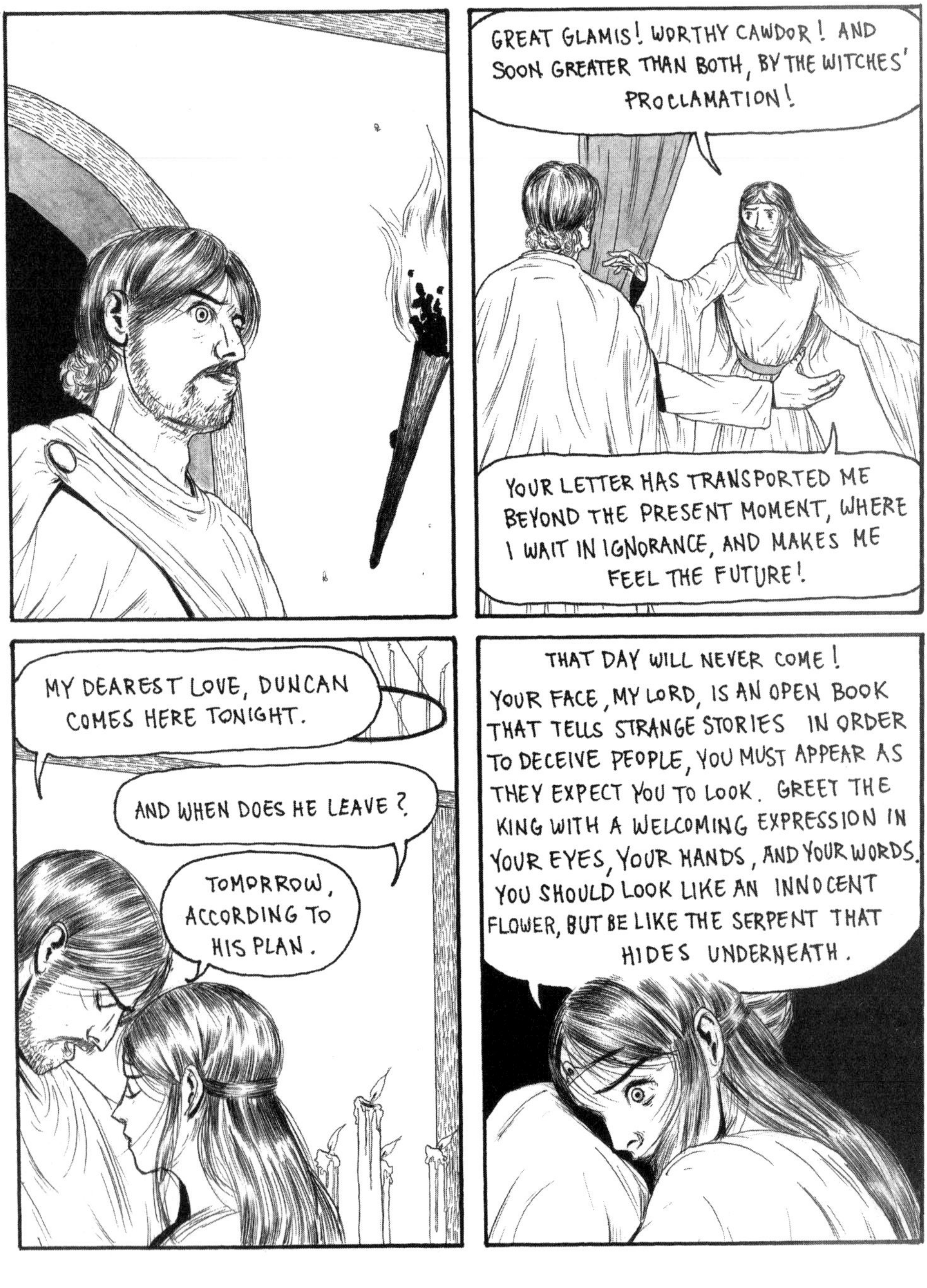
GREAT GLAMIS! WORTHY CAWDOR! AND SOON GREATER THAN BOTH, BY THE WITCHES' PROCLAMATION!
YOUR LETTER HAS TRANSPORTED ME BEYOND THE PRESENT MOMENT, WHERE I WAIT IN IGNORANCE, AND MAKES ME FEEL THE FUTURE!
MY DEAREST LOVE, DUNCAN COMES HERE TONIGHT.
AND WHEN DOES HE LEAVE?
TOMORROW, ACCORDING TO HIS PLAN.
THAT DAY WILL NEVER COME! YOUR FACE, MY LORD, IS AN OPEN BOOK THAT TELLS STRANGE STORIES. IN ORDER TO DECEIVE PEOPLE, YOU MUST APPEAR AS THEY EXPECT YOU TO LOOK. GREET THE KING WITH A WELCOMING EXPRESSION IN YOUR EYES, YOUR HANDS, AND YOUR WORDS. YOU SHOULD LOOK LIKE AN INNOCENT FLOWER, BUT BE LIKE THE SERPENT THAT HIDES UNDERNEATH.

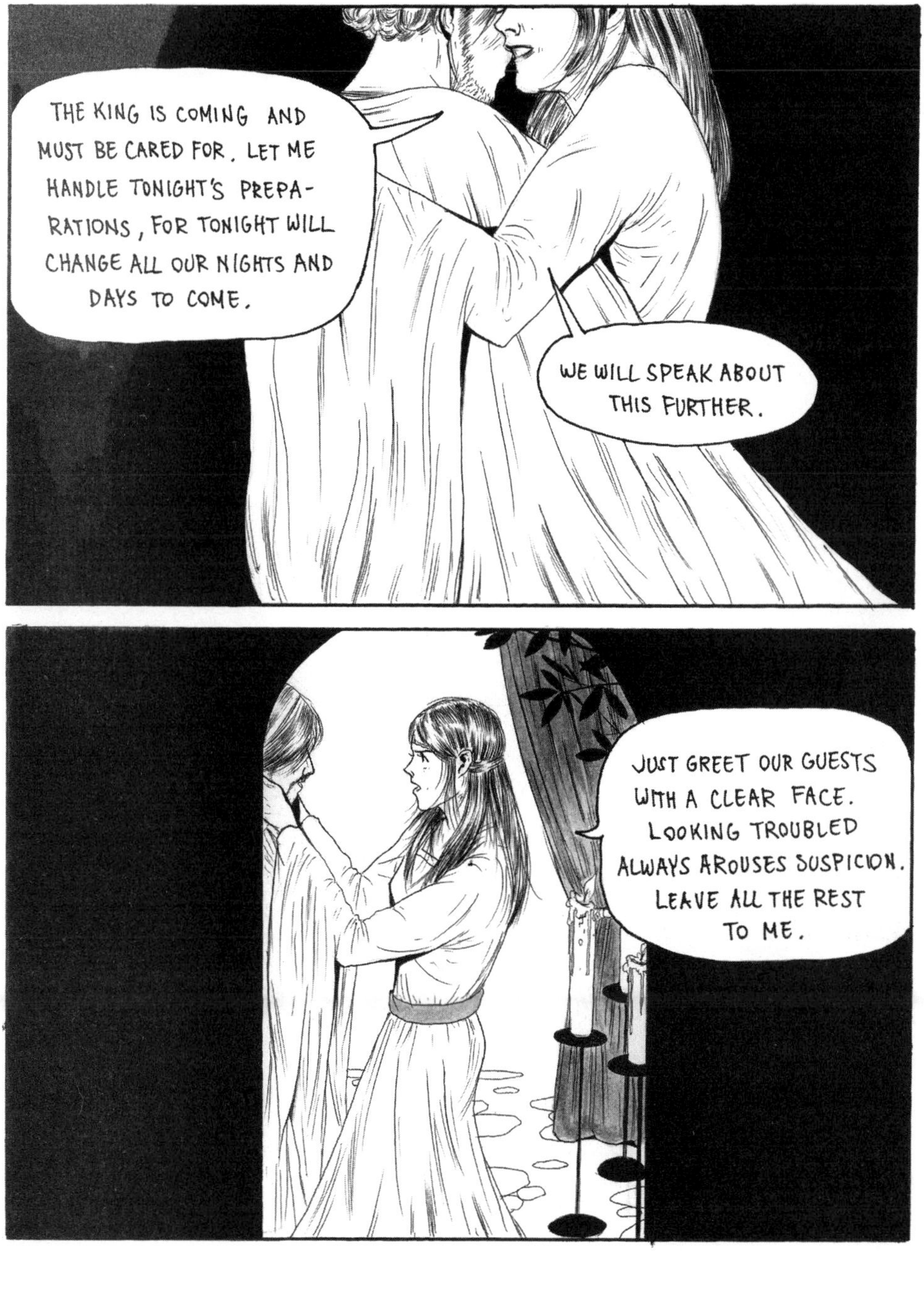
THE KING IS COMING AND MUST BE CARED FOR. LET ME HANDLE TONIGHT'S PREPARATIONS, FOR TONIGHT WILL CHANGE ALL OUR NIGHTS AND DAYS TO COME.
WE WILL SPEAK ABOUT THIS FURTHER.
JUST GREET OUR GUESTS WITH A CLEAR FACE. LOOKING TROUBLED ALWAYS AROUSES SUSPICION. LEAVE ALL THE REST TO ME.

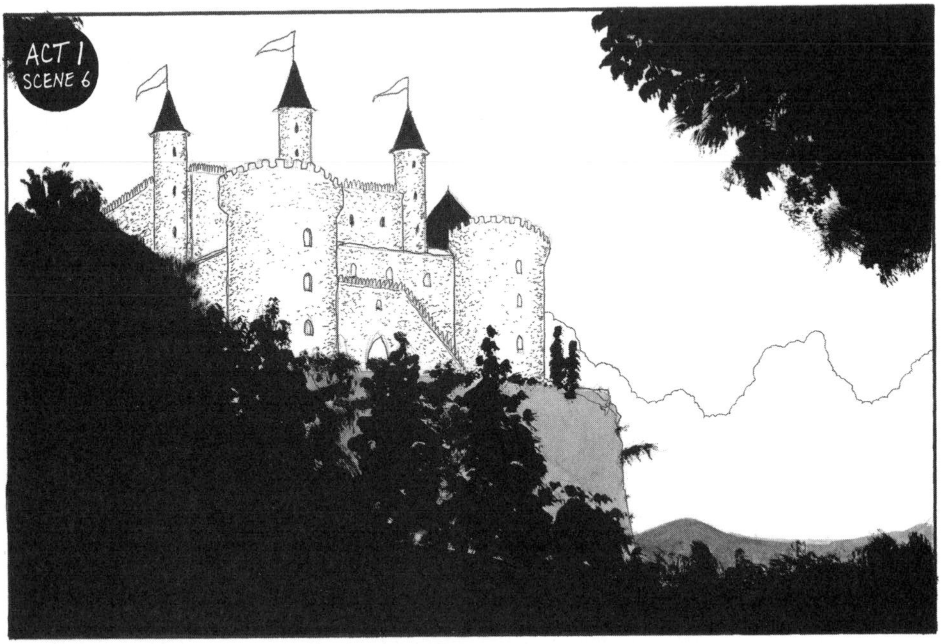
ACT I
SCENE 6

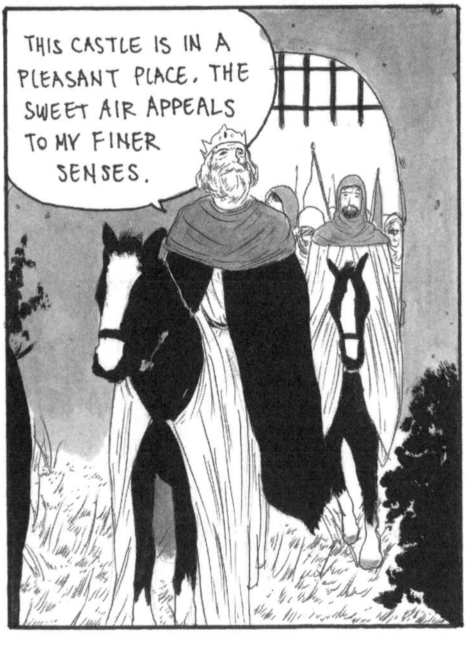
THIS CASTLE IS IN A PLEASANT PLACE. THE SWEET AIR APPEALS TO MY FINER SENSES.

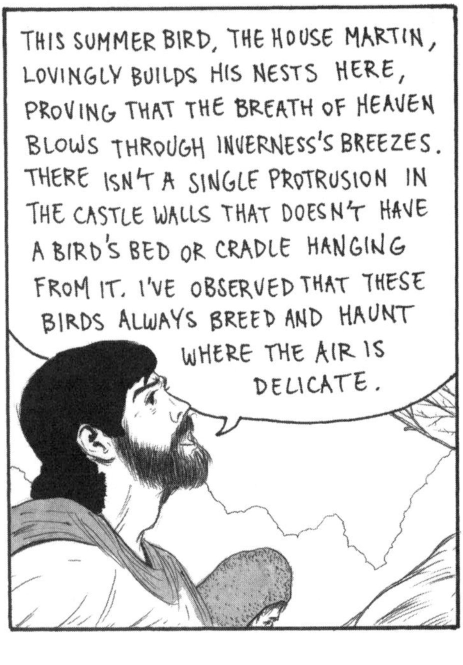
THIS SUMMER BIRD, THE HOUSE MARTIN, LOVINGLY BUILDS HIS NESTS HERE, PROVING THAT THE BREATH OF HEAVEN BLOWS THROUGH INVERNESS'S BREEZES. THERE ISN'T A SINGLE PROTRUSION IN THE CASTLE WALLS THAT DOESN'T HAVE A BIRD'S BED OR CRADLE HANGING FROM IT. I'VE OBSERVED THAT THESE BIRDS ALWAYS BREED AND HAUNT WHERE THE AIR IS DELICATE.

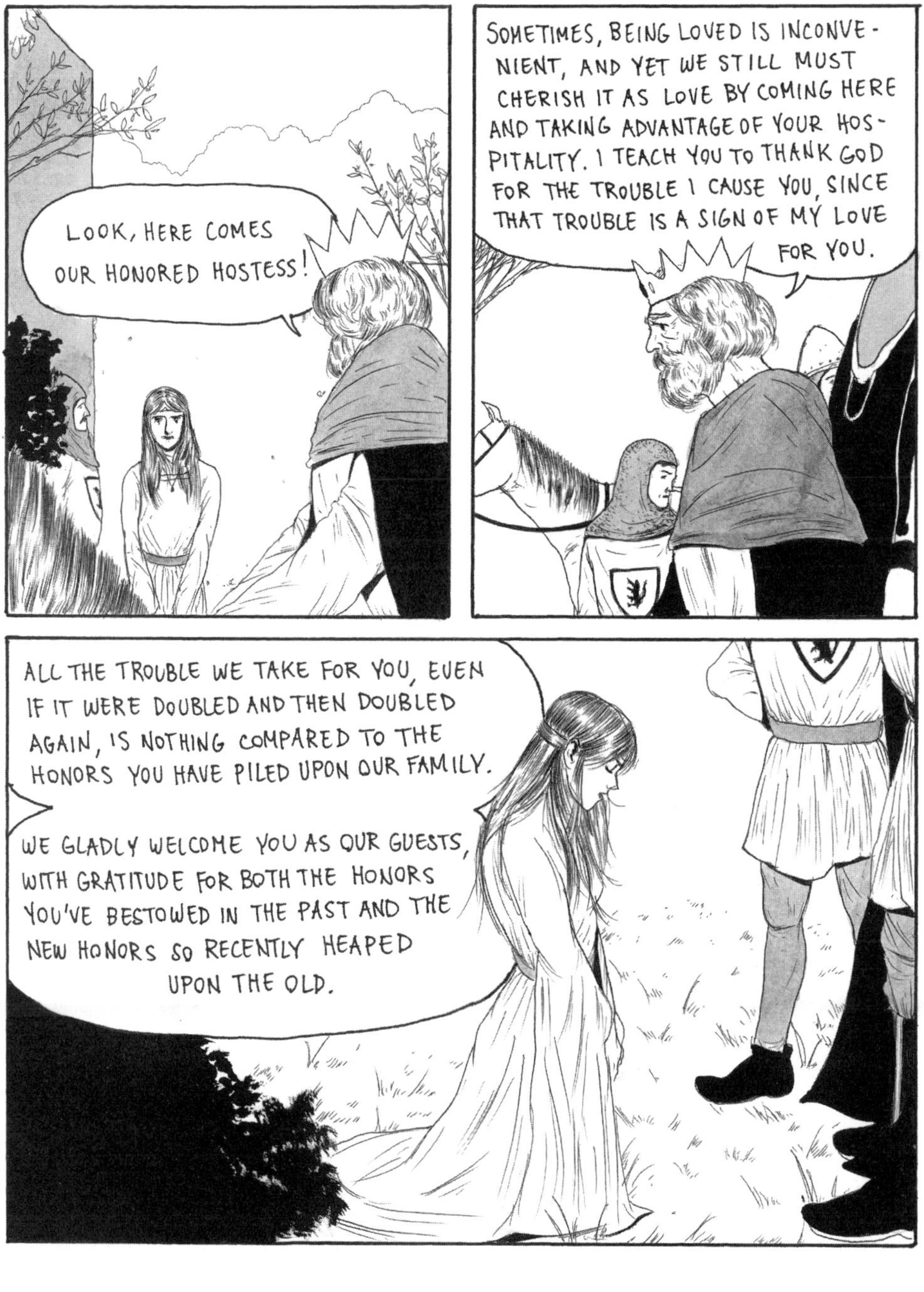
LOOK, HERE COMES OUR HONORED HOSTESS!
SOMETIMES, BEING LOVED IS INCONVE-NIENT, AND YET WE STILL MUST CHERISH IT AS LOVE BY COMING HERE AND TAKING ADVANTAGE OF YOUR HOS-PITALITY. I TEACH YOU TO THANK GOD FOR THE TROUBLE I CAUSE YOU, SINCE THAT TROUBLE IS A SIGN OF MY LOVE FOR YOU.
ALL THE TROUBLE WE TAKE FOR YOU, EVEN IF IT WERE DOUBLED AND THEN DOUBLED AGAIN, IS NOTHING COMPARED TO THE HONORS YOU HAVE PILED UPON OUR FAMILY.
WE GLADLY WELCOME YOU AS OUR GUESTS, WITH GRATITUDE FOR BOTH THE HONORS YOU'VE BESTOWED IN THE PAST AND THE NEW HONORS SO RECENTLY HEAPED UPON THE OLD.

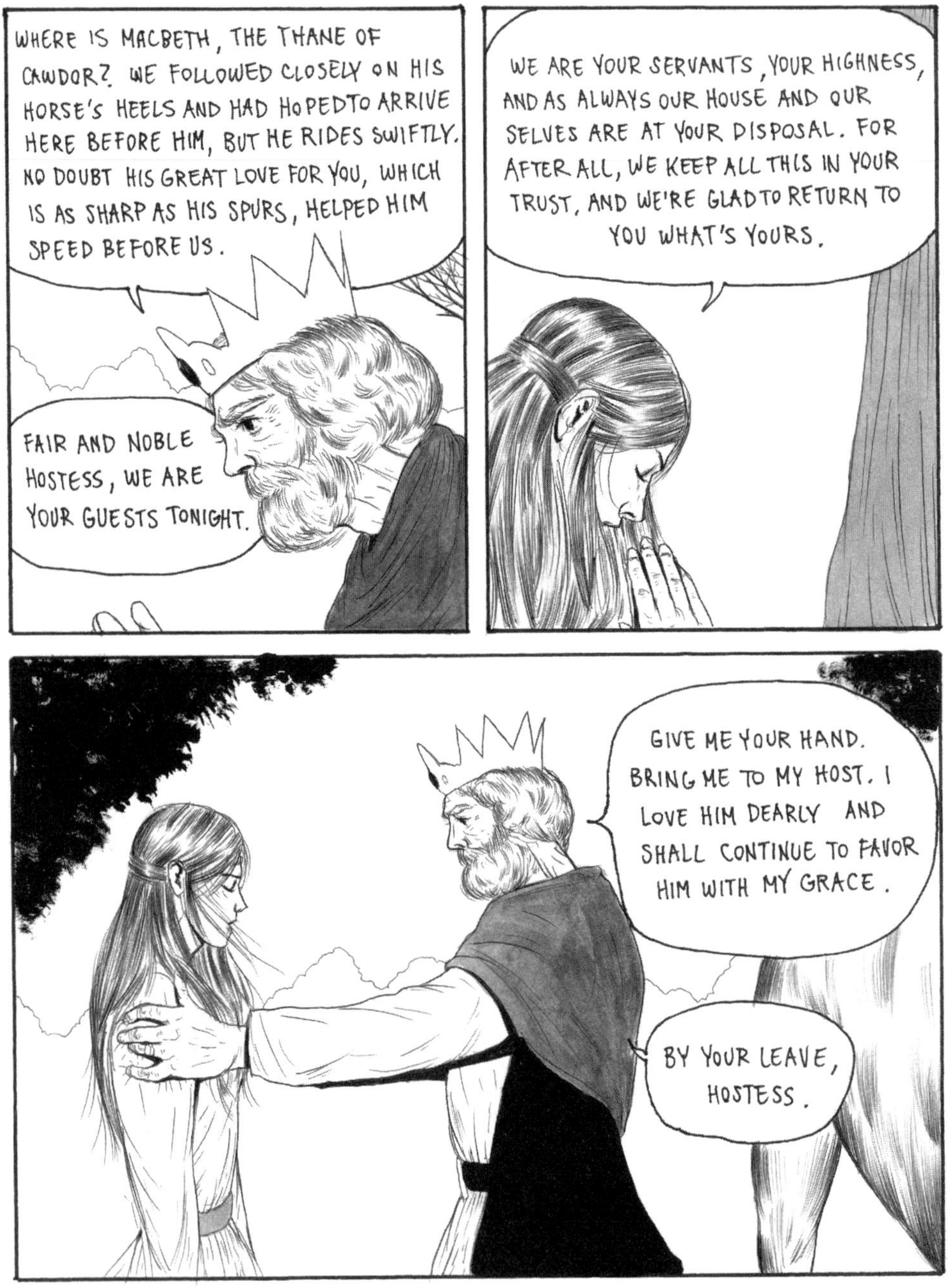
WHERE IS MACBETH, THE THANE OF CAWDOR? WE FOLLOWED CLOSELY ON HIS HORSE'S HEELS AND HAD HOPED TO ARRIVE HERE BEFORE HIM, BUT HE RIDES SWIFTLY. NO DOUBT HIS GREAT LOVE FOR YOU, WHICH IS AS SHARP AS HIS SPURS, HELPED HIM SPEED BEFORE US.
FAIR AND NOBLE HOSTESS, WE ARE YOUR GUESTS TONIGHT.
WE ARE YOUR SERVANTS, YOUR HIGHNESS, AND AS ALWAYS OUR HOUSE AND OUR SELVES ARE AT YOUR DISPOSAL. FOR AFTER ALL, WE KEEP ALL THIS IN YOUR TRUST, AND WE'RE GLAD TO RETURN TO YOU WHAT'S YOURS.
GIVE ME YOUR HAND. BRING ME TO MY HOST. I LOVE HIM DEARLY AND SHALL CONTINUE TO FAVOR HIM WITH MY GRACE.
BY YOUR LEAVE, HOSTESS.

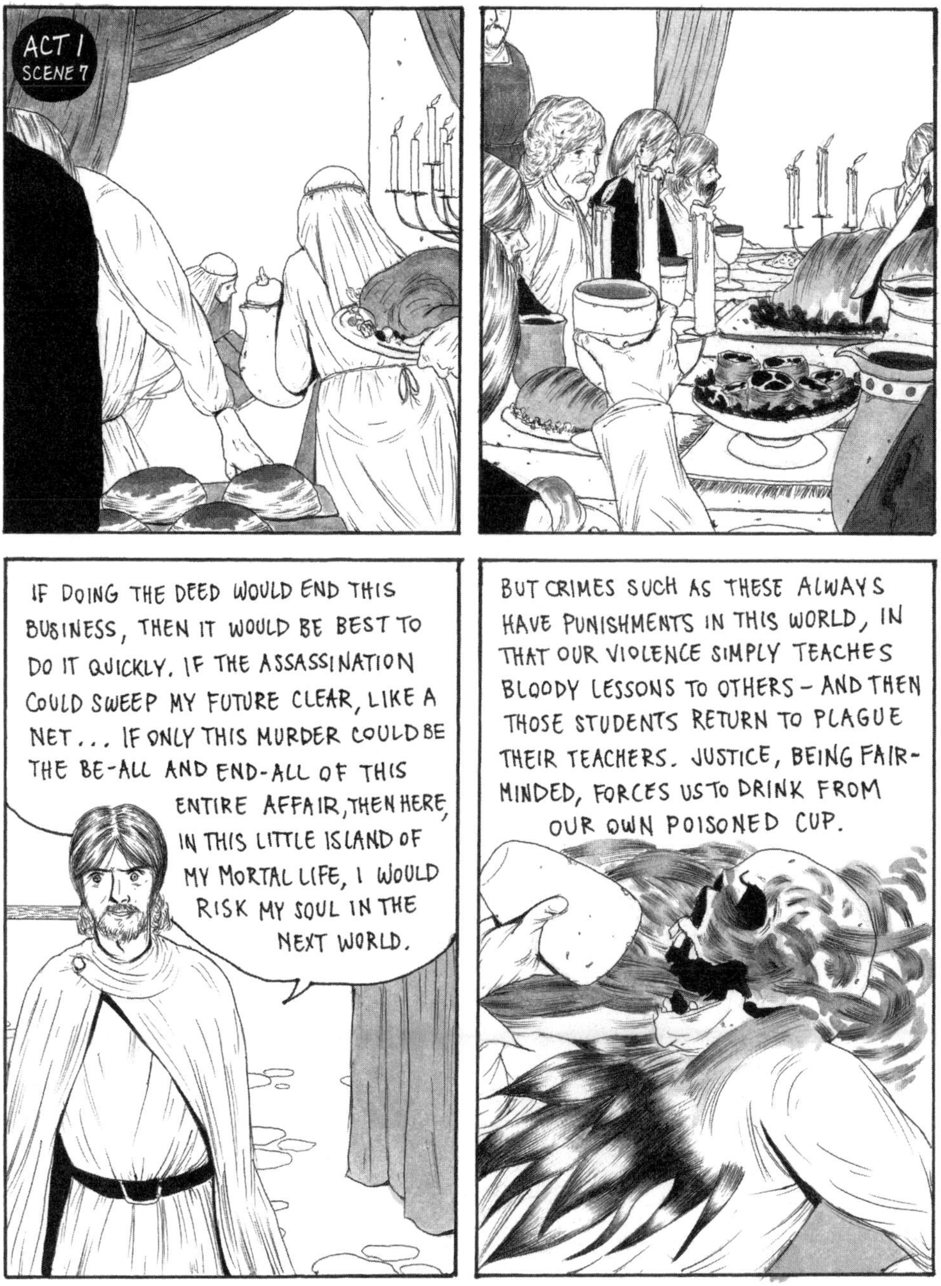
ACT I
SCENE 7
IF DOING THE DEED WOULD END THIS BUSINESS, THEN IT WOULD BE BEST TO DO IT QUICKLY. IF THE ASSASSINATION COULD SWEEP MY FUTURE CLEAR, LIKE A NET... IF ONLY THIS MURDER COULD BE THE BE-ALL AND END-ALL OF THIS ENTIRE AFFAIR, THEN HERE, IN THIS LITTLE ISLAND OF MY MORTAL LIFE, I WOULD RISK MY SOUL IN THE NEXT WORLD.
BUT CRIMES SUCH AS THESE ALWAYS HAVE PUNISHMENTS IN THIS WORLD, IN THAT OUR VIOLENCE SIMPLY TEACHES BLOODY LESSONS TO OTHERS - AND THEN THOSE STUDENTS RETURN TO PLAGUE THEIR TEACHERS. JUSTICE, BEING FAIR-MINDED, FORCES US TO DRINK FROM OUR OWN POISONED CUP.

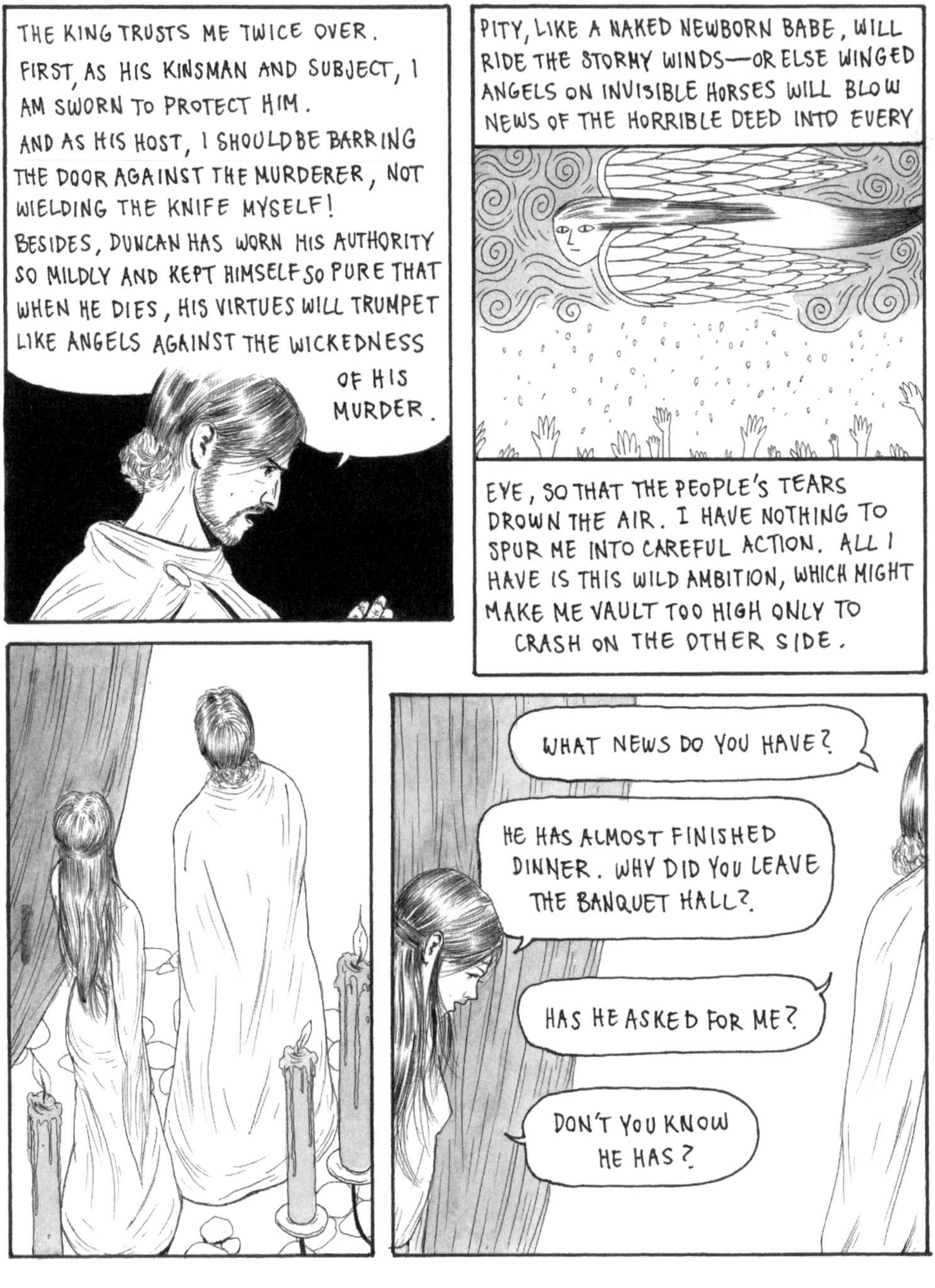
THE KING TRUSTS ME TWICE OVER. FIRST, AS HIS KINSMAN AND SUBJECT, I AM SWORN TO PROTECT HIM. AND AS HIS HOST, I SHOULD BE BARRING THE DOOR AGAINST THE MURDERER, NOT WIELDING THE KNIFE MYSELF! BESIDES, DUNCAN HAS WORN HIS AUTHORITY SO MILDLY AND KEPT HIMSELF SO PURE THAT WHEN HE DIES, HIS VIRTUES WILL TRUMPET LIKE ANGELS AGAINST THE WICKEDNESS OF HIS MURDER.
PITY, LIKE A NAKED NEWBORN BABE, WILL RIDE THE STORMY WINDS—OR ELSE WINGED ANGELS ON INVISIBLE HORSES WILL BLOW NEWS OF THE HORRIBLE DEED INTO EVERY
EYE, SO THAT THE PEOPLE'S TEARS DROWN THE AIR. I HAVE NOTHING TO SPUR ME INTO CAREFUL ACTION. ALL I HAVE IS THIS WILD AMBITION, WHICH MIGHT MAKE ME VAULT TOO HIGH ONLY TO CRASH ON THE OTHER SIDE.
WHAT NEWS DO YOU HAVE?
HE HAS ALMOST FINISHED DINNER. WHY DID YOU LEAVE THE BANQUET HALL?
HAS HE ASKED FOR ME?
DON'T YOU KNOW HE HAS?

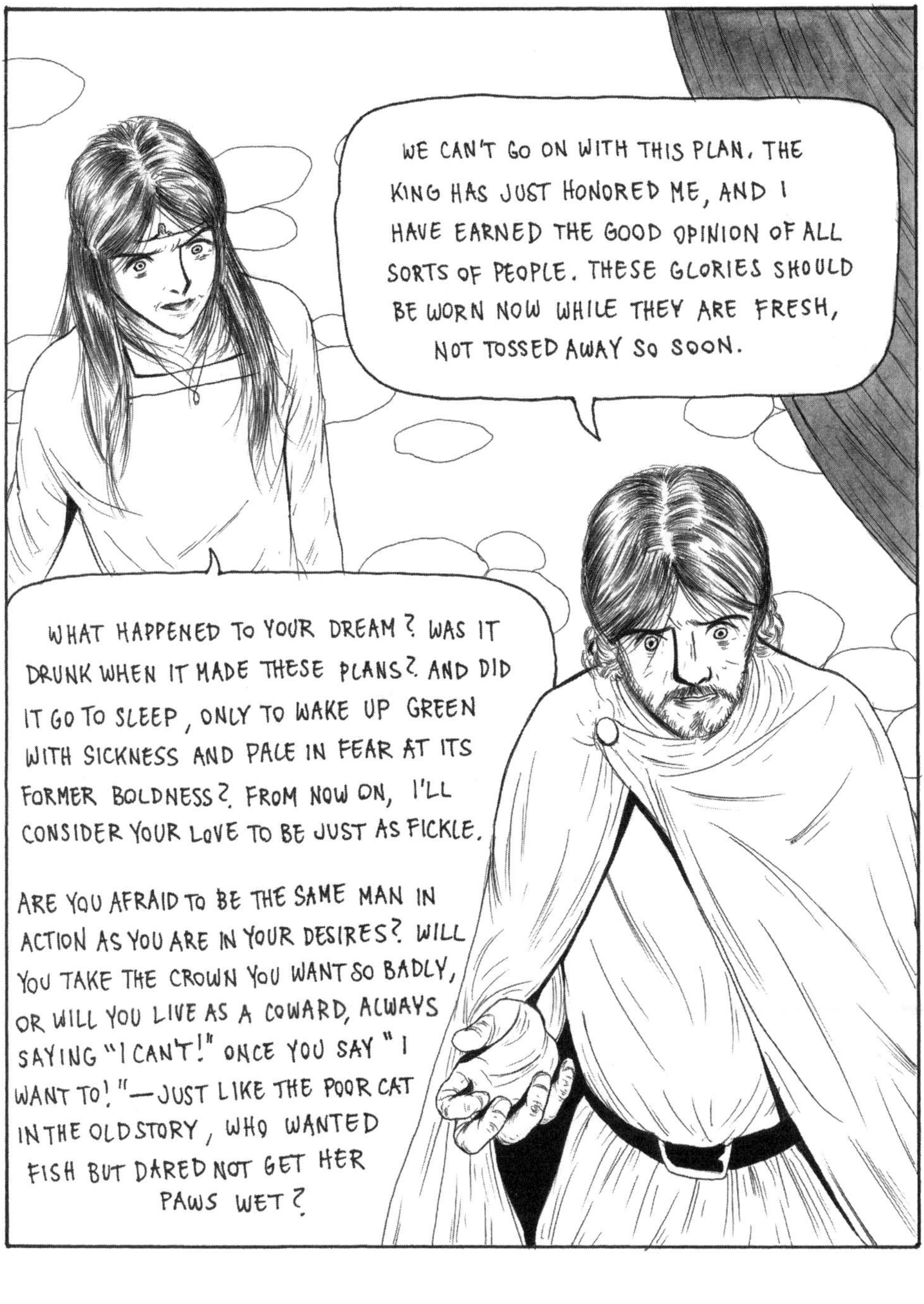
WE CAN'T GO ON WITH THIS PLAN. THE KING HAS JUST HONORED ME, AND I HAVE EARNED THE GOOD OPINION OF ALL SORTS OF PEOPLE. THESE GLORIES SHOULD BE WORN NOW WHILE THEY ARE FRESH, NOT TOSSED AWAY SO SOON.
WHAT HAPPENED TO YOUR DREAM? WAS IT DRUNK WHEN IT MADE THESE PLANS? AND DID IT GO TO SLEEP, ONLY TO WAKE UP GREEN WITH SICKNESS AND PALE IN FEAR AT ITS FORMER BOLDNESS? FROM NOW ON, I'LL CONSIDER YOUR LOVE TO BE JUST AS FICKLE.
ARE YOU AFRAID TO BE THE SAME MAN IN ACTION AS YOU ARE IN YOUR DESIRES? WILL YOU TAKE THE CROWN YOU WANT SO BADLY, OR WILL YOU LIVE AS A COWARD, ALWAYS SAYING "I CAN'T!" ONCE YOU SAY "I WANT TO!"—JUST LIKE THE POOR CAT IN THE OLD STORY, WHO WANTED FISH BUT DARED NOT GET HER PAWS WET?

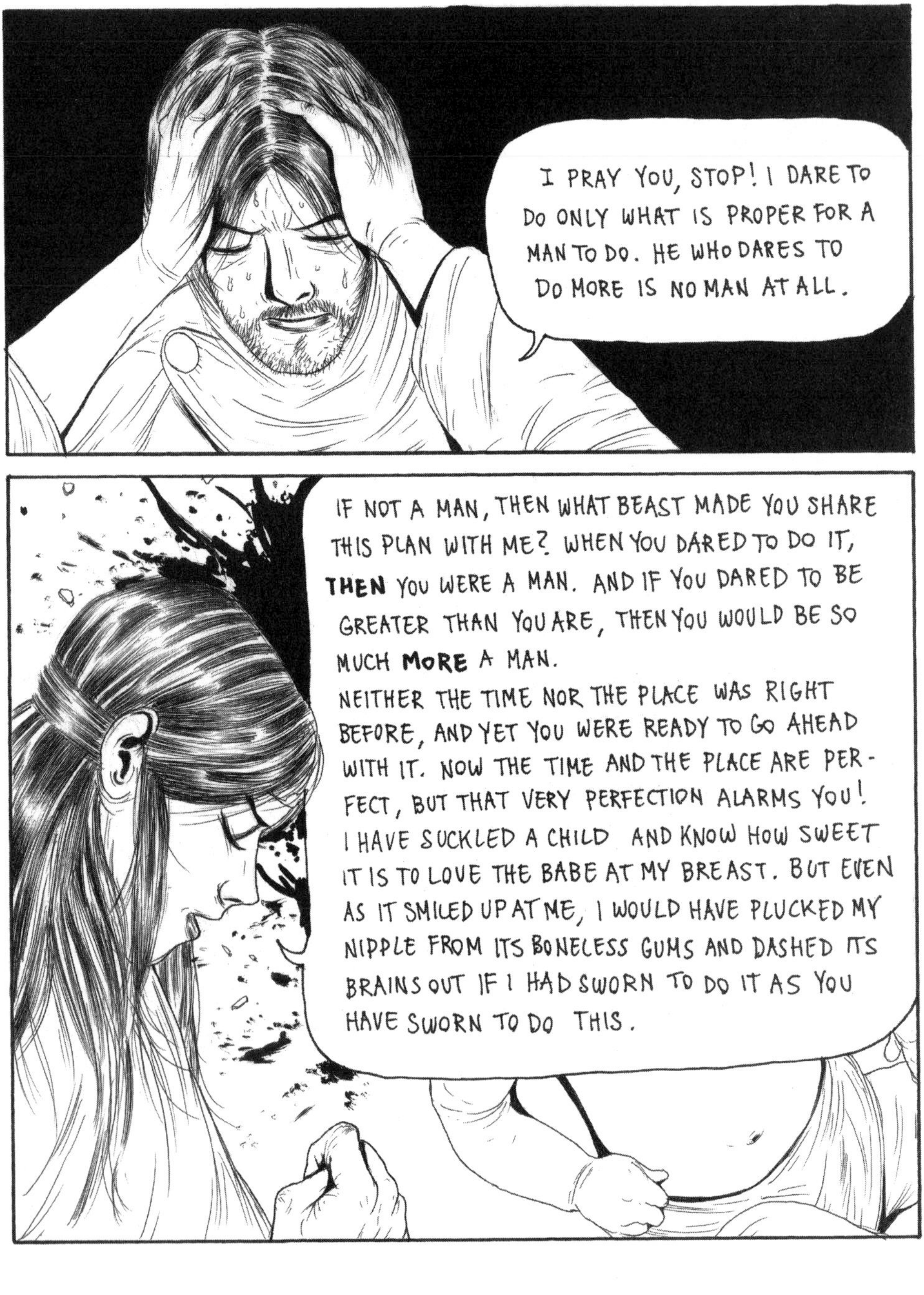
I PRAY YOU, STOP! I DARE TO DO ONLY WHAT IS PROPER FOR A MAN TO DO. HE WHO DARES TO DO MORE IS NO MAN AT ALL.
IF NOT A MAN, THEN WHAT BEAST MADE YOU SHARE THIS PLAN WITH ME? WHEN YOU DARED TO DO IT, **THEN** YOU WERE A MAN. AND IF YOU DARED TO BE GREATER THAN YOU ARE, THEN YOU WOULD BE SO MUCH **MORE** A MAN.
NEITHER THE TIME NOR THE PLACE WAS RIGHT BEFORE, AND YET YOU WERE READY TO GO AHEAD WITH IT. NOW THE TIME AND THE PLACE ARE PERFECT, BUT THAT VERY PERFECTION ALARMS YOU!
I HAVE SUCKLED A CHILD AND KNOW HOW SWEET IT IS TO LOVE THE BABE AT MY BREAST. BUT EVEN AS IT SMILED UP AT ME, I WOULD HAVE PLUCKED MY NIPPLE FROM ITS BONELESS GUMS AND DASHED ITS BRAINS OUT IF I HAD SWORN TO DO IT AS YOU HAVE SWORN TO DO THIS.

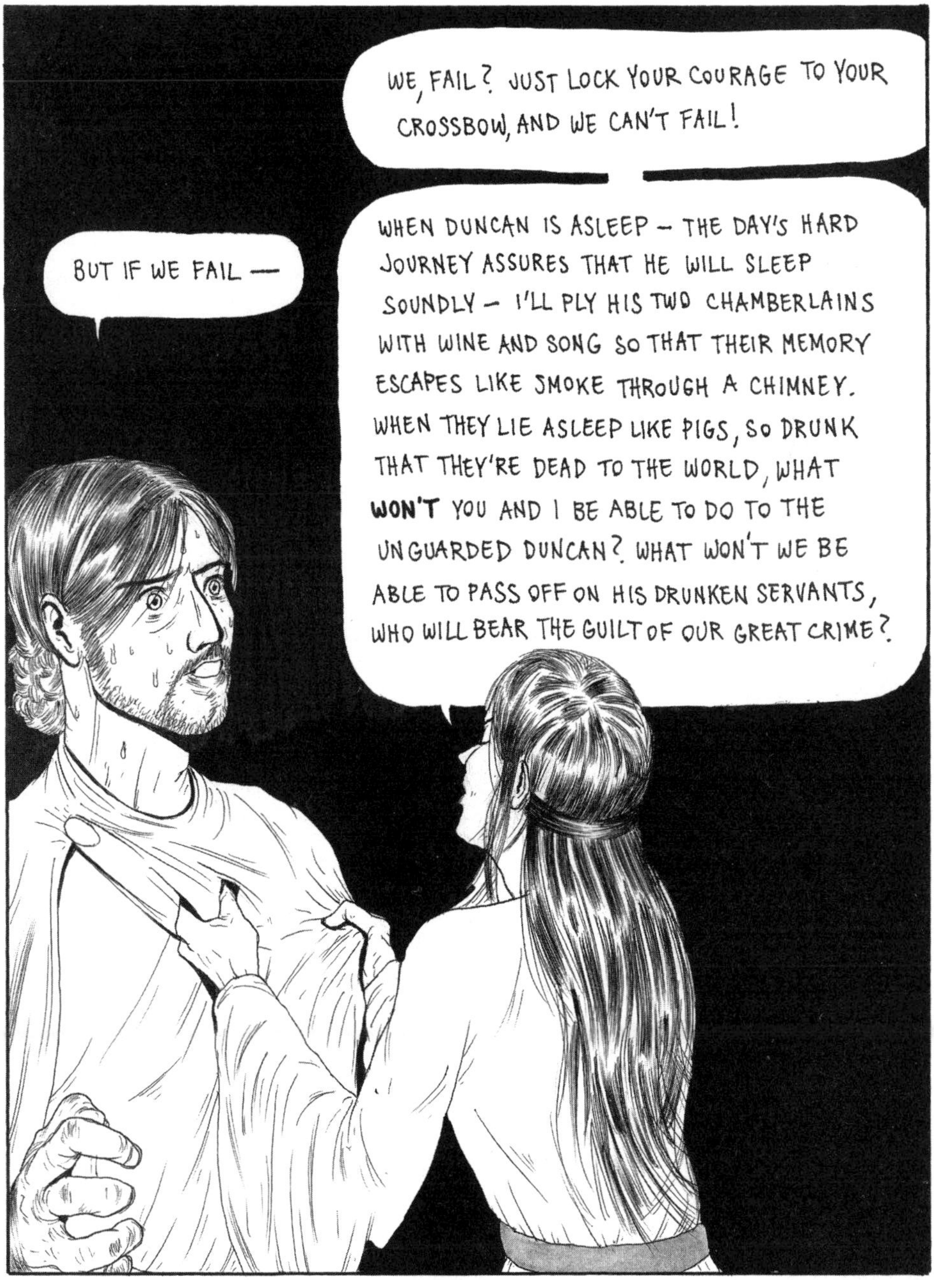
BUT IF WE FAIL —
WE, FAIL? JUST LOCK YOUR COURAGE TO YOUR CROSSBOW, AND WE CAN'T FAIL!
WHEN DUNCAN IS ASLEEP – THE DAY'S HARD JOURNEY ASSURES THAT HE WILL SLEEP SOUNDLY – I'LL PLY HIS TWO CHAMBERLAINS WITH WINE AND SONG SO THAT THEIR MEMORY ESCAPES LIKE SMOKE THROUGH A CHIMNEY. WHEN THEY LIE ASLEEP LIKE PIGS, SO DRUNK THAT THEY'RE DEAD TO THE WORLD, WHAT **WON'T** YOU AND I BE ABLE TO DO TO THE UNGUARDED DUNCAN? WHAT WON'T WE BE ABLE TO PASS OFF ON HIS DRUNKEN SERVANTS, WHO WILL BEAR THE GUILT OF OUR GREAT CRIME?

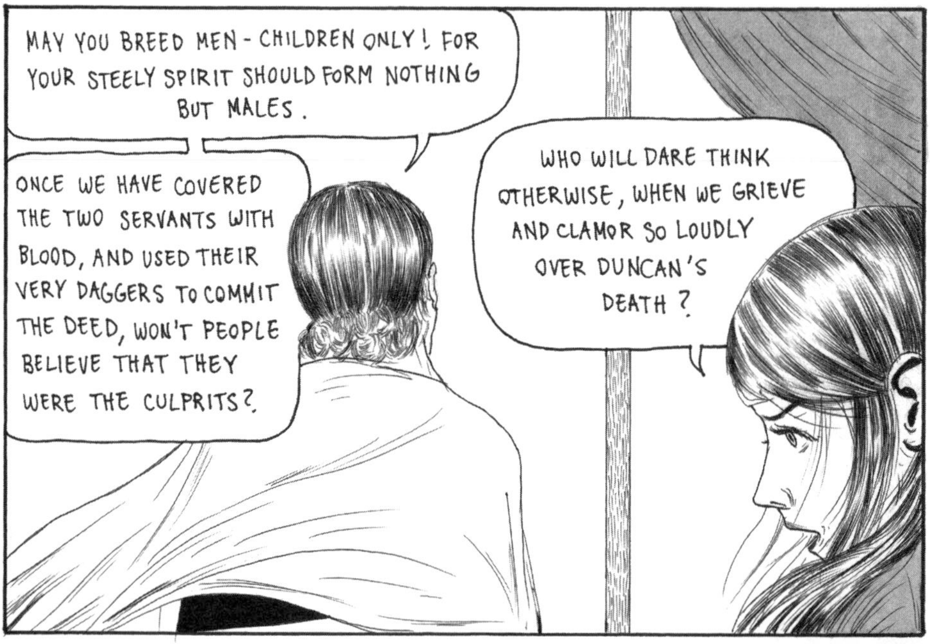
MAY YOU BREED MEN-CHILDREN ONLY! FOR YOUR STEELY SPIRIT SHOULD FORM NOTHING BUT MALES.
ONCE WE HAVE COVERED THE TWO SERVANTS WITH BLOOD, AND USED THEIR VERY DAGGERS TO COMMIT THE DEED, WON'T PEOPLE BELIEVE THAT THEY WERE THE CULPRITS?
WHO WILL DARE THINK OTHERWISE, WHEN WE GRIEVE AND CLAMOR SO LOUDLY OVER DUNCAN'S DEATH?

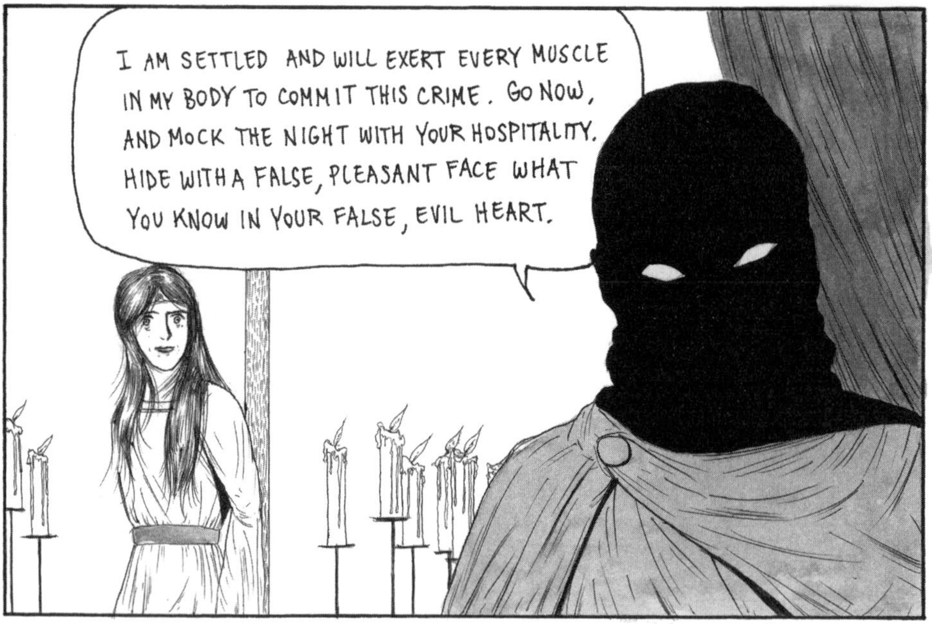
I AM SETTLED AND WILL EXERT EVERY MUSCLE IN MY BODY TO COMMIT THIS CRIME. GO NOW, AND MOCK THE NIGHT WITH YOUR HOSPITALITY. HIDE WITH A FALSE, PLEASANT FACE WHAT YOU KNOW IN YOUR FALSE, EVIL HEART.

ACT II

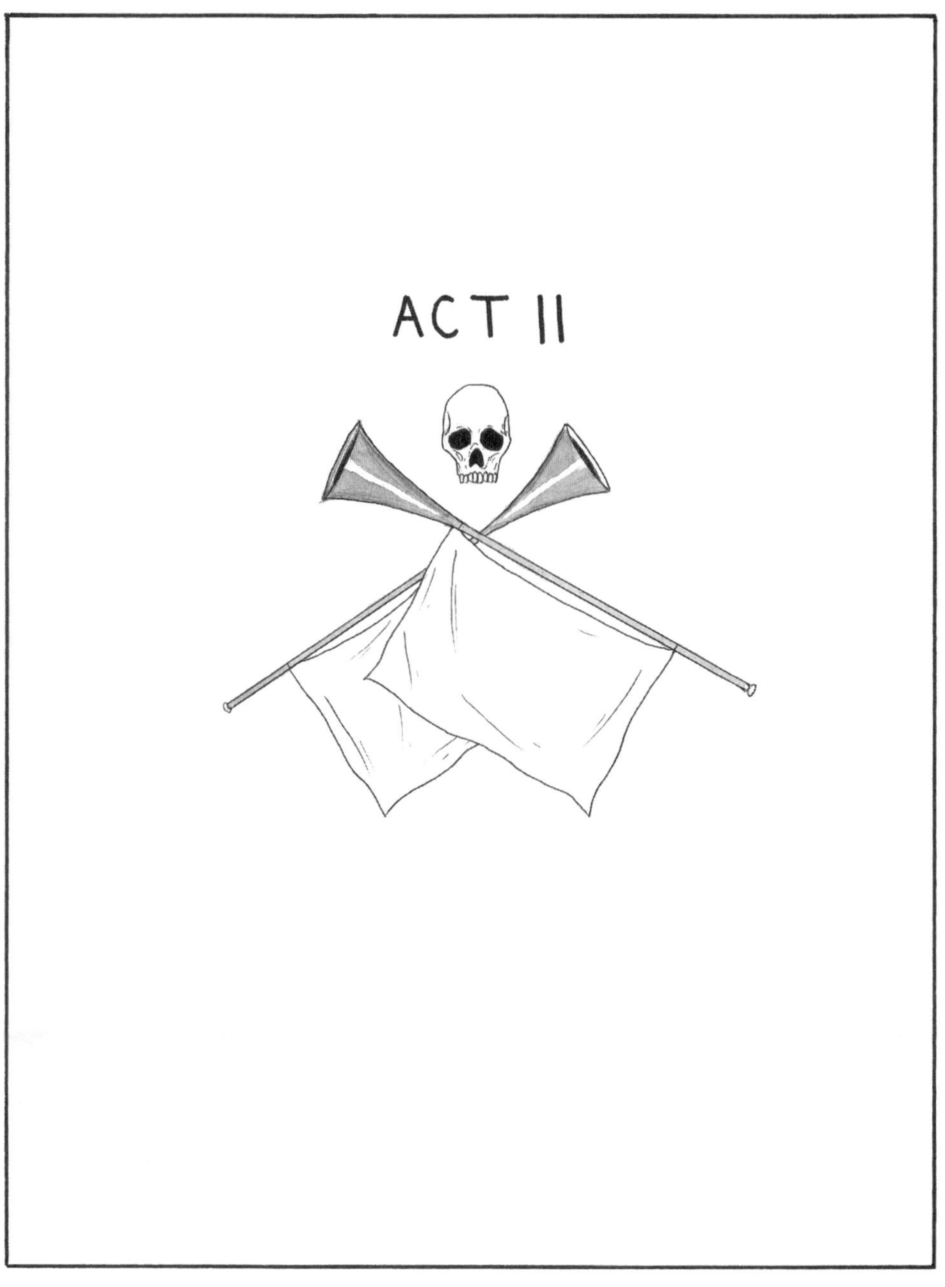

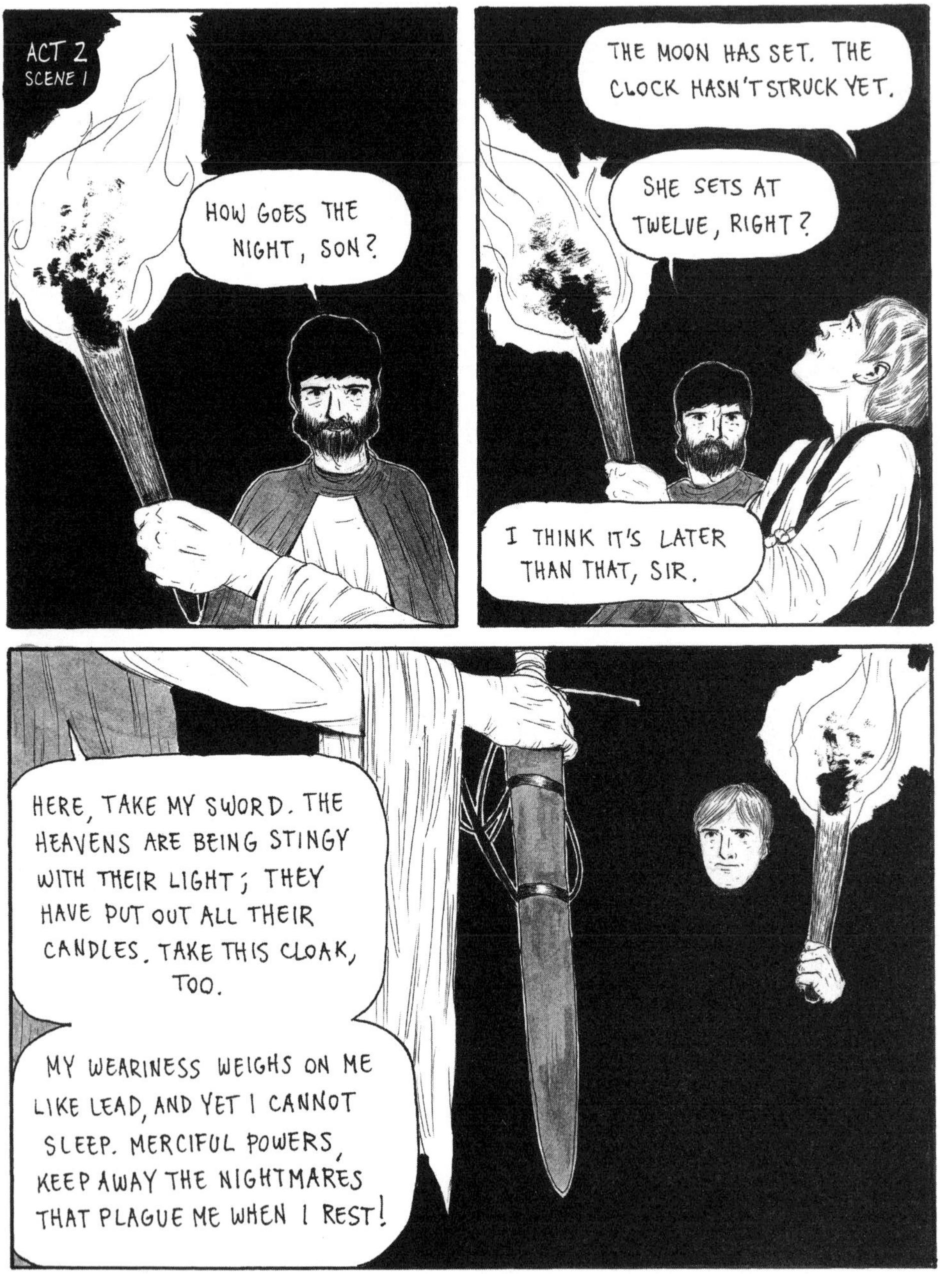
ACT 2
SCENE 1
HOW GOES THE NIGHT, SON?
THE MOON HAS SET. THE CLOCK HASN'T STRUCK YET.
SHE SETS AT TWELVE, RIGHT?
I THINK IT'S LATER THAN THAT, SIR.
HERE, TAKE MY SWORD. THE HEAVENS ARE BEING STINGY WITH THEIR LIGHT; THEY HAVE PUT OUT ALL THEIR CANDLES. TAKE THIS CLOAK, TOO.
MY WEARINESS WEIGHS ON ME LIKE LEAD, AND YET I CANNOT SLEEP. MERCIFUL POWERS, KEEP AWAY THE NIGHTMARES THAT PLAGUE ME WHEN I REST!

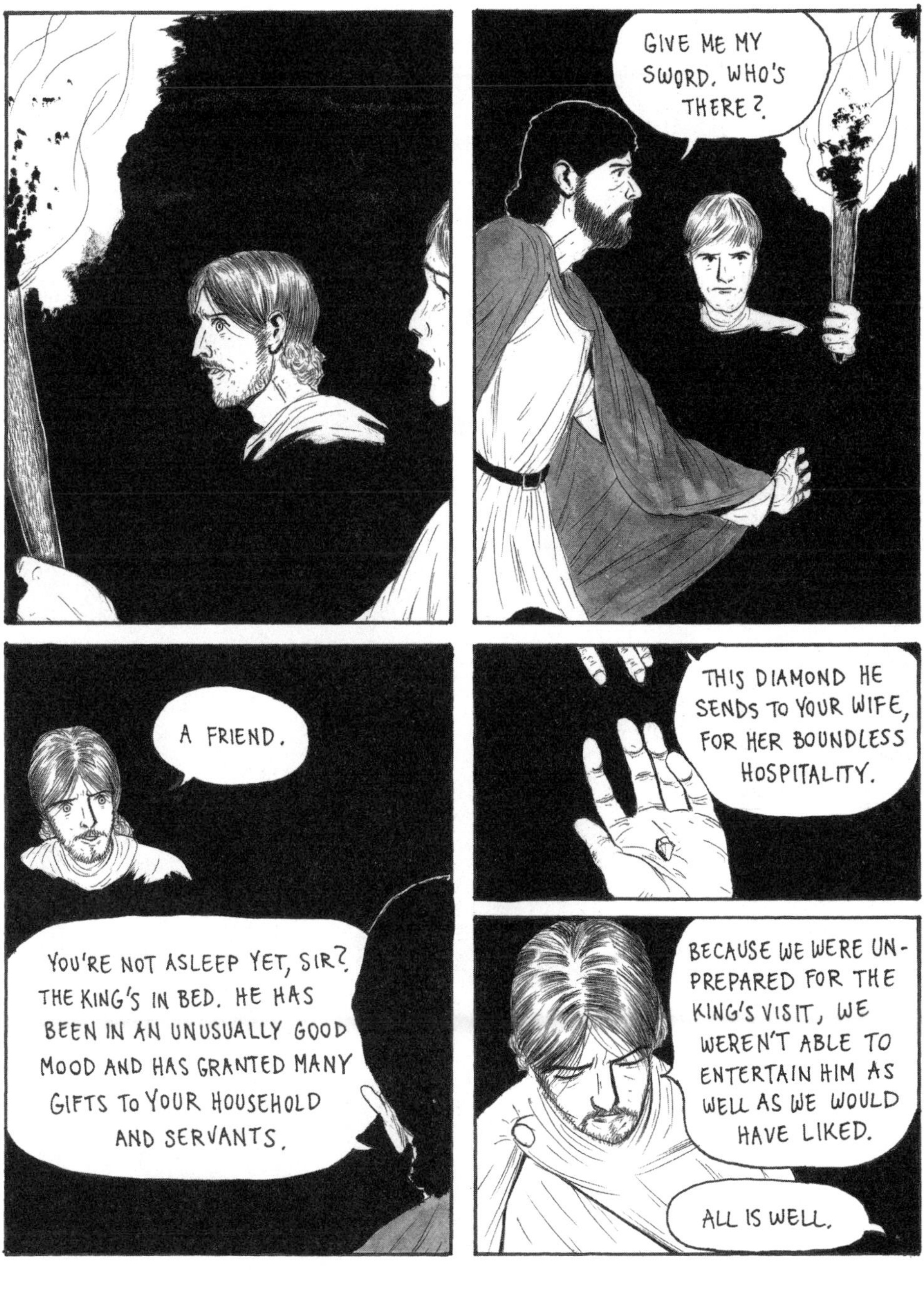
GIVE ME MY SWORD. WHO'S THERE?
A FRIEND.
THIS DIAMOND HE SENDS TO YOUR WIFE, FOR HER BOUNDLESS HOSPITALITY.
YOU'RE NOT ASLEEP YET, SIR? THE KING'S IN BED. HE HAS BEEN IN AN UNUSUALLY GOOD MOOD AND HAS GRANTED MANY GIFTS TO YOUR HOUSEHOLD AND SERVANTS.
BECAUSE WE WERE UN-PREPARED FOR THE KING'S VISIT, WE WEREN'T ABLE TO ENTERTAIN HIM AS WELL AS WE WOULD HAVE LIKED.
ALL IS WELL.

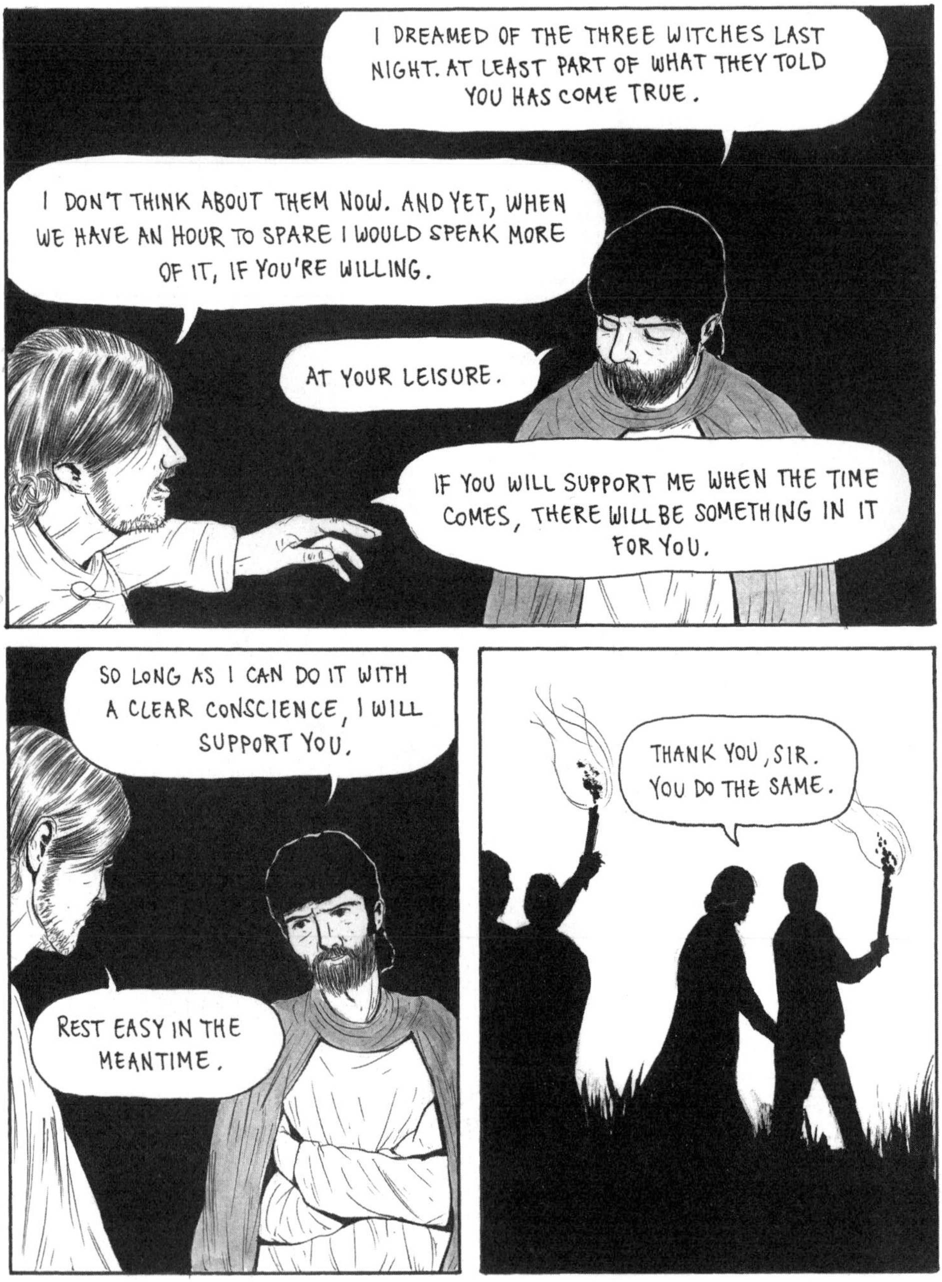
I DREAMED OF THE THREE WITCHES LAST NIGHT. AT LEAST PART OF WHAT THEY TOLD YOU HAS COME TRUE.
I DON'T THINK ABOUT THEM NOW. AND YET, WHEN WE HAVE AN HOUR TO SPARE I WOULD SPEAK MORE OF IT, IF YOU'RE WILLING.
AT YOUR LEISURE.
IF YOU WILL SUPPORT ME WHEN THE TIME COMES, THERE WILL BE SOMETHING IN IT FOR YOU.
SO LONG AS I CAN DO IT WITH A CLEAR CONSCIENCE, I WILL SUPPORT YOU.
REST EASY IN THE MEANTIME.
THANK YOU, SIR. YOU DO THE SAME.

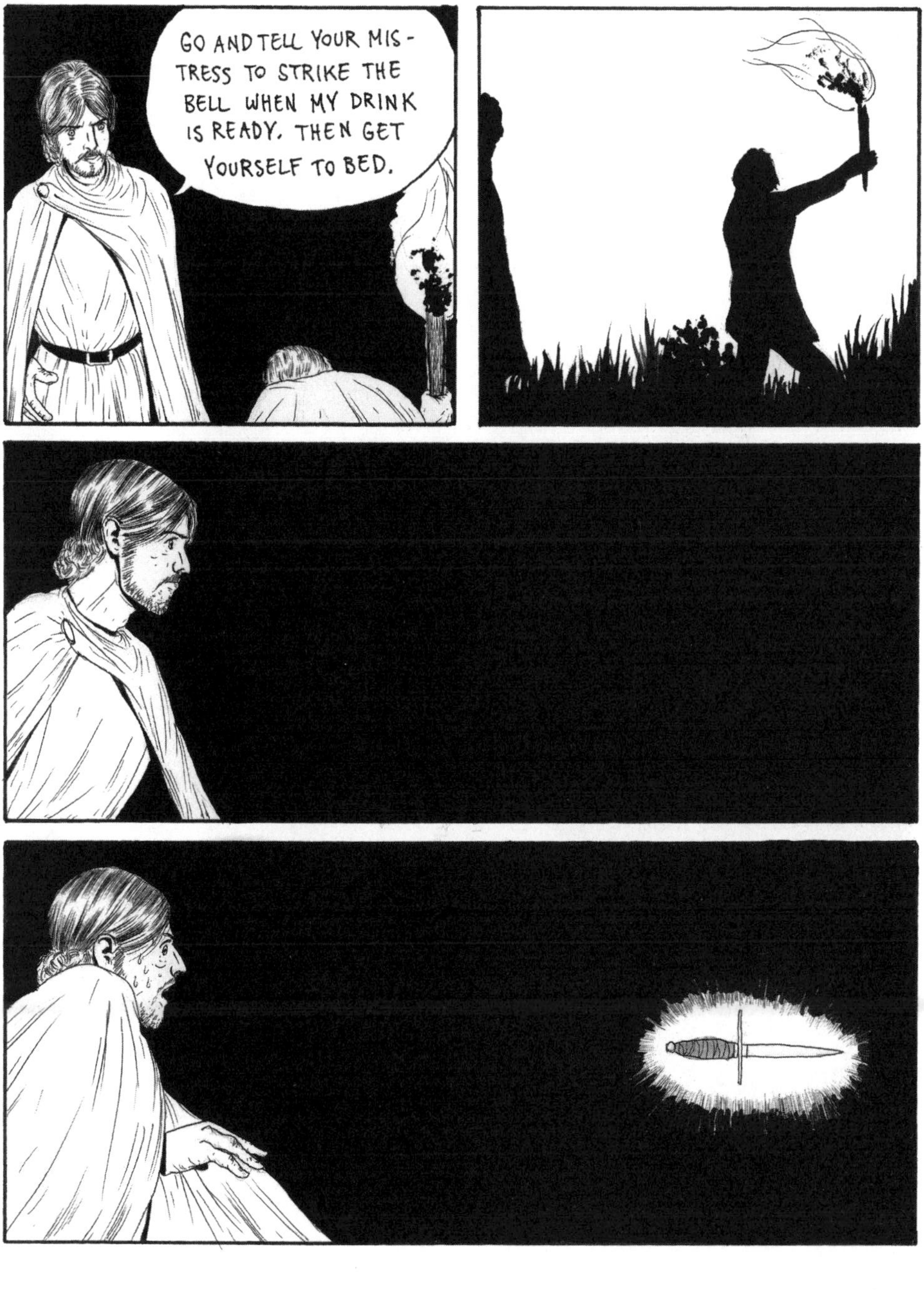
GO AND TELL YOUR MIS-TRESS TO STRIKE THE BELL WHEN MY DRINK IS READY. THEN GET YOURSELF TO BED.

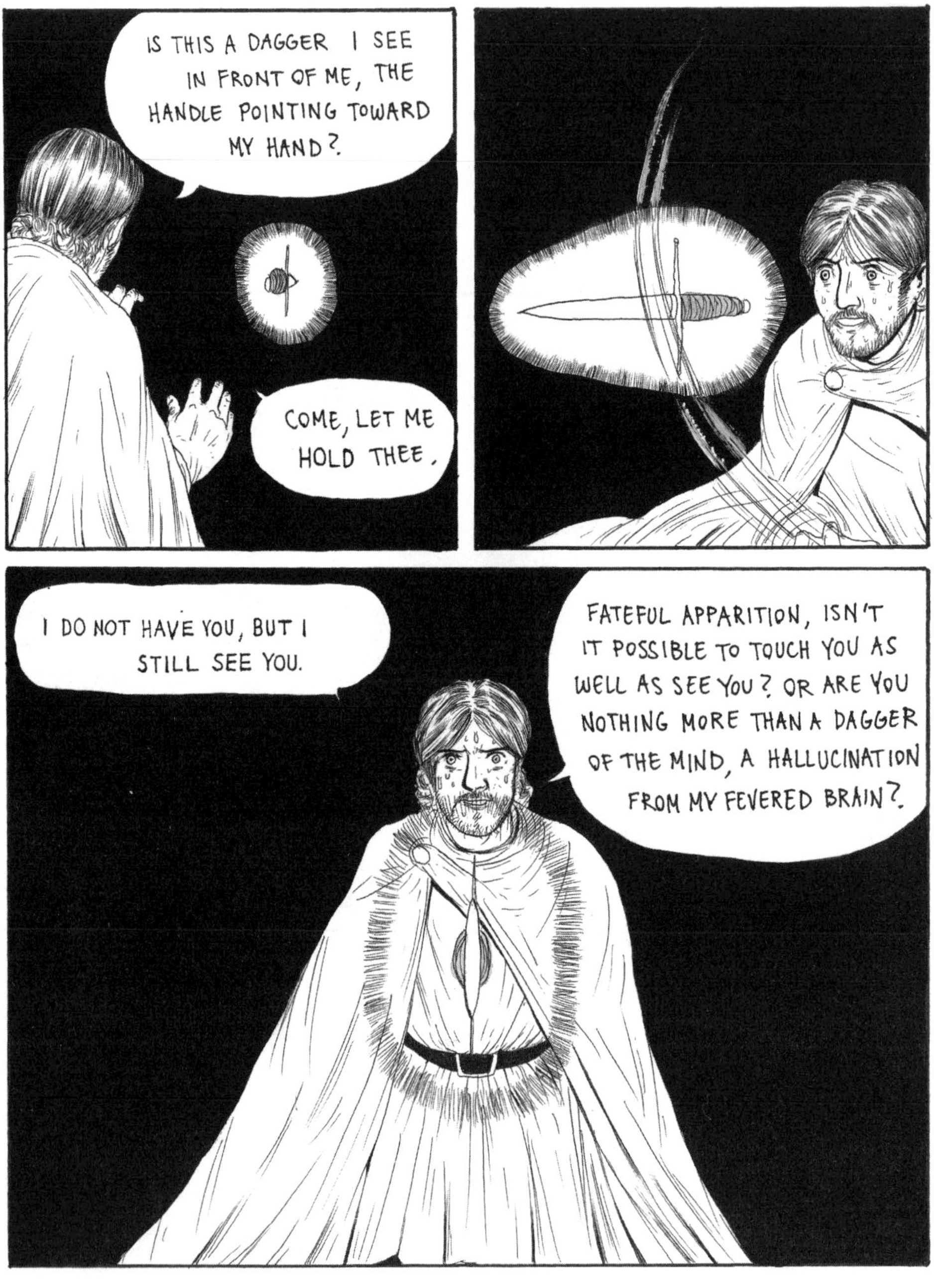
IS THIS A DAGGER I SEE IN FRONT OF ME, THE HANDLE POINTING TOWARD MY HAND?
COME, LET ME HOLD THEE.
I DO NOT HAVE YOU, BUT I STILL SEE YOU.
FATEFUL APPARITION, ISN'T IT POSSIBLE TO TOUCH YOU AS WELL AS SEE YOU? OR ARE YOU NOTHING MORE THAN A DAGGER OF THE MIND, A HALLUCINATION FROM MY FEVERED BRAIN?

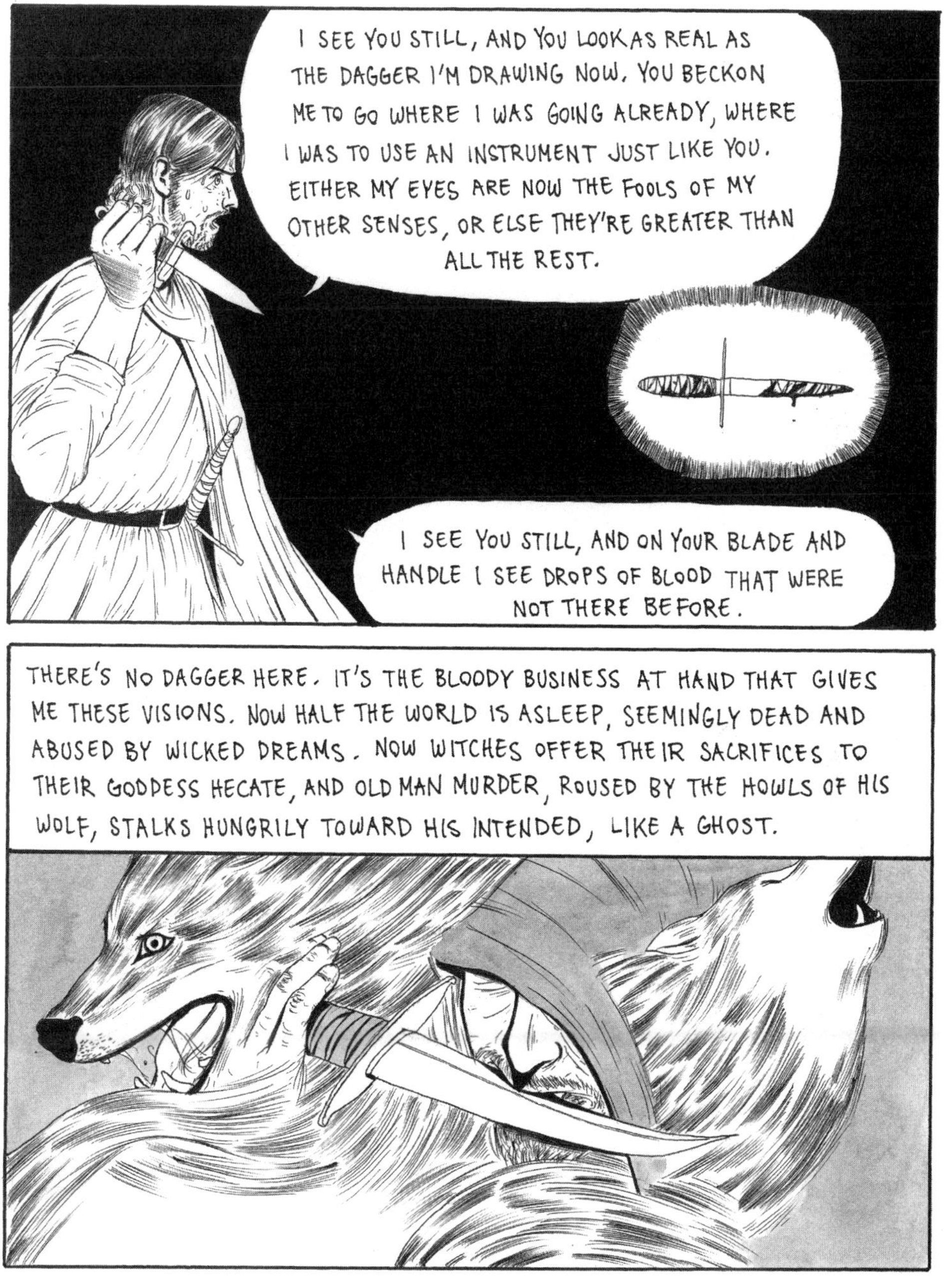
I SEE YOU STILL, AND YOU LOOK AS REAL AS THE DAGGER I'M DRAWING NOW. YOU BECKON ME TO GO WHERE I WAS GOING ALREADY, WHERE I WAS TO USE AN INSTRUMENT JUST LIKE YOU. EITHER MY EYES ARE NOW THE FOOLS OF MY OTHER SENSES, OR ELSE THEY'RE GREATER THAN ALL THE REST.
I SEE YOU STILL, AND ON YOUR BLADE AND HANDLE I SEE DROPS OF BLOOD THAT WERE NOT THERE BEFORE.
THERE'S NO DAGGER HERE. IT'S THE BLOODY BUSINESS AT HAND THAT GIVES ME THESE VISIONS. NOW HALF THE WORLD IS ASLEEP, SEEMINGLY DEAD AND ABUSED BY WICKED DREAMS. NOW WITCHES OFFER THEIR SACRIFICES TO THEIR GODDESS HECATE, AND OLD MAN MURDER, ROUSED BY THE HOWLS OF HIS WOLF, STALKS HUNGRILY TOWARD HIS INTENDED, LIKE A GHOST.

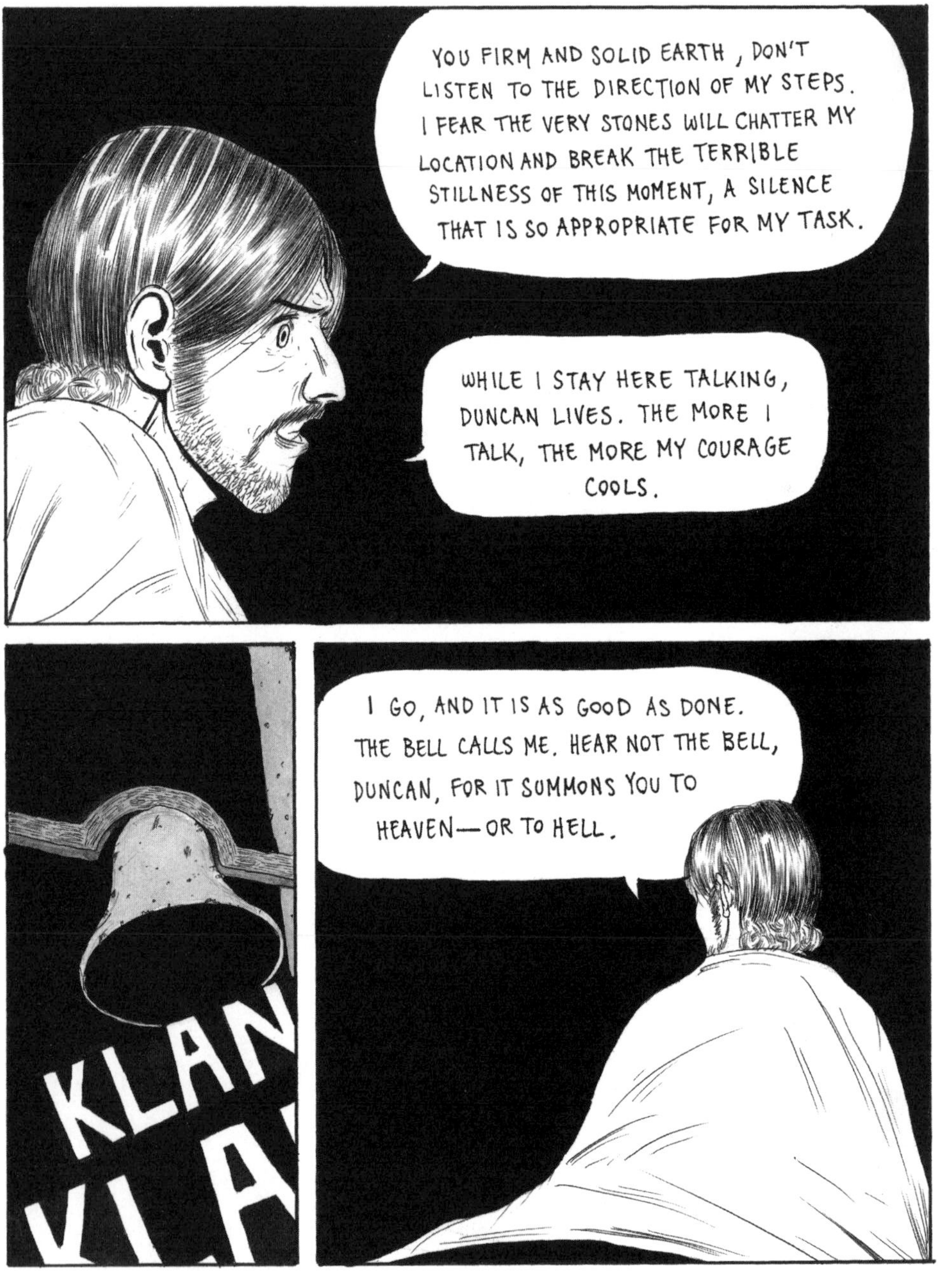
YOU FIRM AND SOLID EARTH, DON'T LISTEN TO THE DIRECTION OF MY STEPS. I FEAR THE VERY STONES WILL CHATTER MY LOCATION AND BREAK THE TERRIBLE STILLNESS OF THIS MOMENT, A SILENCE THAT IS SO APPROPRIATE FOR MY TASK.
WHILE I STAY HERE TALKING, DUNCAN LIVES. THE MORE I TALK, THE MORE MY COURAGE COOLS.
KLAN
I GO, AND IT IS AS GOOD AS DONE. THE BELL CALLS ME. HEAR NOT THE BELL, DUNCAN, FOR IT SUMMONS YOU TO HEAVEN—OR TO HELL.

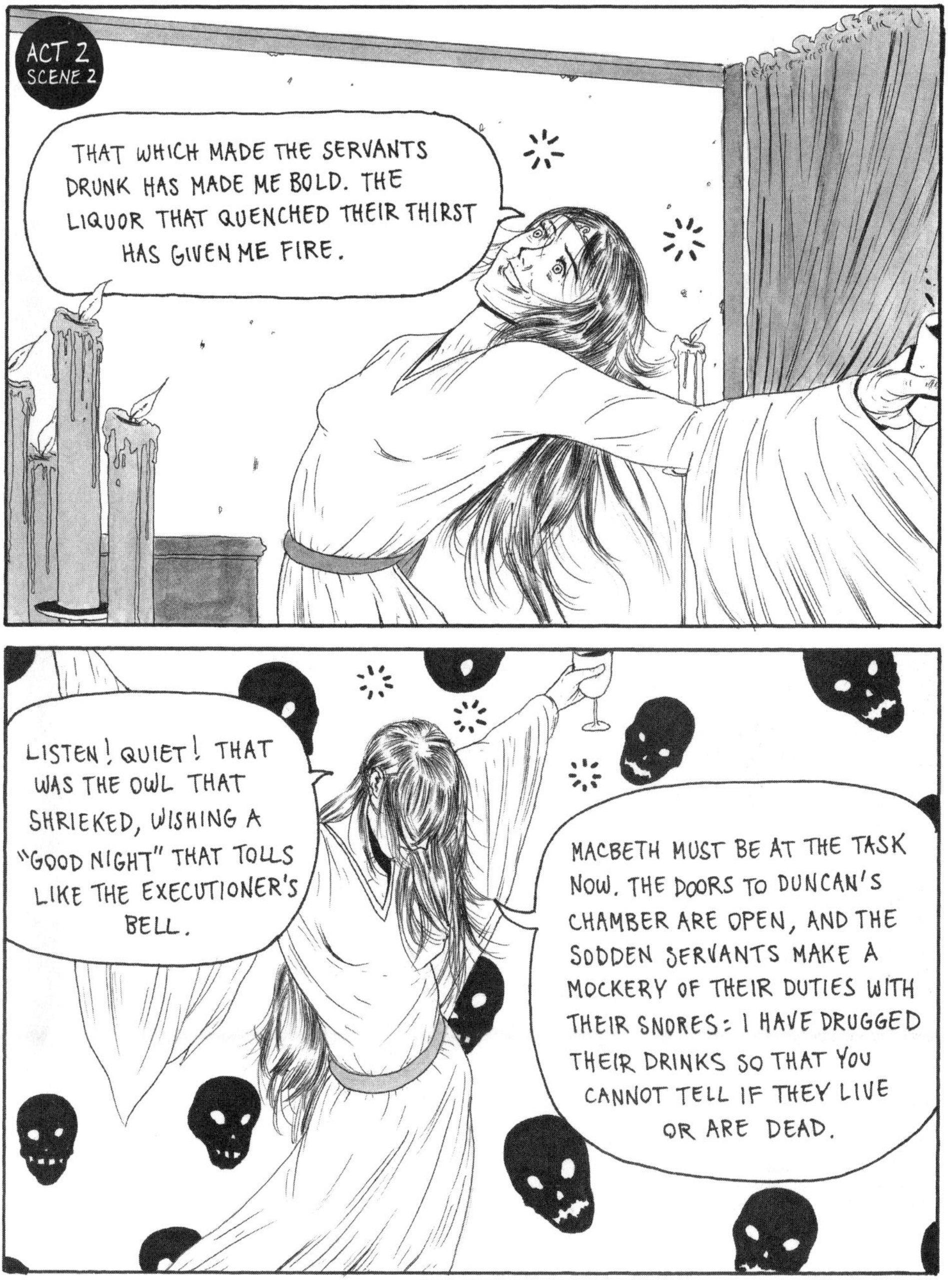
ACT 2 SCENE 2
THAT WHICH MADE THE SERVANTS DRUNK HAS MADE ME BOLD. THE LIQUOR THAT QUENCHED THEIR THIRST HAS GIVEN ME FIRE.
LISTEN! QUIET! THAT WAS THE OWL THAT SHRIEKED, WISHING A "GOOD NIGHT" THAT TOLLS LIKE THE EXECUTIONER'S BELL.
MACBETH MUST BE AT THE TASK NOW. THE DOORS TO DUNCAN'S CHAMBER ARE OPEN, AND THE SODDEN SERVANTS MAKE A MOCKERY OF THEIR DUTIES WITH THEIR SNORES: I HAVE DRUGGED THEIR DRINKS SO THAT YOU CANNOT TELL IF THEY LIVE OR ARE DEAD.

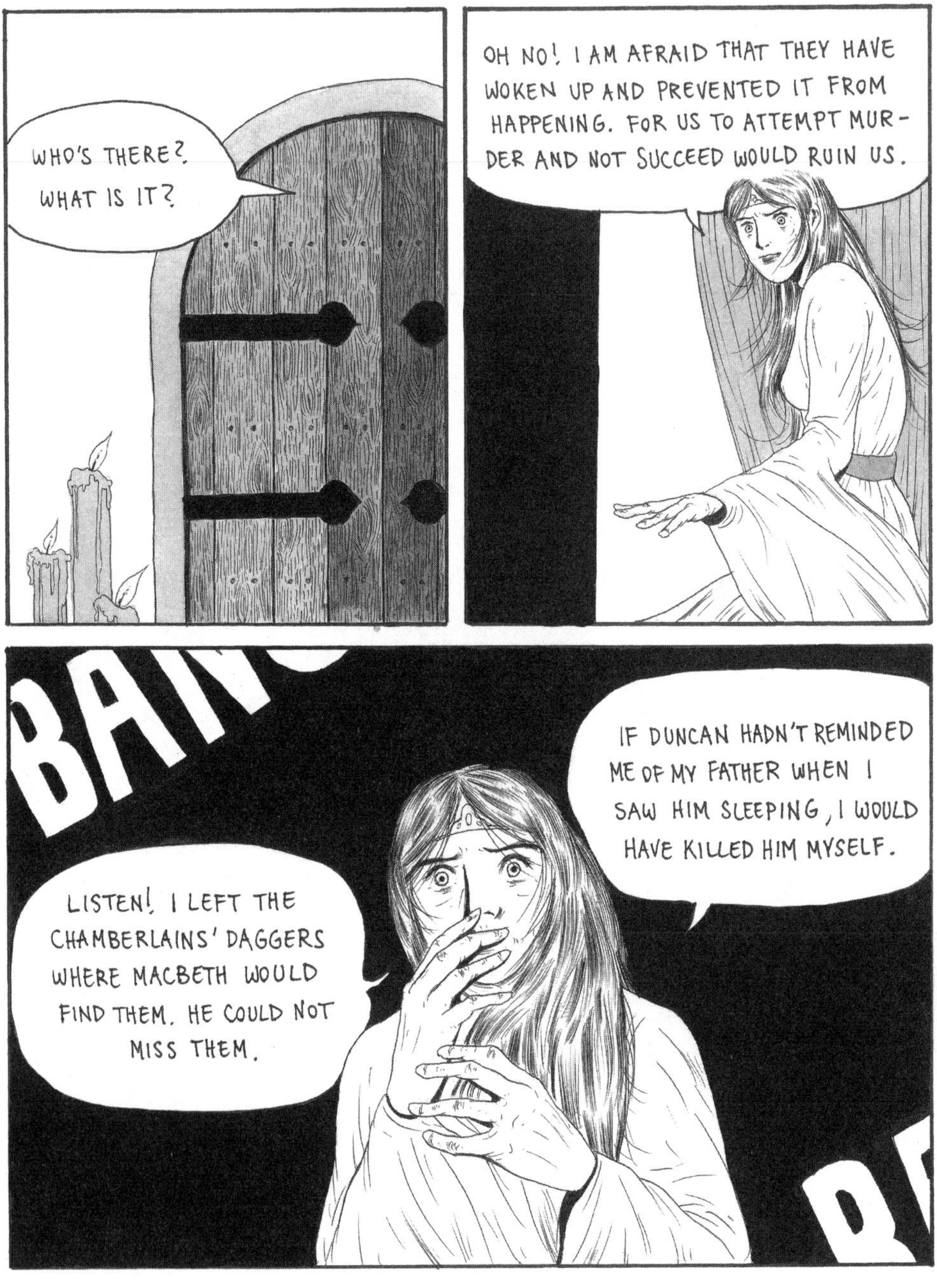
WHO'S THERE? WHAT IS IT?
OH NO! I AM AFRAID THAT THEY HAVE WOKEN UP AND PREVENTED IT FROM HAPPENING. FOR US TO ATTEMPT MURDER AND NOT SUCCEED WOULD RUIN US.
LISTEN! I LEFT THE CHAMBERLAINS' DAGGERS WHERE MACBETH WOULD FIND THEM. HE COULD NOT MISS THEM.
IF DUNCAN HADN'T REMINDED ME OF MY FATHER WHEN I SAW HIM SLEEPING, I WOULD HAVE KILLED HIM MYSELF.

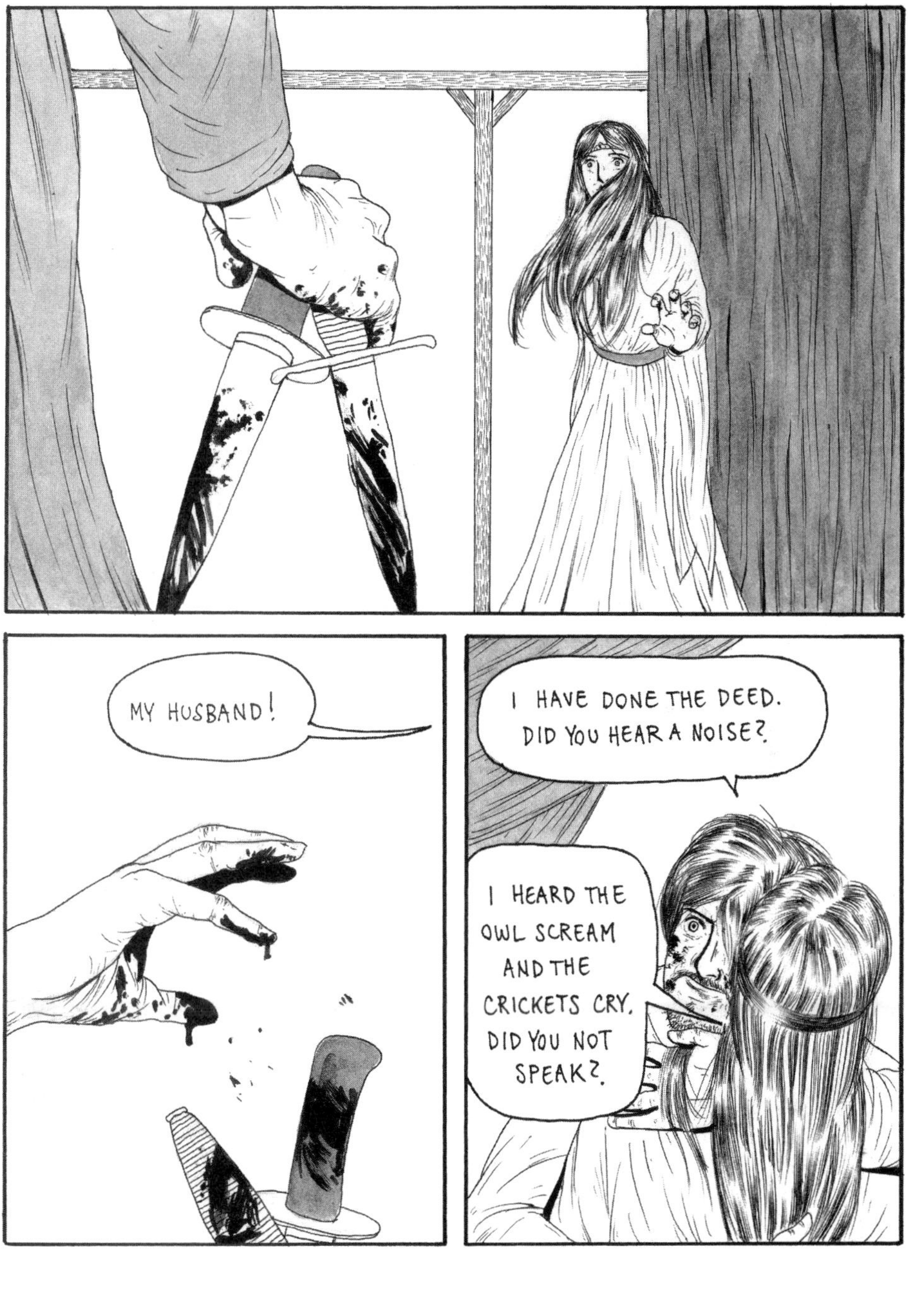
MY HUSBAND!
I HAVE DONE THE DEED. DID YOU HEAR A NOISE?
I HEARD THE OWL SCREAM AND THE CRICKETS CRY. DID YOU NOT SPEAK?

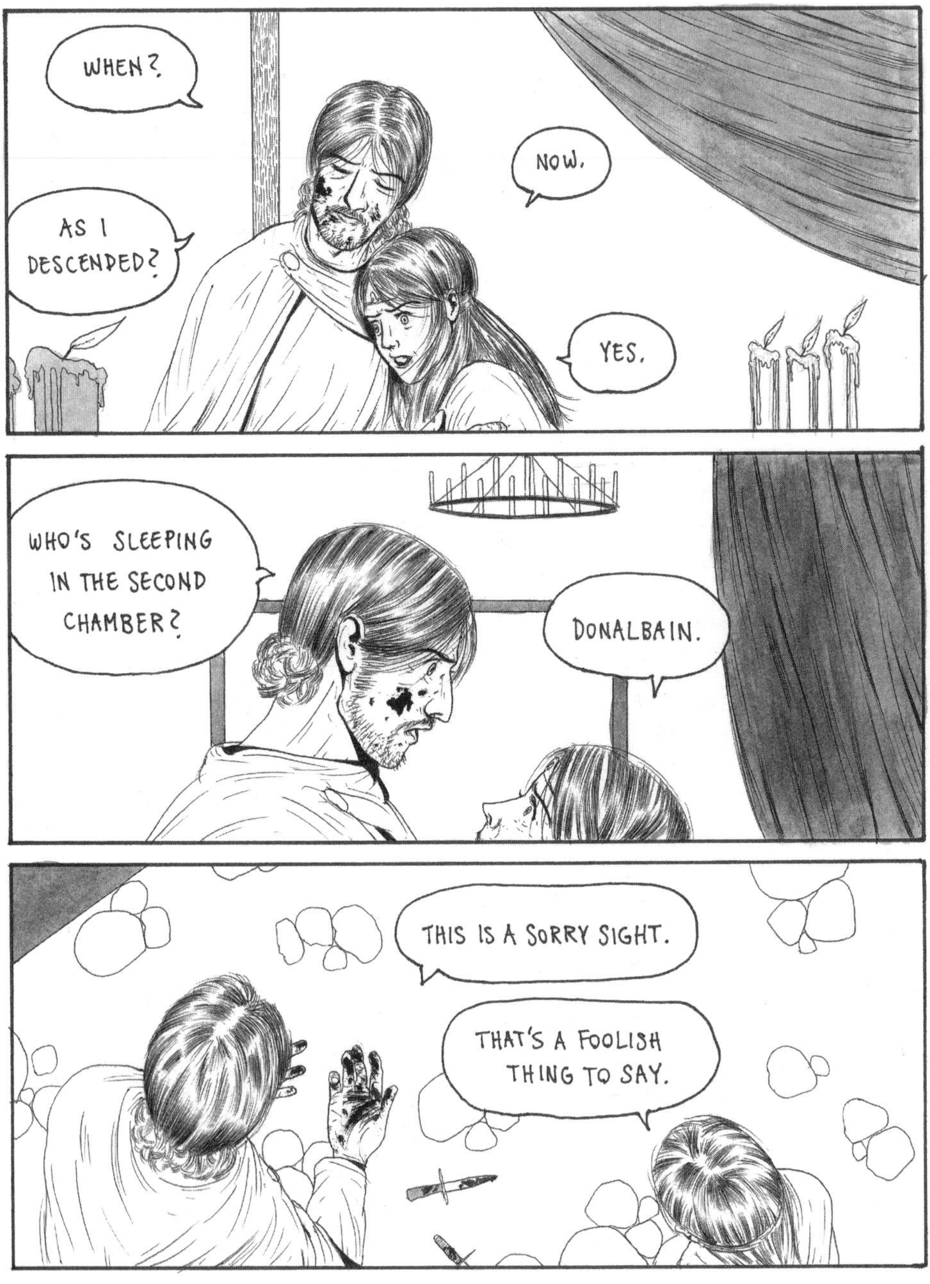
WHEN?
NOW.
AS I DESCENDED?
YES.
WHO'S SLEEPING IN THE SECOND CHAMBER?
DONALBAIN.
THIS IS A SORRY SIGHT.
THAT'S A FOOLISH THING TO SAY.

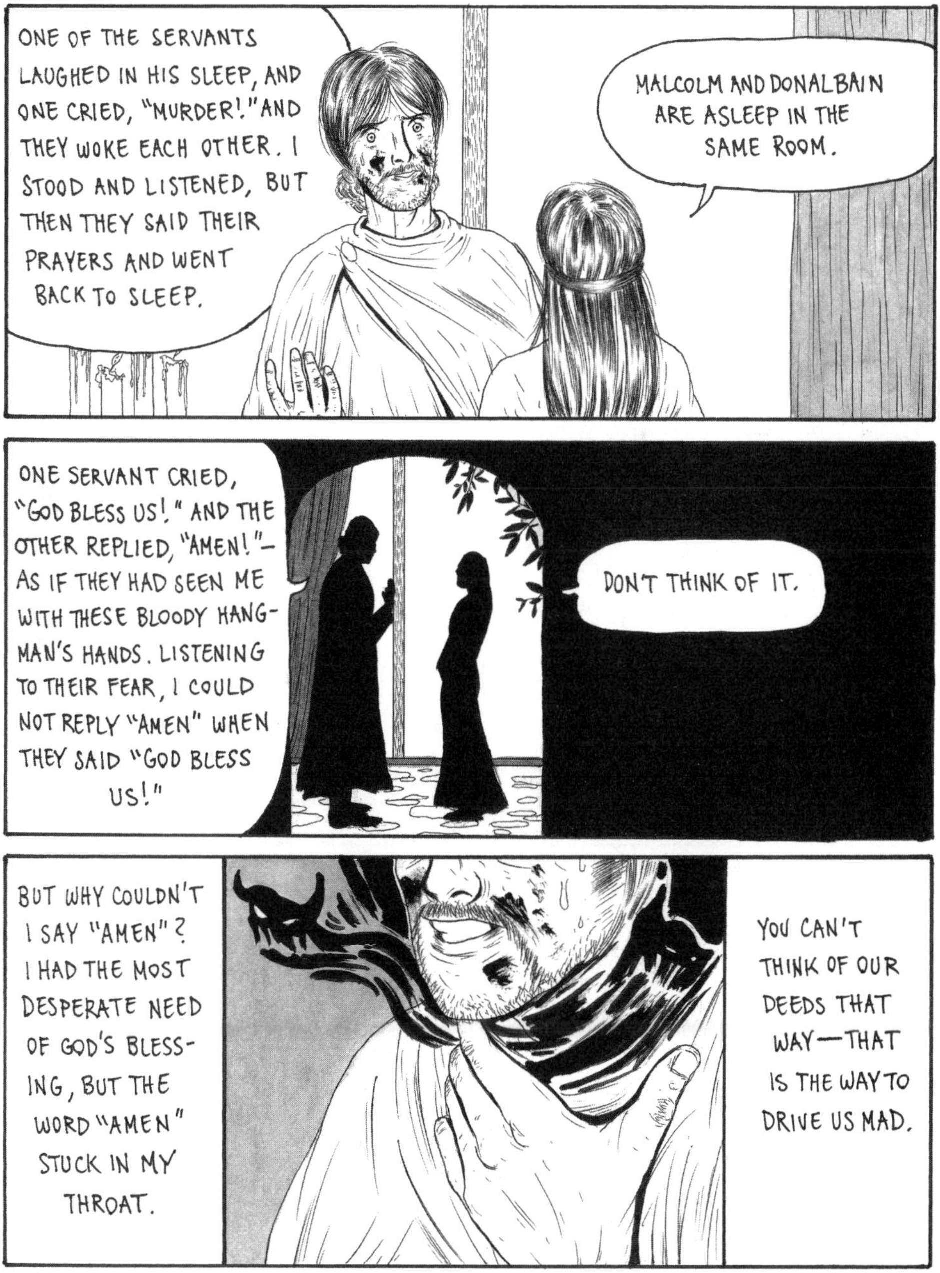
ONE OF THE SERVANTS LAUGHED IN HIS SLEEP, AND ONE CRIED, "MURDER!" AND THEY WOKE EACH OTHER. I STOOD AND LISTENED, BUT THEN THEY SAID THEIR PRAYERS AND WENT BACK TO SLEEP.
MALCOLM AND DONALBAIN ARE ASLEEP IN THE SAME ROOM.
ONE SERVANT CRIED, "GOD BLESS US!" AND THE OTHER REPLIED, "AMEN!"— AS IF THEY HAD SEEN ME WITH THESE BLOODY HANGMAN'S HANDS. LISTENING TO THEIR FEAR, I COULD NOT REPLY "AMEN" WHEN THEY SAID "GOD BLESS US!"
DON'T THINK OF IT.
BUT WHY COULDN'T I SAY "AMEN"? I HAD THE MOST DESPERATE NEED OF GOD'S BLESSING, BUT THE WORD "AMEN" STUCK IN MY THROAT.
YOU CAN'T THINK OF OUR DEEDS THAT WAY—THAT IS THE WAY TO DRIVE US MAD.

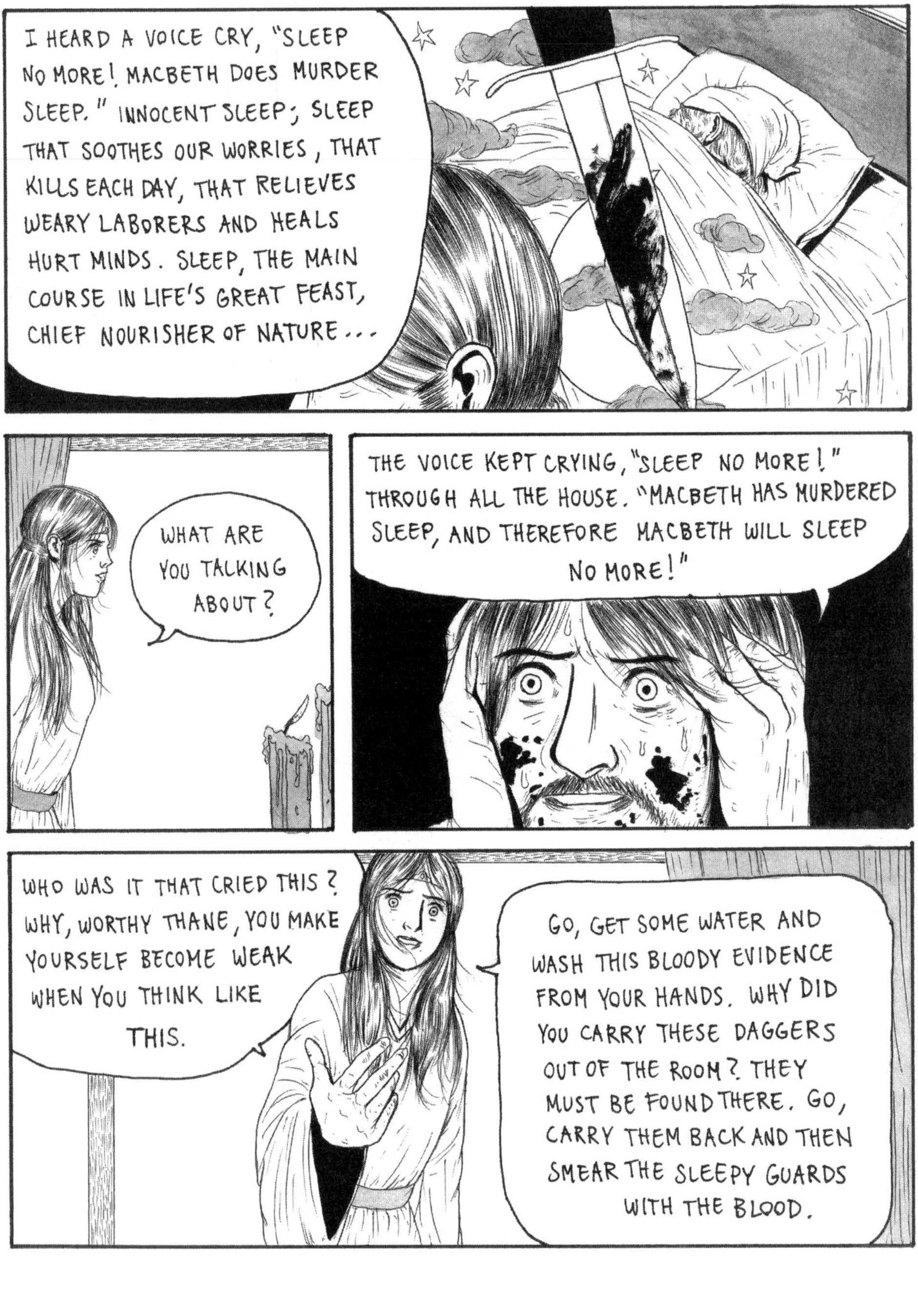
I HEARD A VOICE CRY, "SLEEP NO MORE! MACBETH DOES MURDER SLEEP." INNOCENT SLEEP; SLEEP THAT SOOTHES OUR WORRIES, THAT KILLS EACH DAY, THAT RELIEVES WEARY LABORERS AND HEALS HURT MINDS. SLEEP, THE MAIN COURSE IN LIFE'S GREAT FEAST, CHIEF NOURISHER OF NATURE...
WHAT ARE YOU TALKING ABOUT?
THE VOICE KEPT CRYING, "SLEEP NO MORE!" THROUGH ALL THE HOUSE. "MACBETH HAS MURDERED SLEEP, AND THEREFORE MACBETH WILL SLEEP NO MORE!"
WHO WAS IT THAT CRIED THIS? WHY, WORTHY THANE, YOU MAKE YOURSELF BECOME WEAK WHEN YOU THINK LIKE THIS.
GO, GET SOME WATER AND WASH THIS BLOODY EVIDENCE FROM YOUR HANDS. WHY DID YOU CARRY THESE DAGGERS OUT OF THE ROOM? THEY MUST BE FOUND THERE. GO, CARRY THEM BACK AND THEN SMEAR THE SLEEPY GUARDS WITH THE BLOOD.

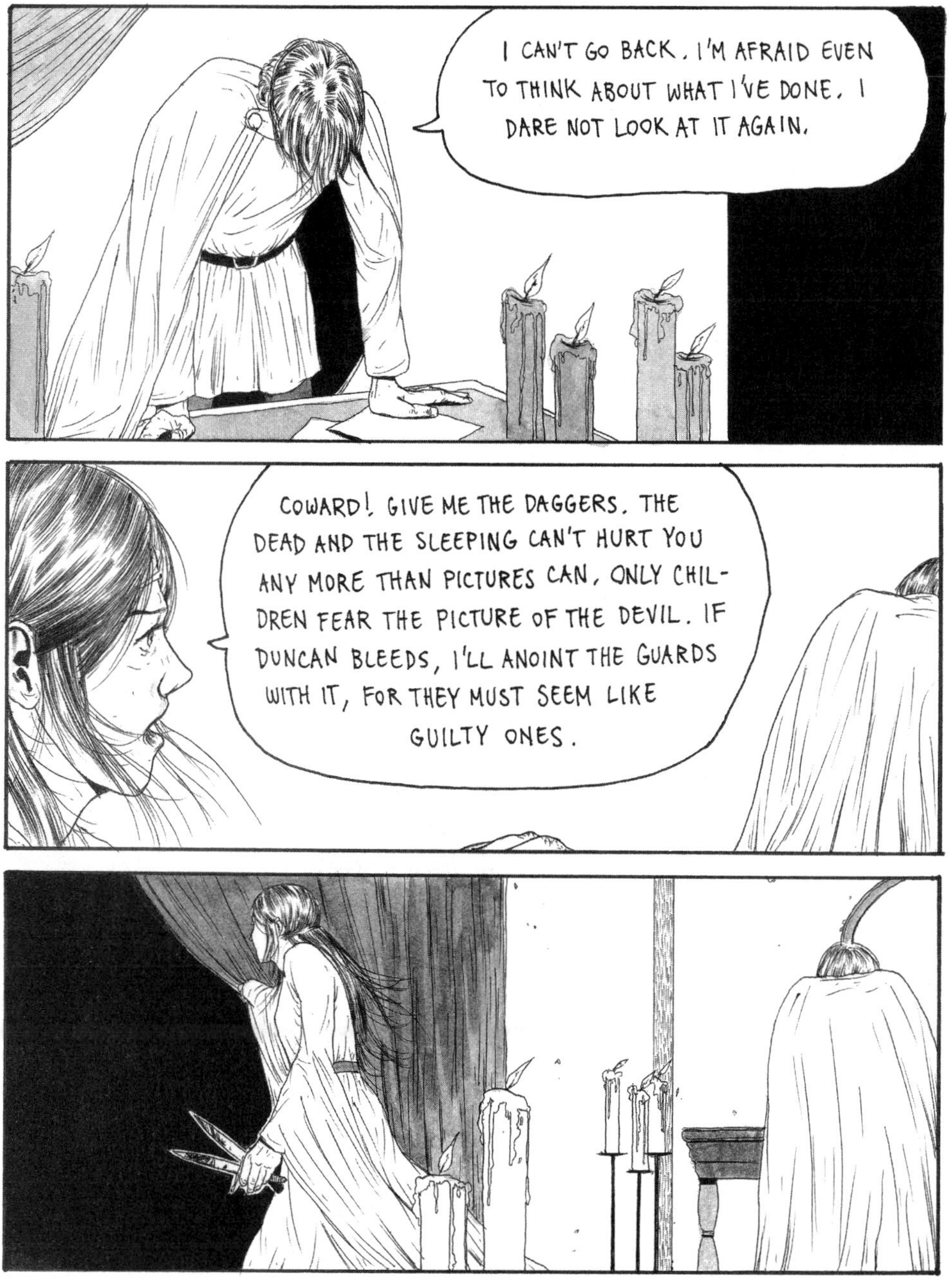
I CAN'T GO BACK. I'M AFRAID EVEN TO THINK ABOUT WHAT I'VE DONE. I DARE NOT LOOK AT IT AGAIN.
COWARD! GIVE ME THE DAGGERS. THE DEAD AND THE SLEEPING CAN'T HURT YOU ANY MORE THAN PICTURES CAN. ONLY CHIL-DREN FEAR THE PICTURE OF THE DEVIL. IF DUNCAN BLEEDS, I'LL ANOINT THE GUARDS WITH IT, FOR THEY MUST SEEM LIKE GUILTY ONES.

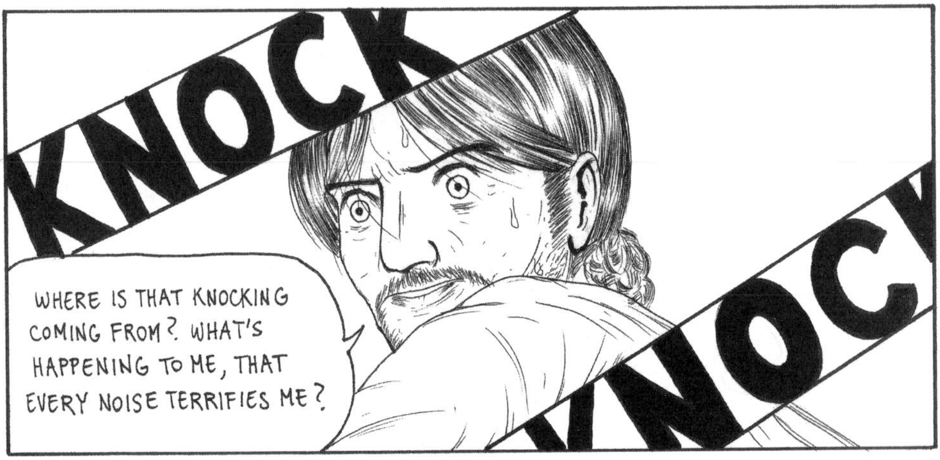
KNOCK
KNOCK
WHERE IS THAT KNOCKING COMING FROM? WHAT'S HAPPENING TO ME, THAT EVERY NOISE TERRIFIES ME?

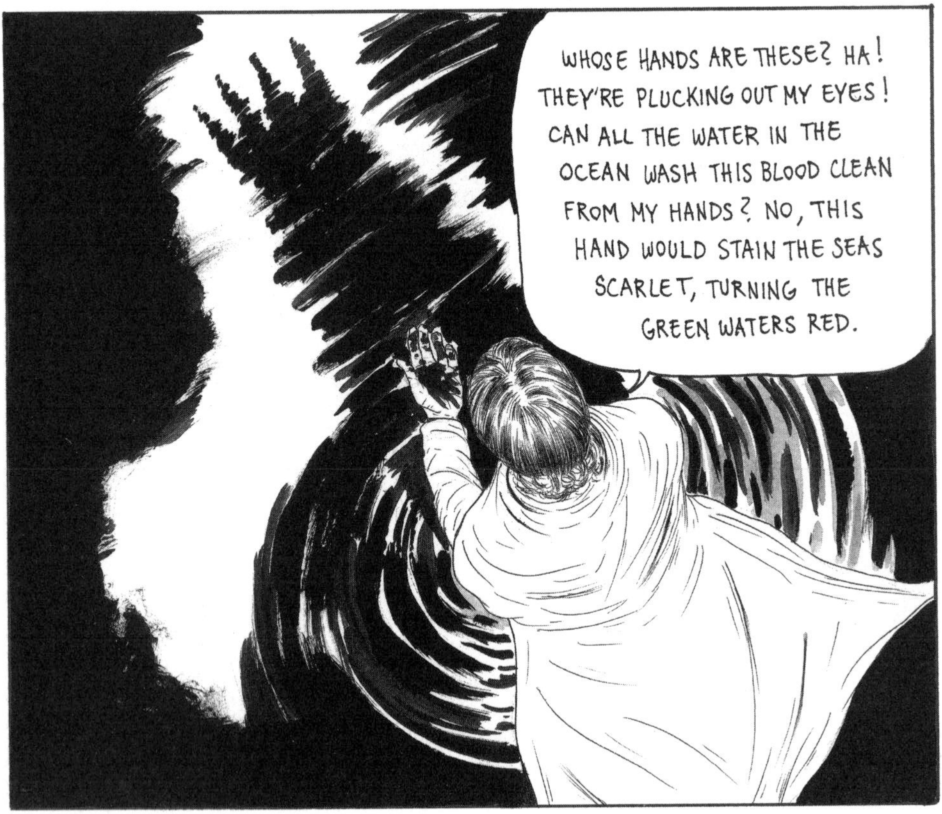
WHOSE HANDS ARE THESE? HA! THEY'RE PLUCKING OUT MY EYES! CAN ALL THE WATER IN THE OCEAN WASH THIS BLOOD CLEAN FROM MY HANDS? NO, THIS HAND WOULD STAIN THE SEAS SCARLET, TURNING THE GREEN WATERS RED.

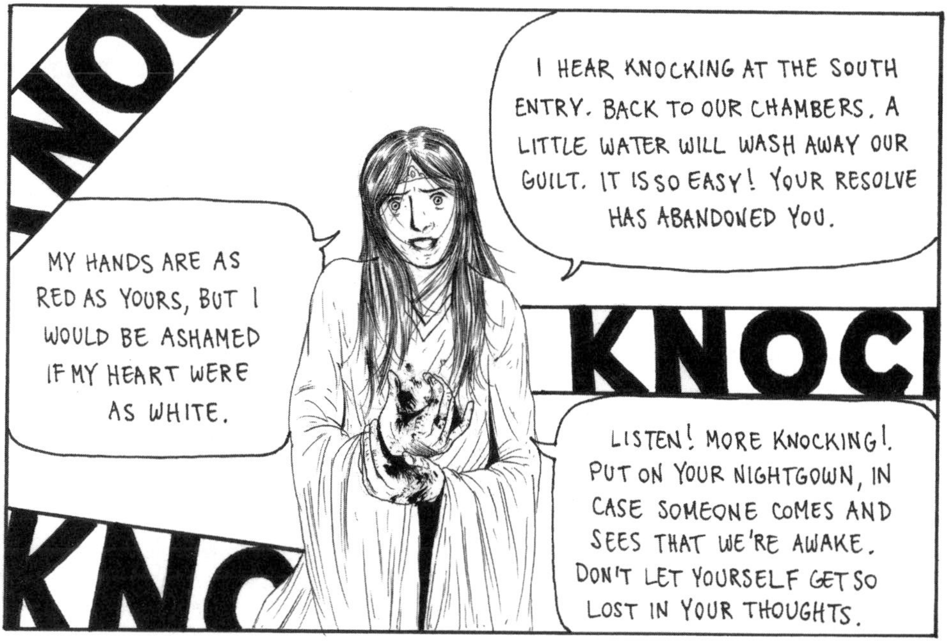
KNOC
I HEAR KNOCKING AT THE SOUTH ENTRY. BACK TO OUR CHAMBERS. A LITTLE WATER WILL WASH AWAY OUR GUILT. IT IS SO EASY! YOUR RESOLVE HAS ABANDONED YOU.
MY HANDS ARE AS RED AS YOURS, BUT I WOULD BE ASHAMED IF MY HEART WERE AS WHITE.
KNOC
LISTEN! MORE KNOCKING!. PUT ON YOUR NIGHTGOWN, IN CASE SOMEONE COMES AND SEES THAT WE'RE AWAKE. DON'T LET YOURSELF GET SO LOST IN YOUR THOUGHTS.
KNOC

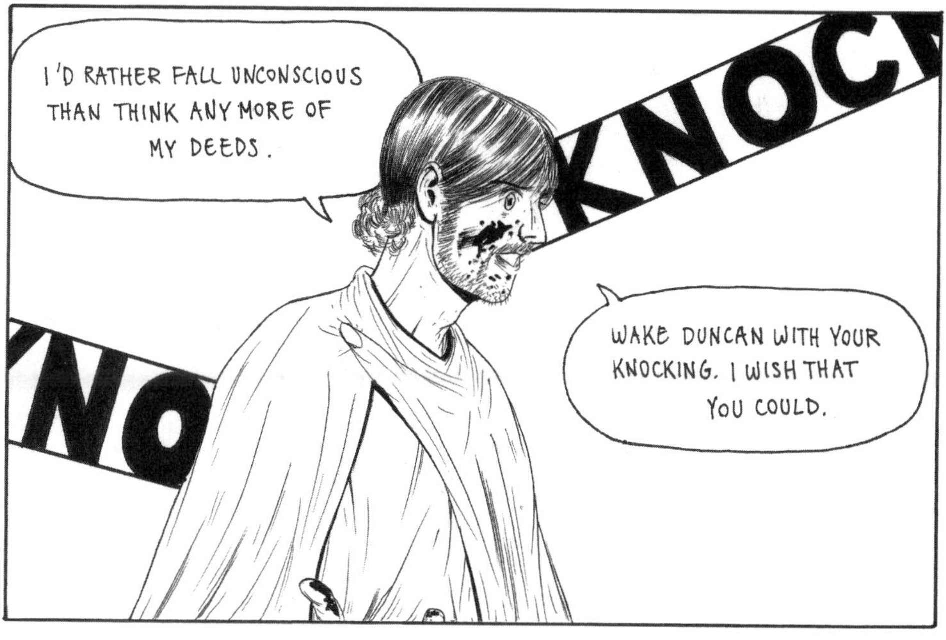
I'D RATHER FALL UNCONSCIOUS THAN THINK ANY MORE OF MY DEEDS.
KNOC
WAKE DUNCAN WITH YOUR KNOCKING. I WISH THAT YOU COULD.
NO

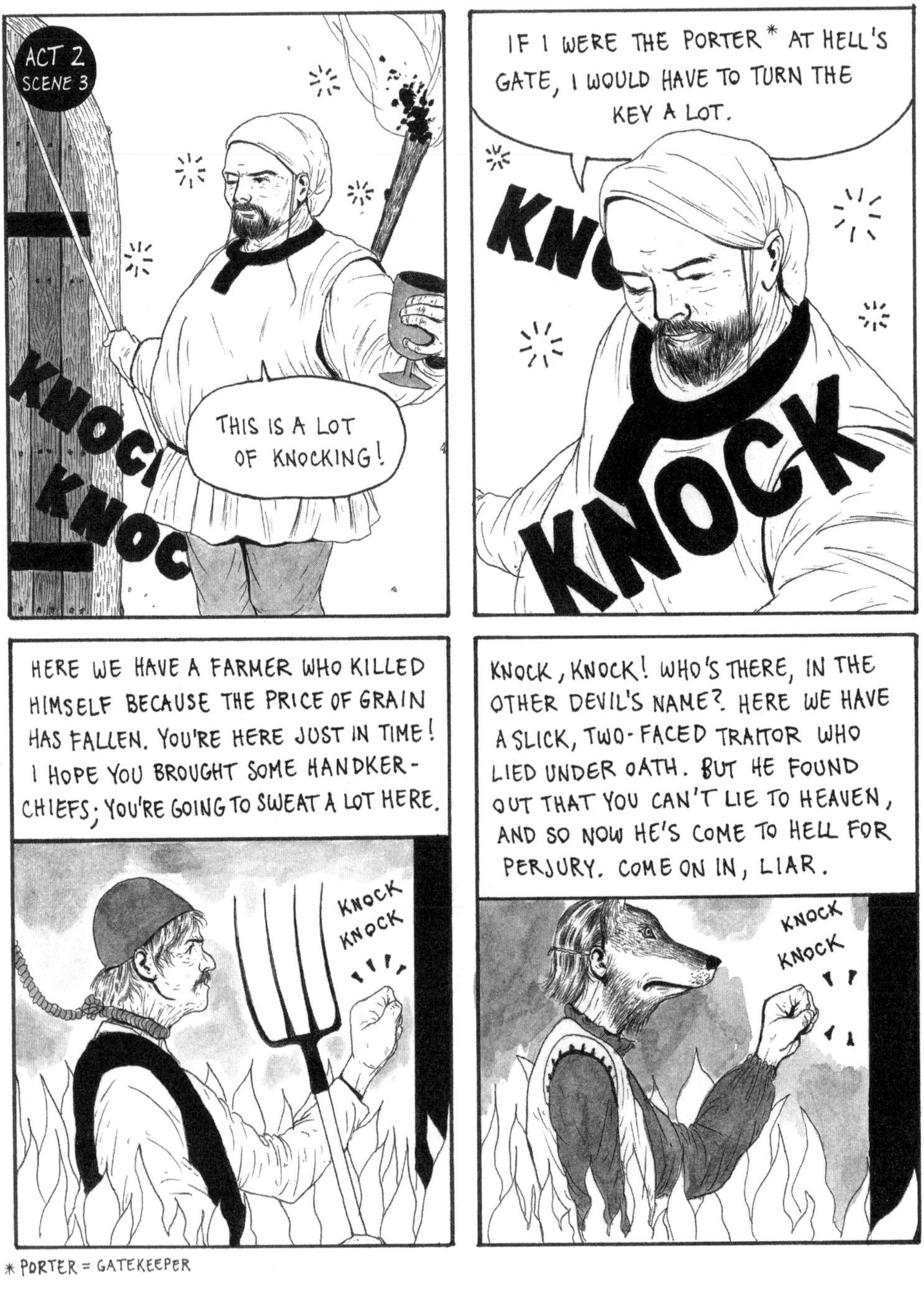
ACT 2
SCENE 3
KNOCK KNOC
THIS IS A LOT OF KNOCKING!
IF I WERE THE PORTER * AT HELL'S GATE, I WOULD HAVE TO TURN THE KEY A LOT.
KNOCK
HERE WE HAVE A FARMER WHO KILLED HIMSELF BECAUSE THE PRICE OF GRAIN HAS FALLEN. YOU'RE HERE JUST IN TIME! I HOPE YOU BROUGHT SOME HANDKERCHIEFS; YOU'RE GOING TO SWEAT A LOT HERE.
KNOCK KNOCK
KNOCK, KNOCK! WHO'S THERE, IN THE OTHER DEVIL'S NAME? HERE WE HAVE A SLICK, TWO-FACED TRAITOR WHO LIED UNDER OATH. BUT HE FOUND OUT THAT YOU CAN'T LIE TO HEAVEN, AND SO NOW HE'S COME TO HELL FOR PERJURY. COME ON IN, LIAR.
KNOCK KNOCK

* PORTER = GATEKEEPER

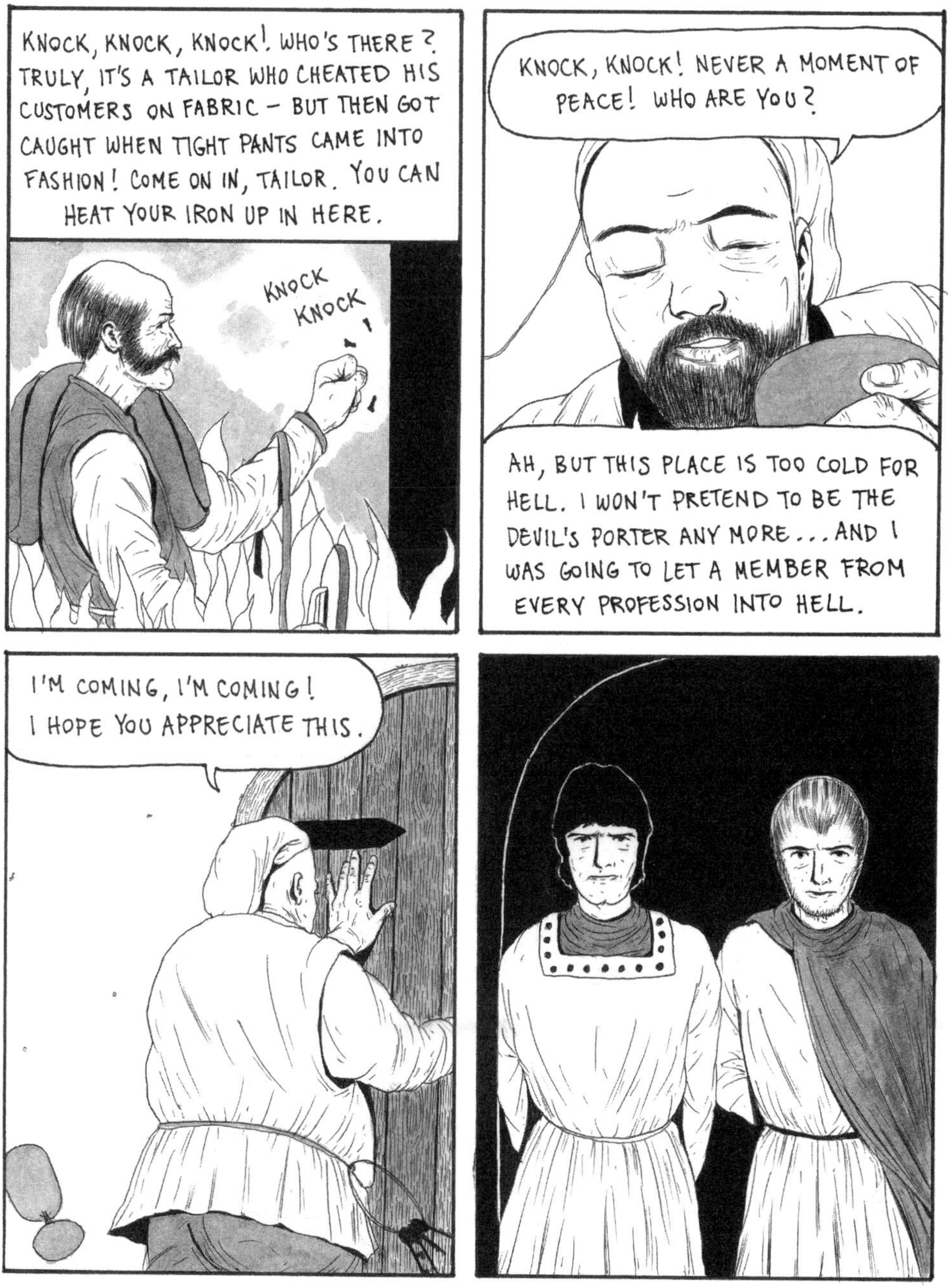
KNOCK, KNOCK, KNOCK! WHO'S THERE? TRULY, IT'S A TAILOR WHO CHEATED HIS CUSTOMERS ON FABRIC - BUT THEN GOT CAUGHT WHEN TIGHT PANTS CAME INTO FASHION! COME ON IN, TAILOR. YOU CAN HEAT YOUR IRON UP IN HERE.
KNOCK KNOCK
KNOCK, KNOCK! NEVER A MOMENT OF PEACE! WHO ARE YOU?
AH, BUT THIS PLACE IS TOO COLD FOR HELL. I WON'T PRETEND TO BE THE DEVIL'S PORTER ANY MORE... AND I WAS GOING TO LET A MEMBER FROM EVERY PROFESSION INTO HELL.
I'M COMING, I'M COMING! I HOPE YOU APPRECIATE THIS.

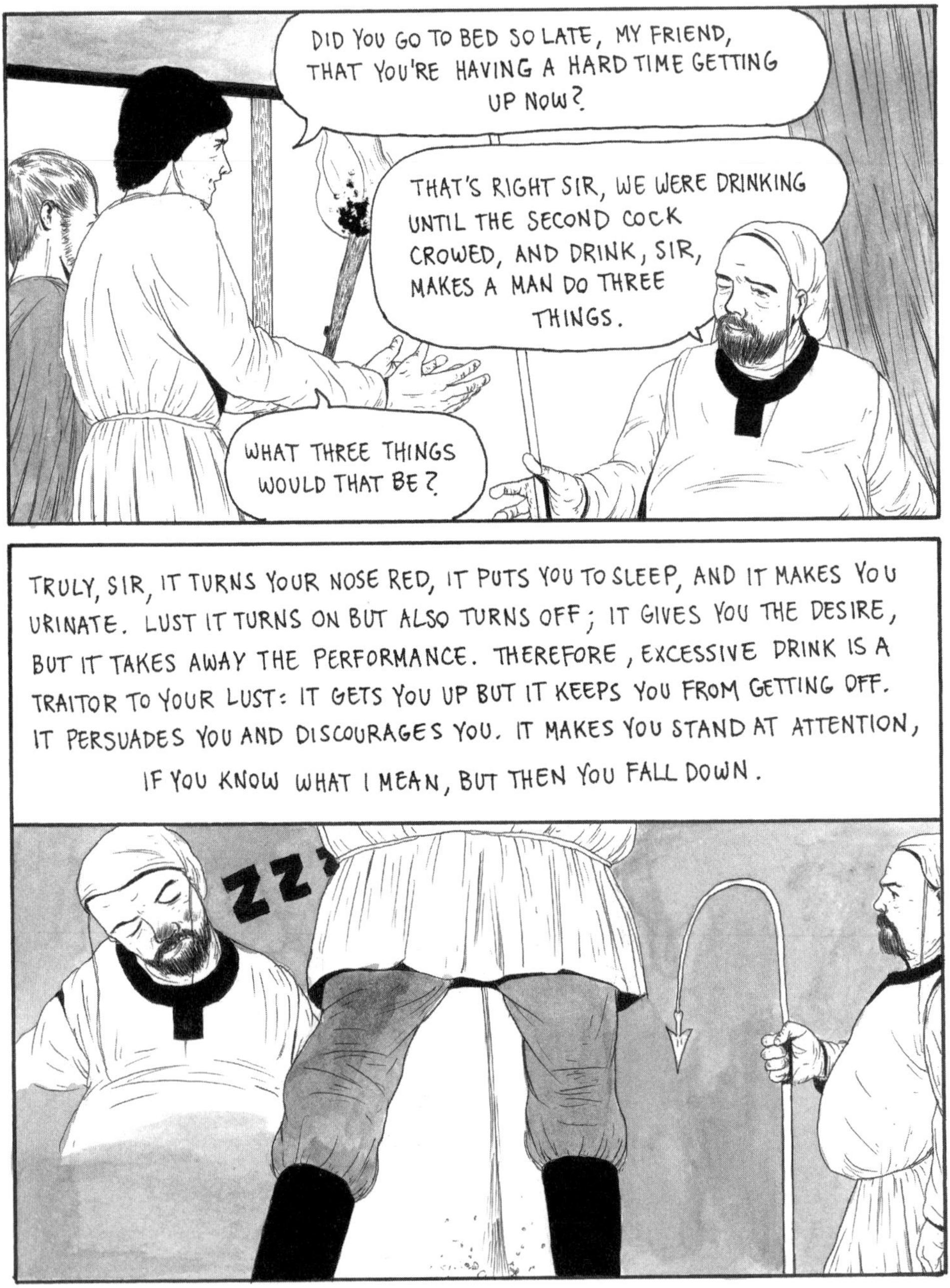
DID YOU GO TO BED SO LATE, MY FRIEND, THAT YOU'RE HAVING A HARD TIME GETTING UP NOW?
THAT'S RIGHT SIR, WE WERE DRINKING UNTIL THE SECOND COCK CROWED, AND DRINK, SIR, MAKES A MAN DO THREE THINGS.
WHAT THREE THINGS WOULD THAT BE?
TRULY, SIR, IT TURNS YOUR NOSE RED, IT PUTS YOU TO SLEEP, AND IT MAKES YOU URINATE. LUST IT TURNS ON BUT ALSO TURNS OFF; IT GIVES YOU THE DESIRE, BUT IT TAKES AWAY THE PERFORMANCE. THEREFORE, EXCESSIVE DRINK IS A TRAITOR TO YOUR LUST: IT GETS YOU UP BUT IT KEEPS YOU FROM GETTING OFF. IT PERSUADES YOU AND DISCOURAGES YOU. IT MAKES YOU STAND AT ATTENTION, IF YOU KNOW WHAT I MEAN, BUT THEN YOU FALL DOWN.
ZZZ

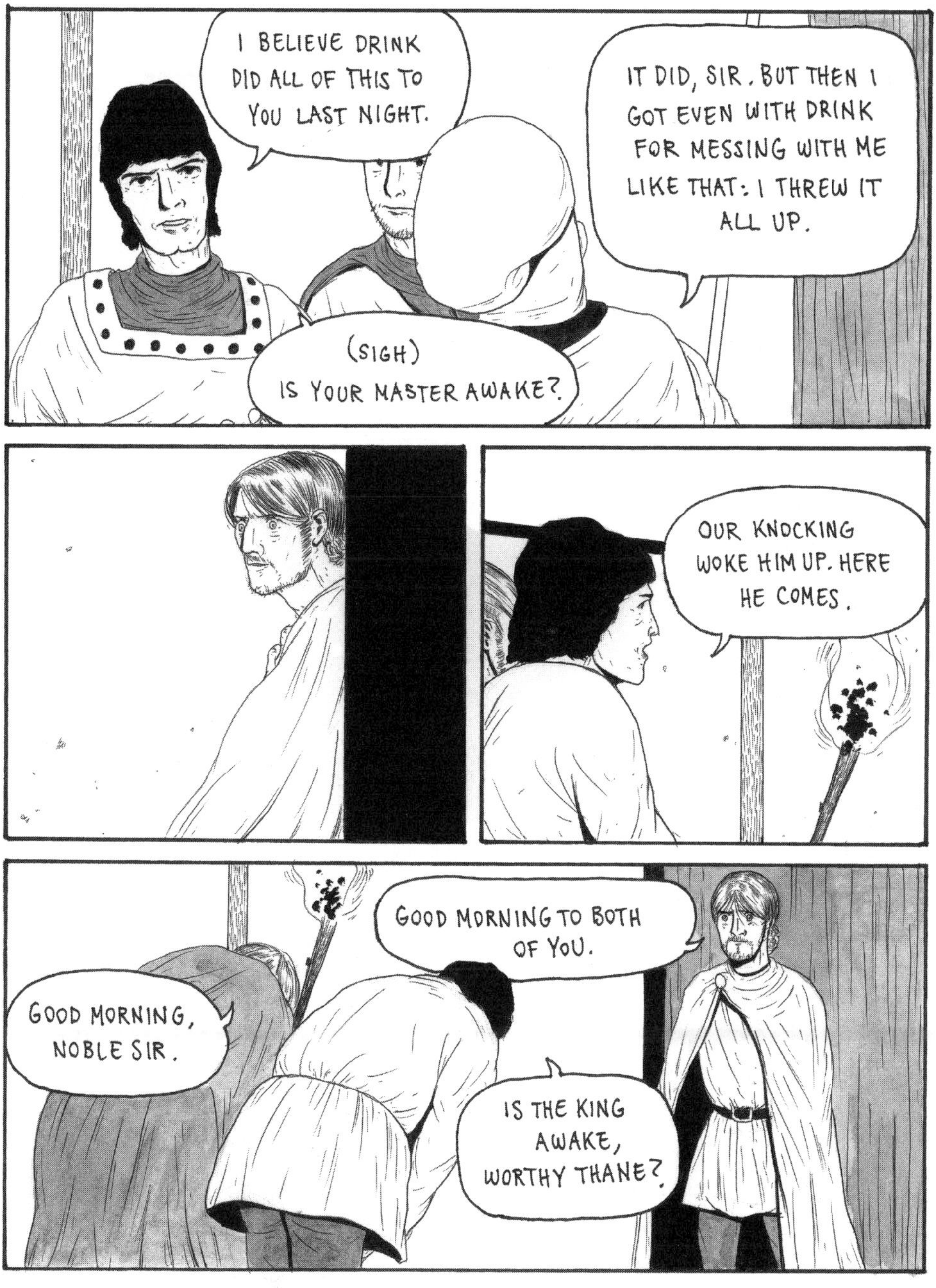

I BELIEVE DRINK DID ALL OF THIS TO YOU LAST NIGHT.
IT DID, SIR. BUT THEN I GOT EVEN WITH DRINK FOR MESSING WITH ME LIKE THAT: I THREW IT ALL UP.
(SIGH) IS YOUR MASTER AWAKE?
OUR KNOCKING WOKE HIM UP. HERE HE COMES.
GOOD MORNING TO BOTH OF YOU.
GOOD MORNING, NOBLE SIR.
IS THE KING AWAKE, WORTHY THANE?

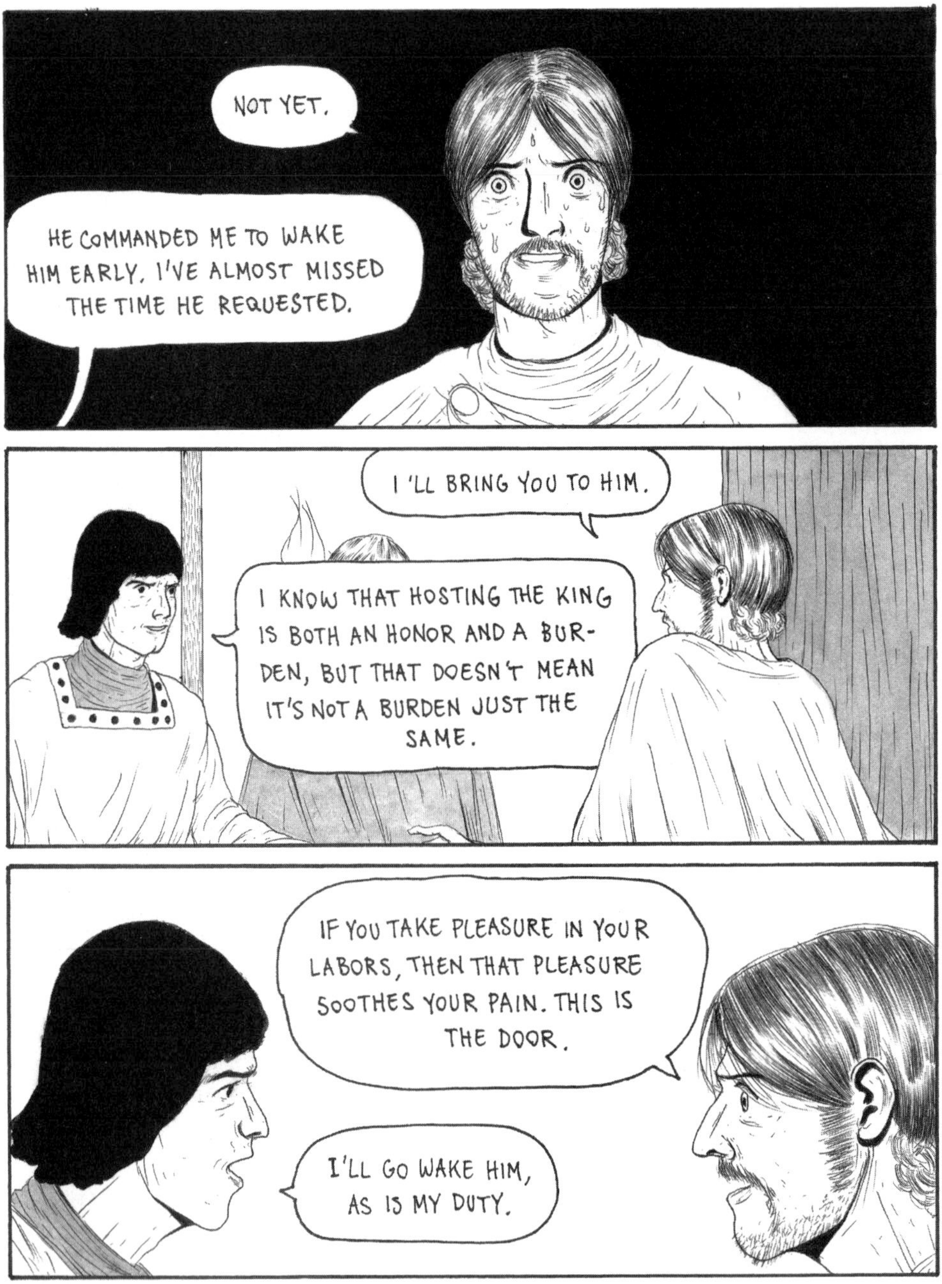
NOT YET.
HE COMMANDED ME TO WAKE HIM EARLY. I'VE ALMOST MISSED THE TIME HE REQUESTED.
I'LL BRING YOU TO HIM.
I KNOW THAT HOSTING THE KING IS BOTH AN HONOR AND A BURDEN, BUT THAT DOESN'T MEAN IT'S NOT A BURDEN JUST THE SAME.
IF YOU TAKE PLEASURE IN YOUR LABORS, THEN THAT PLEASURE SOOTHES YOUR PAIN. THIS IS THE DOOR.
I'LL GO WAKE HIM, AS IS MY DUTY.

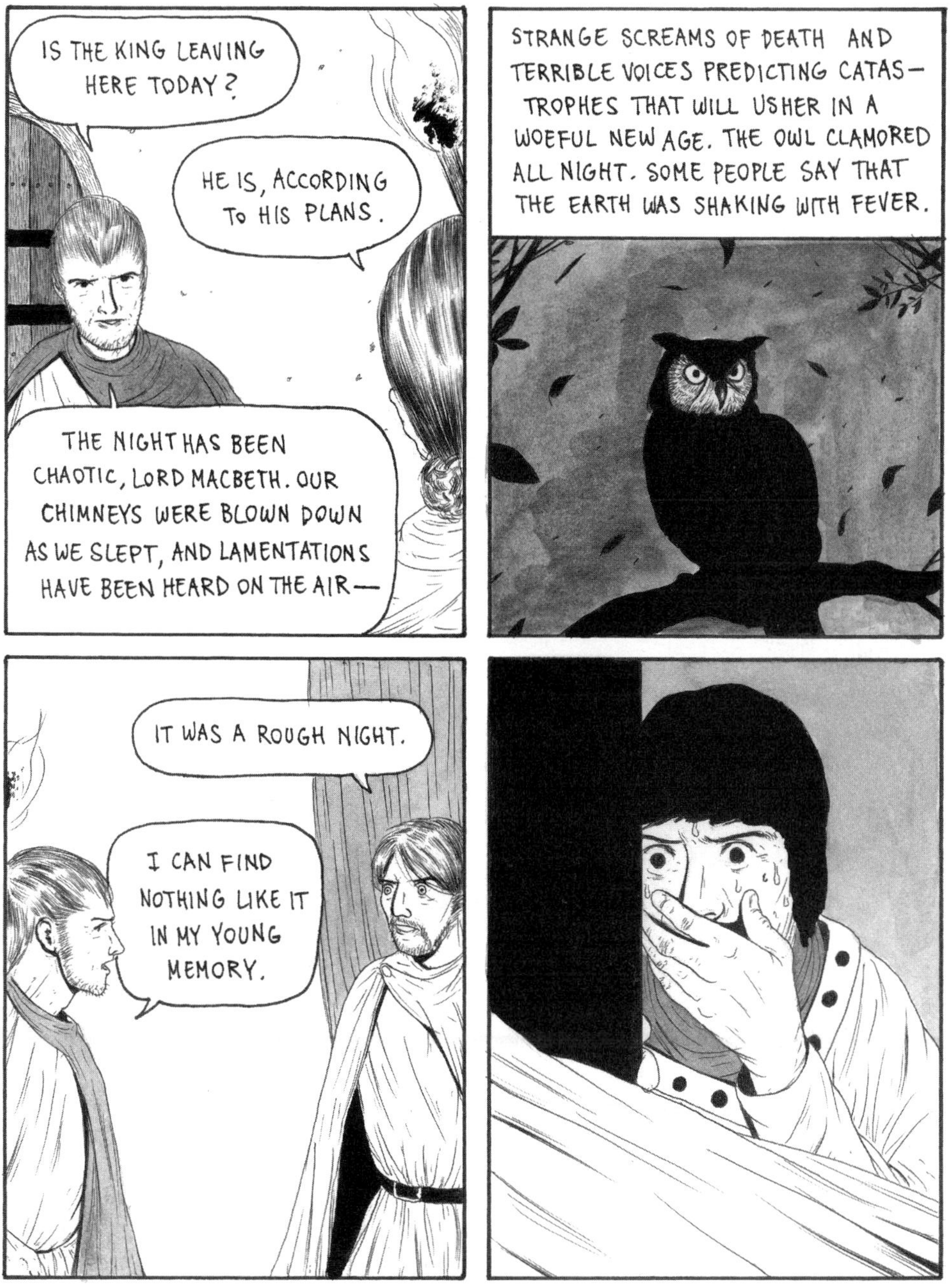

IS THE KING LEAVING HERE TODAY?
HE IS, ACCORDING TO HIS PLANS.
THE NIGHT HAS BEEN CHAOTIC, LORD MACBETH. OUR CHIMNEYS WERE BLOWN DOWN AS WE SLEPT, AND LAMENTATIONS HAVE BEEN HEARD ON THE AIR—
STRANGE SCREAMS OF DEATH AND TERRIBLE VOICES PREDICTING CATAS-TROPHES THAT WILL USHER IN A WOEFUL NEW AGE. THE OWL CLAMORED ALL NIGHT. SOME PEOPLE SAY THAT THE EARTH WAS SHAKING WITH FEVER.
IT WAS A ROUGH NIGHT.
I CAN FIND NOTHING LIKE IT IN MY YOUNG MEMORY.

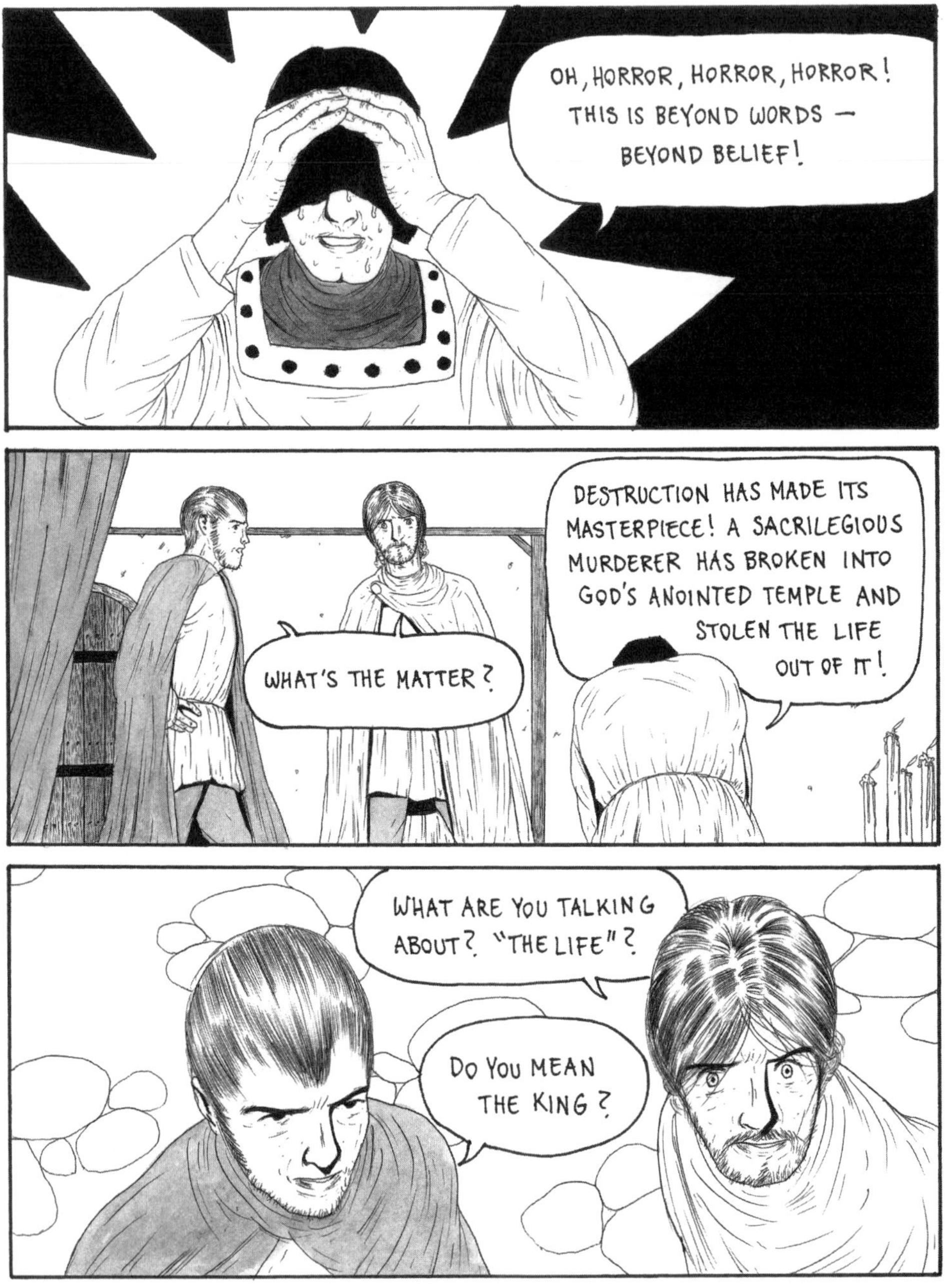
OH, HORROR, HORROR, HORROR! THIS IS BEYOND WORDS — BEYOND BELIEF!
WHAT'S THE MATTER?
DESTRUCTION HAS MADE ITS MASTERPIECE! A SACRILEGIOUS MURDERER HAS BROKEN INTO GOD'S ANOINTED TEMPLE AND STOLEN THE LIFE OUT OF IT!
WHAT ARE YOU TALKING ABOUT? "THE LIFE"?
DO YOU MEAN THE KING?

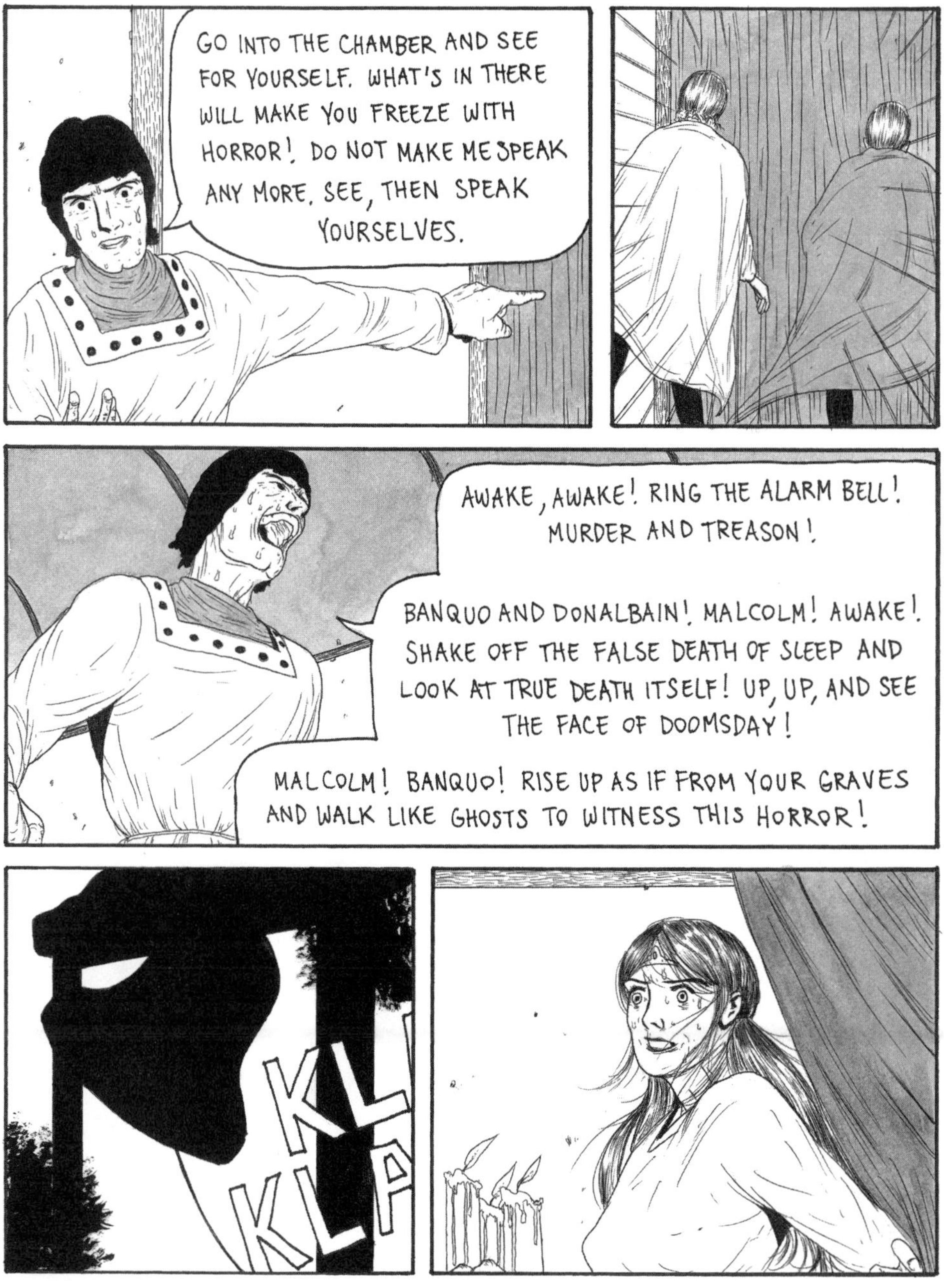
GO INTO THE CHAMBER AND SEE FOR YOURSELF. WHAT'S IN THERE WILL MAKE YOU FREEZE WITH HORROR! DO NOT MAKE ME SPEAK ANY MORE. SEE, THEN SPEAK YOURSELVES.
AWAKE, AWAKE! RING THE ALARM BELL! MURDER AND TREASON!
BANQUO AND DONALBAIN! MALCOLM! AWAKE! SHAKE OFF THE FALSE DEATH OF SLEEP AND LOOK AT TRUE DEATH ITSELF! UP, UP, AND SEE THE FACE OF DOOMSDAY!
MALCOLM! BANQUO! RISE UP AS IF FROM YOUR GRAVES AND WALK LIKE GHOSTS TO WITNESS THIS HORROR!

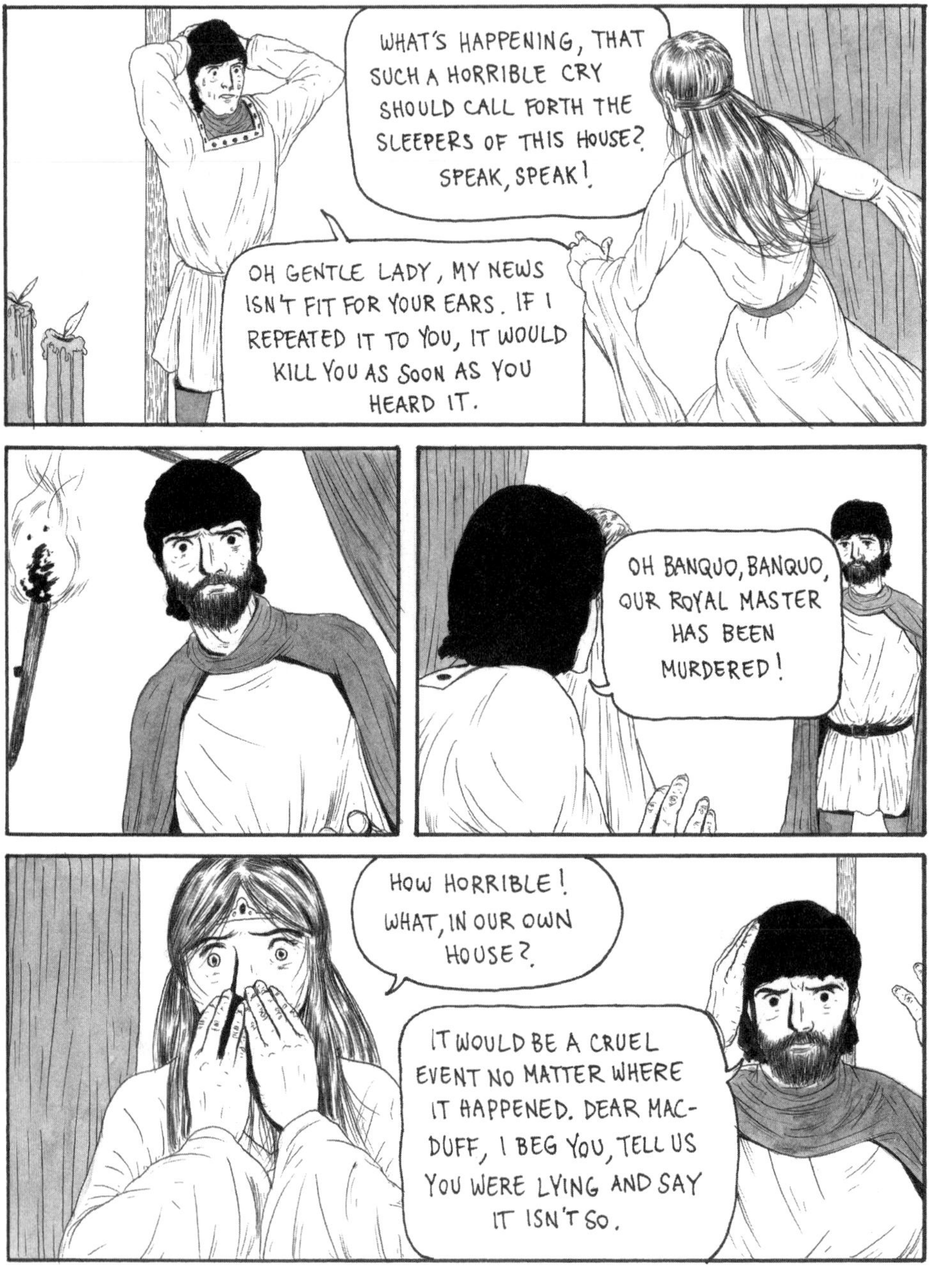
WHAT'S HAPPENING, THAT SUCH A HORRIBLE CRY SHOULD CALL FORTH THE SLEEPERS OF THIS HOUSE? SPEAK, SPEAK!
OH GENTLE LADY, MY NEWS ISN'T FIT FOR YOUR EARS. IF I REPEATED IT TO YOU, IT WOULD KILL YOU AS SOON AS YOU HEARD IT.
OH BANQUO, BANQUO, OUR ROYAL MASTER HAS BEEN MURDERED!
HOW HORRIBLE! WHAT, IN OUR OWN HOUSE?
IT WOULD BE A CRUEL EVENT NO MATTER WHERE IT HAPPENED. DEAR MAC-DUFF, I BEG YOU, TELL US YOU WERE LYING AND SAY IT ISN'T SO.

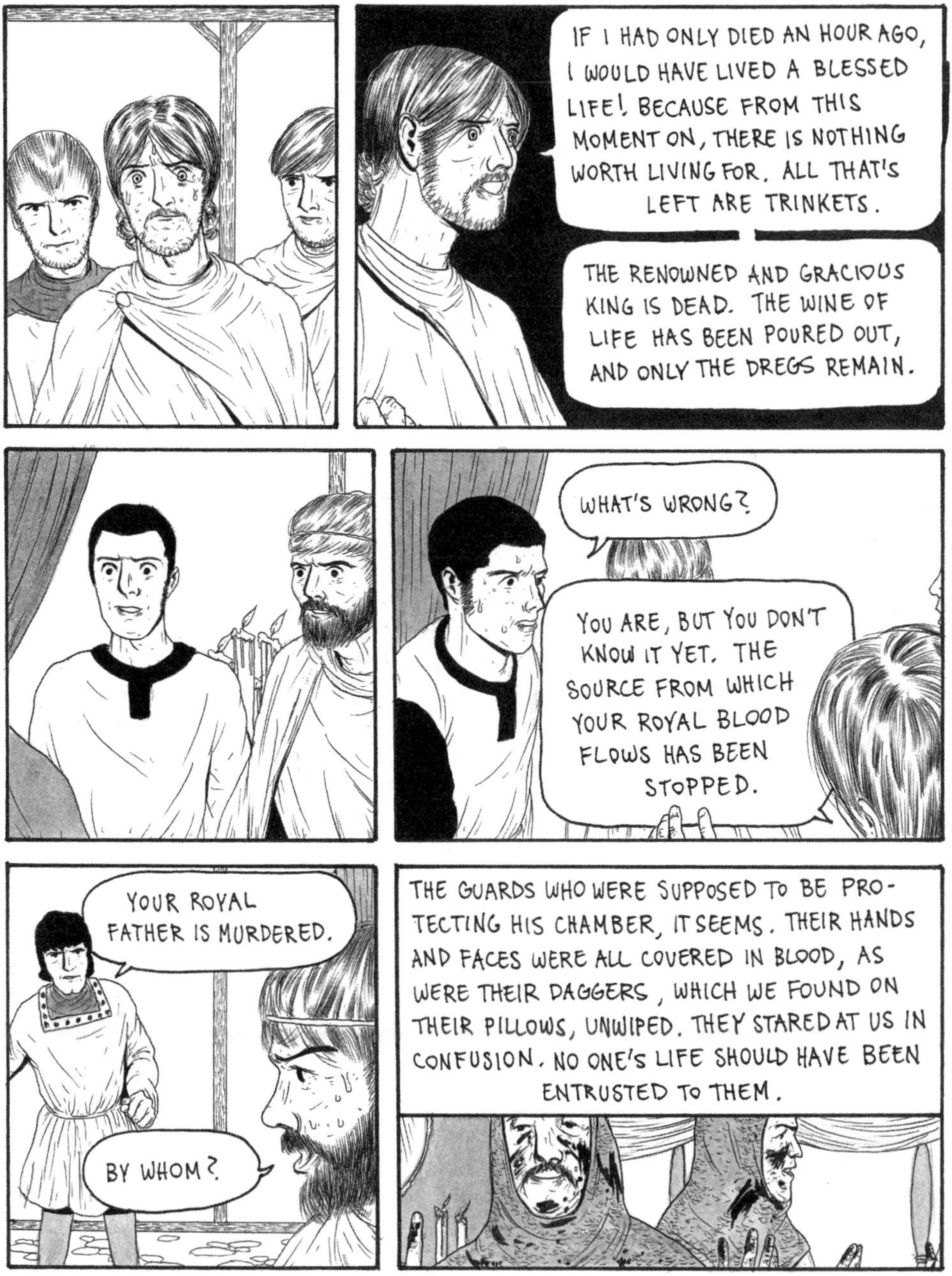
IF I HAD ONLY DIED AN HOUR AGO, I WOULD HAVE LIVED A BLESSED LIFE! BECAUSE FROM THIS MOMENT ON, THERE IS NOTHING WORTH LIVING FOR. ALL THAT'S LEFT ARE TRINKETS.
THE RENOWNED AND GRACIOUS KING IS DEAD. THE WINE OF LIFE HAS BEEN POURED OUT, AND ONLY THE DREGS REMAIN.
WHAT'S WRONG?
YOU ARE, BUT YOU DON'T KNOW IT YET. THE SOURCE FROM WHICH YOUR ROYAL BLOOD FLOWS HAS BEEN STOPPED.
YOUR ROYAL FATHER IS MURDERED.
BY WHOM?
THE GUARDS WHO WERE SUPPOSED TO BE PROTECTING HIS CHAMBER, IT SEEMS. THEIR HANDS AND FACES WERE ALL COVERED IN BLOOD, AS WERE THEIR DAGGERS, WHICH WE FOUND ON THEIR PILLOWS, UNWIPED. THEY STARED AT US IN CONFUSION. NO ONE'S LIFE SHOULD HAVE BEEN ENTRUSTED TO THEM.

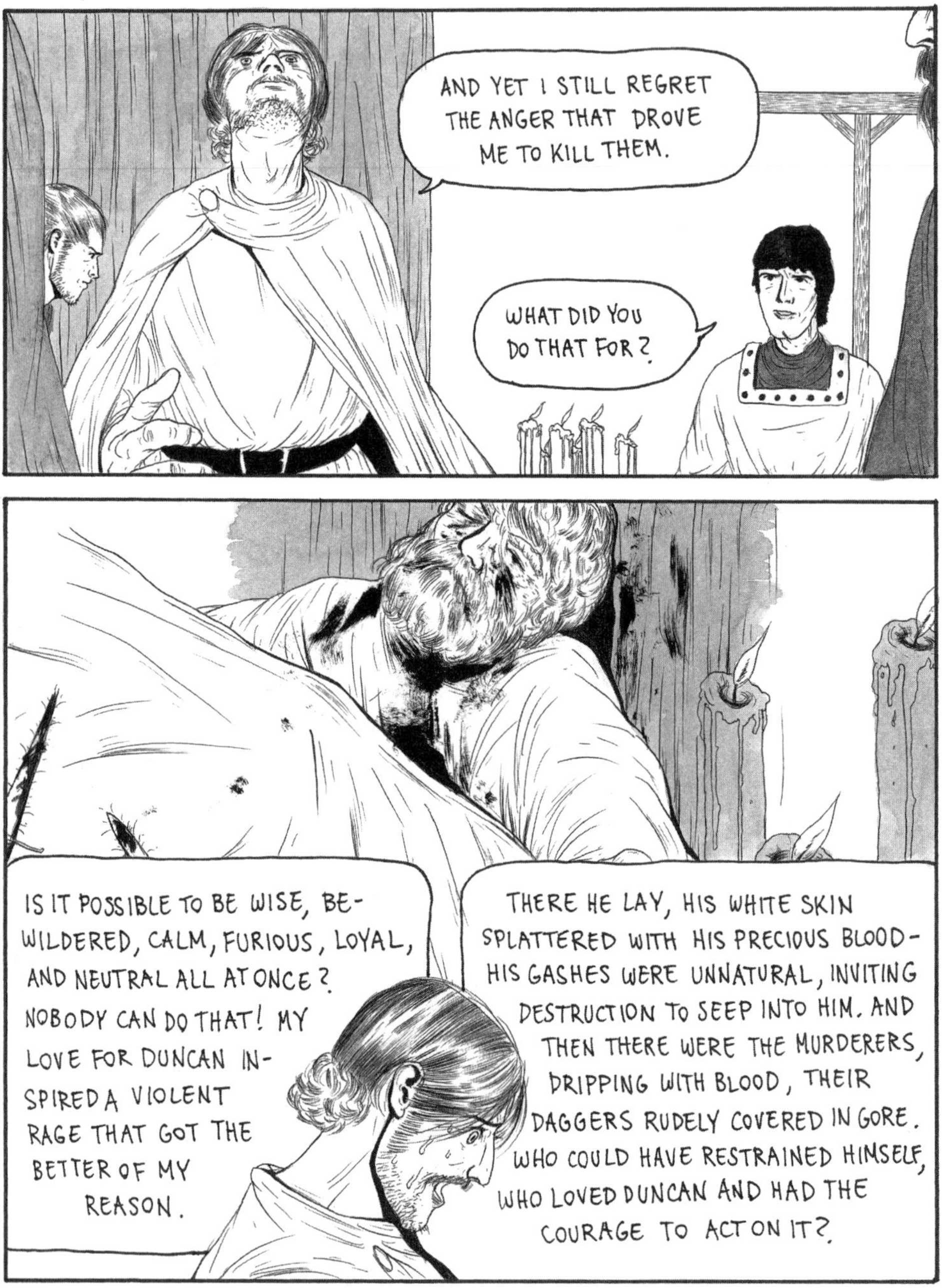
AND YET I STILL REGRET THE ANGER THAT DROVE ME TO KILL THEM.
WHAT DID YOU DO THAT FOR?
IS IT POSSIBLE TO BE WISE, BEWILDERED, CALM, FURIOUS, LOYAL, AND NEUTRAL ALL AT ONCE? NOBODY CAN DO THAT! MY LOVE FOR DUNCAN INSPIRED A VIOLENT RAGE THAT GOT THE BETTER OF MY REASON.
THERE HE LAY, HIS WHITE SKIN SPLATTERED WITH HIS PRECIOUS BLOOD- HIS GASHES WERE UNNATURAL, INVITING DESTRUCTION TO SEEP INTO HIM. AND THEN THERE WERE THE MURDERERS, DRIPPING WITH BLOOD, THEIR DAGGERS RUDELY COVERED IN GORE. WHO COULD HAVE RESTRAINED HIMSELF, WHO LOVED DUNCAN AND HAD THE COURAGE TO ACT ON IT?

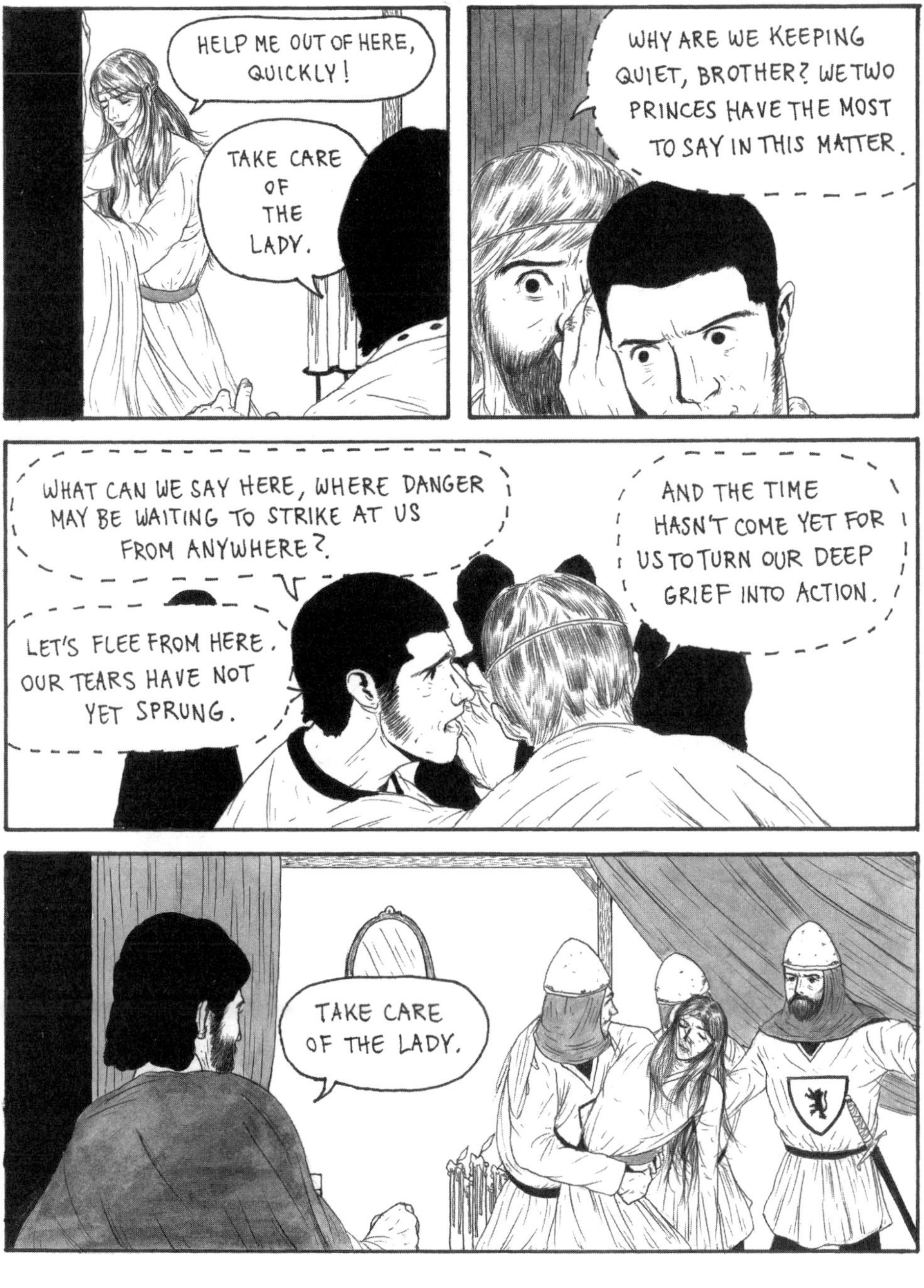
HELP ME OUT OF HERE, QUICKLY!
TAKE CARE OF THE LADY.
WHY ARE WE KEEPING QUIET, BROTHER? WE TWO PRINCES HAVE THE MOST TO SAY IN THIS MATTER.
WHAT CAN WE SAY HERE, WHERE DANGER MAY BE WAITING TO STRIKE AT US FROM ANYWHERE?
LET'S FLEE FROM HERE. OUR TEARS HAVE NOT YET SPRUNG.
AND THE TIME HASN'T COME YET FOR US TO TURN OUR DEEP GRIEF INTO ACTION.
TAKE CARE OF THE LADY.

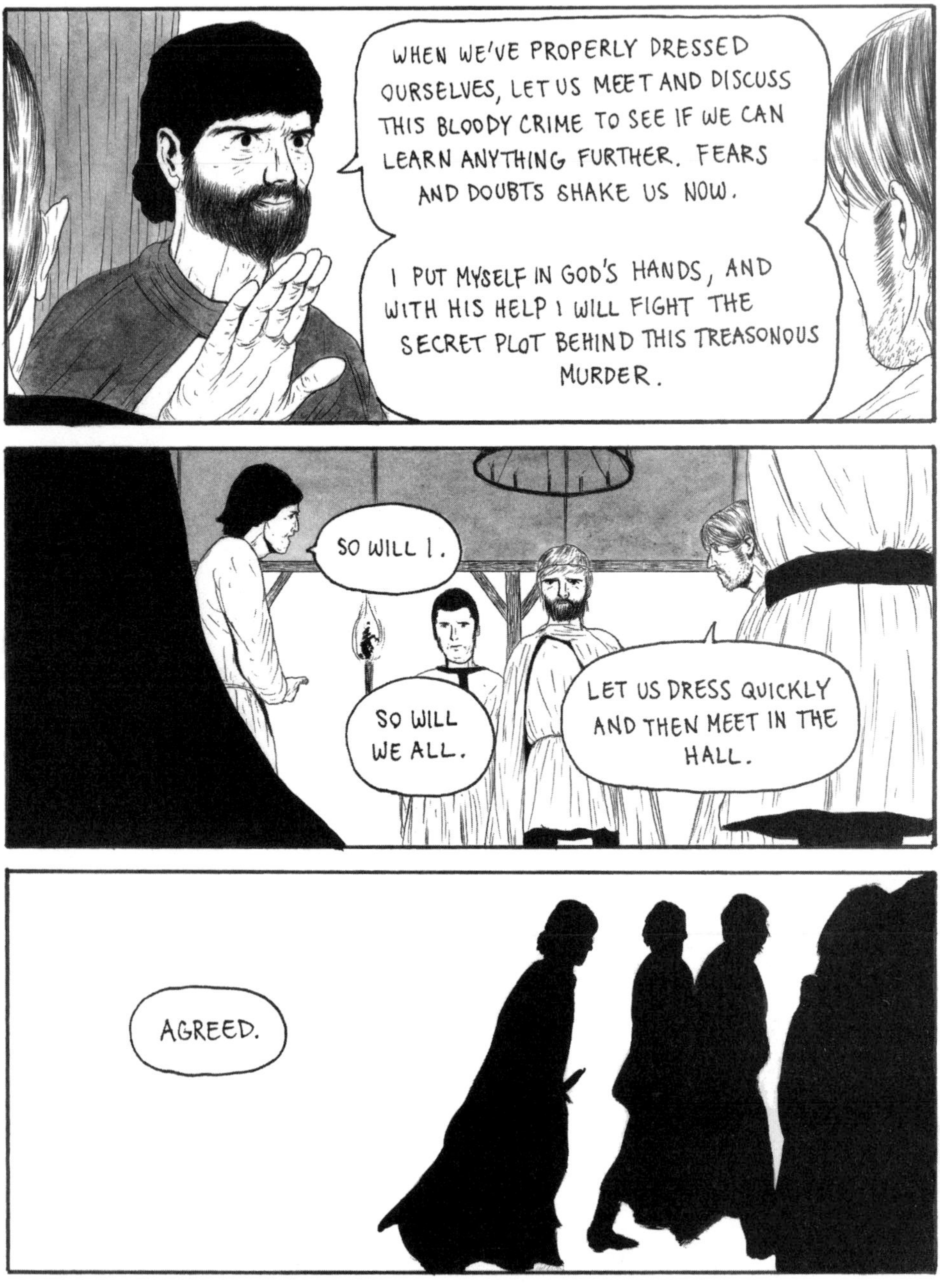
WHEN WE'VE PROPERLY DRESSED OURSELVES, LET US MEET AND DISCUSS THIS BLOODY CRIME TO SEE IF WE CAN LEARN ANYTHING FURTHER. FEARS AND DOUBTS SHAKE US NOW.
I PUT MYSELF IN GOD'S HANDS, AND WITH HIS HELP I WILL FIGHT THE SECRET PLOT BEHIND THIS TREASONOUS MURDER.
SO WILL I.
SO WILL WE ALL.
LET US DRESS QUICKLY AND THEN MEET IN THE HALL.
AGREED.

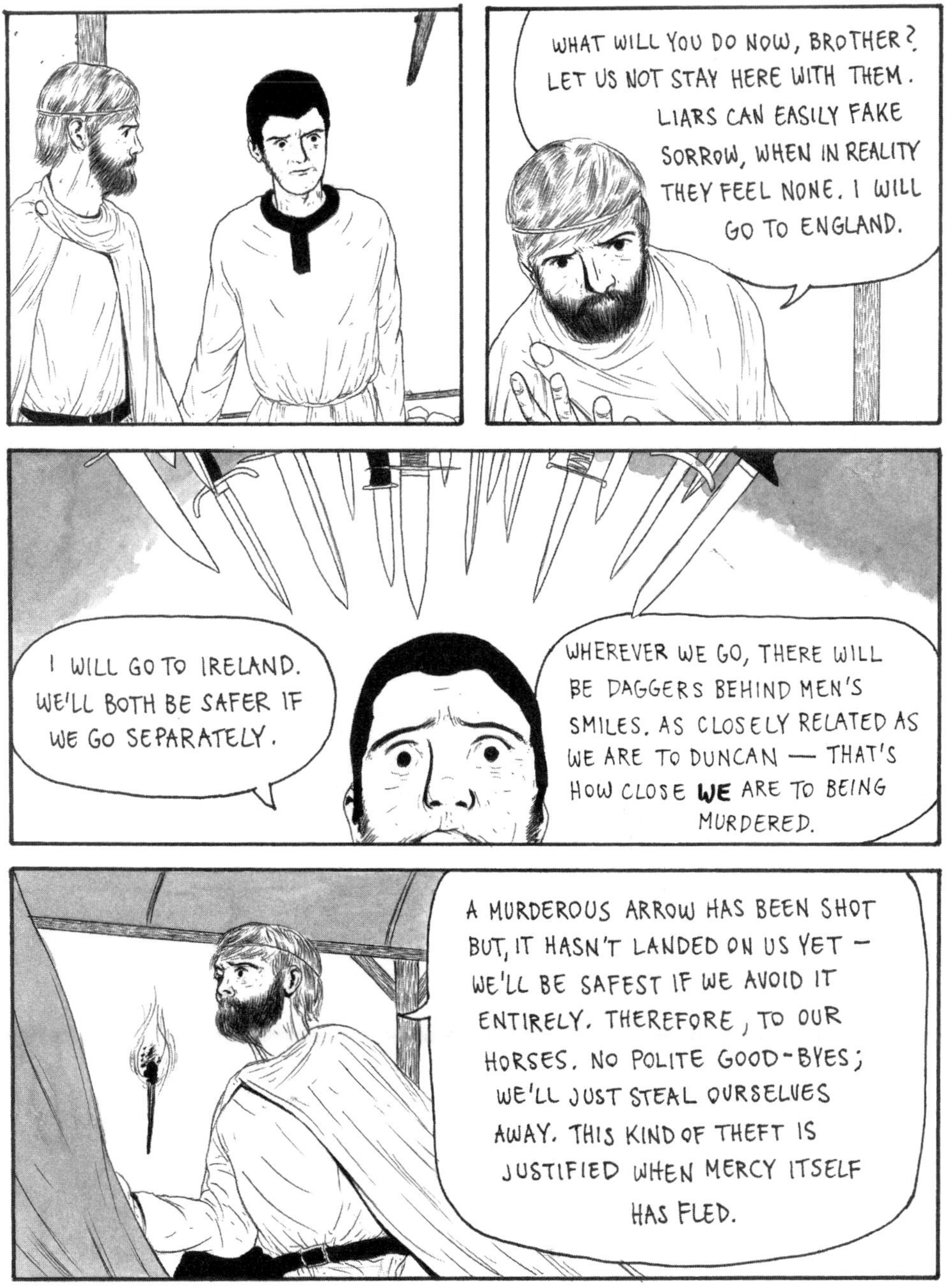
WHAT WILL YOU DO NOW, BROTHER? LET US NOT STAY HERE WITH THEM. LIARS CAN EASILY FAKE SORROW, WHEN IN REALITY THEY FEEL NONE. I WILL GO TO ENGLAND.
I WILL GO TO IRELAND. WE'LL BOTH BE SAFER IF WE GO SEPARATELY.
WHEREVER WE GO, THERE WILL BE DAGGERS BEHIND MEN'S SMILES. AS CLOSELY RELATED AS WE ARE TO DUNCAN — THAT'S HOW CLOSE **WE** ARE TO BEING MURDERED.
A MURDEROUS ARROW HAS BEEN SHOT BUT, IT HASN'T LANDED ON US YET — WE'LL BE SAFEST IF WE AVOID IT ENTIRELY. THEREFORE, TO OUR HORSES. NO POLITE GOOD-BYES; WE'LL JUST STEAL OURSELVES AWAY. THIS KIND OF THEFT IS JUSTIFIED WHEN MERCY ITSELF HAS FLED.

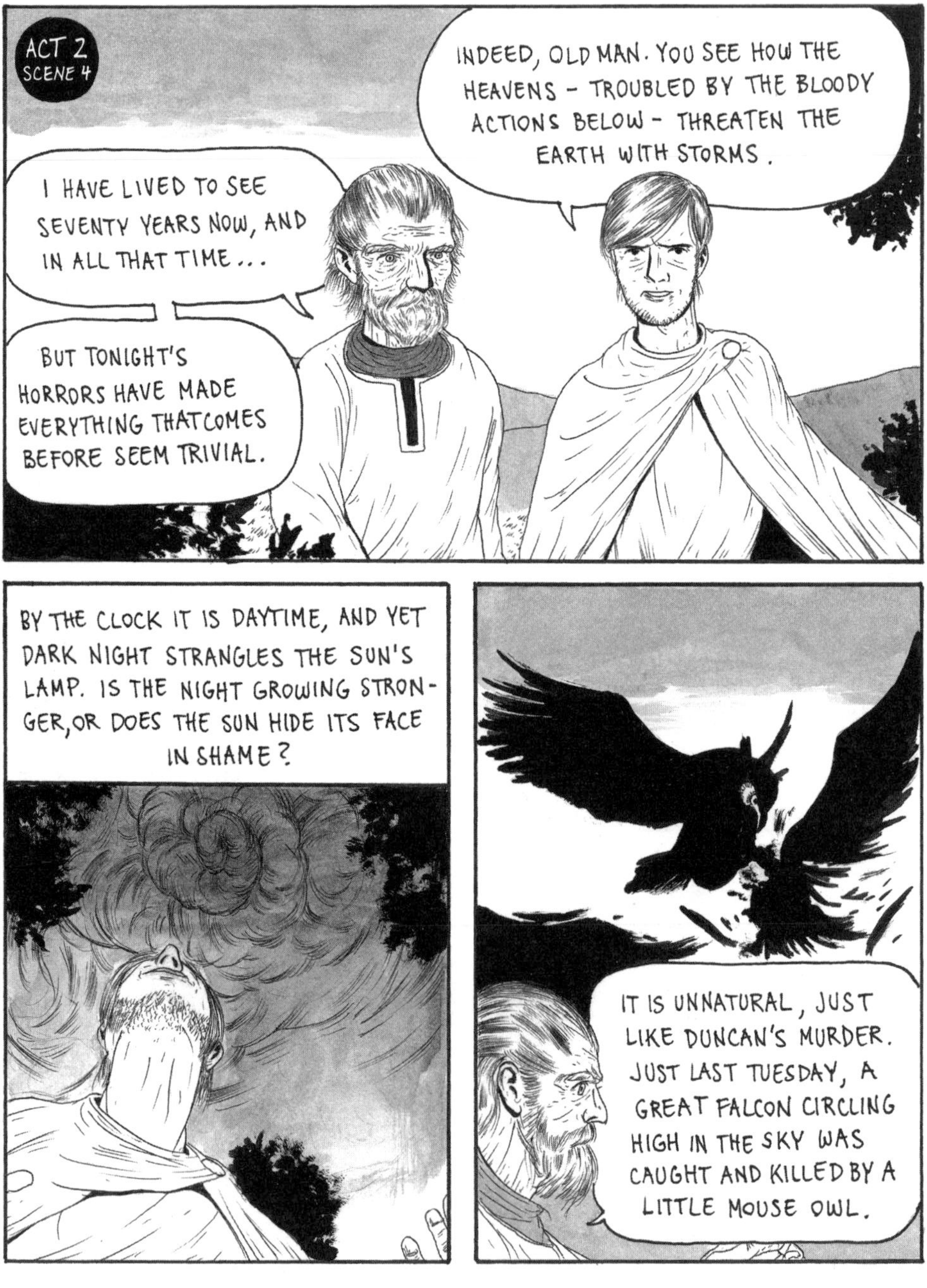
ACT 2 SCENE 4
I HAVE LIVED TO SEE SEVENTY YEARS NOW, AND IN ALL THAT TIME...
BUT TONIGHT'S HORRORS HAVE MADE EVERYTHING THATCOMES BEFORE SEEM TRIVIAL.
INDEED, OLD MAN. YOU SEE HOW THE HEAVENS - TROUBLED BY THE BLOODY ACTIONS BELOW - THREATEN THE EARTH WITH STORMS.
BY THE CLOCK IT IS DAYTIME, AND YET DARK NIGHT STRANGLES THE SUN'S LAMP. IS THE NIGHT GROWING STRONGER, OR DOES THE SUN HIDE ITS FACE IN SHAME?
IT IS UNNATURAL, JUST LIKE DUNCAN'S MURDER. JUST LAST TUESDAY, A GREAT FALCON CIRCLING HIGH IN THE SKY WAS CAUGHT AND KILLED BY A LITTLE MOUSE OWL.

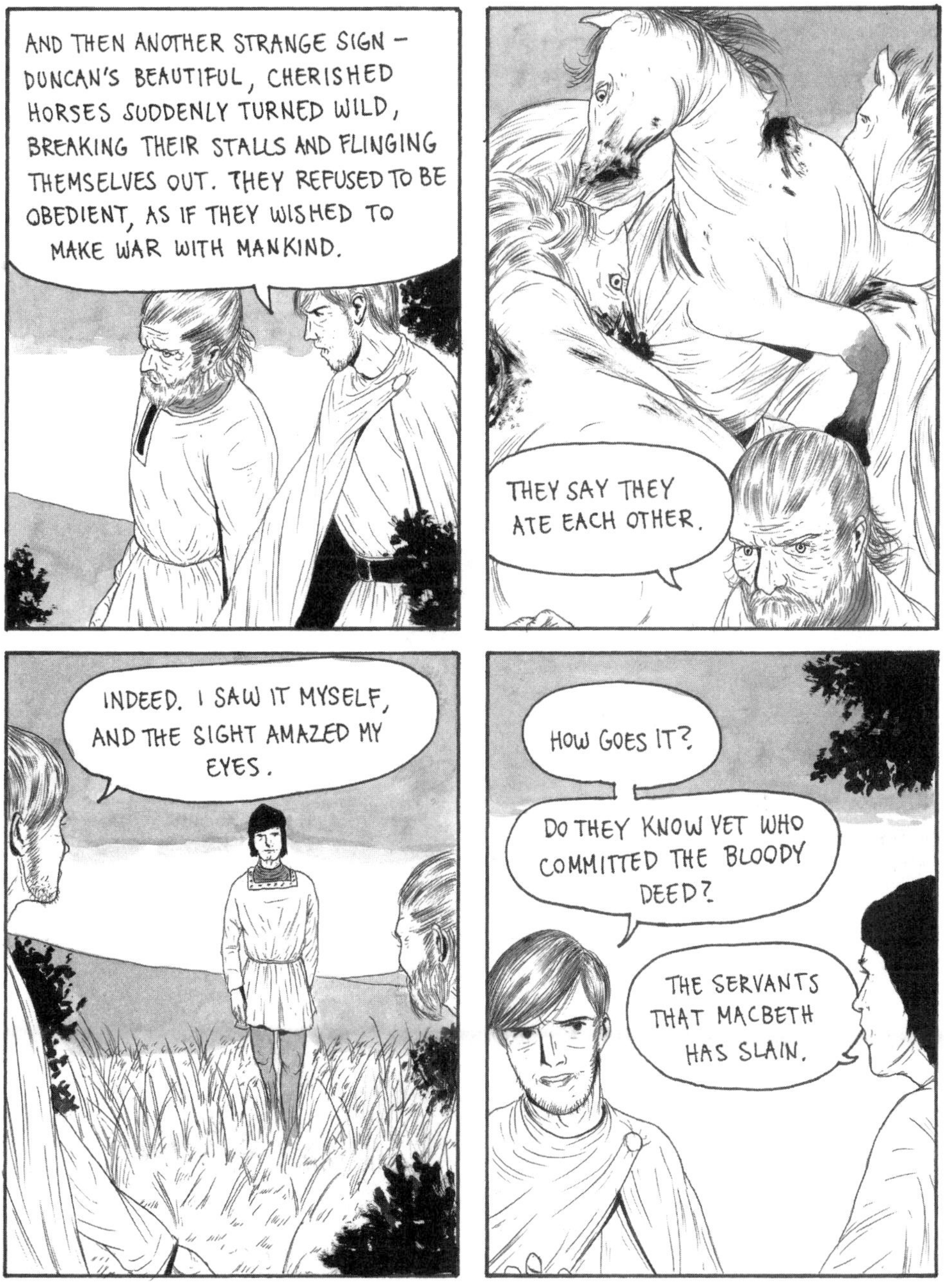
AND THEN ANOTHER STRANGE SIGN - DUNCAN'S BEAUTIFUL, CHERISHED HORSES SUDDENLY TURNED WILD, BREAKING THEIR STALLS AND FLINGING THEMSELVES OUT. THEY REFUSED TO BE OBEDIENT, AS IF THEY WISHED TO MAKE WAR WITH MANKIND.
THEY SAY THEY ATE EACH OTHER.
INDEED. I SAW IT MYSELF, AND THE SIGHT AMAZED MY EYES.
HOW GOES IT?
DO THEY KNOW YET WHO COMMITTED THE BLOODY DEED?
THE SERVANTS THAT MACBETH HAS SLAIN.

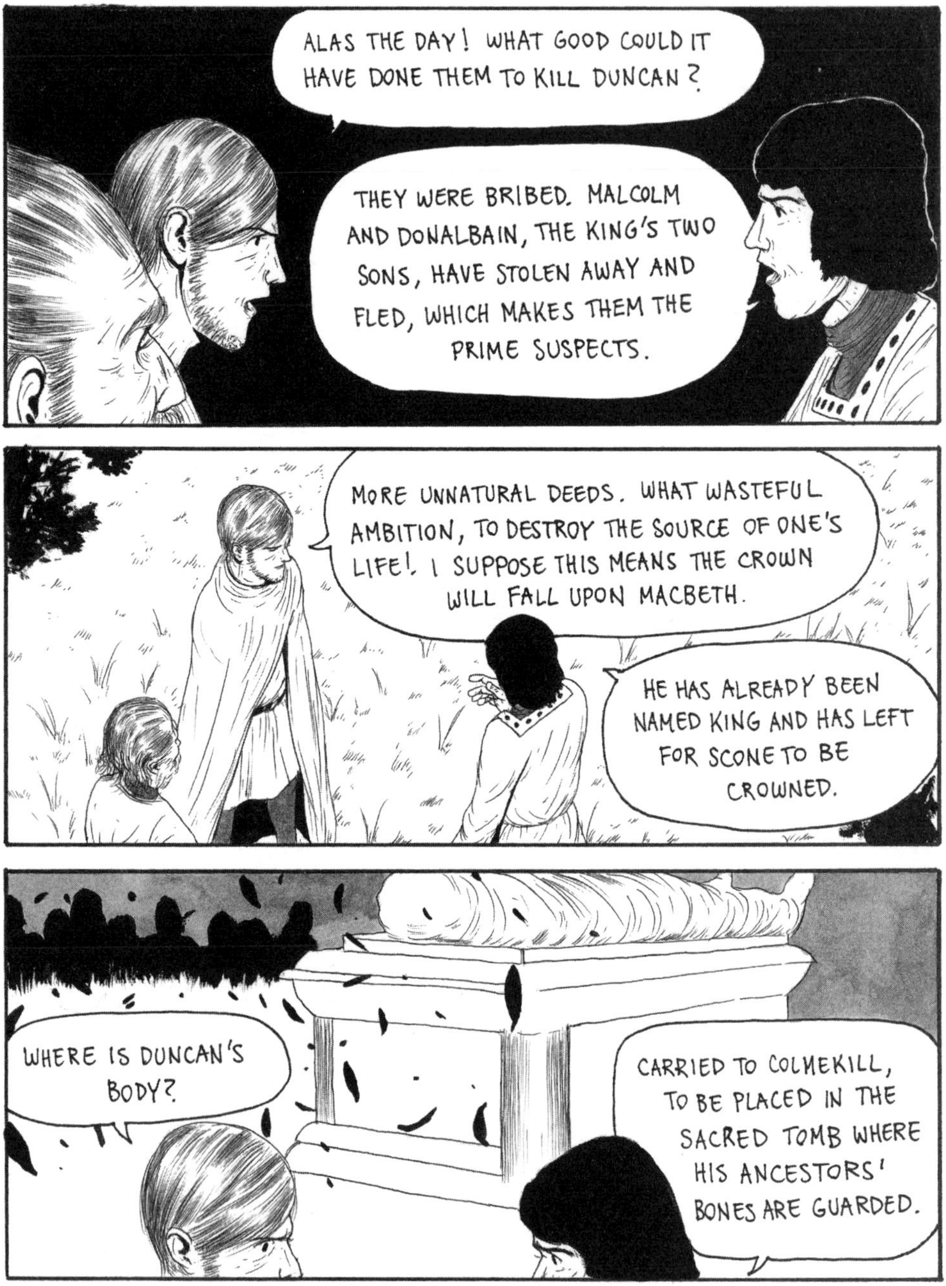
ALAS THE DAY! WHAT GOOD COULD IT HAVE DONE THEM TO KILL DUNCAN?
THEY WERE BRIBED. MALCOLM AND DONALBAIN, THE KING'S TWO SONS, HAVE STOLEN AWAY AND FLED, WHICH MAKES THEM THE PRIME SUSPECTS.
MORE UNNATURAL DEEDS. WHAT WASTEFUL AMBITION, TO DESTROY THE SOURCE OF ONE'S LIFE! I SUPPOSE THIS MEANS THE CROWN WILL FALL UPON MACBETH.
HE HAS ALREADY BEEN NAMED KING AND HAS LEFT FOR SCONE TO BE CROWNED.
WHERE IS DUNCAN'S BODY?
CARRIED TO COLMEKILL, TO BE PLACED IN THE SACRED TOMB WHERE HIS ANCESTORS' BONES ARE GUARDED.

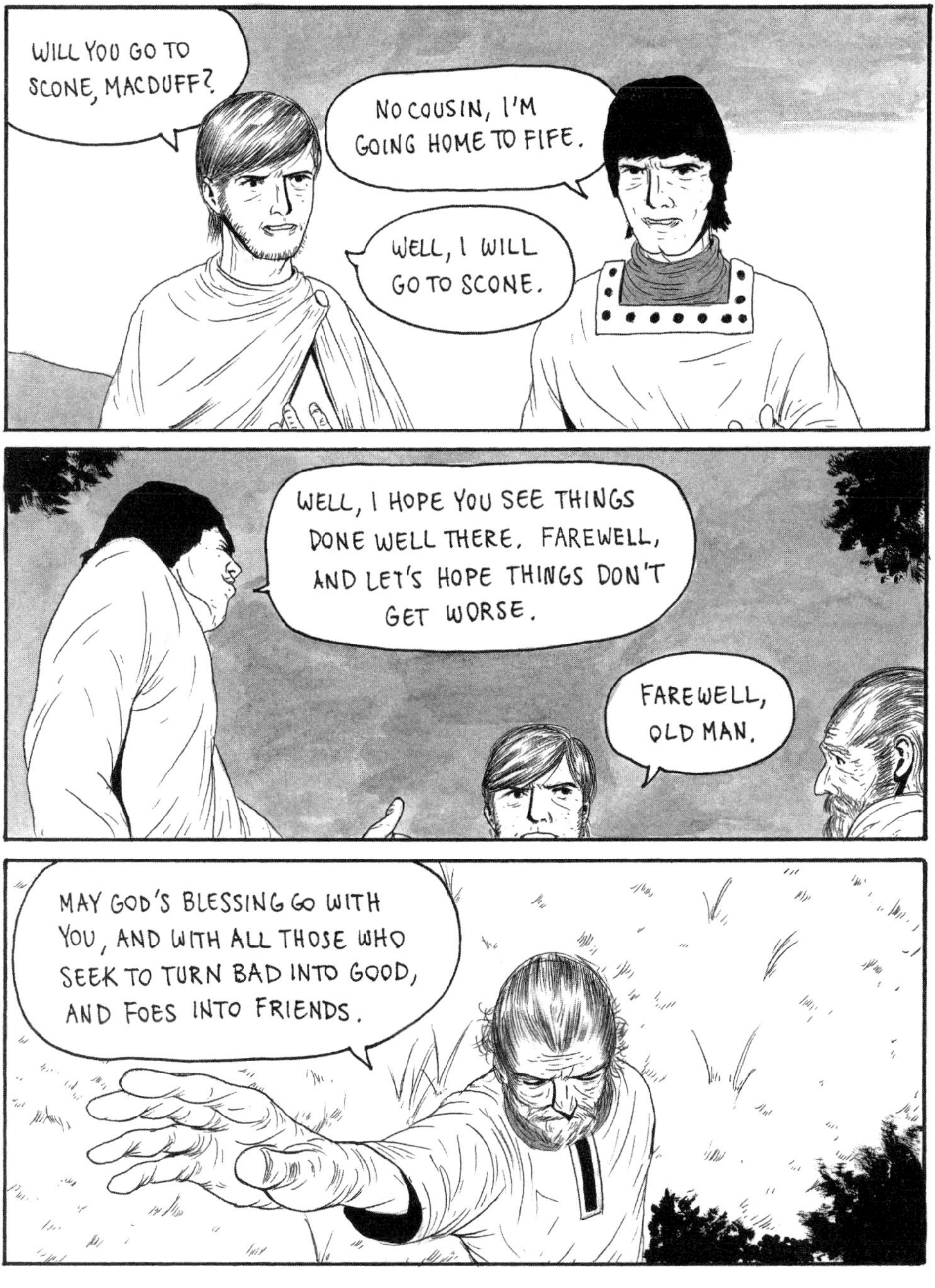
WILL YOU GO TO SCONE, MACDUFF?
NO COUSIN, I'M GOING HOME TO FIFE.
WELL, I WILL GO TO SCONE.
WELL, I HOPE YOU SEE THINGS DONE WELL THERE. FAREWELL, AND LET'S HOPE THINGS DON'T GET WORSE.
FAREWELL, OLD MAN.
MAY GOD'S BLESSING GO WITH YOU, AND WITH ALL THOSE WHO SEEK TO TURN BAD INTO GOOD, AND FOES INTO FRIENDS.

ACT III

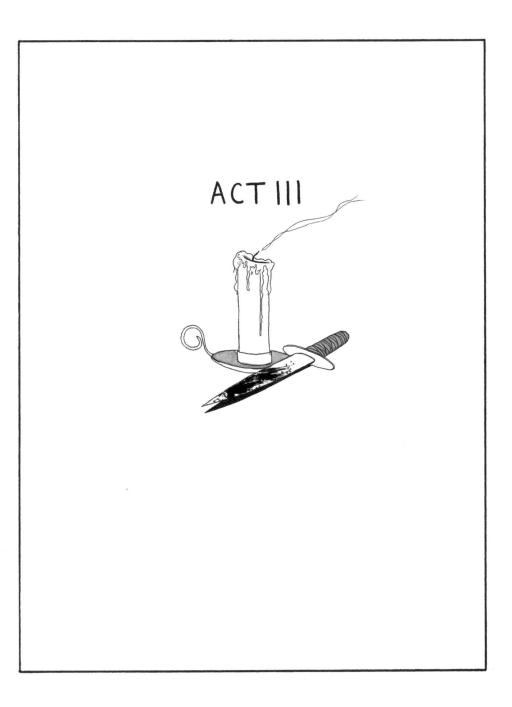

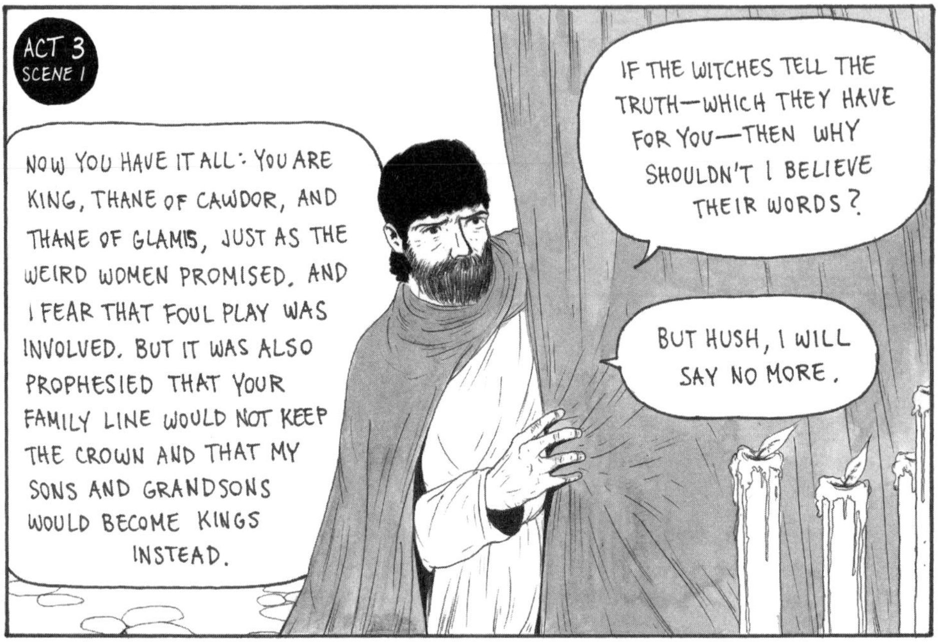
ACT 3
SCENE 1
NOW YOU HAVE IT ALL: YOU ARE KING, THANE OF CAWDOR, AND THANE OF GLAMIS, JUST AS THE WEIRD WOMEN PROMISED. AND I FEAR THAT FOUL PLAY WAS INVOLVED. BUT IT WAS ALSO PROPHESIED THAT YOUR FAMILY LINE WOULD NOT KEEP THE CROWN AND THAT MY SONS AND GRANDSONS WOULD BECOME KINGS INSTEAD.
IF THE WITCHES TELL THE TRUTH—WHICH THEY HAVE FOR YOU—THEN WHY SHOULDN'T I BELIEVE THEIR WORDS?
BUT HUSH, I WILL SAY NO MORE.

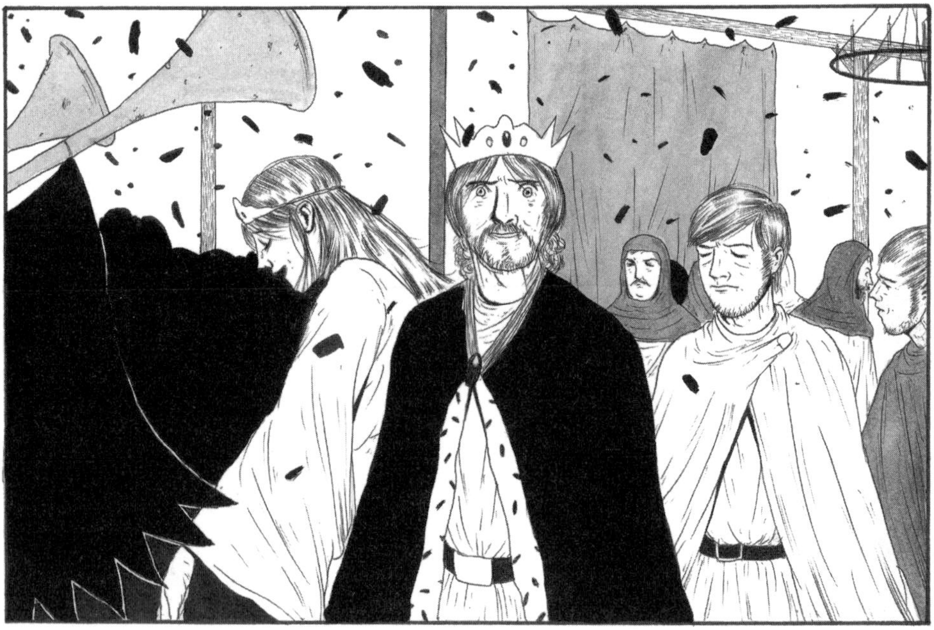

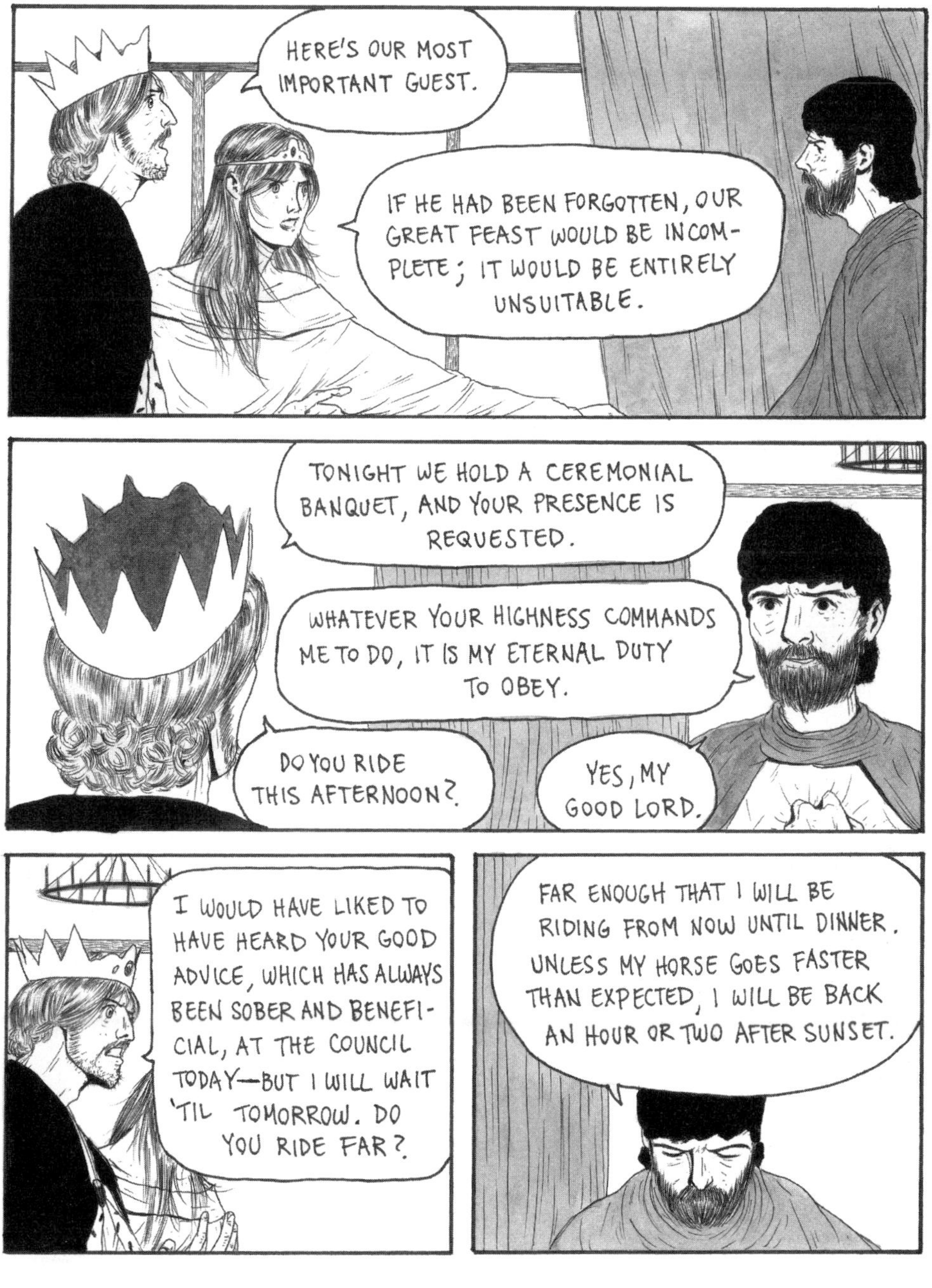
HERE'S OUR MOST IMPORTANT GUEST.
IF HE HAD BEEN FORGOTTEN, OUR GREAT FEAST WOULD BE INCOMPLETE; IT WOULD BE ENTIRELY UNSUITABLE.
TONIGHT WE HOLD A CEREMONIAL BANQUET, AND YOUR PRESENCE IS REQUESTED.
WHATEVER YOUR HIGHNESS COMMANDS ME TO DO, IT IS MY ETERNAL DUTY TO OBEY.
DO YOU RIDE THIS AFTERNOON?
YES, MY GOOD LORD.
I WOULD HAVE LIKED TO HAVE HEARD YOUR GOOD ADVICE, WHICH HAS ALWAYS BEEN SOBER AND BENEFICIAL, AT THE COUNCIL TODAY—BUT I WILL WAIT 'TIL TOMORROW. DO YOU RIDE FAR?
FAR ENOUGH THAT I WILL BE RIDING FROM NOW UNTIL DINNER. UNLESS MY HORSE GOES FASTER THAN EXPECTED, I WILL BE BACK AN HOUR OR TWO AFTER SUNSET.

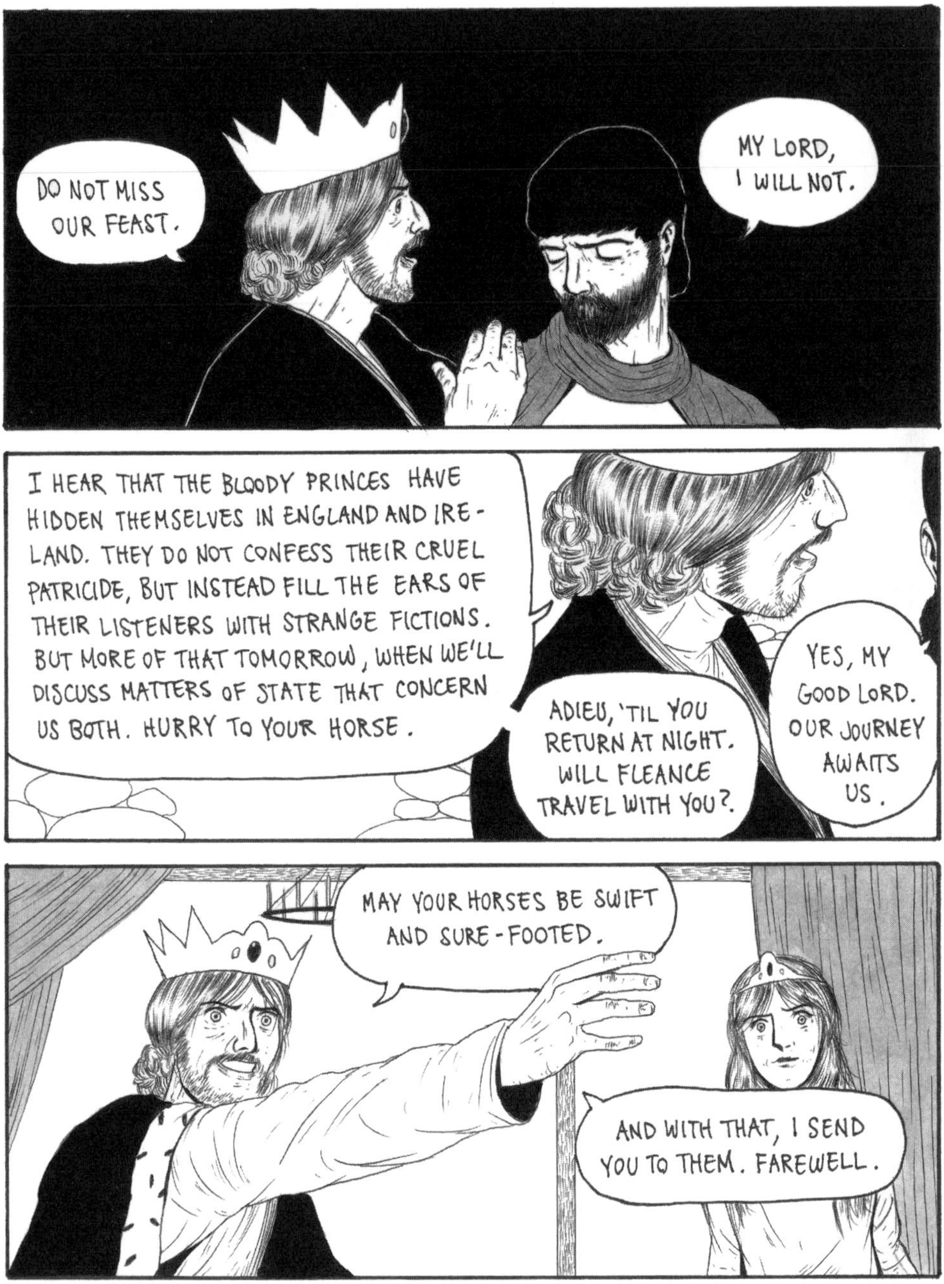
DO NOT MISS OUR FEAST.
MY LORD, I WILL NOT.
I HEAR THAT THE BLOODY PRINCES HAVE HIDDEN THEMSELVES IN ENGLAND AND IRE-LAND. THEY DO NOT CONFESS THEIR CRUEL PATRICIDE, BUT INSTEAD FILL THE EARS OF THEIR LISTENERS WITH STRANGE FICTIONS. BUT MORE OF THAT TOMORROW, WHEN WE'LL DISCUSS MATTERS OF STATE THAT CONCERN US BOTH. HURRY TO YOUR HORSE.
ADIEU, 'TIL YOU RETURN AT NIGHT. WILL FLEANCE TRAVEL WITH YOU?
YES, MY GOOD LORD. OUR JOURNEY AWAITS US.
MAY YOUR HORSES BE SWIFT AND SURE-FOOTED.
AND WITH THAT, I SEND YOU TO THEM. FAREWELL.

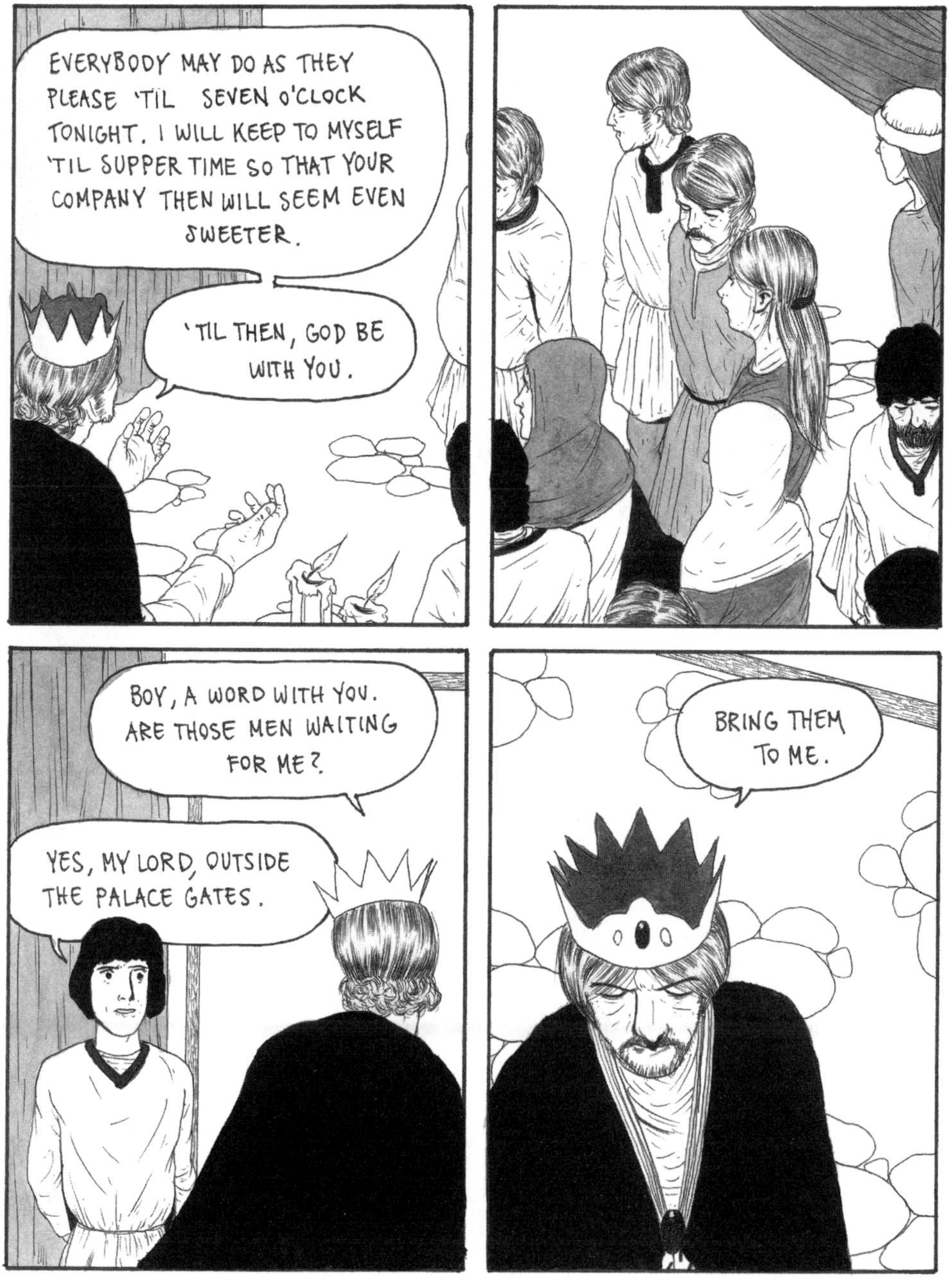
EVERYBODY MAY DO AS THEY PLEASE 'TIL SEVEN O'CLOCK TONIGHT. I WILL KEEP TO MYSELF 'TIL SUPPER TIME SO THAT YOUR COMPANY THEN WILL SEEM EVEN SWEETER.
'TIL THEN, GOD BE WITH YOU.
BOY, A WORD WITH YOU. ARE THOSE MEN WAITING FOR ME?
YES, MY LORD, OUTSIDE THE PALACE GATES.
BRING THEM TO ME.

TO BE KING IS NOTHING IF MY POSITION IS NOT SECURE. MY FEAR OF BANQUO HITS ME DEEP—HE HAS A NOBILITY OF NATURE THAT I FEAR. HE'S WILLING TO TAKE RISKS, AND, ALONG WITH A BOLD MIND, HE HAS THE WISDOM TO MATCH HIS BRAVERY WITH CAUTION.
I FEAR NONE BUT HIM—HE MAKES MY GUARDIAN ANGEL TREMBLE, AS OCTAVIUS CAESAR DID MARK ANTONY'S.
HE CHIDED THE WITCHES WHEN THEY FIRST CALLED ME KING, BIDDING THEM TO SPEAK TO HIM. THEN, PROPHET-LIKE, THEY TOLD HIM HE WOULD BE FATHER TO A LINE OF KINGS. THEY GAVE ME A CROWN AND A SCEPTER THAT WILL WITHER WITH ME.
POWER WILL BE WRENCHED FROM MY HAND BY A STRANGER, NOT A SON OF MY OWN. IF THIS IS TRUE, THEN I HAVE DEFILED MY MIND AND MURDERED THE GRACIOUS DUNCAN FOR BANQUO'S SONS—I'VE RUINED MY OWN PEACE FOR THEIR BENEFIT.
I'VE GIVEN MY SOUL, THAT EVER-LASTING JEWEL, TO THE DEVIL SO THAT **THEY** MIGHT BE KINGS! THE SEEDS OF BANQUO—KINGS! FATE, I CHALLENGE YOU! COME AND I WILL BATTLE YOU TO THE DEATH!

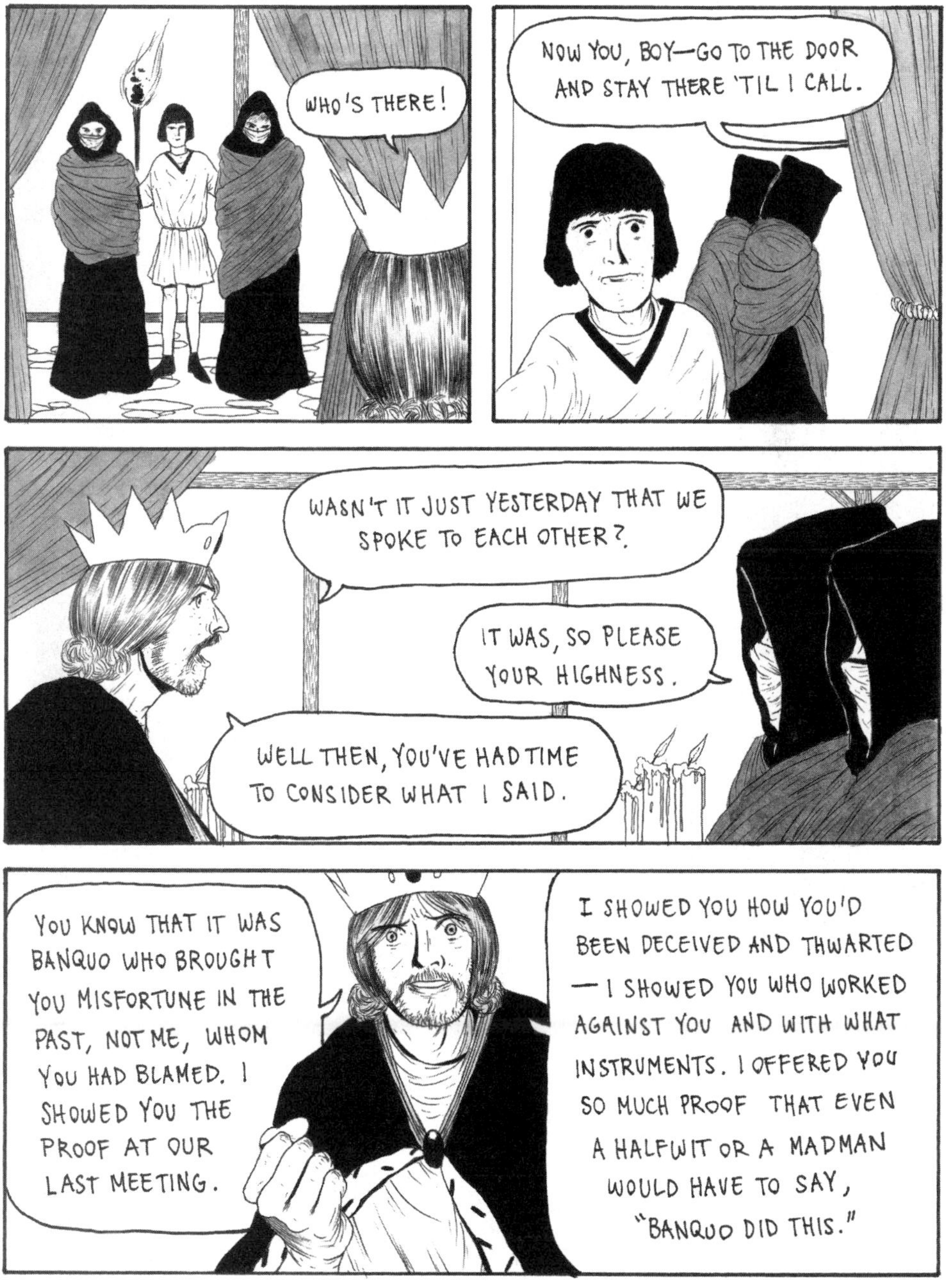
WHO'S THERE!
NOW YOU, BOY—GO TO THE DOOR AND STAY THERE 'TIL I CALL.
WASN'T IT JUST YESTERDAY THAT WE SPOKE TO EACH OTHER?
IT WAS, SO PLEASE YOUR HIGHNESS.
WELL THEN, YOU'VE HAD TIME TO CONSIDER WHAT I SAID.
YOU KNOW THAT IT WAS BANQUO WHO BROUGHT YOU MISFORTUNE IN THE PAST, NOT ME, WHOM YOU HAD BLAMED. I SHOWED YOU THE PROOF AT OUR LAST MEETING.
I SHOWED YOU HOW YOU'D BEEN DECEIVED AND THWARTED —I SHOWED YOU WHO WORKED AGAINST YOU AND WITH WHAT INSTRUMENTS. I OFFERED YOU SO MUCH PROOF THAT EVEN A HALFWIT OR A MADMAN WOULD HAVE TO SAY, "BANQUO DID THIS."

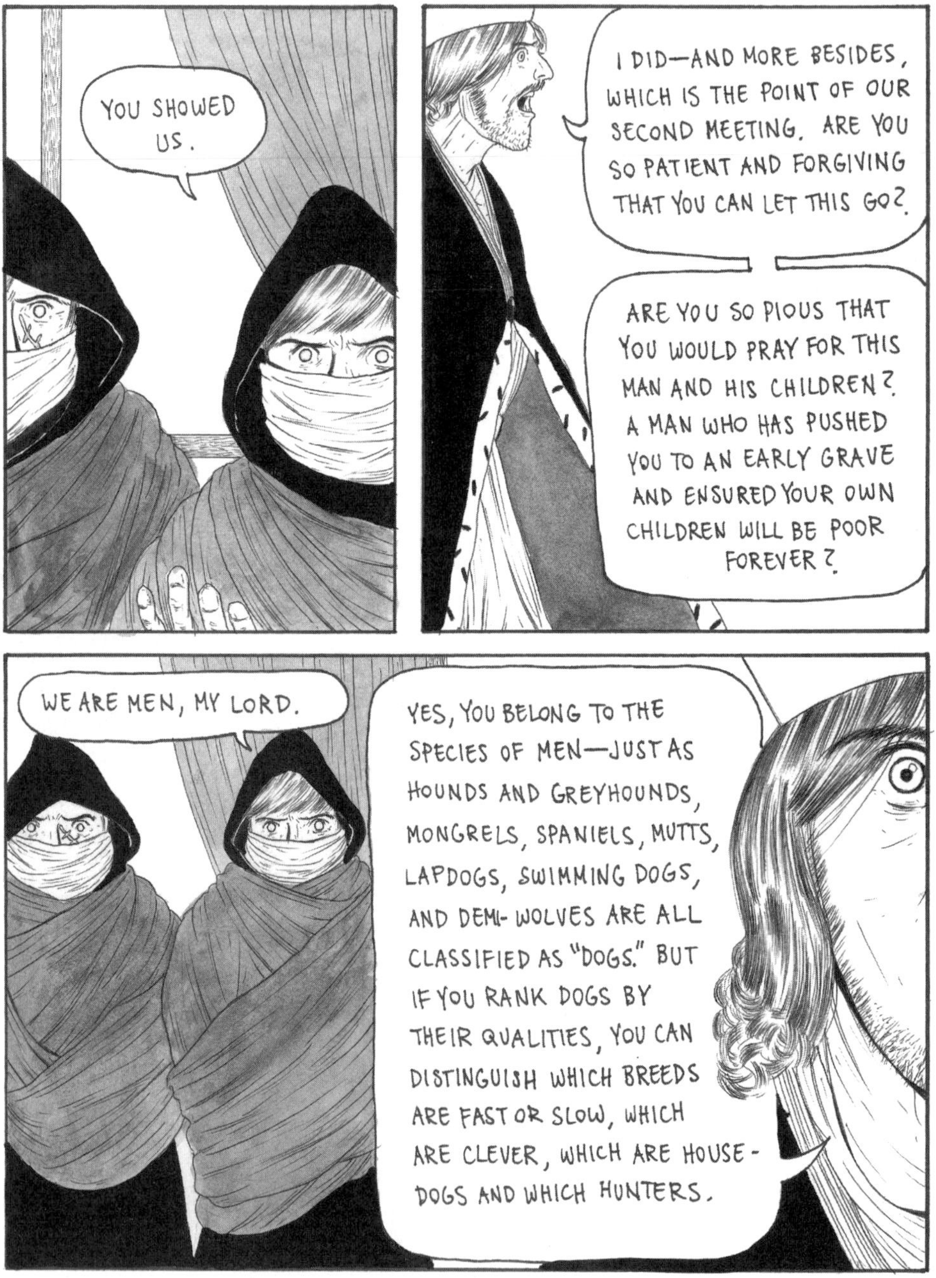
YOU SHOWED US.
I DID—AND MORE BESIDES, WHICH IS THE POINT OF OUR SECOND MEETING. ARE YOU SO PATIENT AND FORGIVING THAT YOU CAN LET THIS GO?
ARE YOU SO PIOUS THAT YOU WOULD PRAY FOR THIS MAN AND HIS CHILDREN? A MAN WHO HAS PUSHED YOU TO AN EARLY GRAVE AND ENSURED YOUR OWN CHILDREN WILL BE POOR FOREVER?
WE ARE MEN, MY LORD.
YES, YOU BELONG TO THE SPECIES OF MEN—JUST AS HOUNDS AND GREYHOUNDS, MONGRELS, SPANIELS, MUTTS, LAPDOGS, SWIMMING DOGS, AND DEMI-WOLVES ARE ALL CLASSIFIED AS "DOGS." BUT IF YOU RANK DOGS BY THEIR QUALITIES, YOU CAN DISTINGUISH WHICH BREEDS ARE FAST OR SLOW, WHICH ARE CLEVER, WHICH ARE HOUSE-DOGS AND WHICH HUNTERS.

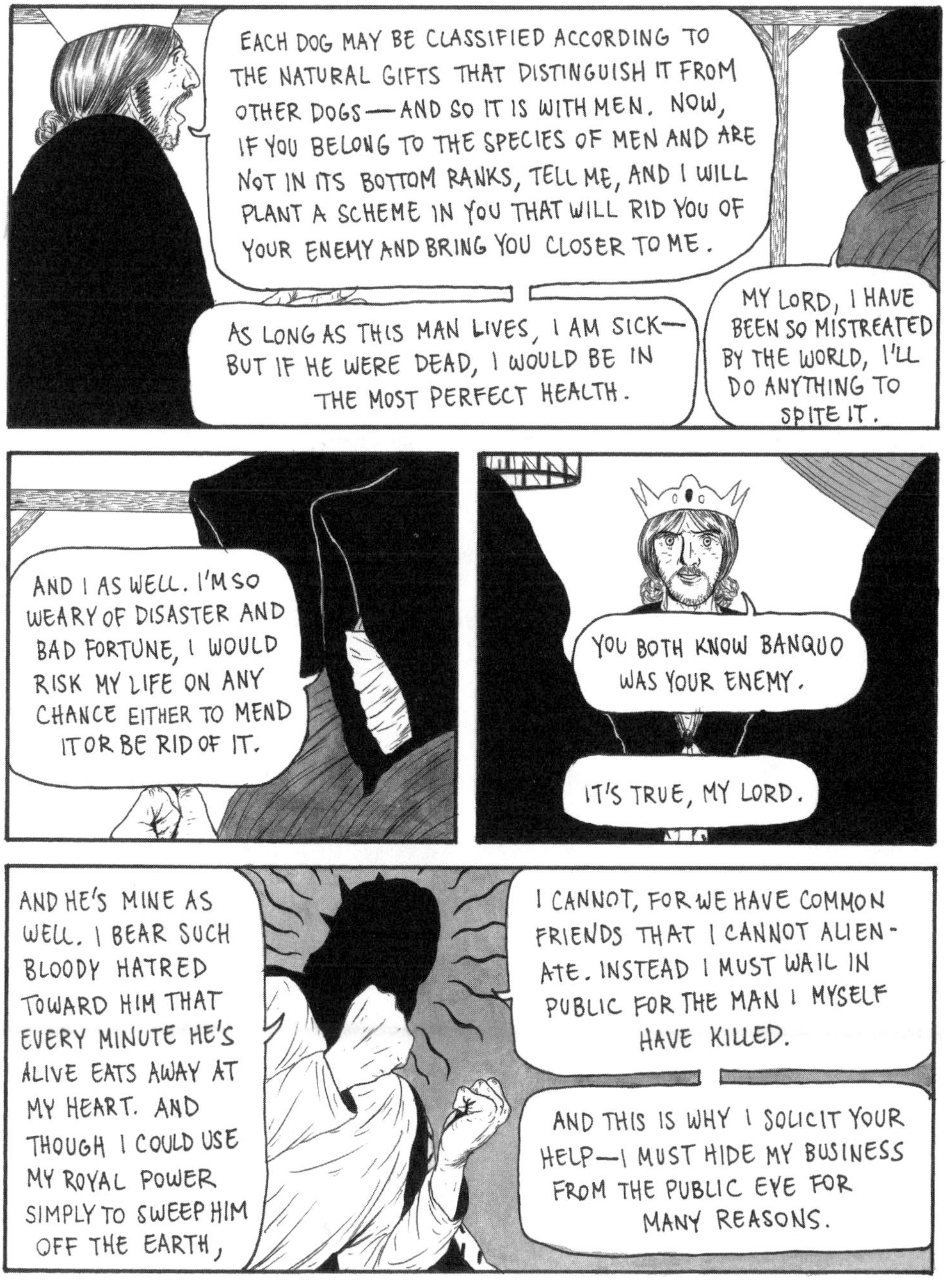
EACH DOG MAY BE CLASSIFIED ACCORDING TO THE NATURAL GIFTS THAT DISTINGUISH IT FROM OTHER DOGS—AND SO IT IS WITH MEN. NOW, IF YOU BELONG TO THE SPECIES OF MEN AND ARE NOT IN ITS BOTTOM RANKS, TELL ME, AND I WILL PLANT A SCHEME IN YOU THAT WILL RID YOU OF YOUR ENEMY AND BRING YOU CLOSER TO ME.
AS LONG AS THIS MAN LIVES, I AM SICK—BUT IF HE WERE DEAD, I WOULD BE IN THE MOST PERFECT HEALTH.
MY LORD, I HAVE BEEN SO MISTREATED BY THE WORLD, I'LL DO ANYTHING TO SPITE IT.
AND I AS WELL. I'M SO WEARY OF DISASTER AND BAD FORTUNE, I WOULD RISK MY LIFE ON ANY CHANCE EITHER TO MEND IT OR BE RID OF IT.
YOU BOTH KNOW BANQUO WAS YOUR ENEMY.
IT'S TRUE, MY LORD.
AND HE'S MINE AS WELL. I BEAR SUCH BLOODY HATRED TOWARD HIM THAT EVERY MINUTE HE'S ALIVE EATS AWAY AT MY HEART. AND THOUGH I COULD USE MY ROYAL POWER SIMPLY TO SWEEP HIM OFF THE EARTH,
I CANNOT, FOR WE HAVE COMMON FRIENDS THAT I CANNOT ALIEN-ATE. INSTEAD I MUST WAIL IN PUBLIC FOR THE MAN I MYSELF HAVE KILLED.
AND THIS IS WHY I SOLICIT YOUR HELP—I MUST HIDE MY BUSINESS FROM THE PUBLIC EYE FOR MANY REASONS.

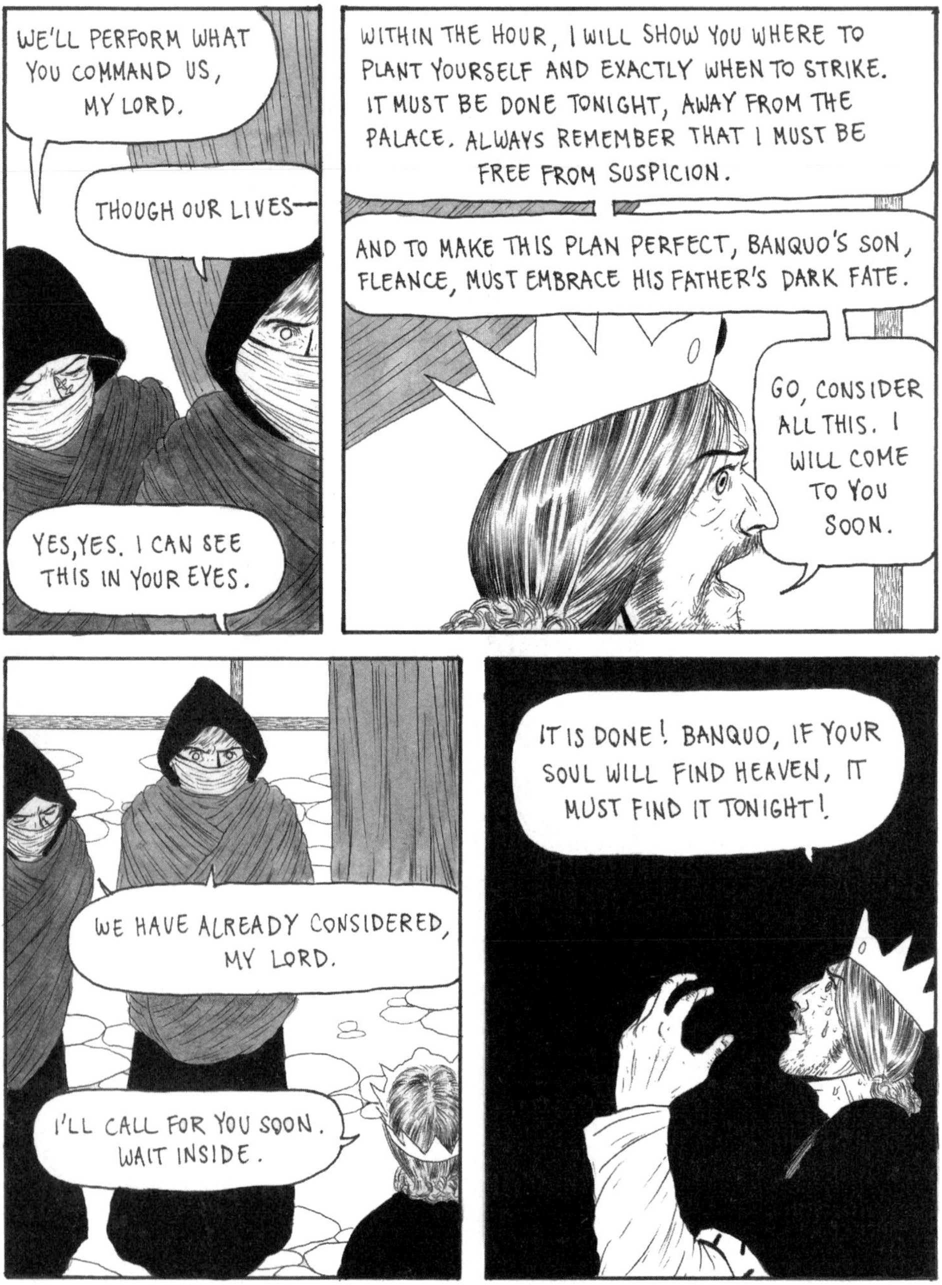
WE'LL PERFORM WHAT YOU COMMAND US, MY LORD.
THOUGH OUR LIVES—
YES, YES. I CAN SEE THIS IN YOUR EYES.
WITHIN THE HOUR, I WILL SHOW YOU WHERE TO PLANT YOURSELF AND EXACTLY WHEN TO STRIKE. IT MUST BE DONE TONIGHT, AWAY FROM THE PALACE. ALWAYS REMEMBER THAT I MUST BE FREE FROM SUSPICION.
AND TO MAKE THIS PLAN PERFECT, BANQUO'S SON, FLEANCE, MUST EMBRACE HIS FATHER'S DARK FATE.
GO, CONSIDER ALL THIS. I WILL COME TO YOU SOON.
WE HAVE ALREADY CONSIDERED, MY LORD.
I'LL CALL FOR YOU SOON. WAIT INSIDE.
IT IS DONE! BANQUO, IF YOUR SOUL WILL FIND HEAVEN, IT MUST FIND IT TONIGHT!

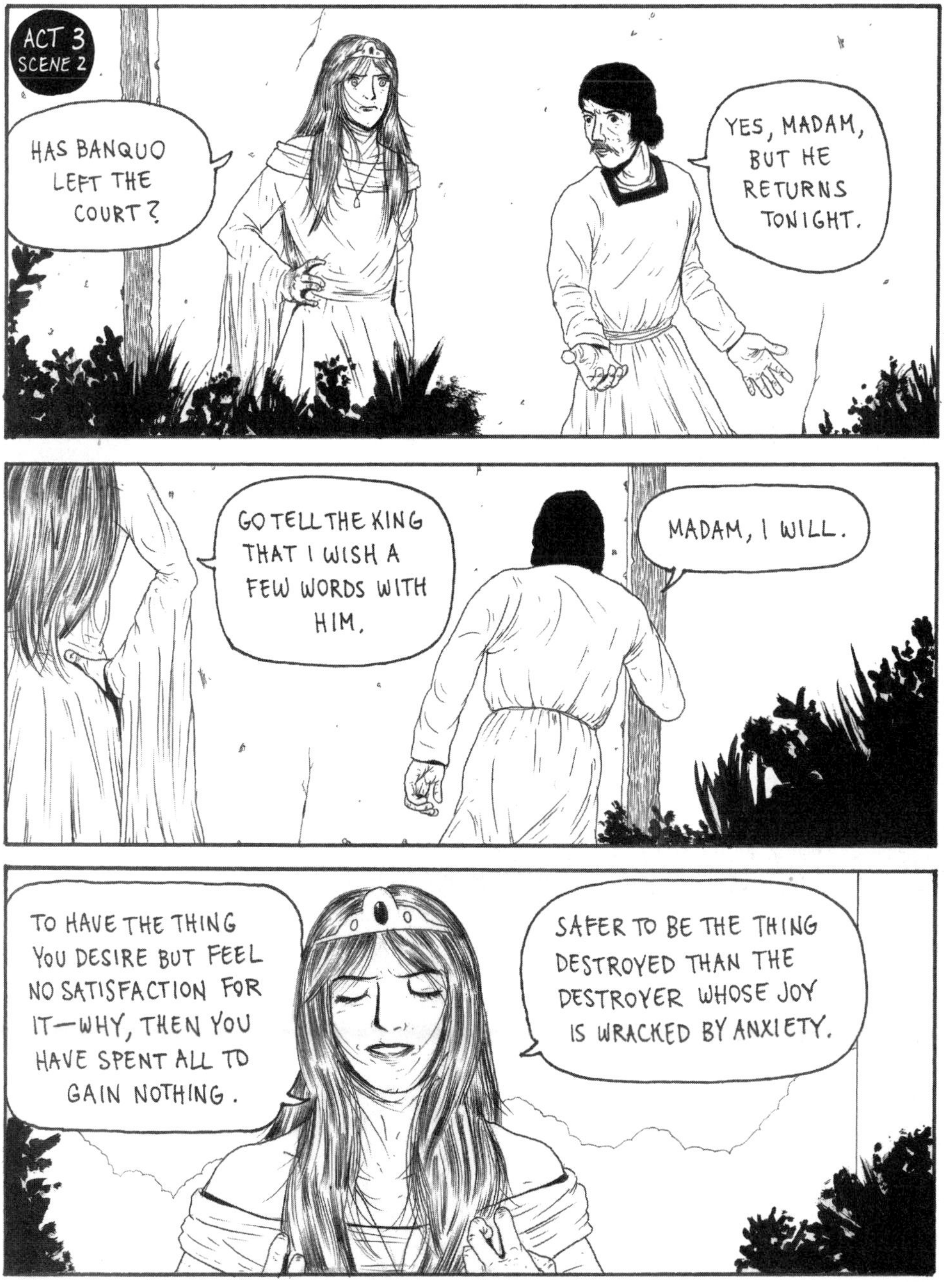
ACT 3
SCENE 2
HAS BANQUO LEFT THE COURT?
YES, MADAM, BUT HE RETURNS TONIGHT.
GO TELL THE KING THAT I WISH A FEW WORDS WITH HIM.
MADAM, I WILL.
TO HAVE THE THING YOU DESIRE BUT FEEL NO SATISFACTION FOR IT—WHY, THEN YOU HAVE SPENT ALL TO GAIN NOTHING.
SAFER TO BE THE THING DESTROYED THAN THE DESTROYER WHOSE JOY IS WRACKED BY ANXIETY.

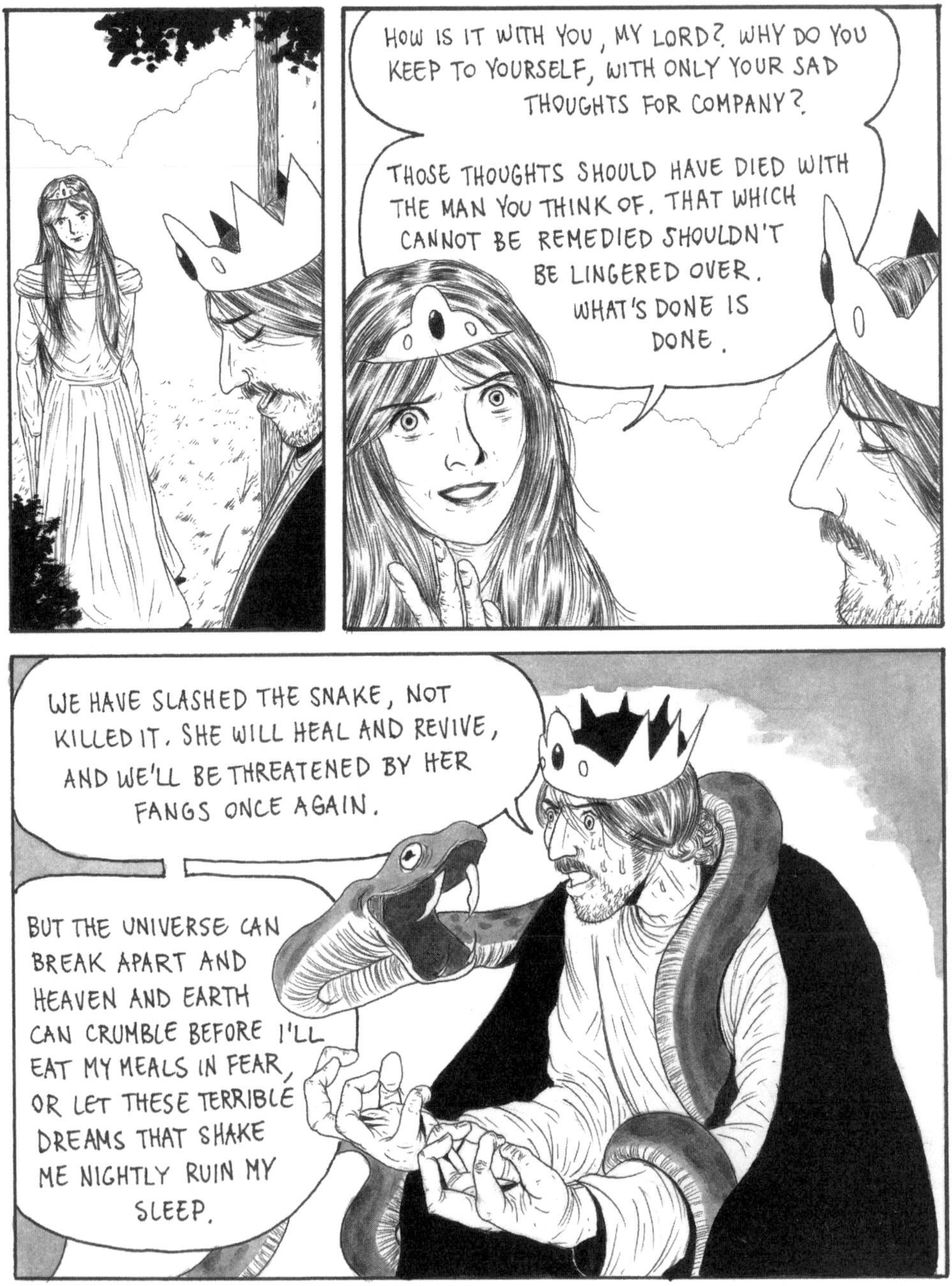
HOW IS IT WITH YOU, MY LORD? WHY DO YOU KEEP TO YOURSELF, WITH ONLY YOUR SAD THOUGHTS FOR COMPANY?
THOSE THOUGHTS SHOULD HAVE DIED WITH THE MAN YOU THINK OF. THAT WHICH CANNOT BE REMEDIED SHOULDN'T BE LINGERED OVER. WHAT'S DONE IS DONE.
WE HAVE SLASHED THE SNAKE, NOT KILLED IT. SHE WILL HEAL AND REVIVE, AND WE'LL BE THREATENED BY HER FANGS ONCE AGAIN.
BUT THE UNIVERSE CAN BREAK APART AND HEAVEN AND EARTH CAN CRUMBLE BEFORE I'LL EAT MY MEALS IN FEAR, OR LET THESE TERRIBLE DREAMS THAT SHAKE ME NIGHTLY RUIN MY SLEEP.

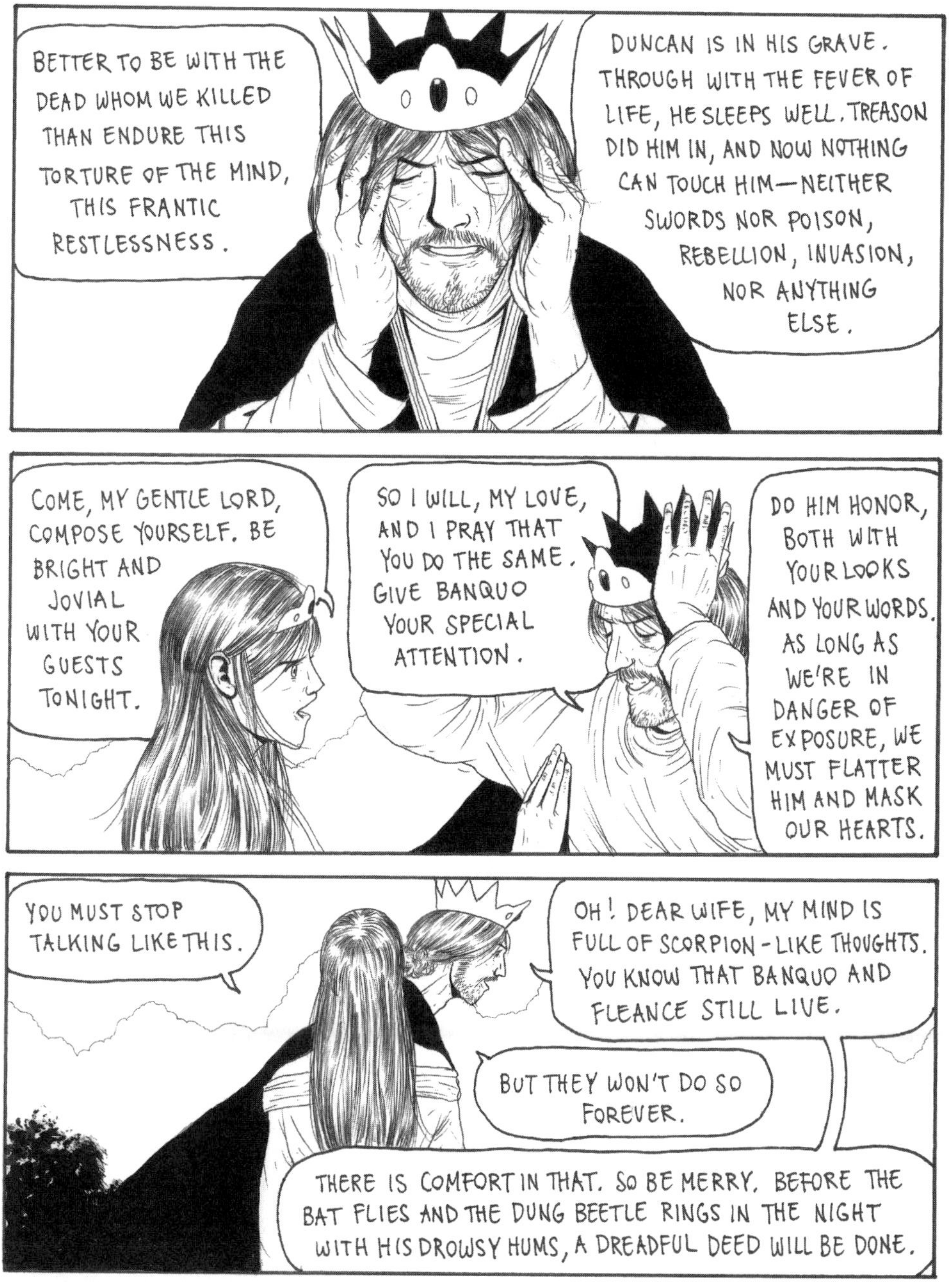
BETTER TO BE WITH THE DEAD WHOM WE KILLED THAN ENDURE THIS TORTURE OF THE MIND, THIS FRANTIC RESTLESSNESS.
DUNCAN IS IN HIS GRAVE. THROUGH WITH THE FEVER OF LIFE, HE SLEEPS WELL. TREASON DID HIM IN, AND NOW NOTHING CAN TOUCH HIM—NEITHER SWORDS NOR POISON, REBELLION, INVASION, NOR ANYTHING ELSE.
COME, MY GENTLE LORD, COMPOSE YOURSELF. BE BRIGHT AND JOVIAL WITH YOUR GUESTS TONIGHT.
SO I WILL, MY LOVE, AND I PRAY THAT YOU DO THE SAME. GIVE BANQUO YOUR SPECIAL ATTENTION.
DO HIM HONOR, BOTH WITH YOUR LOOKS AND YOUR WORDS. AS LONG AS WE'RE IN DANGER OF EXPOSURE, WE MUST FLATTER HIM AND MASK OUR HEARTS.
YOU MUST STOP TALKING LIKE THIS.
OH! DEAR WIFE, MY MIND IS FULL OF SCORPION-LIKE THOUGHTS. YOU KNOW THAT BANQUO AND FLEANCE STILL LIVE.
BUT THEY WON'T DO SO FOREVER.
THERE IS COMFORT IN THAT. SO BE MERRY. BEFORE THE BAT FLIES AND THE DUNG BEETLE RINGS IN THE NIGHT WITH HIS DROWSY HUMS, A DREADFUL DEED WILL BE DONE.

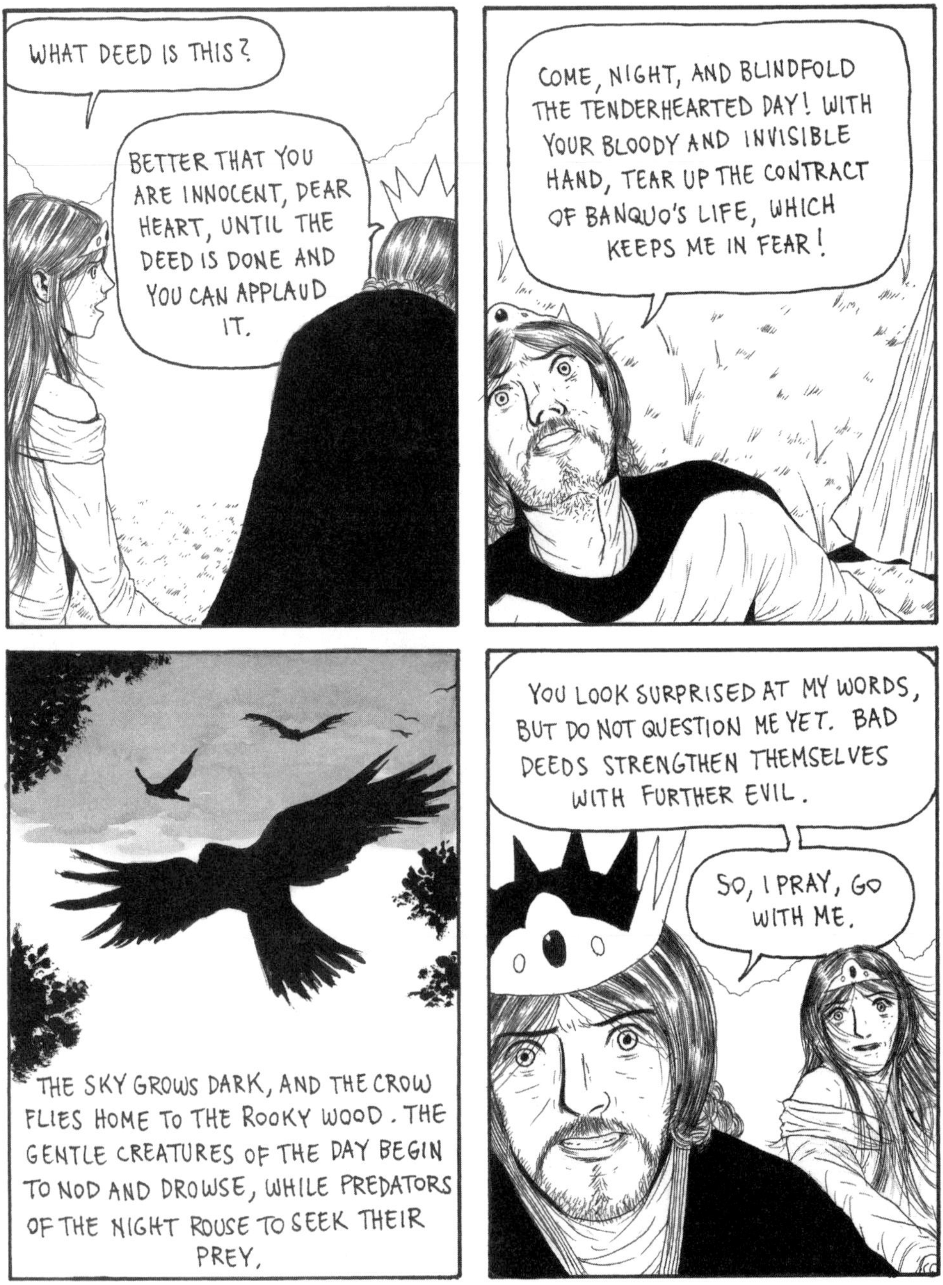
WHAT DEED IS THIS?
BETTER THAT YOU ARE INNOCENT, DEAR HEART, UNTIL THE DEED IS DONE AND YOU CAN APPLAUD IT.
COME, NIGHT, AND BLINDFOLD THE TENDERHEARTED DAY! WITH YOUR BLOODY AND INVISIBLE HAND, TEAR UP THE CONTRACT OF BANQUO'S LIFE, WHICH KEEPS ME IN FEAR!
THE SKY GROWS DARK, AND THE CROW FLIES HOME TO THE ROOKY WOOD. THE GENTLE CREATURES OF THE DAY BEGIN TO NOD AND DROWSE, WHILE PREDATORS OF THE NIGHT ROUSE TO SEEK THEIR PREY.
YOU LOOK SURPRISED AT MY WORDS, BUT DO NOT QUESTION ME YET. BAD DEEDS STRENGTHEN THEMSELVES WITH FURTHER EVIL.
SO, I PRAY, GO WITH ME.

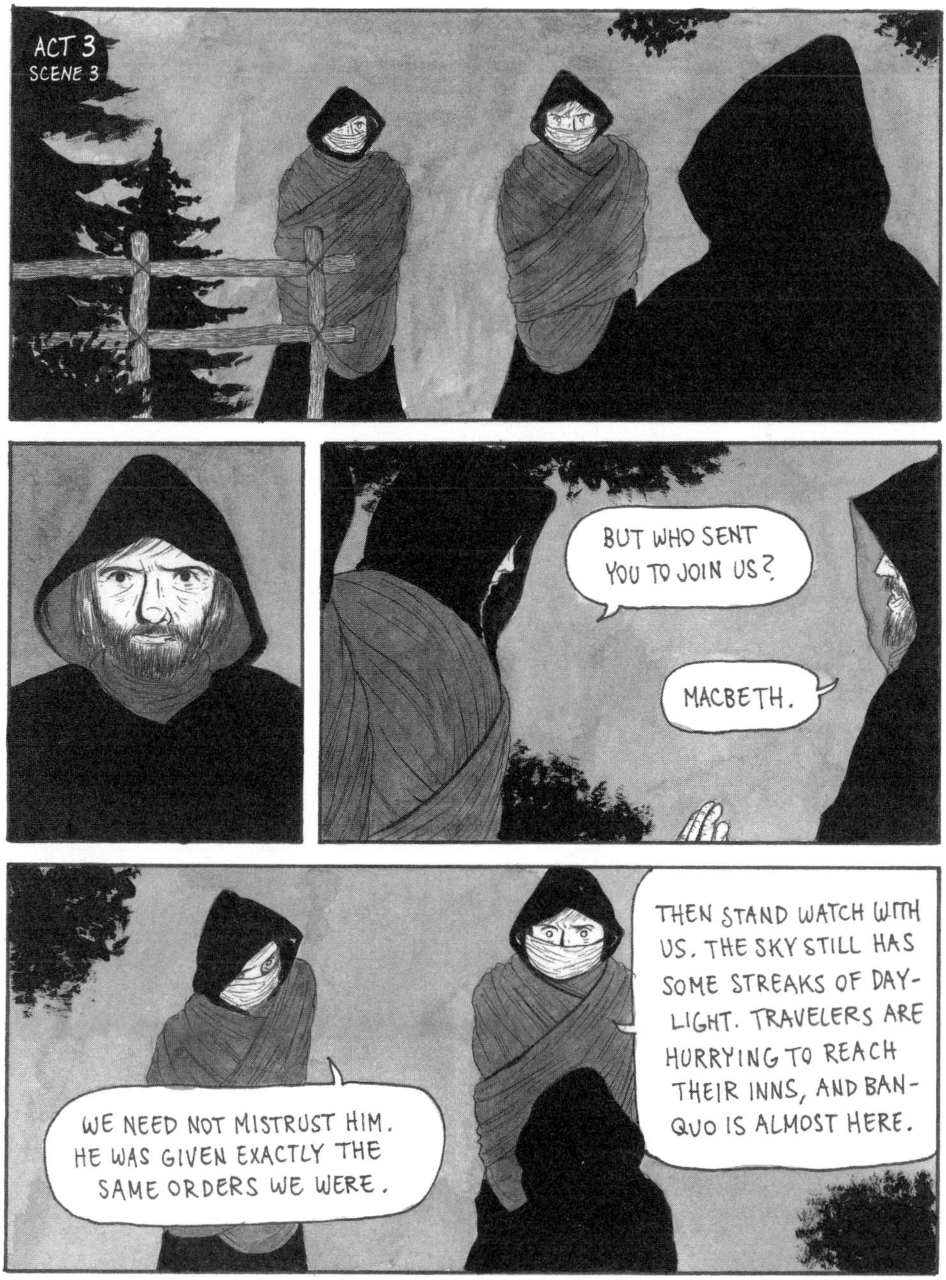
ACT 3
SCENE 3
BUT WHO SENT YOU TO JOIN US?
MACBETH.
THEN STAND WATCH WITH US. THE SKY STILL HAS SOME STREAKS OF DAY-LIGHT. TRAVELERS ARE HURRYING TO REACH THEIR INNS, AND BAN-QUO IS ALMOST HERE.
WE NEED NOT MISTRUST HIM. HE WAS GIVEN EXACTLY THE SAME ORDERS WE WERE.

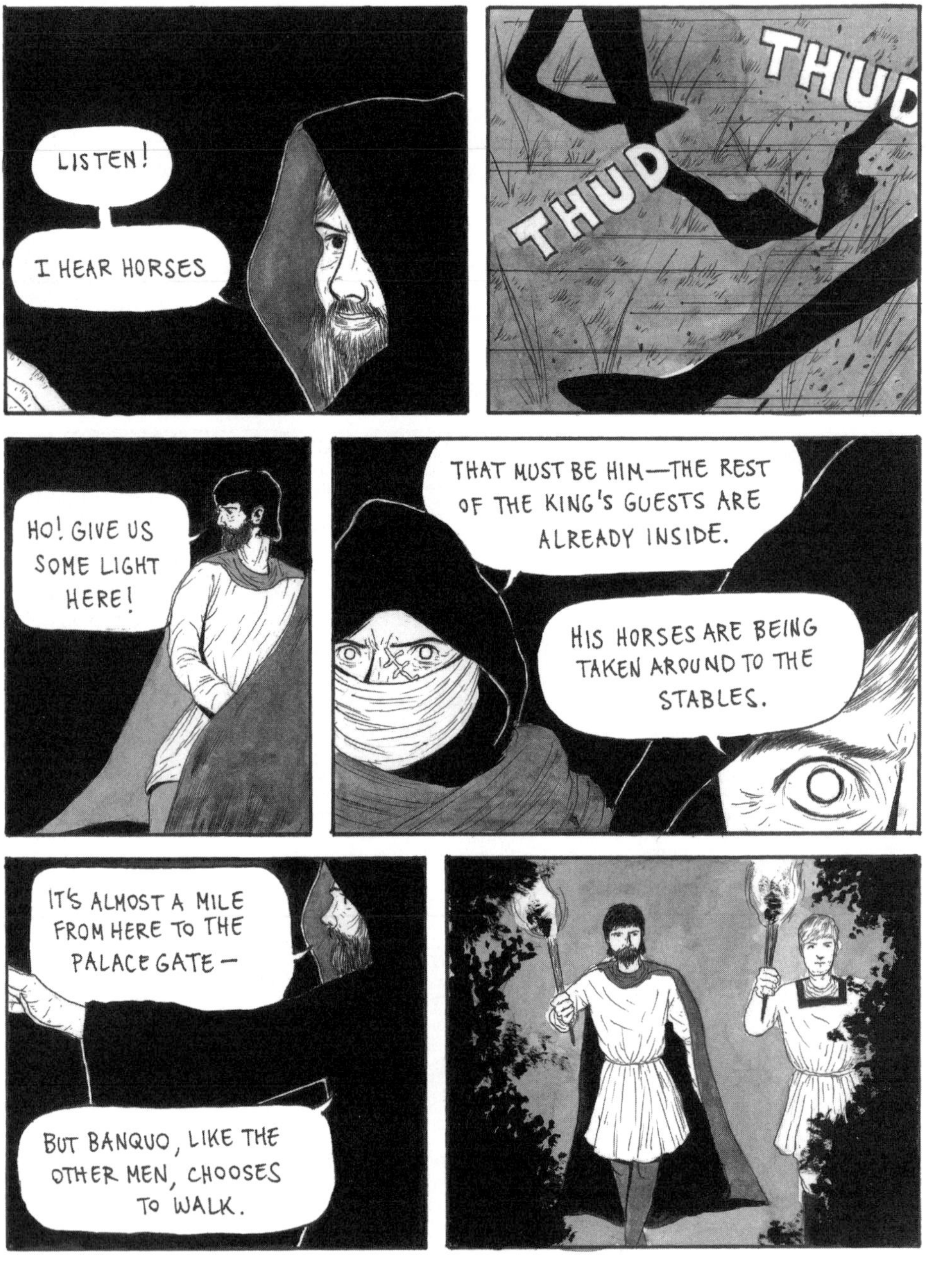
LISTEN!
I HEAR HORSES
THUD
THUD
HO! GIVE US SOME LIGHT HERE!
THAT MUST BE HIM—THE REST OF THE KING'S GUESTS ARE ALREADY INSIDE.
HIS HORSES ARE BEING TAKEN AROUND TO THE STABLES.
IT'S ALMOST A MILE FROM HERE TO THE PALACE GATE—
BUT BANQUO, LIKE THE OTHER MEN, CHOOSES TO WALK.

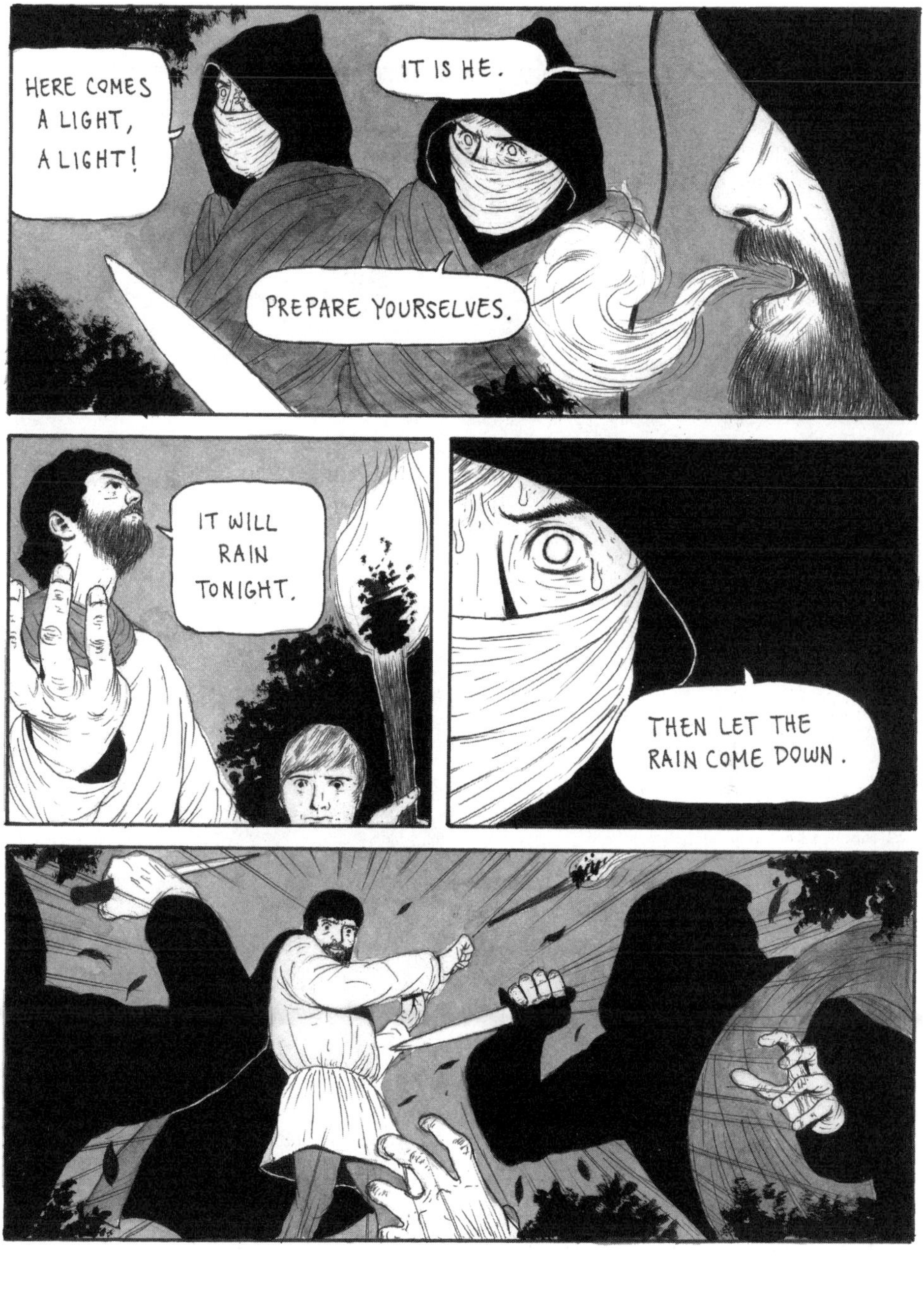
HERE COMES A LIGHT, A LIGHT!
IT IS HE.
PREPARE YOURSELVES.
IT WILL RAIN TONIGHT.
THEN LET THE RAIN COME DOWN.

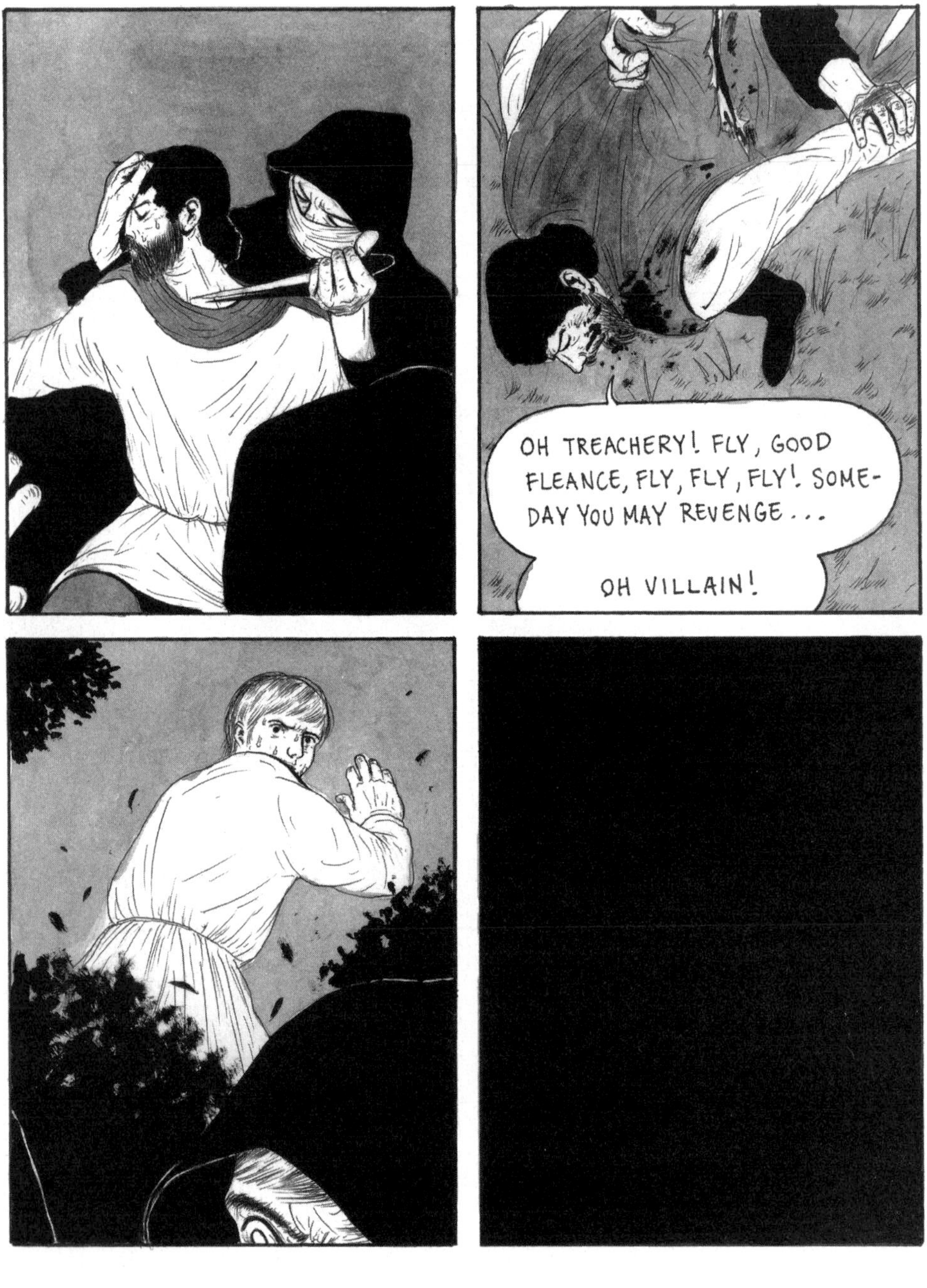
OH TREACHERY! FLY, GOOD FLEANCE, FLY, FLY, FLY! SOMEDAY YOU MAY REVENGE...
OH VILLAIN!

WHO STRUCK OUT THE LIGHT?
WASN'T THAT THE PLAN?
THERE'S ONLY ONE BODY HERE. THE SON HAS FLED.
WE HAVE FAILED IN HALF OUR MISSION.
WELL, LET'S BE GONE, TO TELL MACBETH WHAT WE DID ACCOMPLISH.

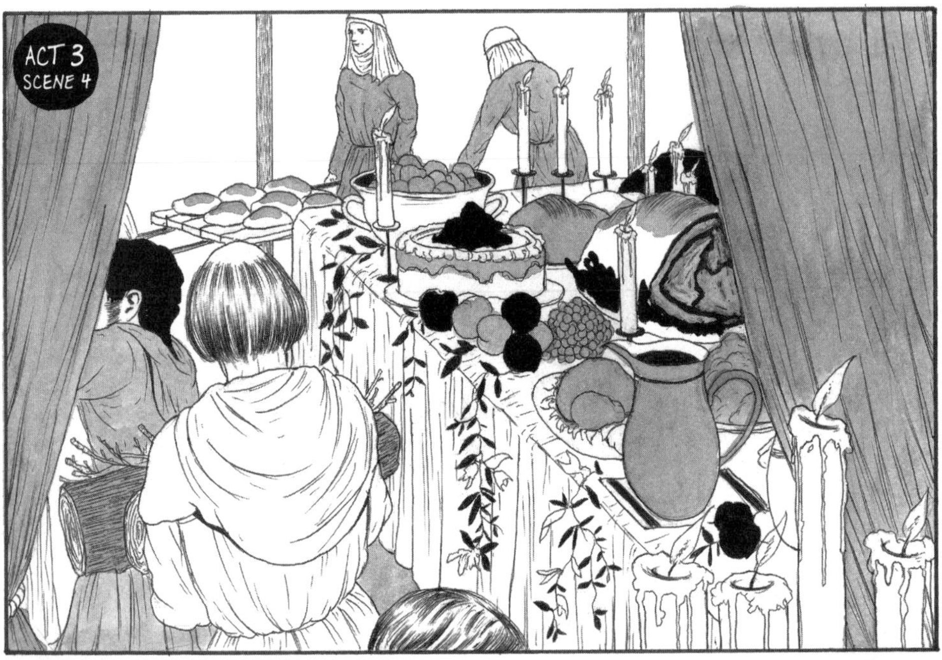
ACT 3
SCENE 4

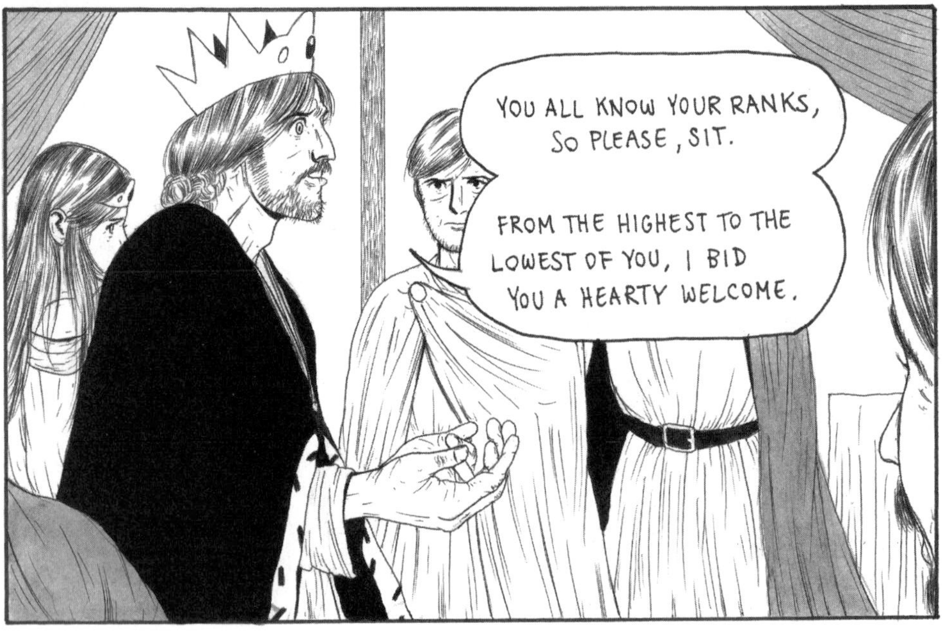
YOU ALL KNOW YOUR RANKS, SO PLEASE, SIT.
FROM THE HIGHEST TO THE LOWEST OF YOU, I BID YOU A HEARTY WELCOME.

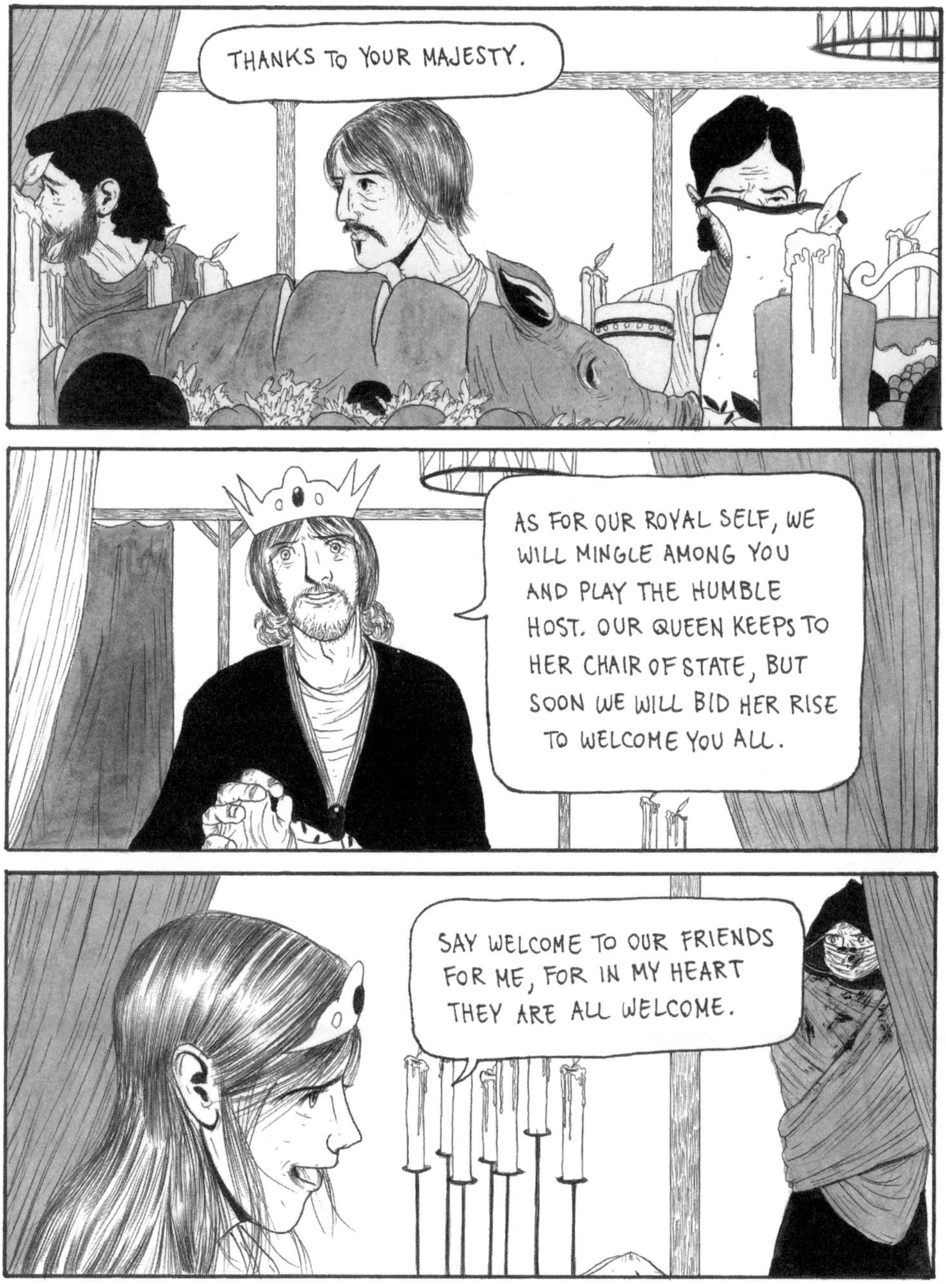
THANKS TO YOUR MAJESTY.
AS FOR OUR ROYAL SELF, WE WILL MINGLE AMONG YOU AND PLAY THE HUMBLE HOST. OUR QUEEN KEEPS TO HER CHAIR OF STATE, BUT SOON WE WILL BID HER RISE TO WELCOME YOU ALL.
SAY WELCOME TO OUR FRIENDS FOR ME, FOR IN MY HEART THEY ARE ALL WELCOME.

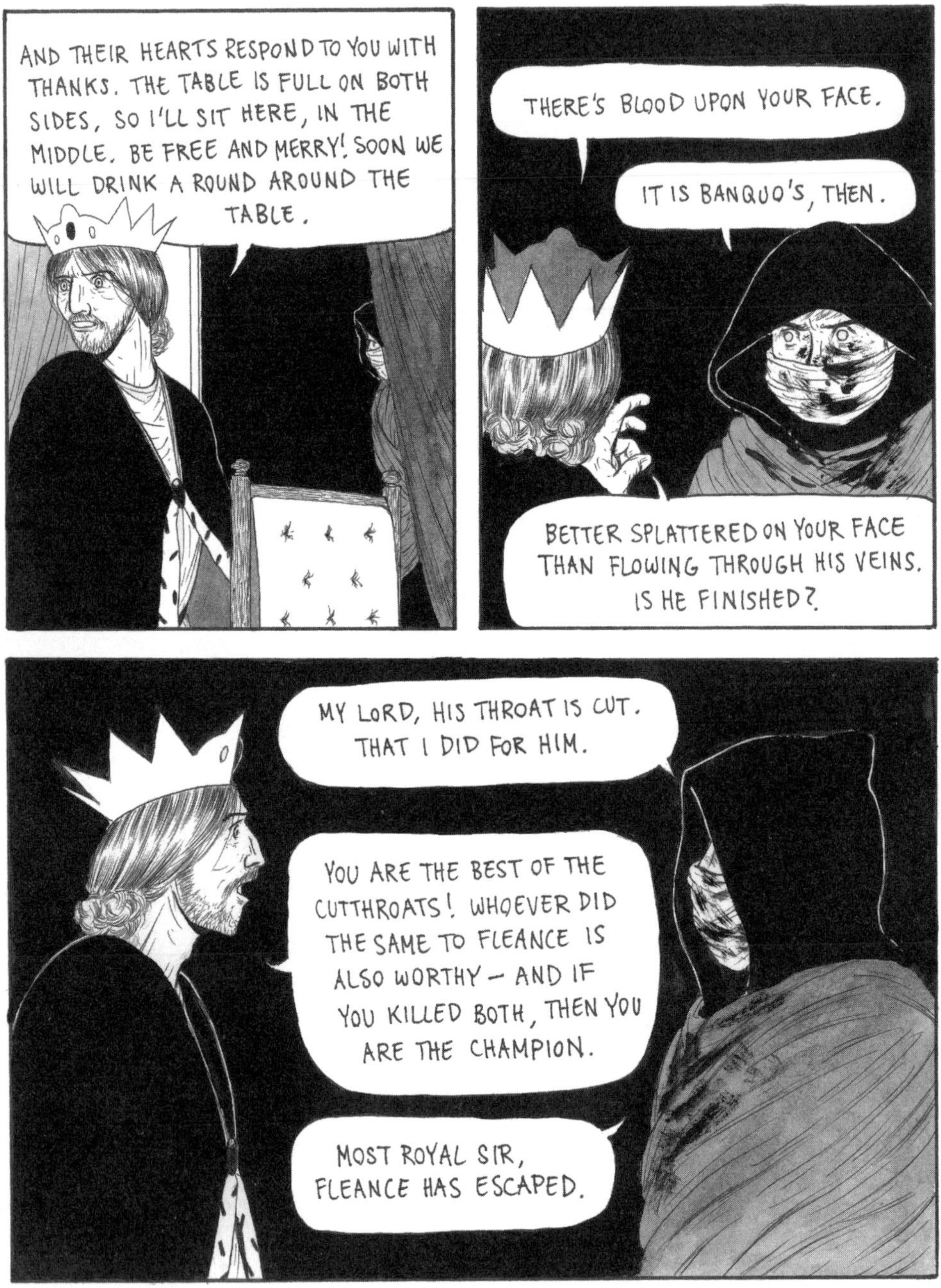
AND THEIR HEARTS RESPOND TO YOU WITH THANKS. THE TABLE IS FULL ON BOTH SIDES, SO I'LL SIT HERE, IN THE MIDDLE. BE FREE AND MERRY! SOON WE WILL DRINK A ROUND AROUND THE TABLE.
THERE'S BLOOD UPON YOUR FACE.
IT IS BANQUO'S, THEN.
BETTER SPLATTERED ON YOUR FACE THAN FLOWING THROUGH HIS VEINS. IS HE FINISHED?
MY LORD, HIS THROAT IS CUT. THAT I DID FOR HIM.
YOU ARE THE BEST OF THE CUTTHROATS! WHOEVER DID THE SAME TO FLEANCE IS ALSO WORTHY – AND IF YOU KILLED BOTH, THEN YOU ARE THE CHAMPION.
MOST ROYAL SIR, FLEANCE HAS ESCAPED.

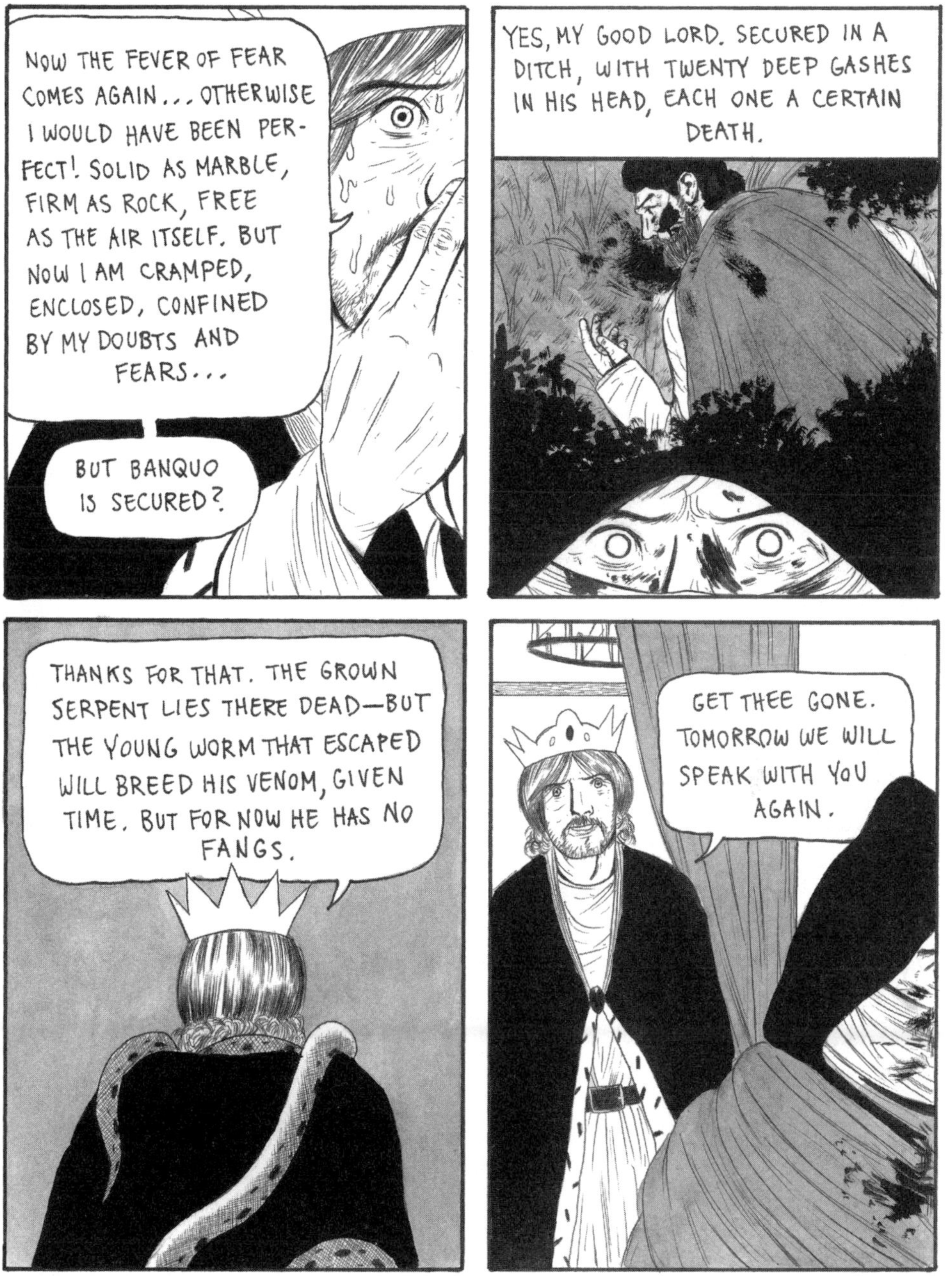
NOW THE FEVER OF FEAR COMES AGAIN... OTHERWISE I WOULD HAVE BEEN PERFECT! SOLID AS MARBLE, FIRM AS ROCK, FREE AS THE AIR ITSELF. BUT NOW I AM CRAMPED, ENCLOSED, CONFINED BY MY DOUBTS AND FEARS...
BUT BANQUO IS SECURED?
YES, MY GOOD LORD. SECURED IN A DITCH, WITH TWENTY DEEP GASHES IN HIS HEAD, EACH ONE A CERTAIN DEATH.
THANKS FOR THAT. THE GROWN SERPENT LIES THERE DEAD—BUT THE YOUNG WORM THAT ESCAPED WILL BREED HIS VENOM, GIVEN TIME. BUT FOR NOW HE HAS NO FANGS.
GET THEE GONE. TOMORROW WE WILL SPEAK WITH YOU AGAIN.

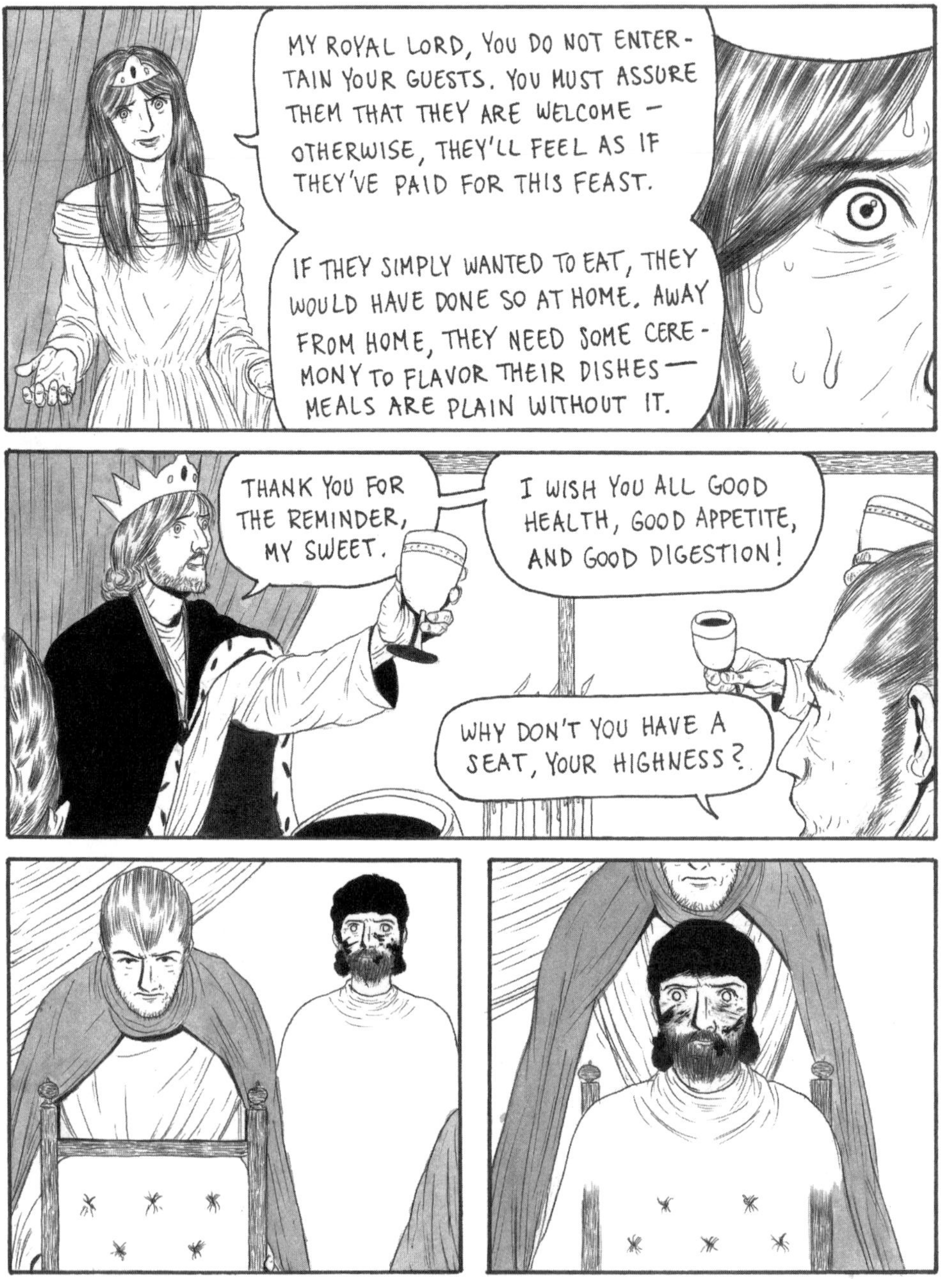
MY ROYAL LORD, YOU DO NOT ENTERTAIN YOUR GUESTS. YOU MUST ASSURE THEM THAT THEY ARE WELCOME — OTHERWISE, THEY'LL FEEL AS IF THEY'VE PAID FOR THIS FEAST.
IF THEY SIMPLY WANTED TO EAT, THEY WOULD HAVE DONE SO AT HOME. AWAY FROM HOME, THEY NEED SOME CEREMONY TO FLAVOR THEIR DISHES — MEALS ARE PLAIN WITHOUT IT.
THANK YOU FOR THE REMINDER, MY SWEET.
I WISH YOU ALL GOOD HEALTH, GOOD APPETITE, AND GOOD DIGESTION!
WHY DON'T YOU HAVE A SEAT, YOUR HIGHNESS?

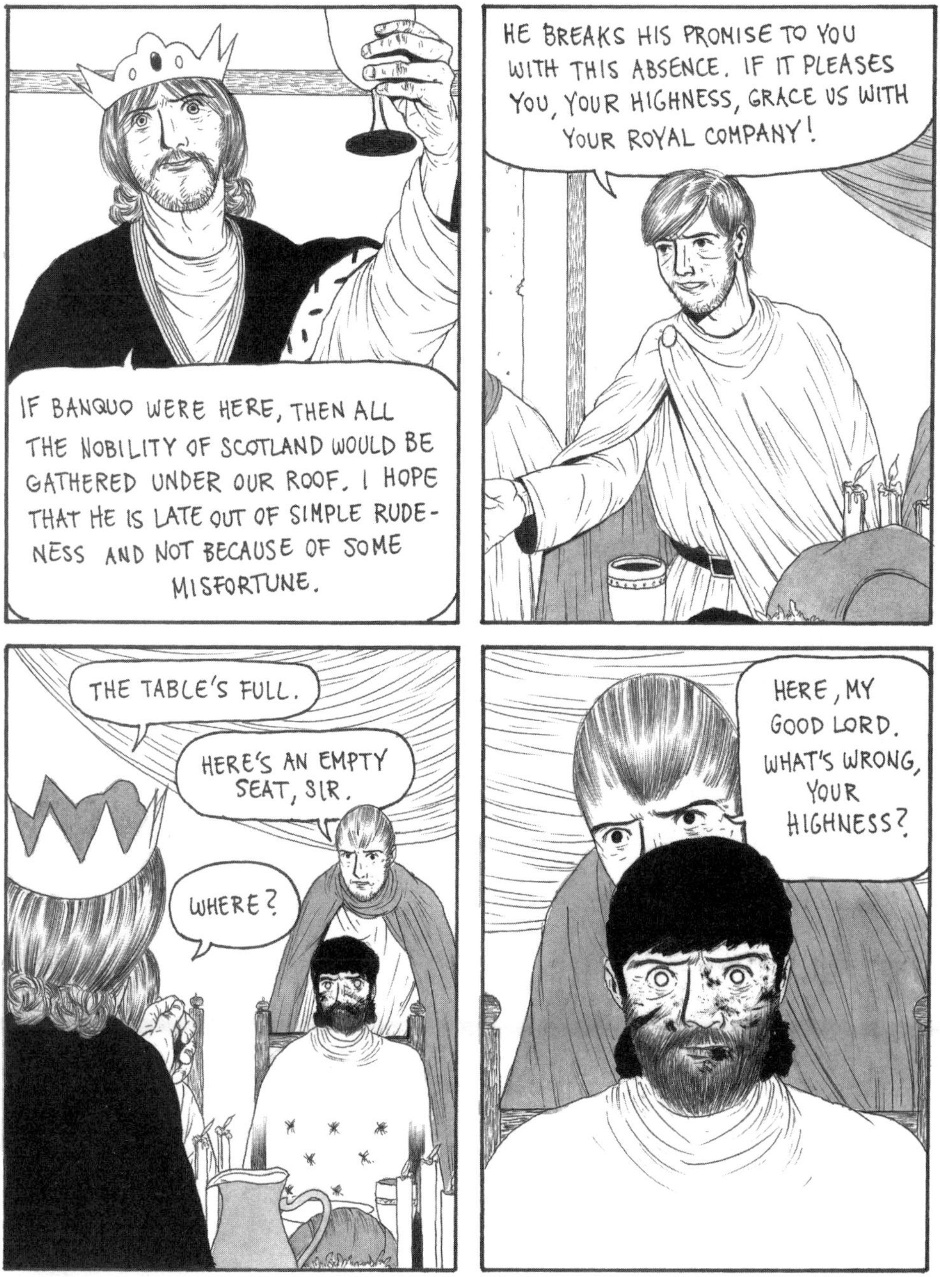
IF BANQUO WERE HERE, THEN ALL THE NOBILITY OF SCOTLAND WOULD BE GATHERED UNDER OUR ROOF. I HOPE THAT HE IS LATE OUT OF SIMPLE RUDENESS AND NOT BECAUSE OF SOME MISFORTUNE.
HE BREAKS HIS PROMISE TO YOU WITH THIS ABSENCE. IF IT PLEASES YOU, YOUR HIGHNESS, GRACE US WITH YOUR ROYAL COMPANY!
THE TABLE'S FULL.
HERE'S AN EMPTY SEAT, SIR.
WHERE?
HERE, MY GOOD LORD. WHAT'S WRONG, YOUR HIGHNESS?

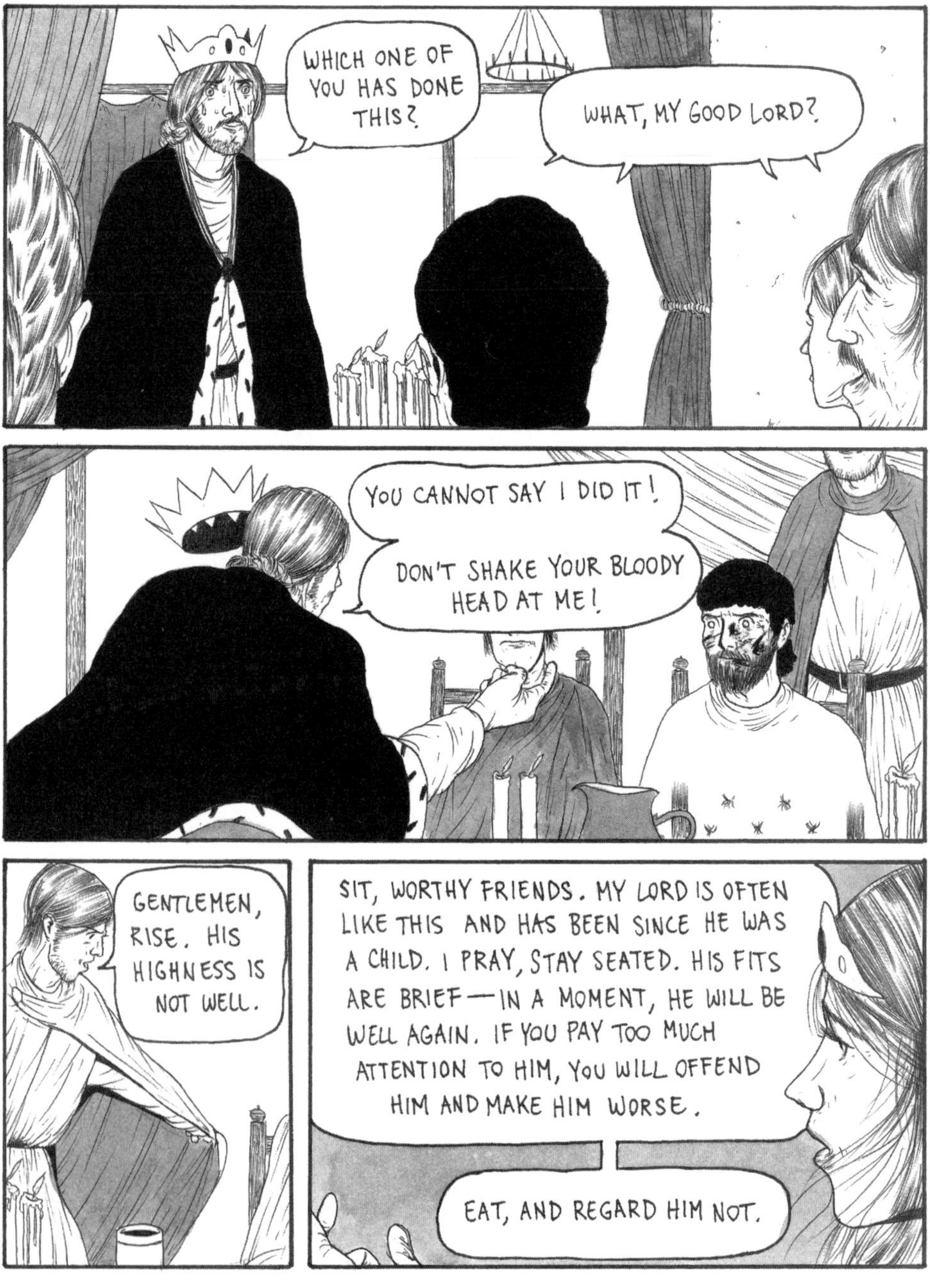
WHICH ONE OF YOU HAS DONE THIS?
WHAT, MY GOOD LORD?
YOU CANNOT SAY I DID IT!
DON'T SHAKE YOUR BLOODY HEAD AT ME!
GENTLEMEN, RISE. HIS HIGHNESS IS NOT WELL.
SIT, WORTHY FRIENDS. MY LORD IS OFTEN LIKE THIS AND HAS BEEN SINCE HE WAS A CHILD. I PRAY, STAY SEATED. HIS FITS ARE BRIEF—IN A MOMENT, HE WILL BE WELL AGAIN. IF YOU PAY TOO MUCH ATTENTION TO HIM, YOU WILL OFFEND HIM AND MAKE HIM WORSE.
EAT, AND REGARD HIM NOT.

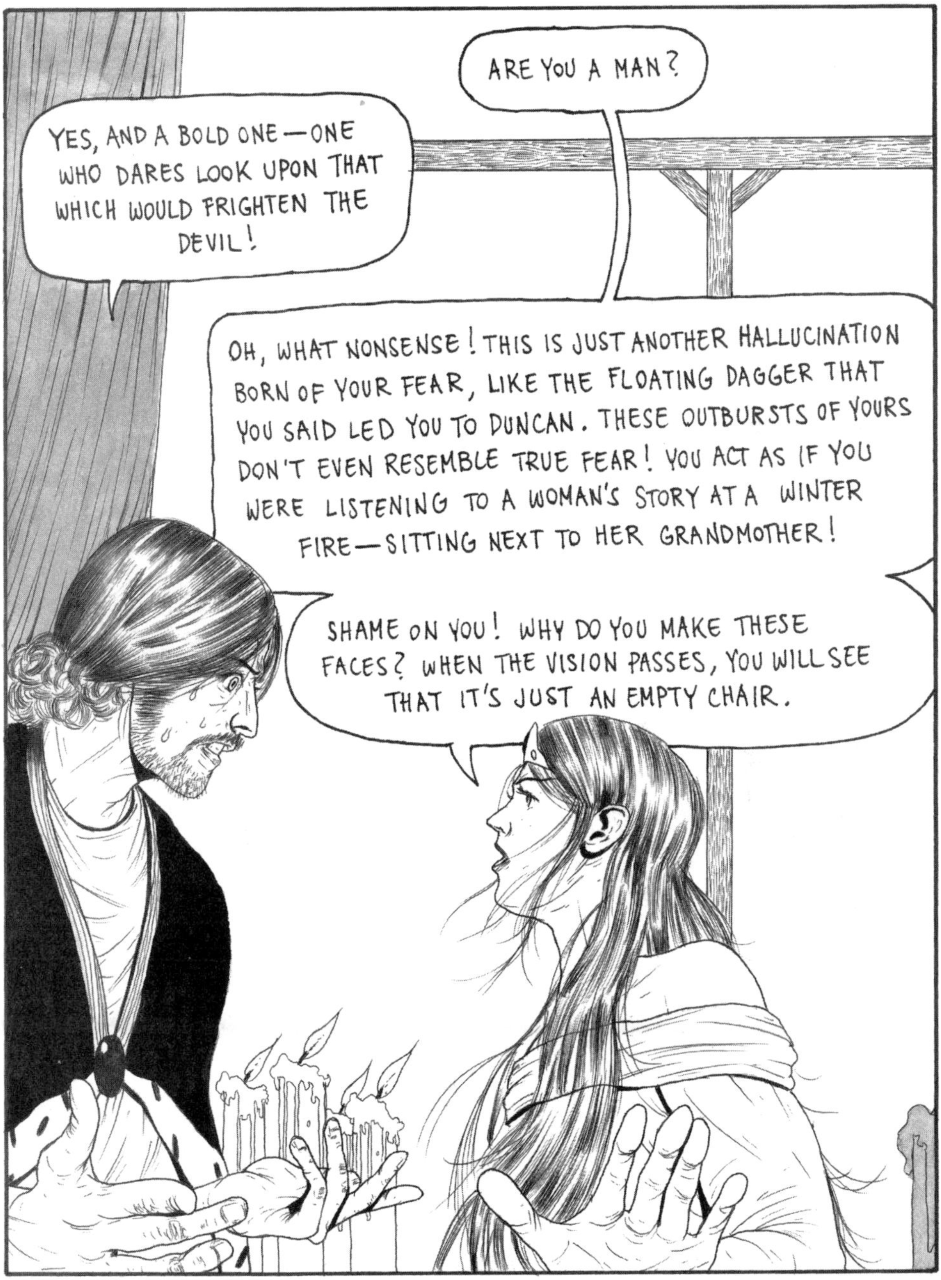
ARE YOU A MAN?
YES, AND A BOLD ONE—ONE WHO DARES LOOK UPON THAT WHICH WOULD FRIGHTEN THE DEVIL!
OH, WHAT NONSENSE! THIS IS JUST ANOTHER HALLUCINATION BORN OF YOUR FEAR, LIKE THE FLOATING DAGGER THAT YOU SAID LED YOU TO DUNCAN. THESE OUTBURSTS OF YOURS DON'T EVEN RESEMBLE TRUE FEAR! YOU ACT AS IF YOU WERE LISTENING TO A WOMAN'S STORY AT A WINTER FIRE—SITTING NEXT TO HER GRANDMOTHER!
SHAME ON YOU! WHY DO YOU MAKE THESE FACES? WHEN THE VISION PASSES, YOU WILL SEE THAT IT'S JUST AN EMPTY CHAIR.

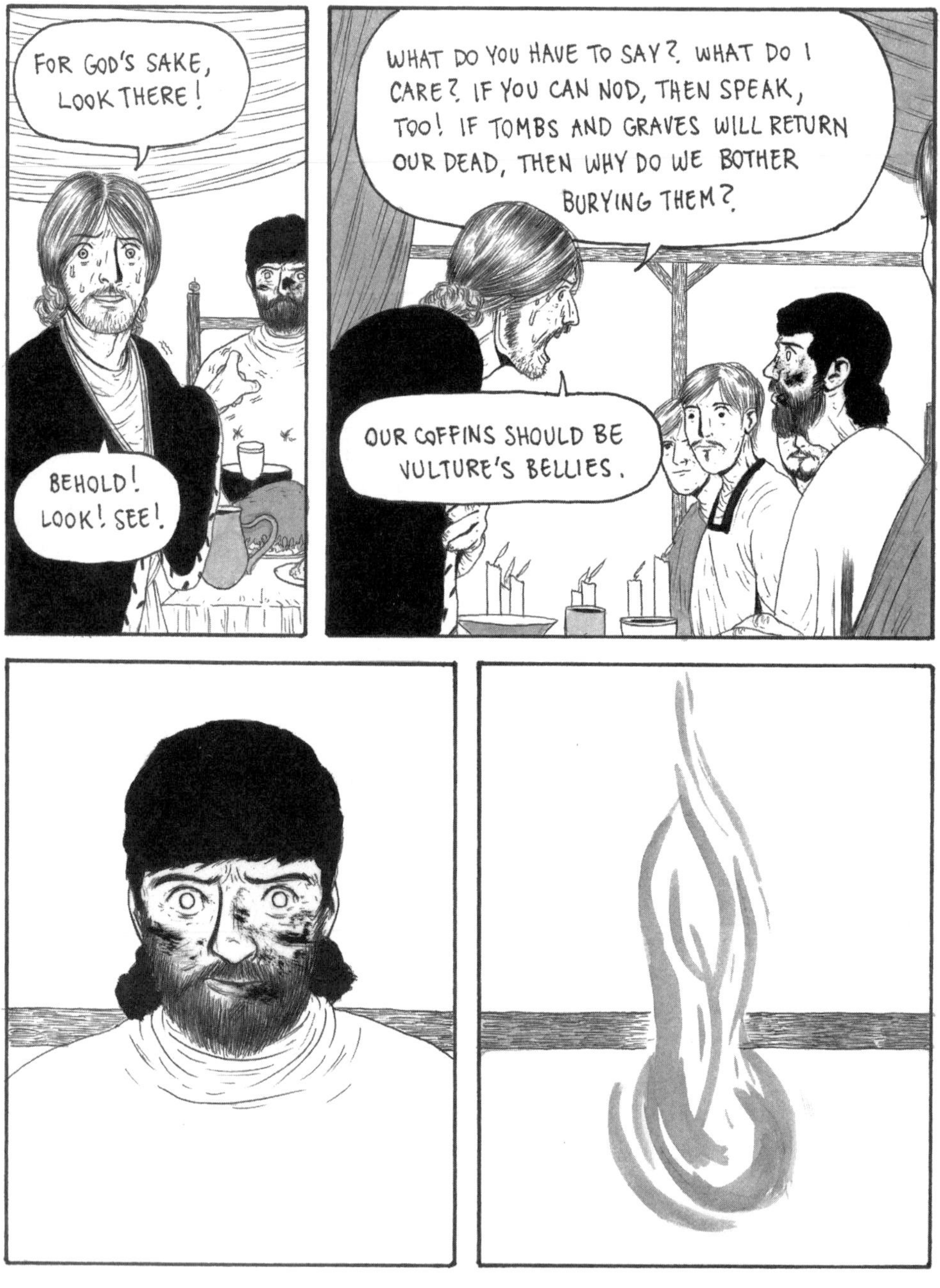
FOR GOD'S SAKE, LOOK THERE!
BEHOLD! LOOK! SEE!
WHAT DO YOU HAVE TO SAY? WHAT DO I CARE? IF YOU CAN NOD, THEN SPEAK, TOO! IF TOMBS AND GRAVES WILL RETURN OUR DEAD, THEN WHY DO WE BOTHER BURYING THEM?
OUR COFFINS SHOULD BE VULTURE'S BELLIES.

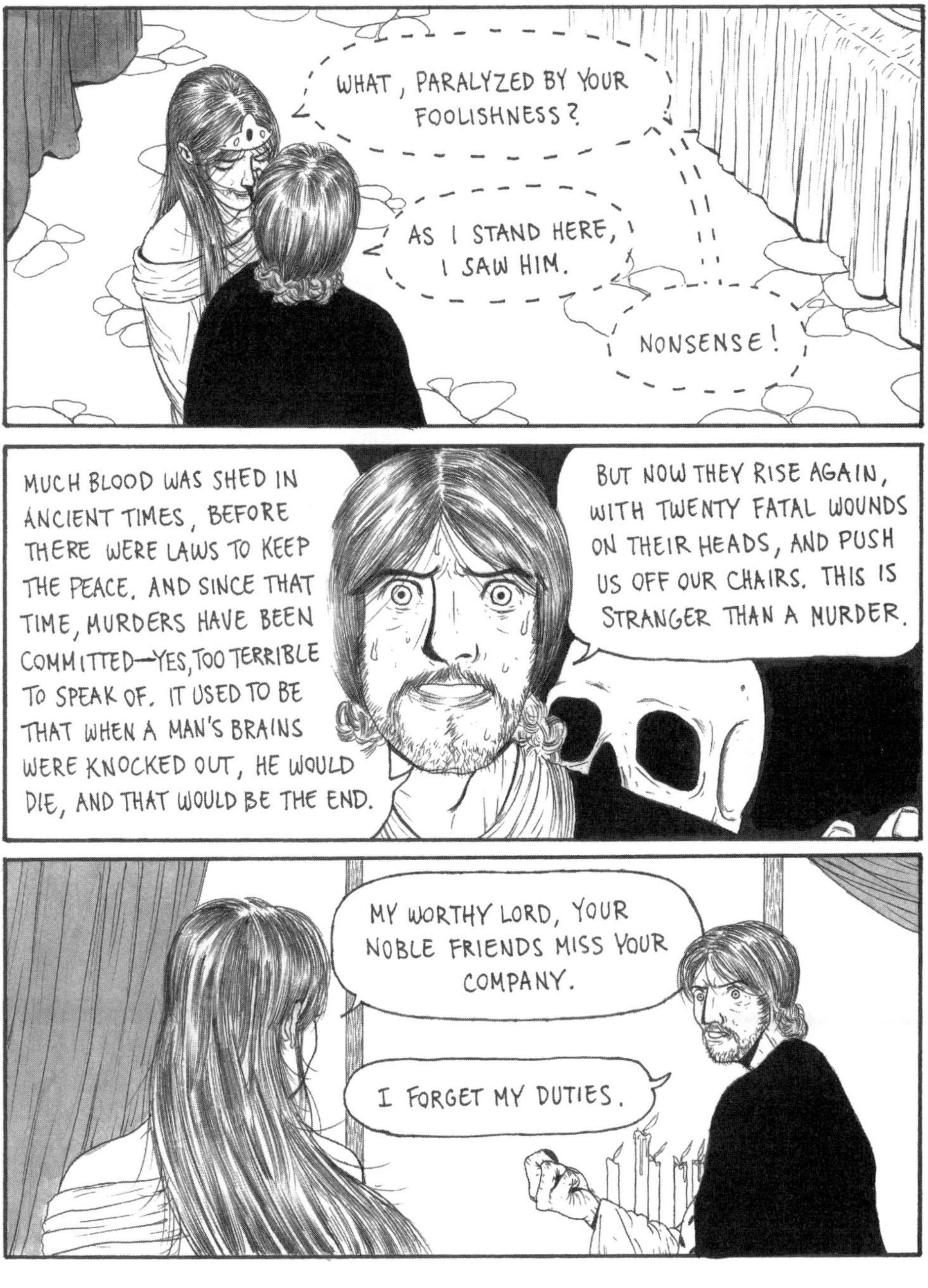
WHAT, PARALYZED BY YOUR FOOLISHNESS?
AS I STAND HERE, I SAW HIM.
NONSENSE!
MUCH BLOOD WAS SHED IN ANCIENT TIMES, BEFORE THERE WERE LAWS TO KEEP THE PEACE. AND SINCE THAT TIME, MURDERS HAVE BEEN COMMITTED—YES, TOO TERRIBLE TO SPEAK OF. IT USED TO BE THAT WHEN A MAN'S BRAINS WERE KNOCKED OUT, HE WOULD DIE, AND THAT WOULD BE THE END.
BUT NOW THEY RISE AGAIN, WITH TWENTY FATAL WOUNDS ON THEIR HEADS, AND PUSH US OFF OUR CHAIRS. THIS IS STRANGER THAN A MURDER.
MY WORTHY LORD, YOUR NOBLE FRIENDS MISS YOUR COMPANY.
I FORGET MY DUTIES.

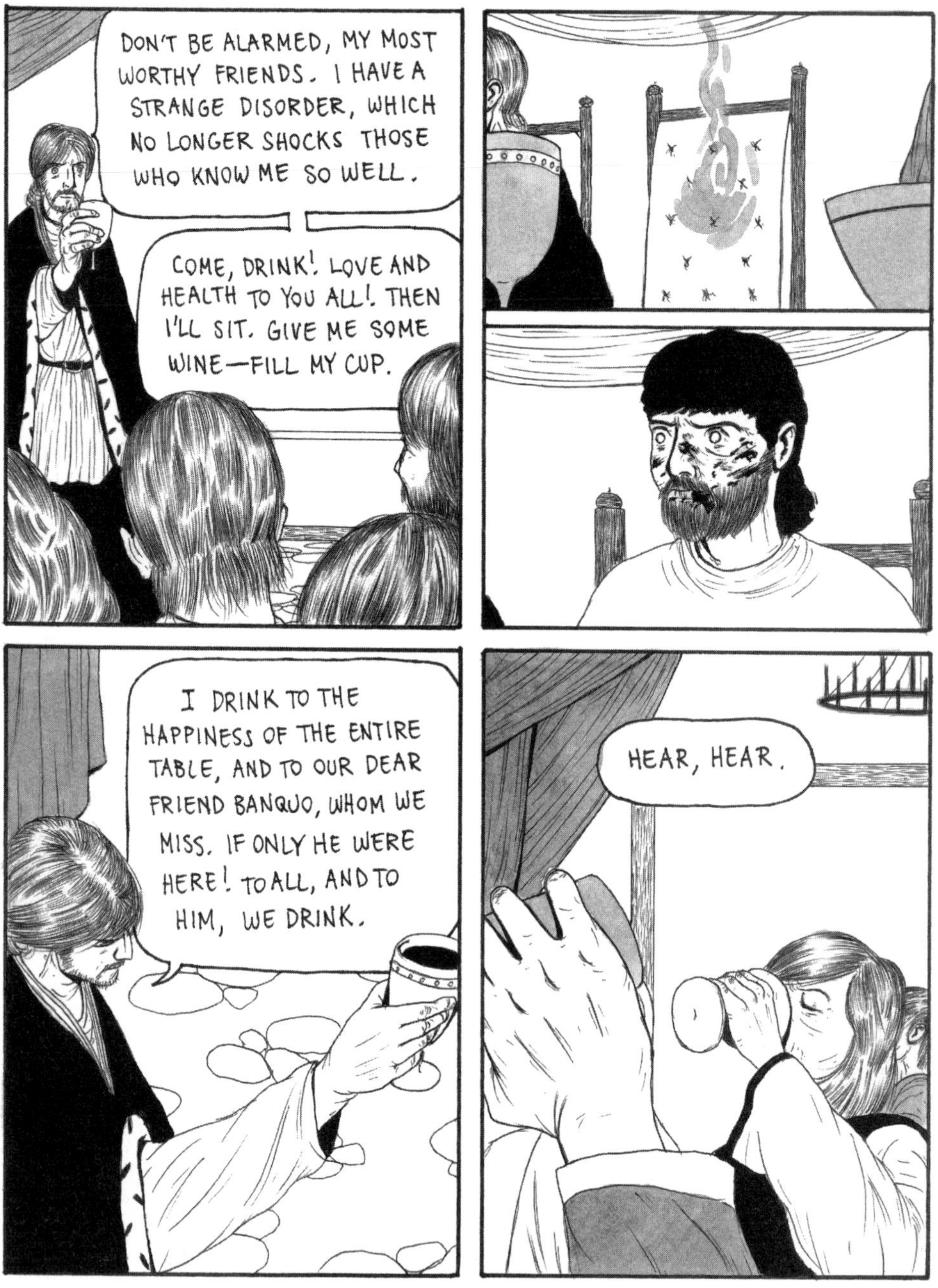
DON'T BE ALARMED, MY MOST WORTHY FRIENDS. I HAVE A STRANGE DISORDER, WHICH NO LONGER SHOCKS THOSE WHO KNOW ME SO WELL.
COME, DRINK! LOVE AND HEALTH TO YOU ALL! THEN I'LL SIT. GIVE ME SOME WINE—FILL MY CUP.
I DRINK TO THE HAPPINESS OF THE ENTIRE TABLE, AND TO OUR DEAR FRIEND BANQUO, WHOM WE MISS. IF ONLY HE WERE HERE! TO ALL, AND TO HIM, WE DRINK.
HEAR, HEAR.

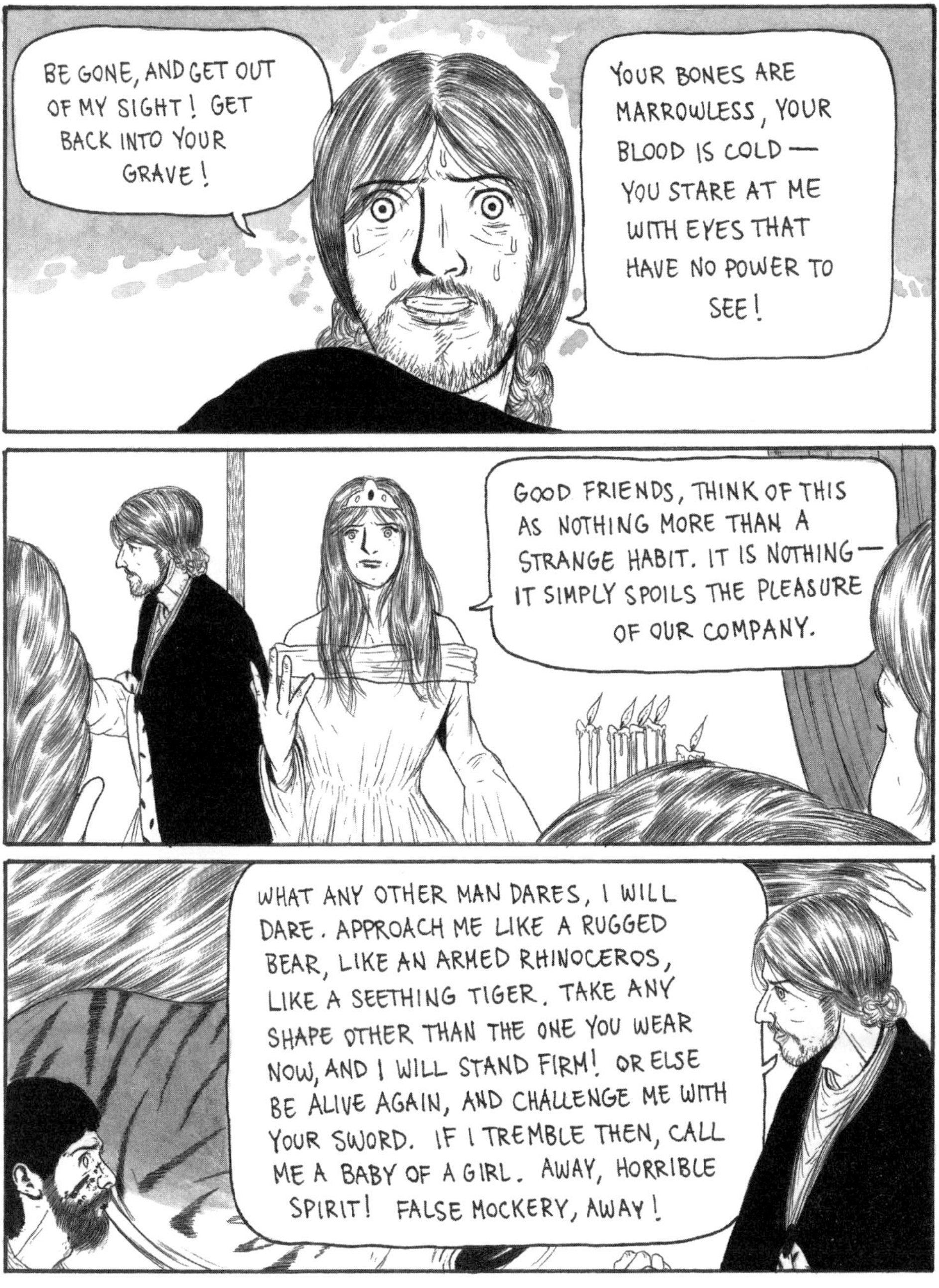
BE GONE, AND GET OUT OF MY SIGHT! GET BACK INTO YOUR GRAVE!
YOUR BONES ARE MARROWLESS, YOUR BLOOD IS COLD— YOU STARE AT ME WITH EYES THAT HAVE NO POWER TO SEE!
GOOD FRIENDS, THINK OF THIS AS NOTHING MORE THAN A STRANGE HABIT. IT IS NOTHING— IT SIMPLY SPOILS THE PLEASURE OF OUR COMPANY.
WHAT ANY OTHER MAN DARES, I WILL DARE. APPROACH ME LIKE A RUGGED BEAR, LIKE AN ARMED RHINOCEROS, LIKE A SEETHING TIGER. TAKE ANY SHAPE OTHER THAN THE ONE YOU WEAR NOW, AND I WILL STAND FIRM! OR ELSE BE ALIVE AGAIN, AND CHALLENGE ME WITH YOUR SWORD. IF I TREMBLE THEN, CALL ME A BABY OF A GIRL. AWAY, HORRIBLE SPIRIT! FALSE MOCKERY, AWAY!

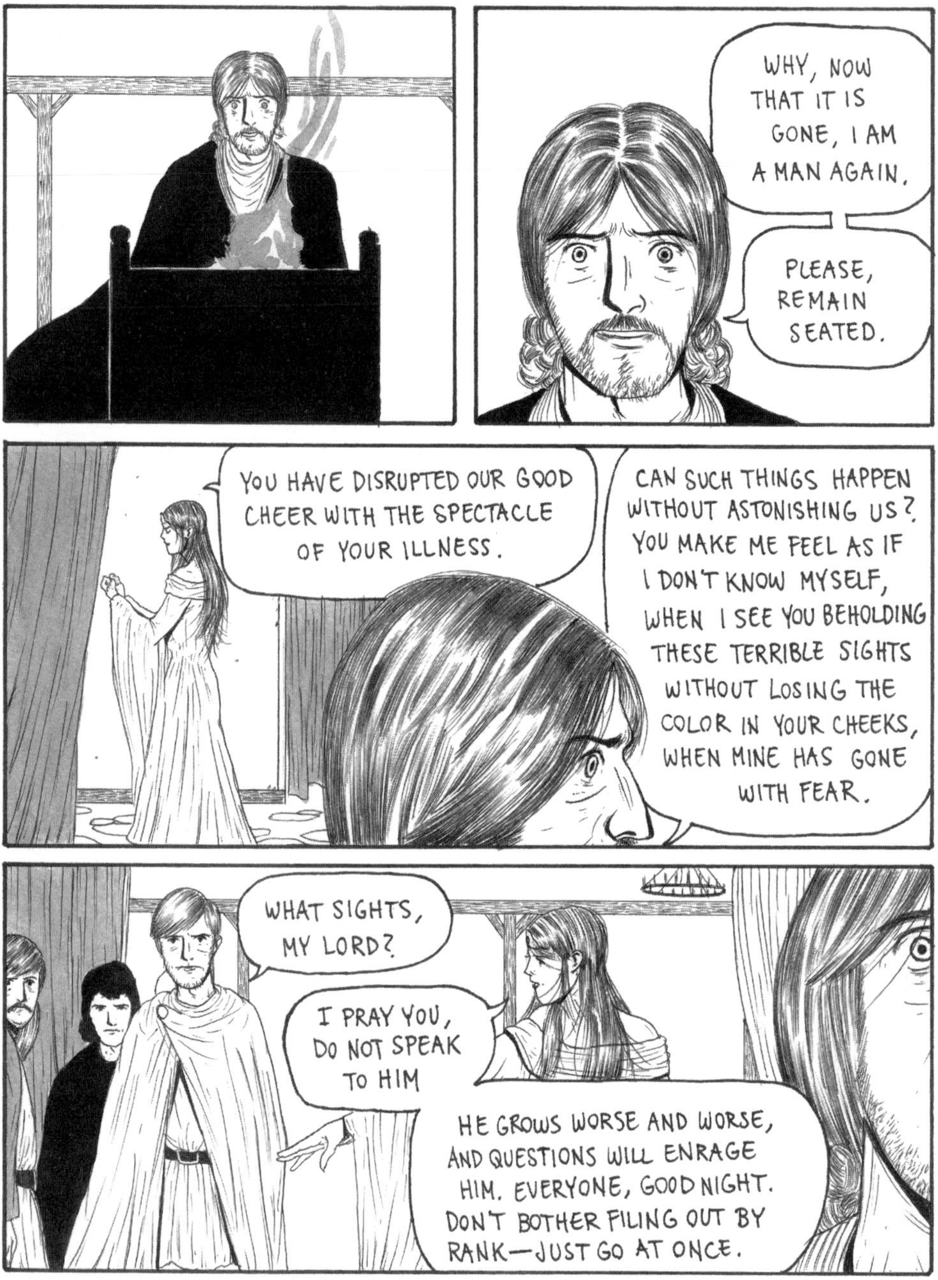
WHY, NOW THAT IT IS GONE, I AM A MAN AGAIN.
PLEASE, REMAIN SEATED.
YOU HAVE DISRUPTED OUR GOOD CHEER WITH THE SPECTACLE OF YOUR ILLNESS.
CAN SUCH THINGS HAPPEN WITHOUT ASTONISHING US? YOU MAKE ME FEEL AS IF I DON'T KNOW MYSELF, WHEN I SEE YOU BEHOLDING THESE TERRIBLE SIGHTS WITHOUT LOSING THE COLOR IN YOUR CHEEKS, WHEN MINE HAS GONE WITH FEAR.
WHAT SIGHTS, MY LORD?
I PRAY YOU, DO NOT SPEAK TO HIM
HE GROWS WORSE AND WORSE, AND QUESTIONS WILL ENRAGE HIM. EVERYONE, GOOD NIGHT. DON'T BOTHER FILING OUT BY RANK—JUST GO AT ONCE.

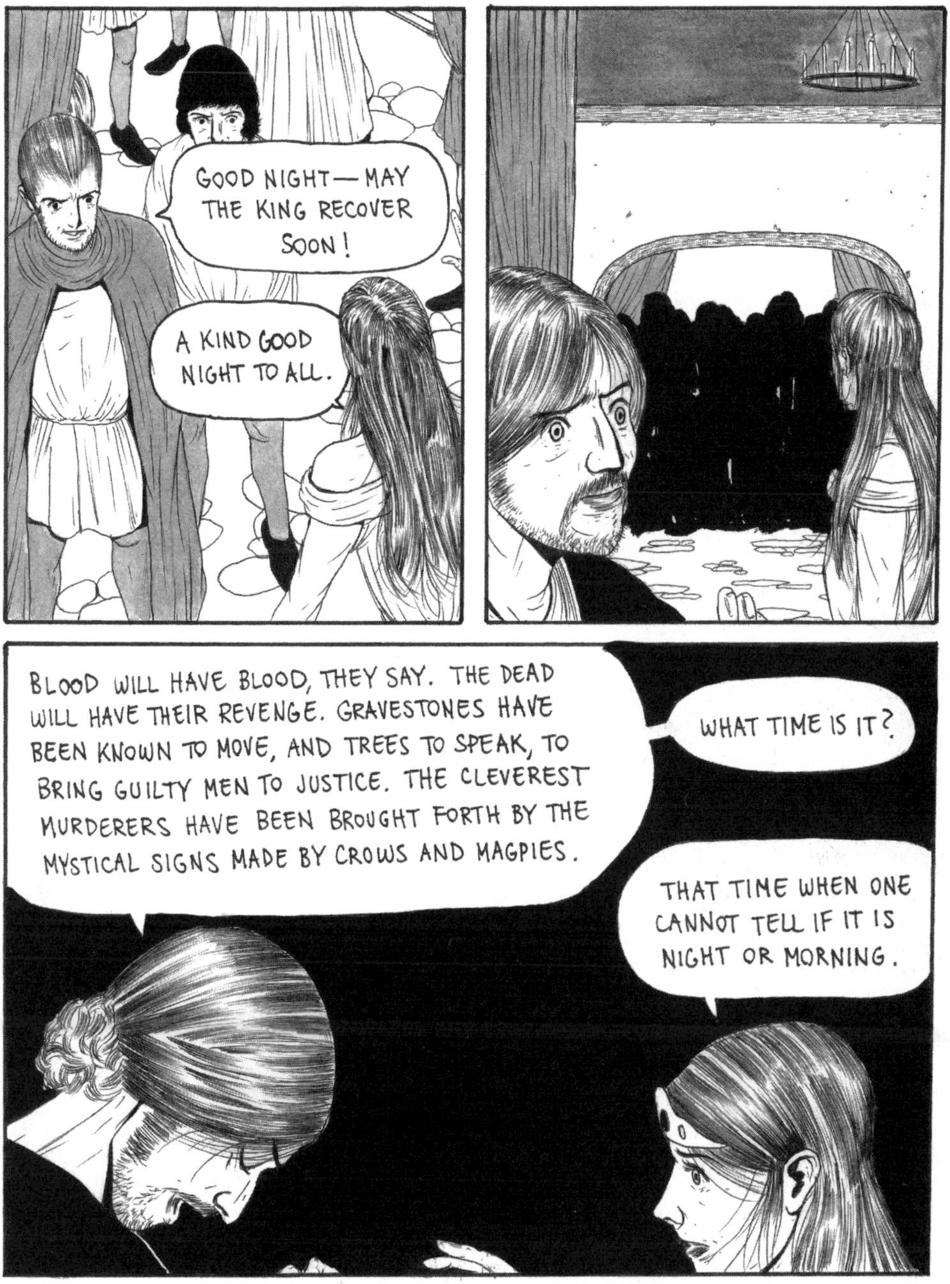
GOOD NIGHT— MAY THE KING RECOVER SOON!
A KIND GOOD NIGHT TO ALL.
BLOOD WILL HAVE BLOOD, THEY SAY. THE DEAD WILL HAVE THEIR REVENGE. GRAVESTONES HAVE BEEN KNOWN TO MOVE, AND TREES TO SPEAK, TO BRING GUILTY MEN TO JUSTICE. THE CLEVEREST MURDERERS HAVE BEEN BROUGHT FORTH BY THE MYSTICAL SIGNS MADE BY CROWS AND MAGPIES.
WHAT TIME IS IT?
THAT TIME WHEN ONE CANNOT TELL IF IT IS NIGHT OR MORNING.

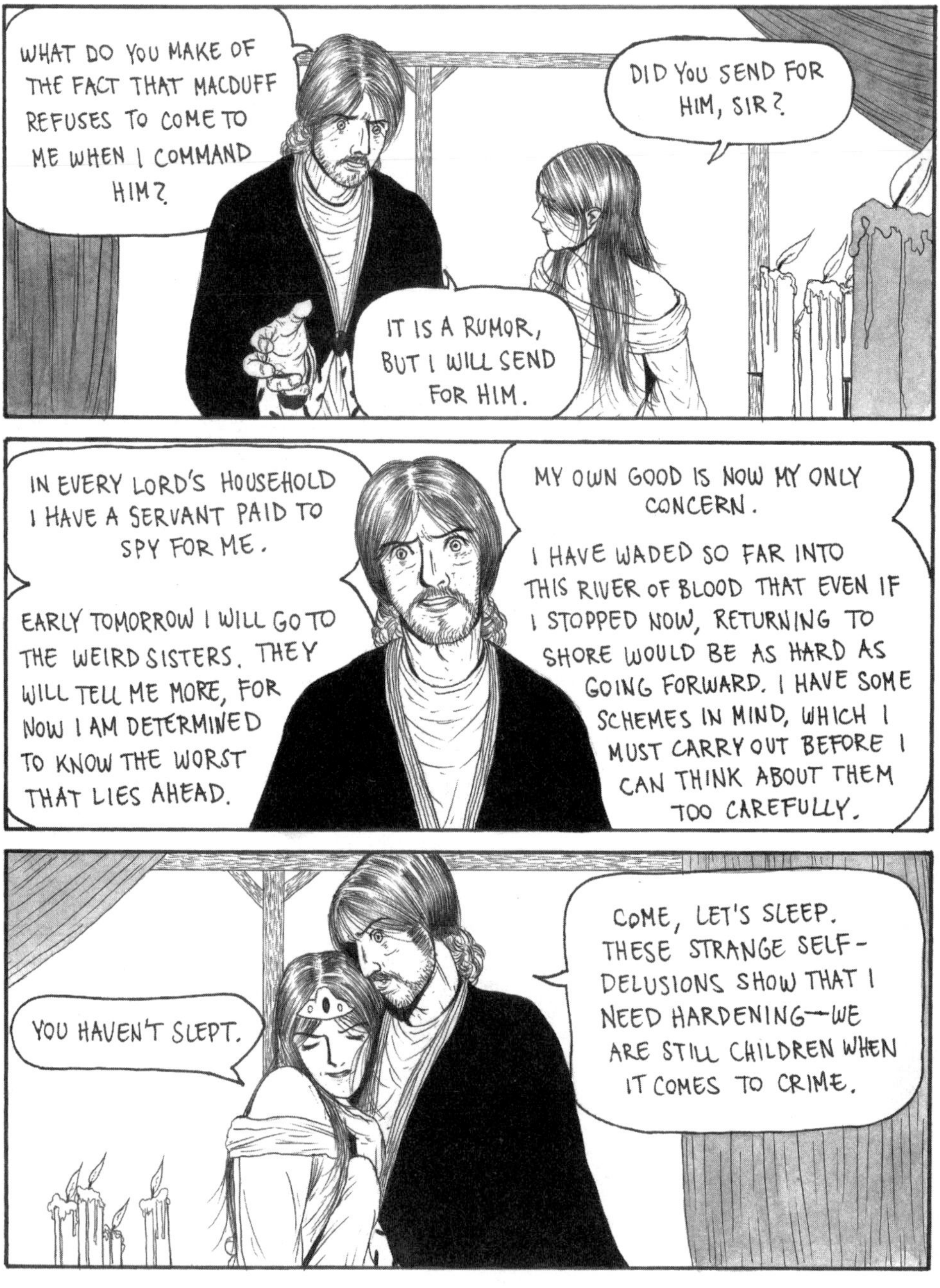
WHAT DO YOU MAKE OF THE FACT THAT MACDUFF REFUSES TO COME TO ME WHEN I COMMAND HIM?
DID YOU SEND FOR HIM, SIR?
IT IS A RUMOR, BUT I WILL SEND FOR HIM.
IN EVERY LORD'S HOUSEHOLD I HAVE A SERVANT PAID TO SPY FOR ME.
EARLY TOMORROW I WILL GO TO THE WEIRD SISTERS. THEY WILL TELL ME MORE, FOR NOW I AM DETERMINED TO KNOW THE WORST THAT LIES AHEAD.
MY OWN GOOD IS NOW MY ONLY CONCERN.
I HAVE WADED SO FAR INTO THIS RIVER OF BLOOD THAT EVEN IF I STOPPED NOW, RETURNING TO SHORE WOULD BE AS HARD AS GOING FORWARD. I HAVE SOME SCHEMES IN MIND, WHICH I MUST CARRY OUT BEFORE I CAN THINK ABOUT THEM TOO CAREFULLY.
YOU HAVEN'T SLEPT.
COME, LET'S SLEEP. THESE STRANGE SELF-DELUSIONS SHOW THAT I NEED HARDENING—WE ARE STILL CHILDREN WHEN IT COMES TO CRIME.

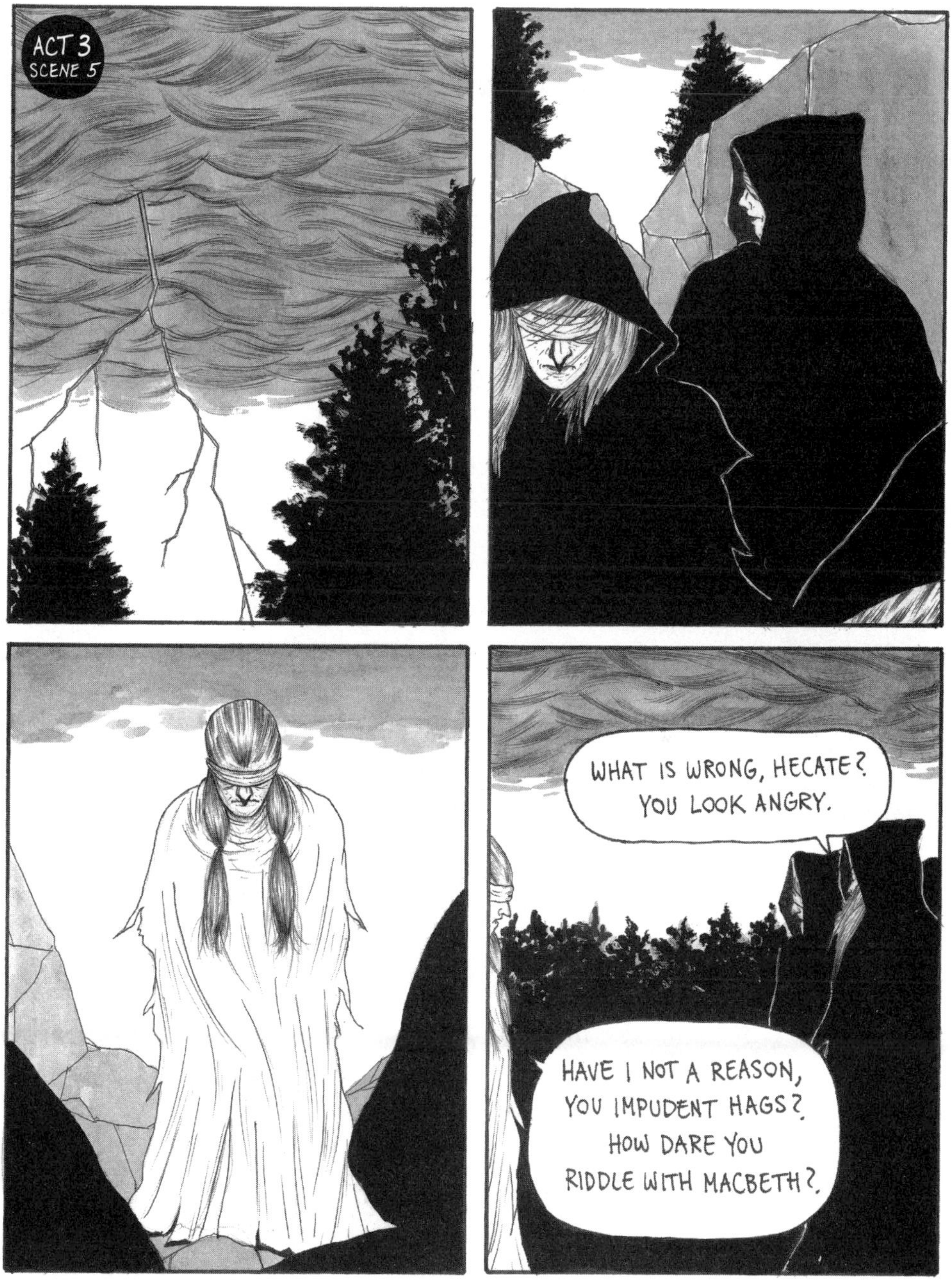
ACT 3
SCENE 5
WHAT IS WRONG, HECATE? YOU LOOK ANGRY.
HAVE I NOT A REASON, YOU IMPUDENT HAGS? HOW DARE YOU RIDDLE WITH MACBETH?

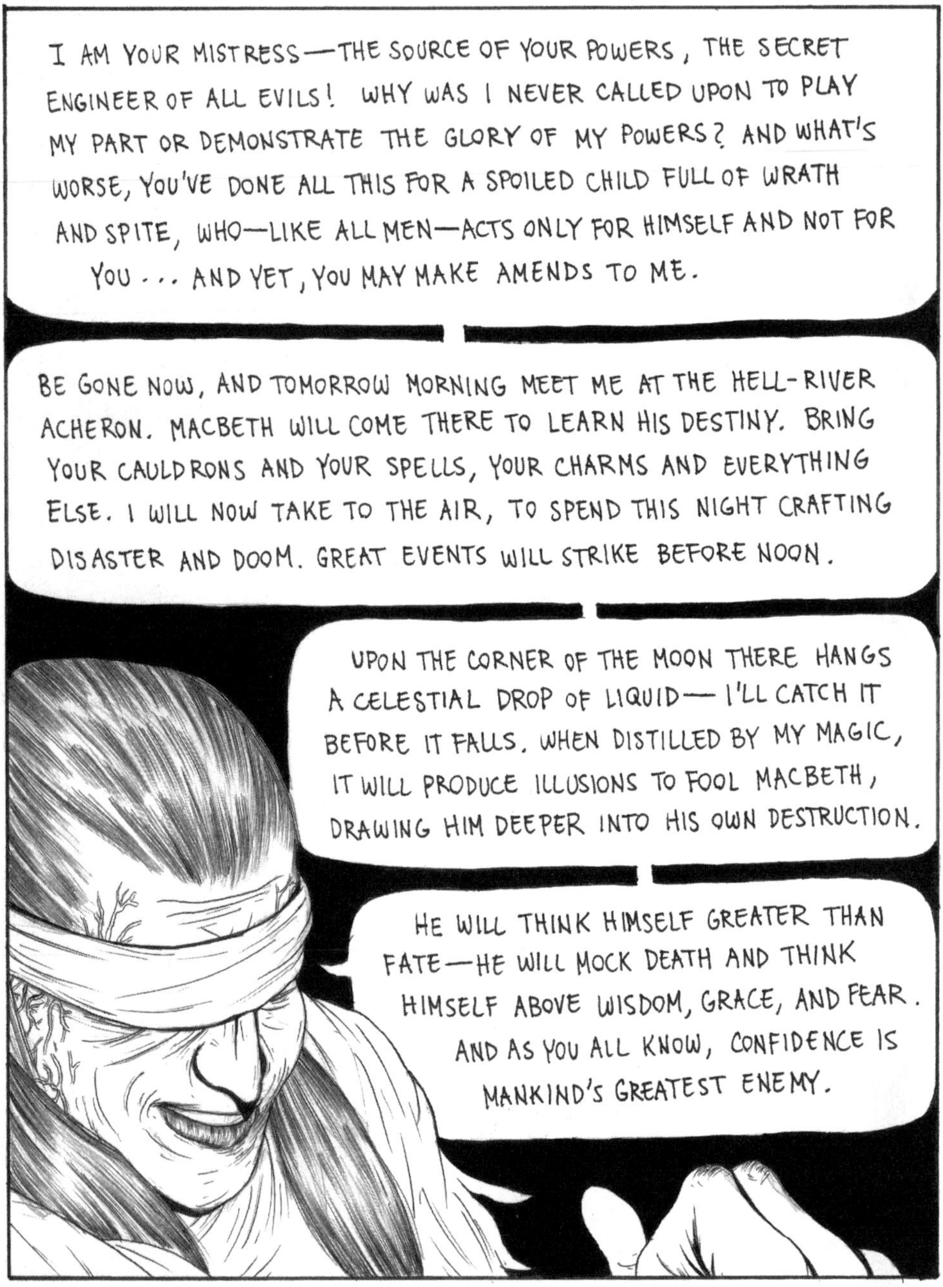
I AM YOUR MISTRESS—THE SOURCE OF YOUR POWERS, THE SECRET ENGINEER OF ALL EVILS! WHY WAS I NEVER CALLED UPON TO PLAY MY PART OR DEMONSTRATE THE GLORY OF MY POWERS? AND WHAT'S WORSE, YOU'VE DONE ALL THIS FOR A SPOILED CHILD FULL OF WRATH AND SPITE, WHO—LIKE ALL MEN—ACTS ONLY FOR HIMSELF AND NOT FOR YOU... AND YET, YOU MAY MAKE AMENDS TO ME.
BE GONE NOW, AND TOMORROW MORNING MEET ME AT THE HELL-RIVER ACHERON. MACBETH WILL COME THERE TO LEARN HIS DESTINY. BRING YOUR CAULDRONS AND YOUR SPELLS, YOUR CHARMS AND EVERYTHING ELSE. I WILL NOW TAKE TO THE AIR, TO SPEND THIS NIGHT CRAFTING DISASTER AND DOOM. GREAT EVENTS WILL STRIKE BEFORE NOON.
UPON THE CORNER OF THE MOON THERE HANGS A CELESTIAL DROP OF LIQUID—I'LL CATCH IT BEFORE IT FALLS. WHEN DISTILLED BY MY MAGIC, IT WILL PRODUCE ILLUSIONS TO FOOL MACBETH, DRAWING HIM DEEPER INTO HIS OWN DESTRUCTION.
HE WILL THINK HIMSELF GREATER THAN FATE—HE WILL MOCK DEATH AND THINK HIMSELF ABOVE WISDOM, GRACE, AND FEAR. AND AS YOU ALL KNOW, CONFIDENCE IS MANKIND'S GREATEST ENEMY.

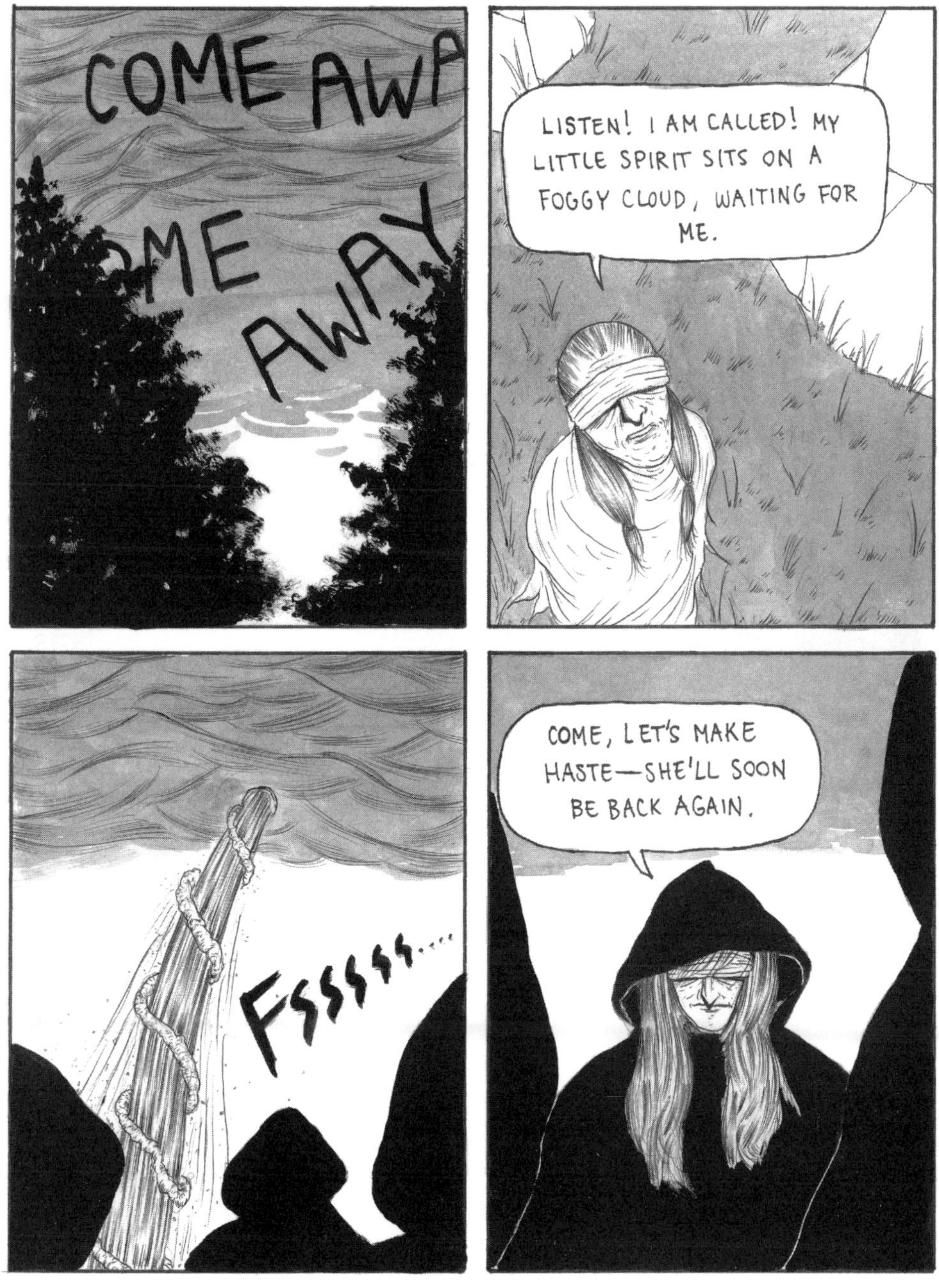
COME AWA
OME AWAY
AWAY
LISTEN! I AM CALLED! MY LITTLE SPIRIT SITS ON A FOGGY CLOUD, WAITING FOR ME.
FSSSSS....
COME, LET'S MAKE HASTE—SHE'LL SOON BE BACK AGAIN.

ACT 3 SCENE 6
IT SEEMS WE ARE OF THE SAME MIND—THEREFORE, YOU MAY DRAW YOUR OWN CONCLUSIONS. ALL I CAN SAY IS THAT SOMETHING STRANGE IS HAPPENING.
MACBETH SHOWED GREAT CONCERN FOR DUNCAN— AFTER HE WAS DEAD.
AND THE EVER-VALIANT BANQUO WENT WALKING TOO LATE AT NIGHT; IF YOU LIKE, YOU MIGHT ASSUME THAT FLEANCE KILLED HIM, SINCE HE HAS FLED THE SCENE OF THE CRIME. CLEARLY, MEN SHOULD AVOID LEAVING THEIR HOUSES TOO LATE AT NIGHT.
AND WHO CAN HELP THINKING HOW MONSTROUS IT WAS FOR MALCOLM AND DONALBAIN TO KILL THEIR GRACIOUS FATHER? A DAMNING CRIME! HOW IT GRIEVED MACBETH . . . DIDN'T HE IMMEDIATELY KILL THOSE TWO DELINQUENT GUARDS IN A PIOUS RAGE? WASN'T THAT NOBLE OF HIM? YES, AND WISE, TOO, FOR WE ALL WOULD HAVE BEEN OUTRAGED TO HEAR THOSE TWO DENY THEIR CRIME.
SO I SAY THAT MACBETH HAS HANDLED THINGS WELL.

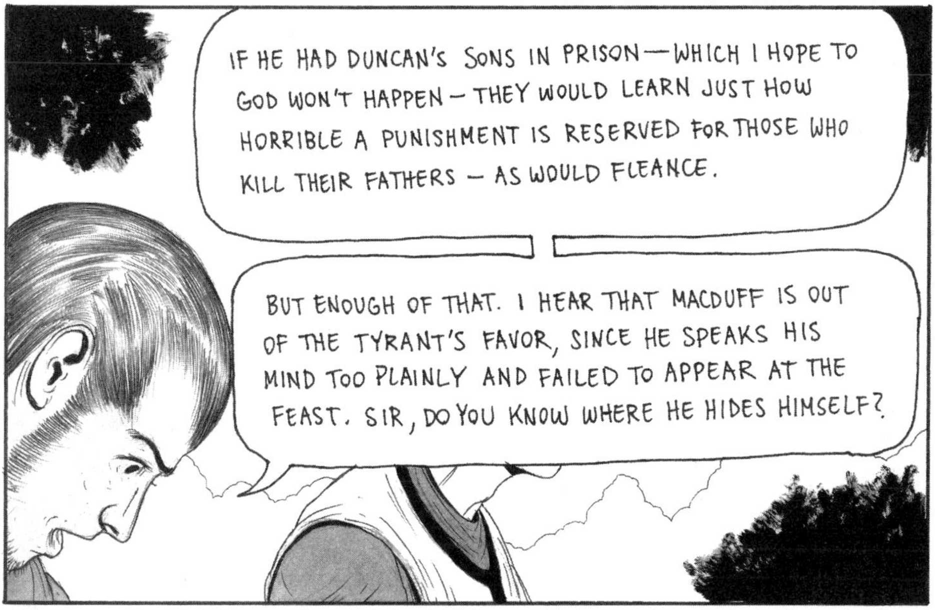
IF HE HAD DUNCAN'S SONS IN PRISON—WHICH I HOPE TO GOD WON'T HAPPEN—THEY WOULD LEARN JUST HOW HORRIBLE A PUNISHMENT IS RESERVED FOR THOSE WHO KILL THEIR FATHERS—AS WOULD FLEANCE.
BUT ENOUGH OF THAT. I HEAR THAT MACDUFF IS OUT OF THE TYRANT'S FAVOR, SINCE HE SPEAKS HIS MIND TOO PLAINLY AND FAILED TO APPEAR AT THE FEAST. SIR, DO YOU KNOW WHERE HE HIDES HIMSELF?

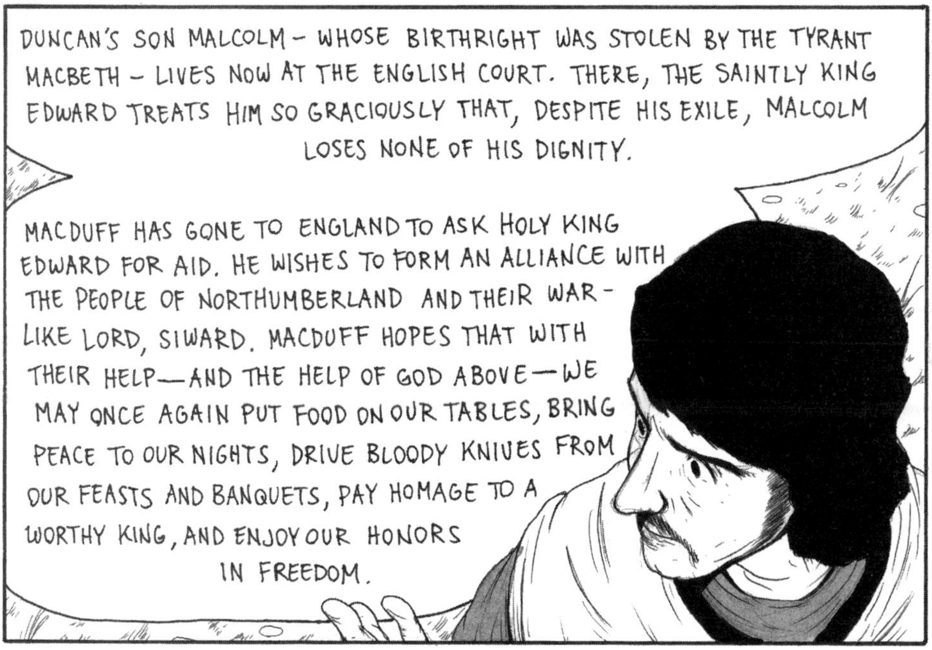
DUNCAN'S SON MALCOLM—WHOSE BIRTHRIGHT WAS STOLEN BY THE TYRANT MACBETH—LIVES NOW AT THE ENGLISH COURT. THERE, THE SAINTLY KING EDWARD TREATS HIM SO GRACIOUSLY THAT, DESPITE HIS EXILE, MALCOLM LOSES NONE OF HIS DIGNITY.
MACDUFF HAS GONE TO ENGLAND TO ASK HOLY KING EDWARD FOR AID. HE WISHES TO FORM AN ALLIANCE WITH THE PEOPLE OF NORTHUMBERLAND AND THEIR WAR-LIKE LORD, SIWARD. MACDUFF HOPES THAT WITH THEIR HELP—AND THE HELP OF GOD ABOVE—WE MAY ONCE AGAIN PUT FOOD ON OUR TABLES, BRING PEACE TO OUR NIGHTS, DRIVE BLOODY KNIVES FROM OUR FEASTS AND BANQUETS, PAY HOMAGE TO A WORTHY KING, AND ENJOY OUR HONORS IN FREEDOM.

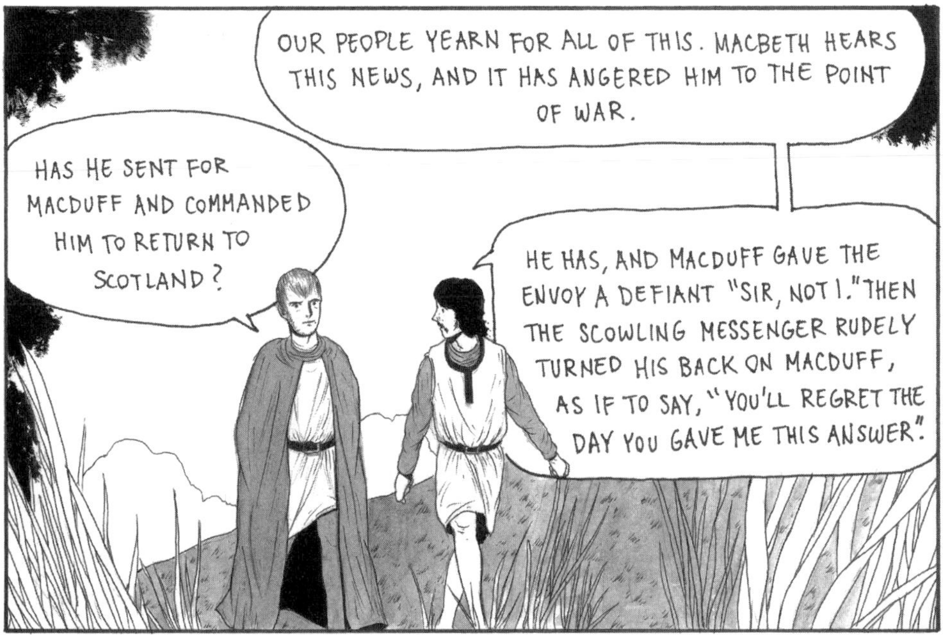
OUR PEOPLE YEARN FOR ALL OF THIS. MACBETH HEARS THIS NEWS, AND IT HAS ANGERED HIM TO THE POINT OF WAR.
HAS HE SENT FOR MACDUFF AND COMMANDED HIM TO RETURN TO SCOTLAND?
HE HAS, AND MACDUFF GAVE THE ENVOY A DEFIANT "SIR, NOT I." THEN THE SCOWLING MESSENGER RUDELY TURNED HIS BACK ON MACDUFF, AS IF TO SAY, "YOU'LL REGRET THE DAY YOU GAVE ME THIS ANSWER."

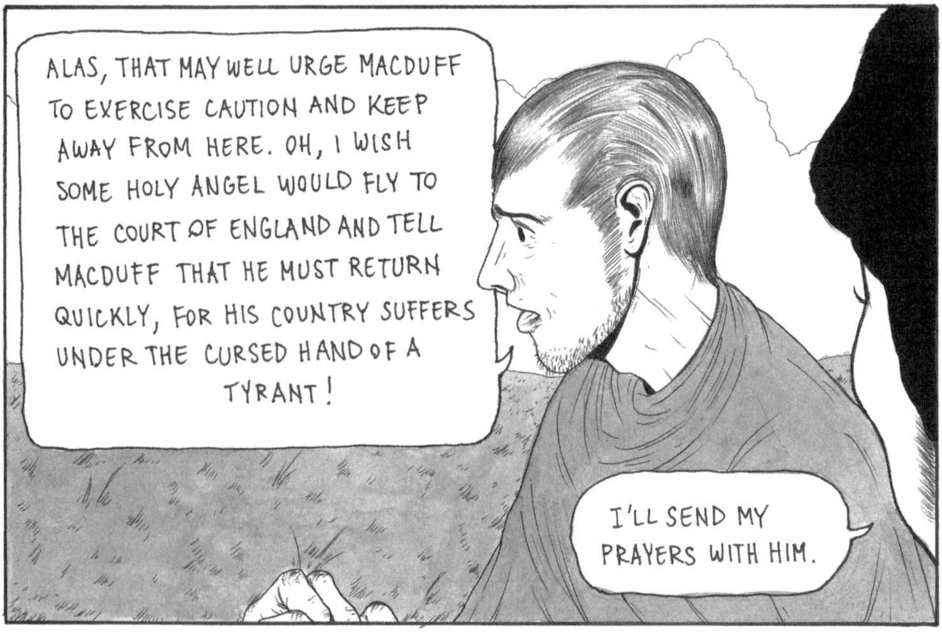
ALAS, THAT MAY WELL URGE MACDUFF TO EXERCISE CAUTION AND KEEP AWAY FROM HERE. OH, I WISH SOME HOLY ANGEL WOULD FLY TO THE COURT OF ENGLAND AND TELL MACDUFF THAT HE MUST RETURN QUICKLY, FOR HIS COUNTRY SUFFERS UNDER THE CURSED HAND OF A TYRANT!
I'LL SEND MY PRAYERS WITH HIM.

ACT IV

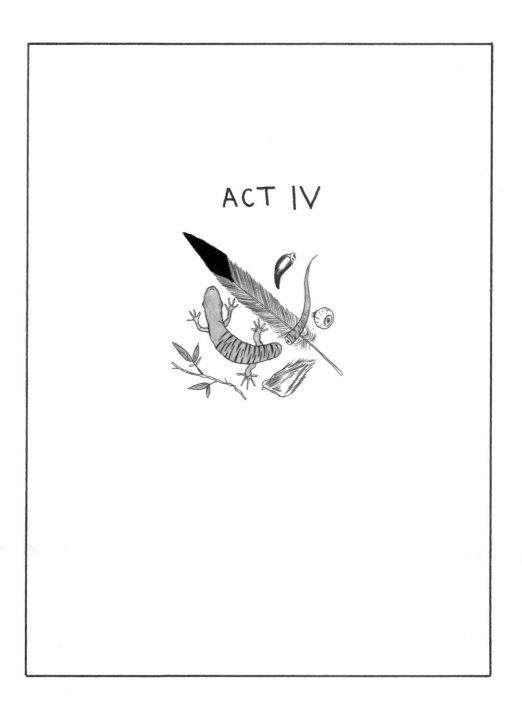

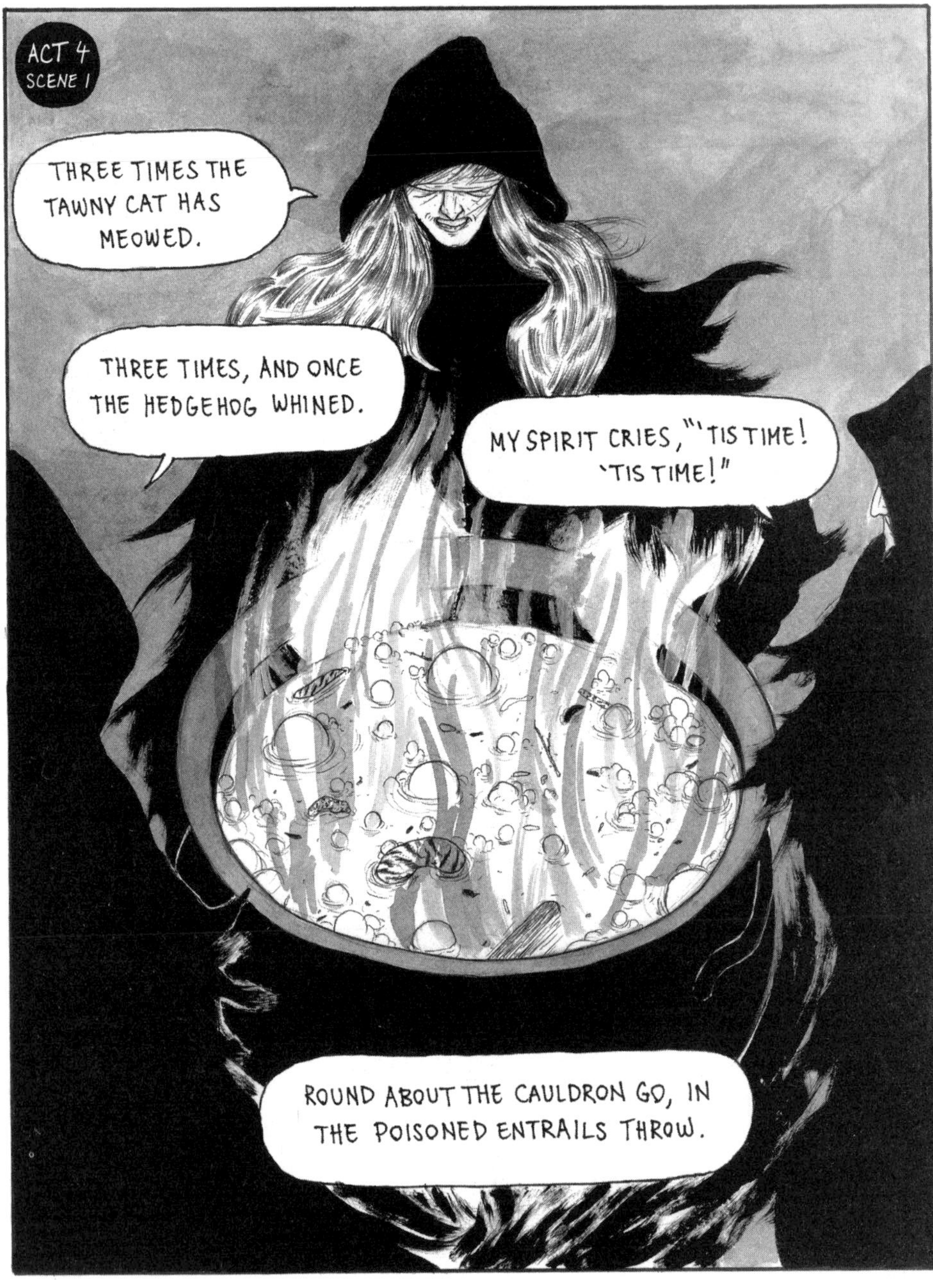
ACT 4
SCENE 1
THREE TIMES THE TAWNY CAT HAS MEOWED.
THREE TIMES, AND ONCE THE HEDGEHOG WHINED.
MY SPIRIT CRIES, "'TIS TIME! 'TIS TIME!"
ROUND ABOUT THE CAULDRON GO, IN THE POISONED ENTRAILS THROW.

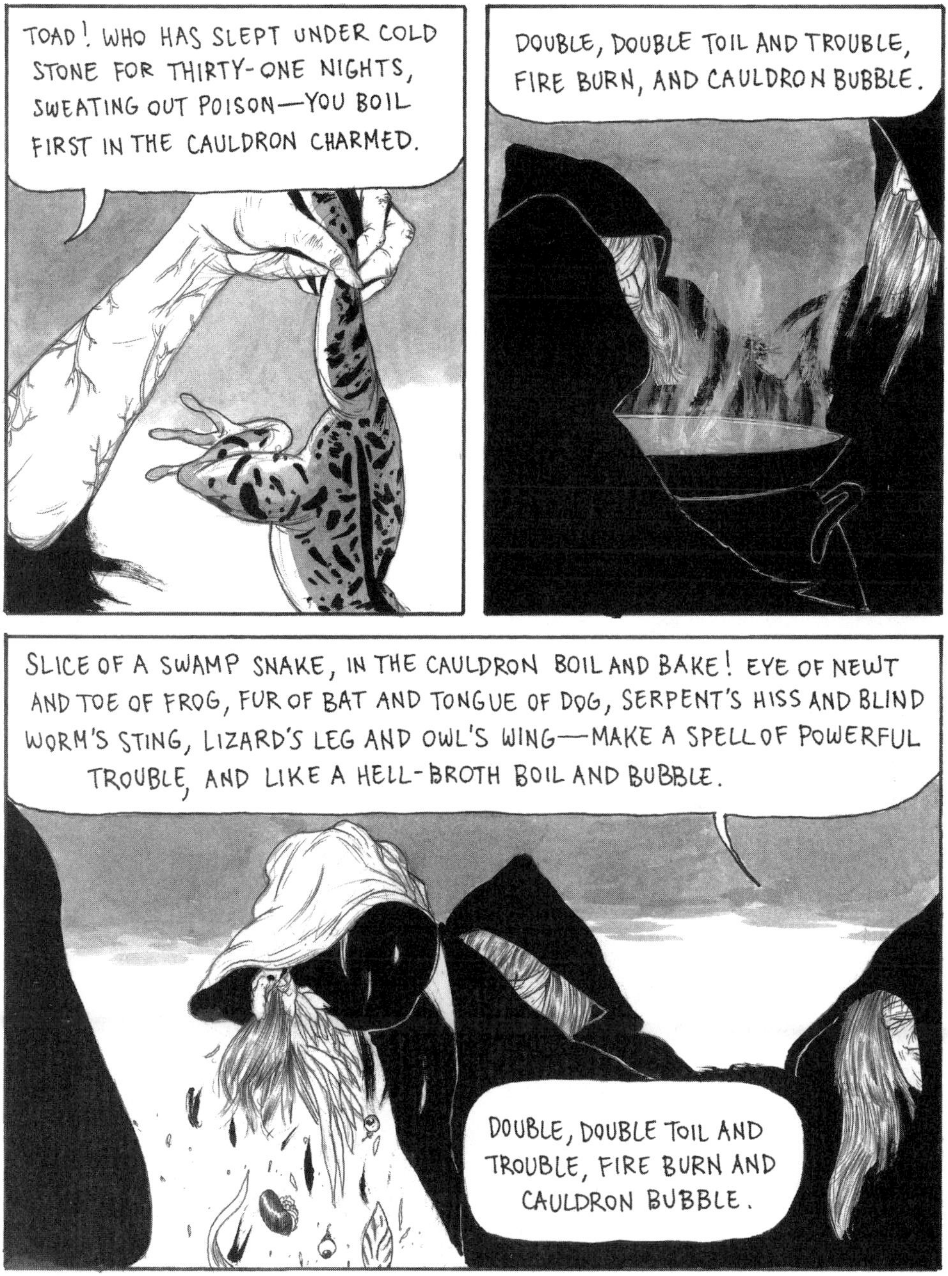
TOAD! WHO HAS SLEPT UNDER COLD STONE FOR THIRTY-ONE NIGHTS, SWEATING OUT POISON—YOU BOIL FIRST IN THE CAULDRON CHARMED.
DOUBLE, DOUBLE TOIL AND TROUBLE, FIRE BURN, AND CAULDRON BUBBLE.
SLICE OF A SWAMP SNAKE, IN THE CAULDRON BOIL AND BAKE! EYE OF NEWT AND TOE OF FROG, FUR OF BAT AND TONGUE OF DOG, SERPENT'S HISS AND BLIND WORM'S STING, LIZARD'S LEG AND OWL'S WING—MAKE A SPELL OF POWERFUL TROUBLE, AND LIKE A HELL-BROTH BOIL AND BUBBLE.
DOUBLE, DOUBLE TOIL AND TROUBLE, FIRE BURN AND CAULDRON BUBBLE.

DRAGON'S SCALE, WOLF'S TOOTH, WITCH'S FLESH... THROAT AND STOMACH OF A SALT-SEA SHARK... ROOT OF HEMLOCK, DUG IN THE DARK... LIVER OF A BLASPHEMOUS JEW... BILE OF GOAT AND TWIGS OF YEW (PEELED OFF IN THE MOON'S ECLIPSE)... NOSE OF TURK AND TARTAR'S LIPS... FINGER OF AN INFANT LEFT DEAD IN A DITCH... MAKE THIS POTION THICK AND TOUGH!

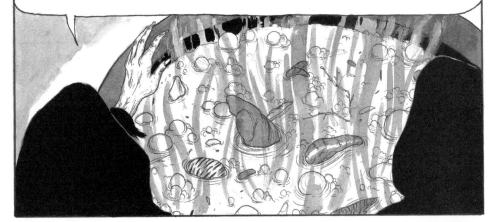

AND LAST, A TIGER'S CHURNING GUTS.

DOUBLE, DOUBLE TOIL AND TROUBLE, FIRE BURN AND CAULDRON BUBBLE.

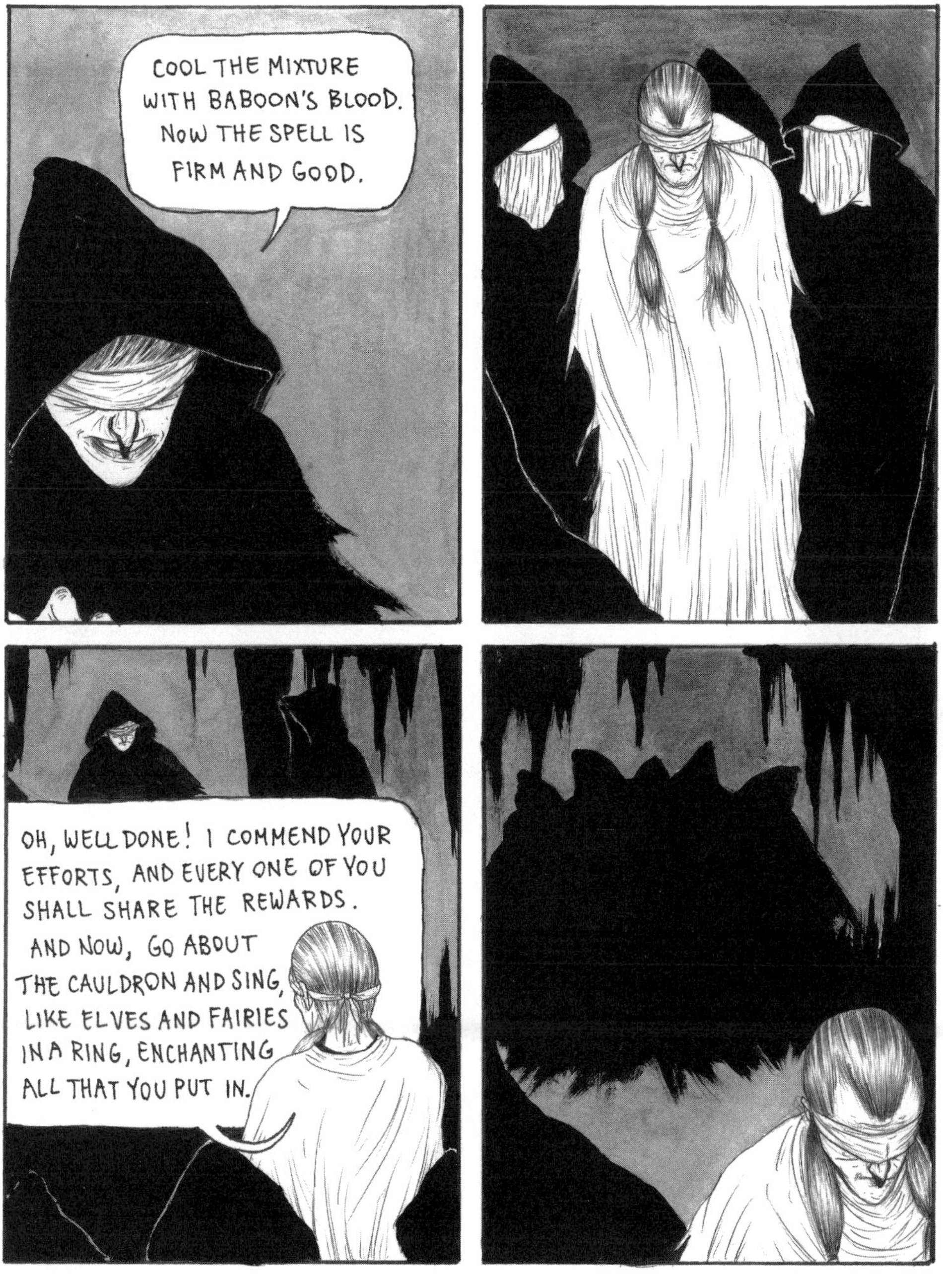
COOL THE MIXTURE WITH BABOON'S BLOOD. NOW THE SPELL IS FIRM AND GOOD.
OH, WELL DONE! I COMMEND YOUR EFFORTS, AND EVERY ONE OF YOU SHALL SHARE THE REWARDS. AND NOW, GO ABOUT THE CAULDRON AND SING, LIKE ELVES AND FAIRIES IN A RING, ENCHANTING ALL THAT YOU PUT IN.

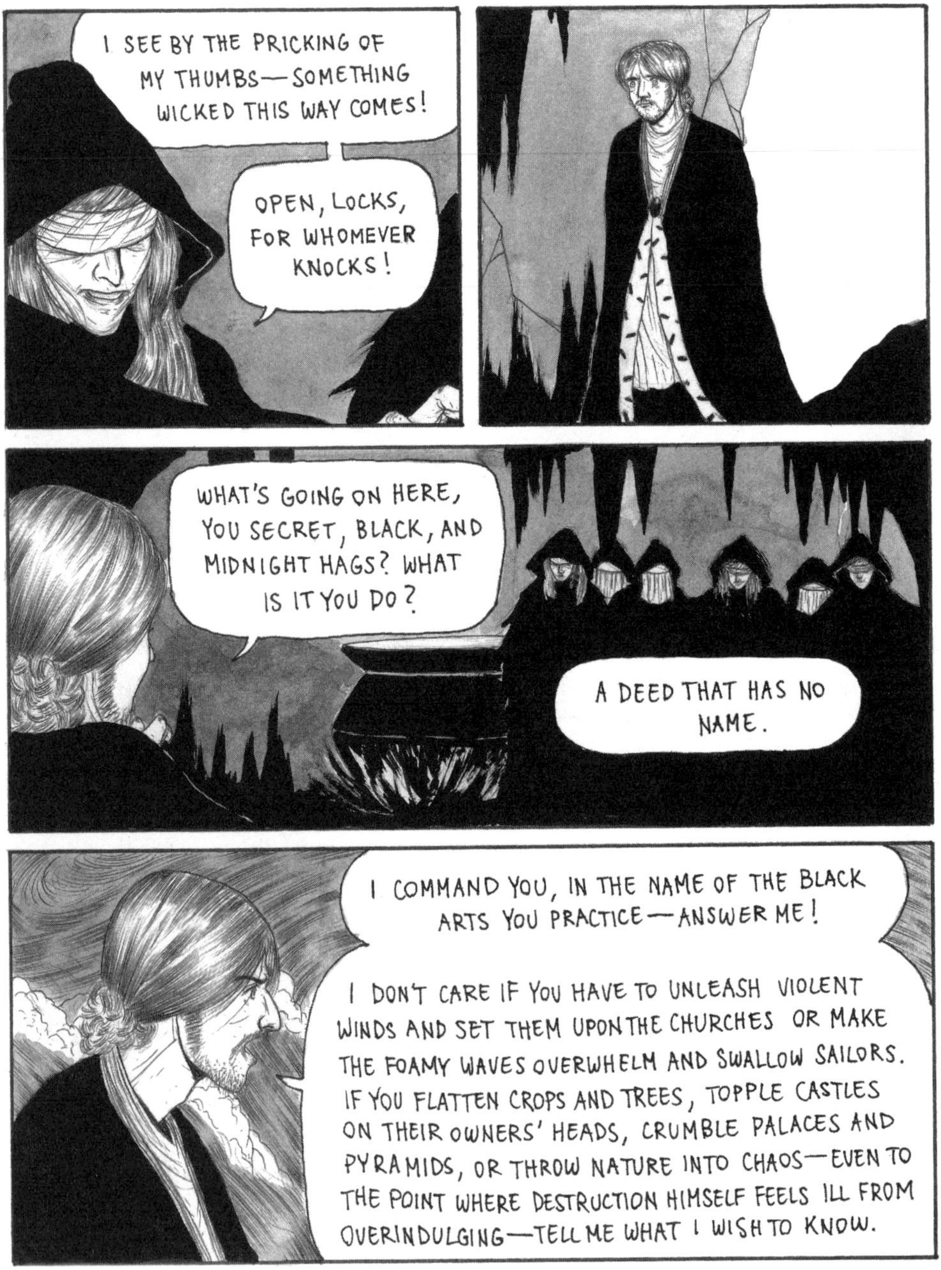
I SEE BY THE PRICKING OF MY THUMBS—SOMETHING WICKED THIS WAY COMES!
OPEN, LOCKS, FOR WHOMEVER KNOCKS!
WHAT'S GOING ON HERE, YOU SECRET, BLACK, AND MIDNIGHT HAGS? WHAT IS IT YOU DO?
A DEED THAT HAS NO NAME.
I COMMAND YOU, IN THE NAME OF THE BLACK ARTS YOU PRACTICE—ANSWER ME!
I DON'T CARE IF YOU HAVE TO UNLEASH VIOLENT WINDS AND SET THEM UPON THE CHURCHES OR MAKE THE FOAMY WAVES OVERWHELM AND SWALLOW SAILORS. IF YOU FLATTEN CROPS AND TREES, TOPPLE CASTLES ON THEIR OWNERS' HEADS, CRUMBLE PALACES AND PYRAMIDS, OR THROW NATURE INTO CHAOS—EVEN TO THE POINT WHERE DESTRUCTION HIMSELF FEELS ILL FROM OVERINDULGING—TELL ME WHAT I WISH TO KNOW.

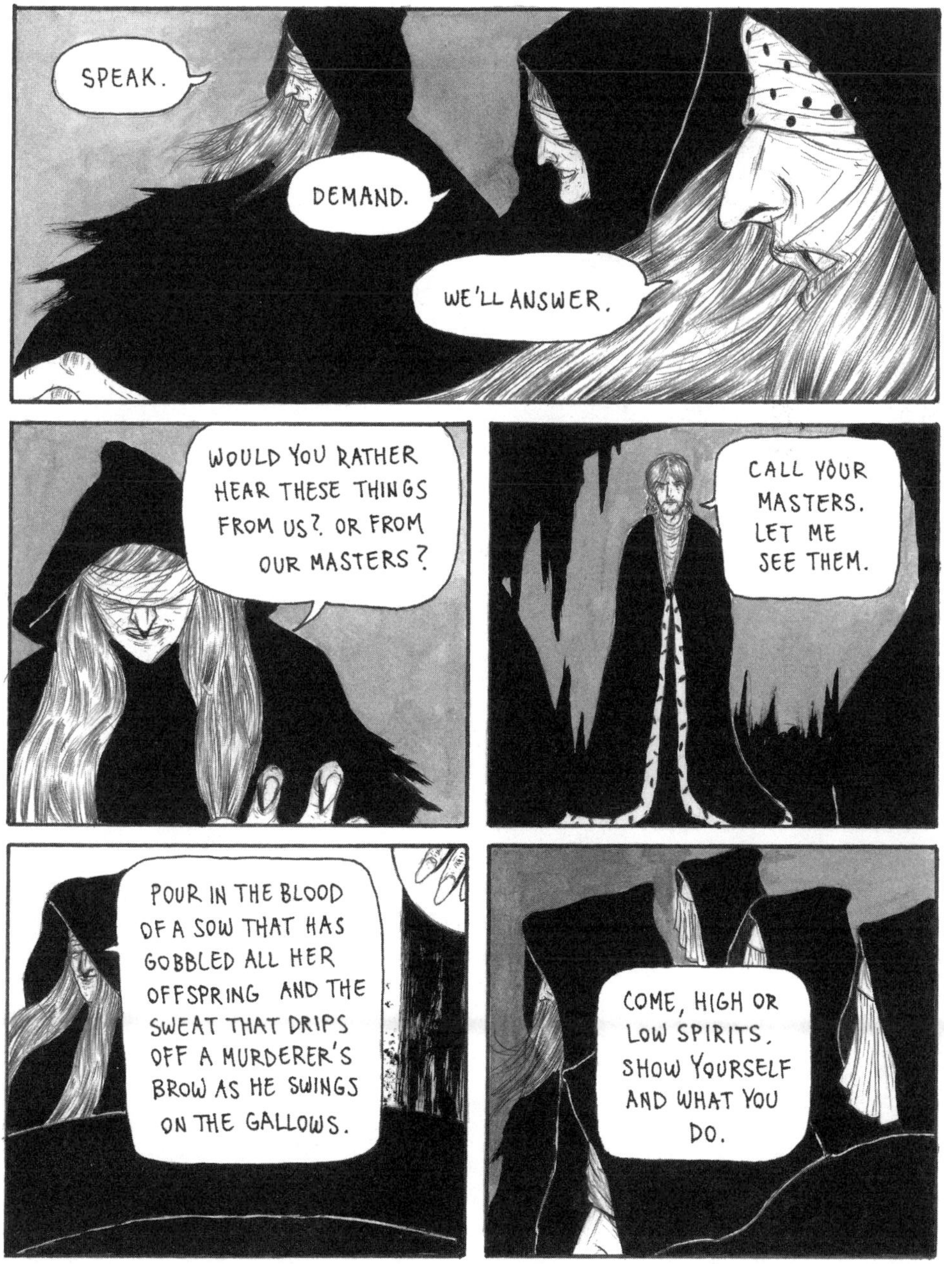
SPEAK.
DEMAND.
WE'LL ANSWER.
WOULD YOU RATHER HEAR THESE THINGS FROM US? OR FROM OUR MASTERS?
CALL YOUR MASTERS. LET ME SEE THEM.
POUR IN THE BLOOD OF A SOW THAT HAS GOBBLED ALL HER OFFSPRING AND THE SWEAT THAT DRIPS OFF A MURDERER'S BROW AS HE SWINGS ON THE GALLOWS.
COME, HIGH OR LOW SPIRITS. SHOW YOURSELF AND WHAT YOU DO.

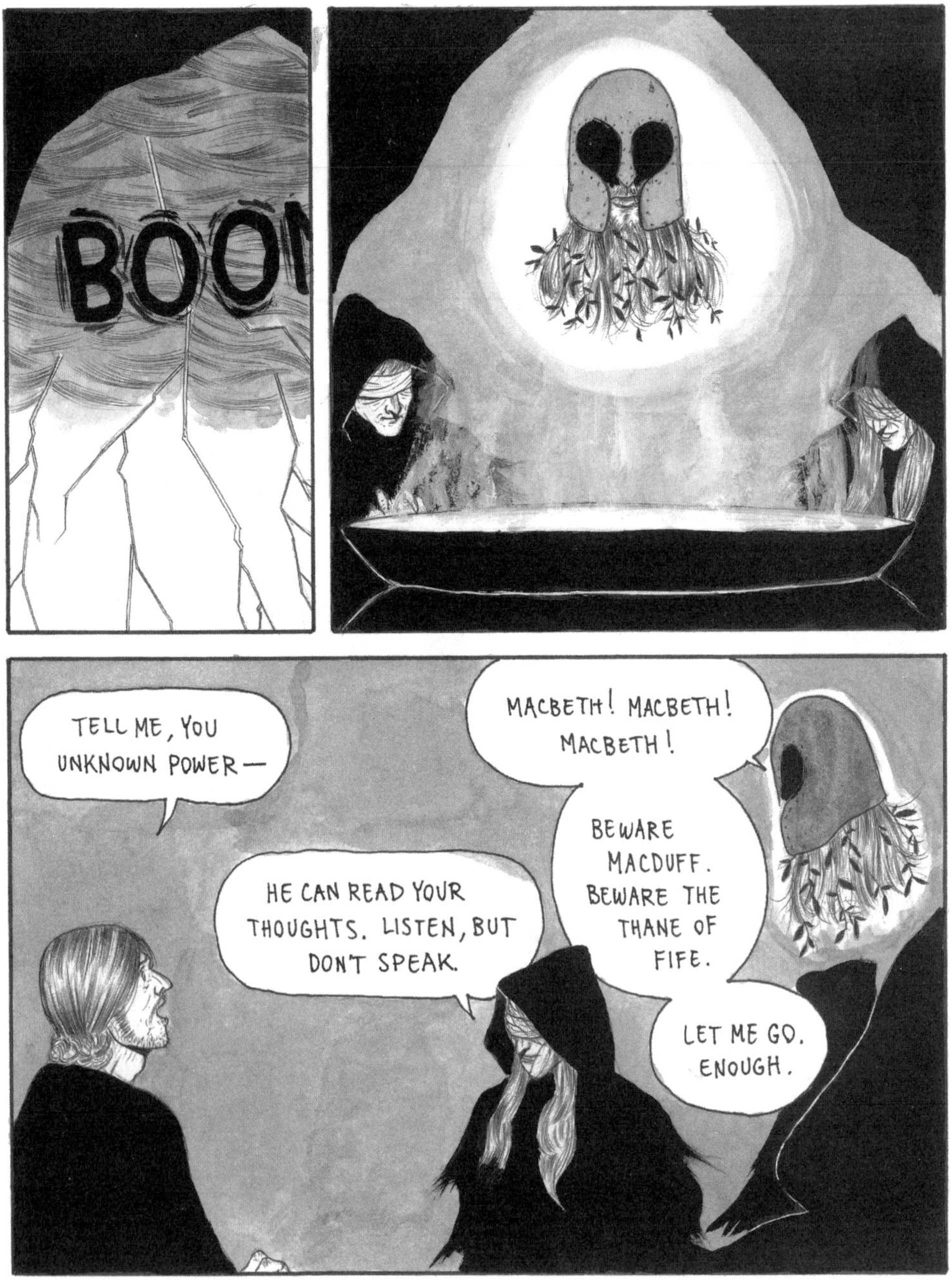
BOOM
TELL ME, YOU UNKNOWN POWER—
MACBETH! MACBETH! MACBETH!
HE CAN READ YOUR THOUGHTS. LISTEN, BUT DON'T SPEAK.
BEWARE MACDUFF. BEWARE THE THANE OF FIFE.
LET ME GO. ENOUGH.

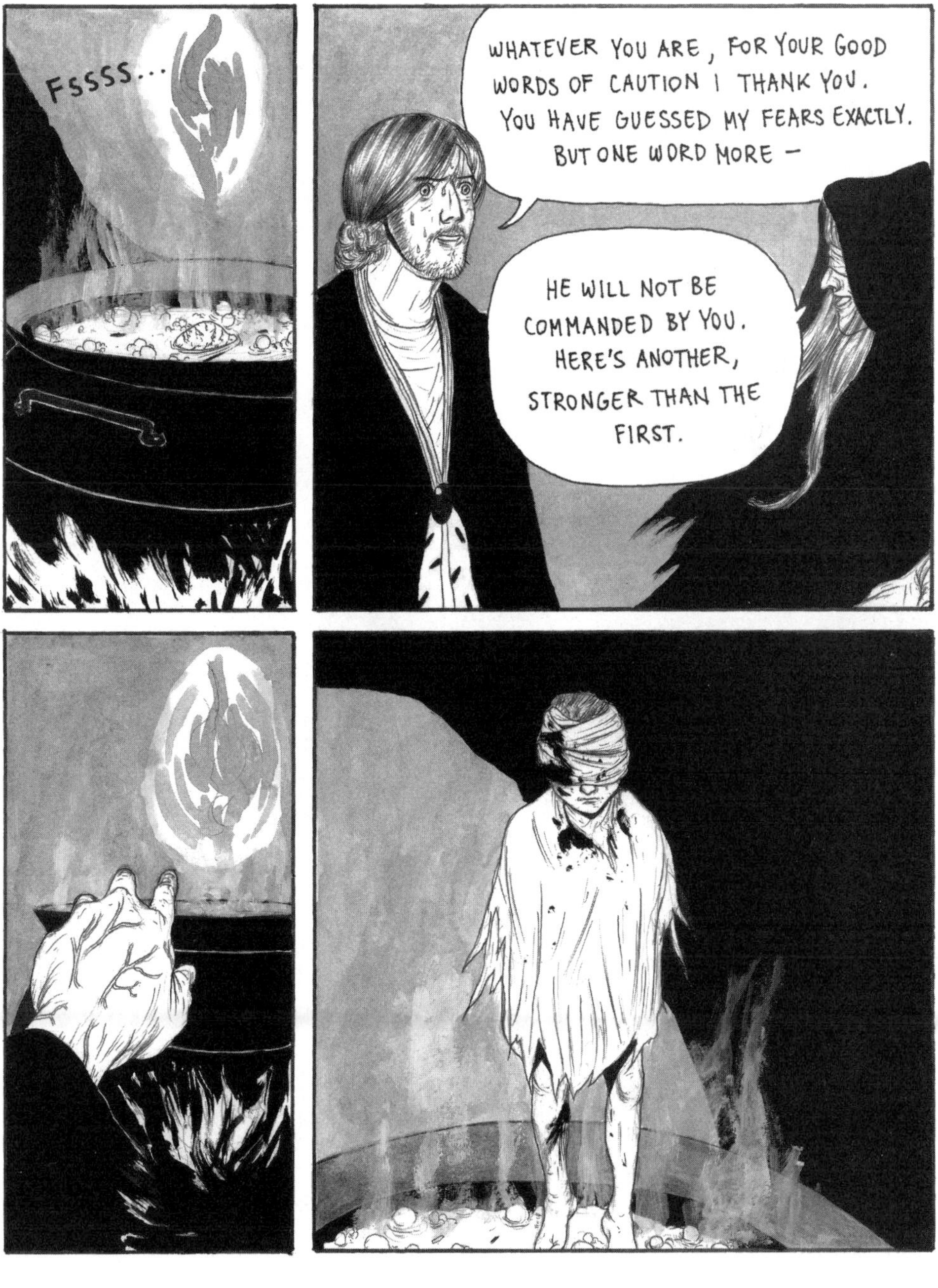
FSSSS...
WHATEVER YOU ARE, FOR YOUR GOOD WORDS OF CAUTION I THANK YOU. YOU HAVE GUESSED MY FEARS EXACTLY. BUT ONE WORD MORE –
HE WILL NOT BE COMMANDED BY YOU. HERE'S ANOTHER, STRONGER THAN THE FIRST.

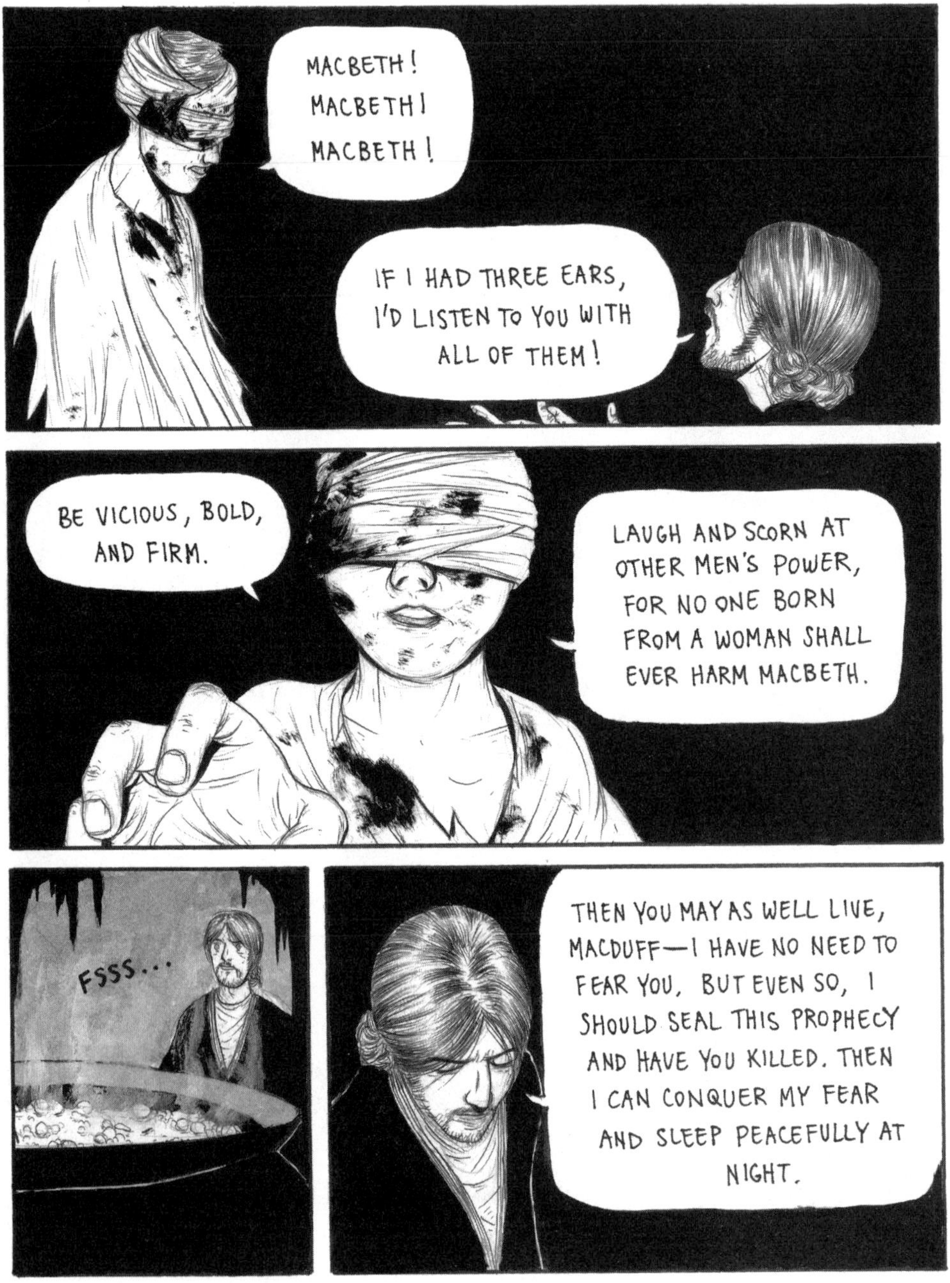
MACBETH! MACBETH! MACBETH!
IF I HAD THREE EARS, I'D LISTEN TO YOU WITH ALL OF THEM!
BE VICIOUS, BOLD, AND FIRM.
LAUGH AND SCORN AT OTHER MEN'S POWER, FOR NO ONE BORN FROM A WOMAN SHALL EVER HARM MACBETH.
FSSS...
THEN YOU MAY AS WELL LIVE, MACDUFF—I HAVE NO NEED TO FEAR YOU. BUT EVEN SO, I SHOULD SEAL THIS PROPHECY AND HAVE YOU KILLED. THEN I CAN CONQUER MY FEAR AND SLEEP PEACEFULLY AT NIGHT.

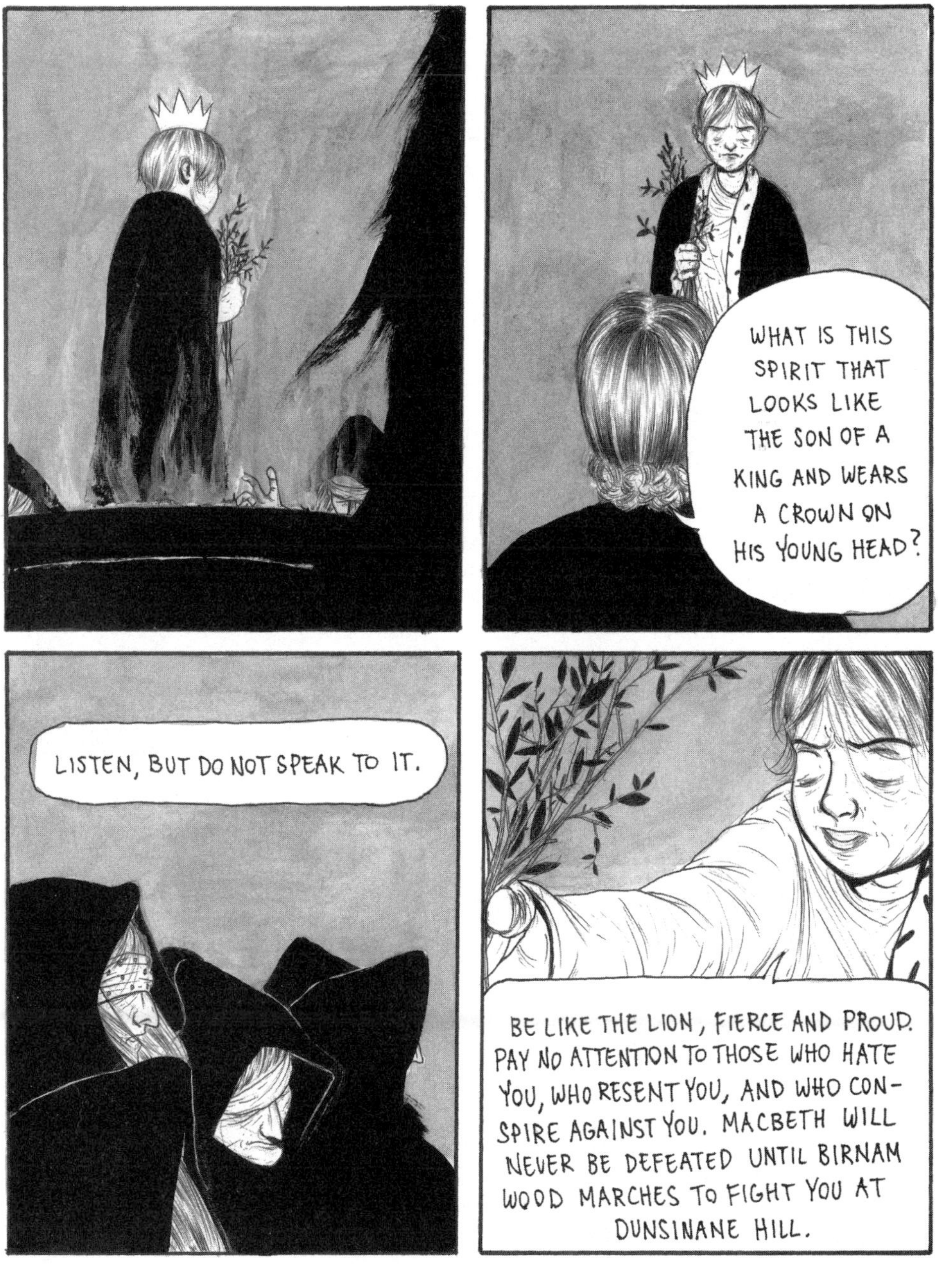
WHAT IS THIS SPIRIT THAT LOOKS LIKE THE SON OF A KING AND WEARS A CROWN ON HIS YOUNG HEAD?
LISTEN, BUT DO NOT SPEAK TO IT.
BE LIKE THE LION, FIERCE AND PROUD. PAY NO ATTENTION TO THOSE WHO HATE YOU, WHO RESENT YOU, AND WHO CONSPIRE AGAINST YOU. MACBETH WILL NEVER BE DEFEATED UNTIL BIRNAM WOOD MARCHES TO FIGHT YOU AT DUNSINANE HILL.

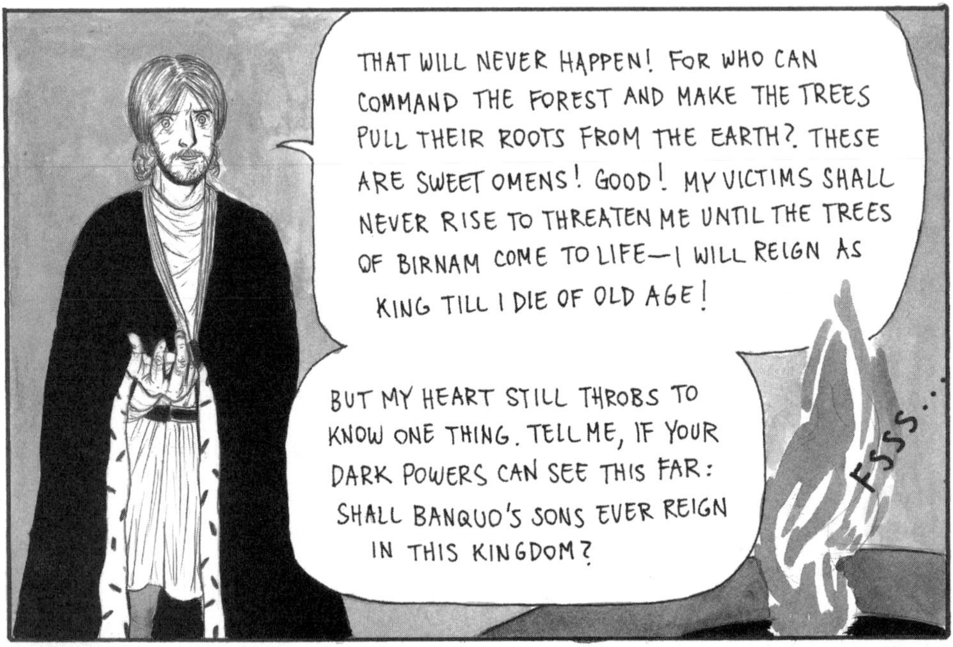
THAT WILL NEVER HAPPEN! FOR WHO CAN COMMAND THE FOREST AND MAKE THE TREES PULL THEIR ROOTS FROM THE EARTH? THESE ARE SWEET OMENS! GOOD! MY VICTIMS SHALL NEVER RISE TO THREATEN ME UNTIL THE TREES OF BIRNAM COME TO LIFE—I WILL REIGN AS KING TILL I DIE OF OLD AGE!
BUT MY HEART STILL THROBS TO KNOW ONE THING. TELL ME, IF YOUR DARK POWERS CAN SEE THIS FAR: SHALL BANQUO'S SONS EVER REIGN IN THIS KINGDOM?
FSSS...

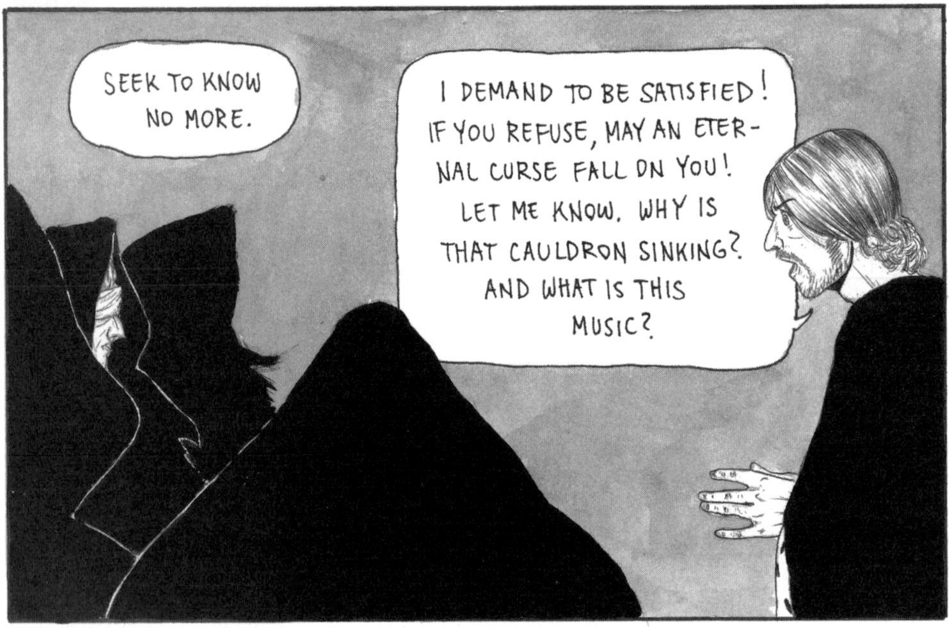
SEEK TO KNOW NO MORE.
I DEMAND TO BE SATISFIED! IF YOU REFUSE, MAY AN ETERNAL CURSE FALL ON YOU! LET ME KNOW. WHY IS THAT CAULDRON SINKING? AND WHAT IS THIS MUSIC?

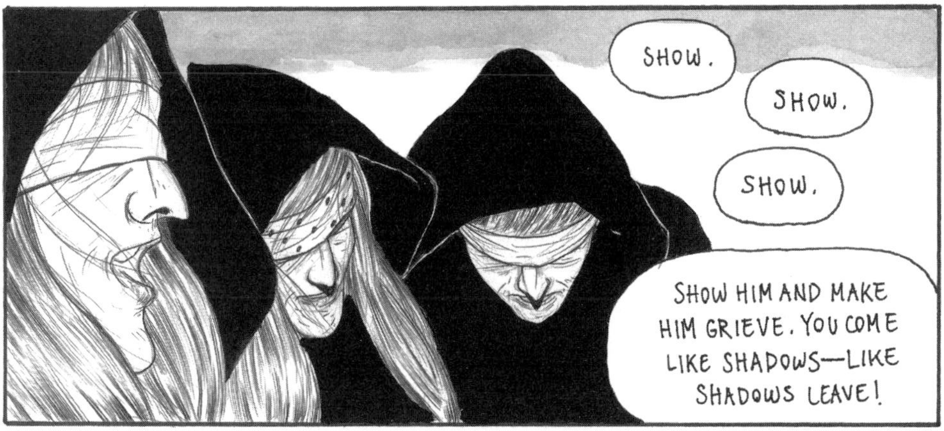
SHOW.
SHOW.
SHOW.
SHOW HIM AND MAKE HIM GRIEVE. YOU COME LIKE SHADOWS—LIKE SHADOWS LEAVE!

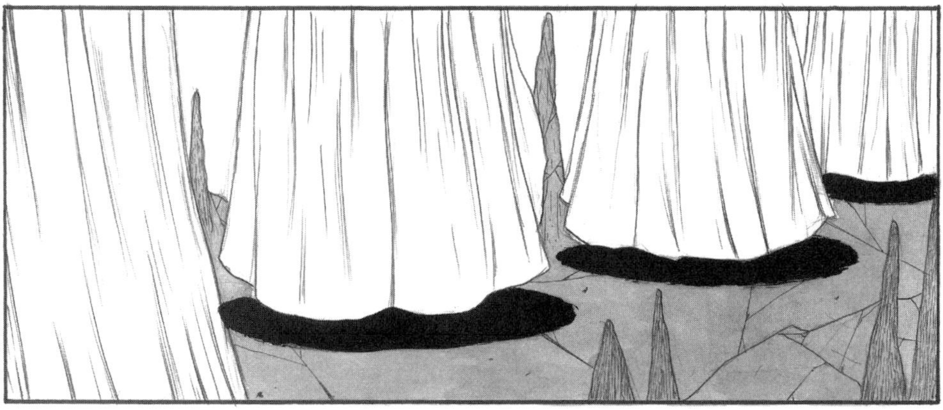

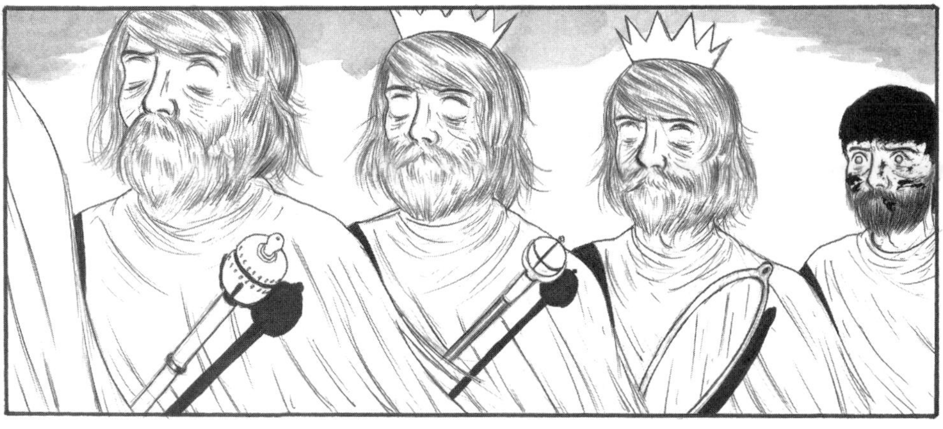

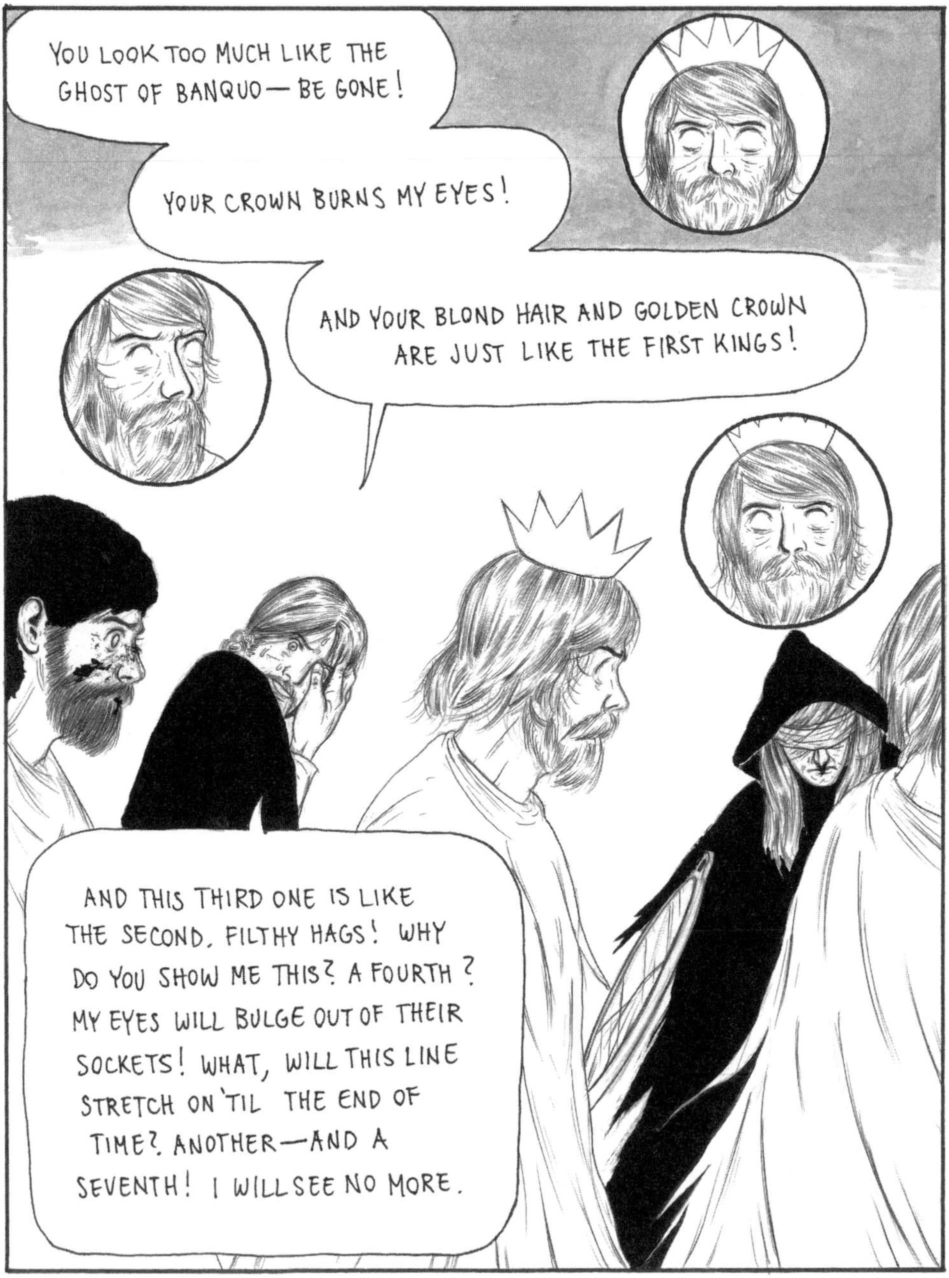
YOU LOOK TOO MUCH LIKE THE GHOST OF BANQUO—BE GONE!
YOUR CROWN BURNS MY EYES!
AND YOUR BLOND HAIR AND GOLDEN CROWN ARE JUST LIKE THE FIRST KINGS!
AND THIS THIRD ONE IS LIKE THE SECOND. FILTHY HAGS! WHY DO YOU SHOW ME THIS? A FOURTH? MY EYES WILL BULGE OUT OF THEIR SOCKETS! WHAT, WILL THIS LINE STRETCH ON 'TIL THE END OF TIME? ANOTHER—AND A SEVENTH! I WILL SEE NO MORE.

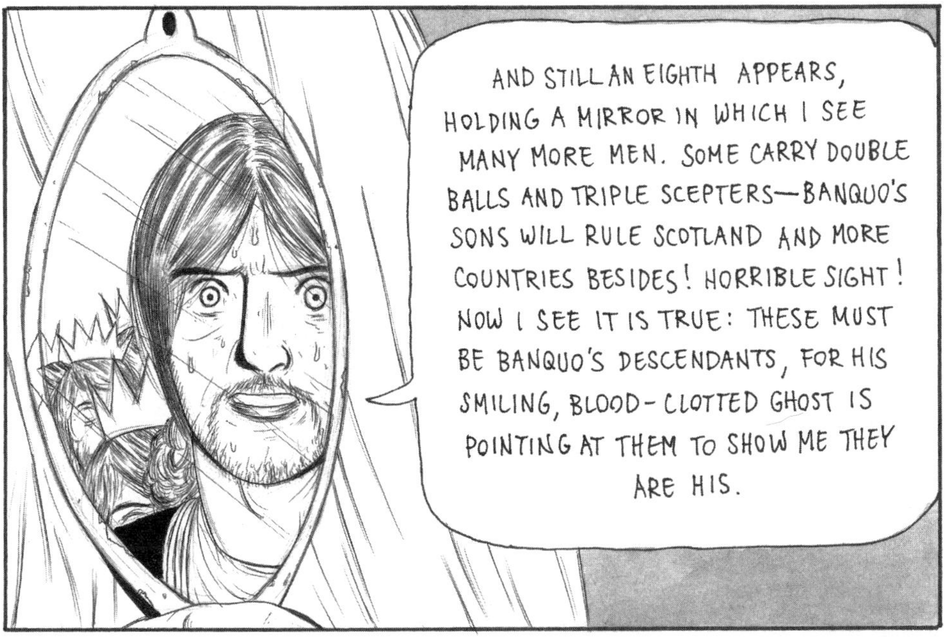
AND STILL AN EIGHTH APPEARS, HOLDING A MIRROR IN WHICH I SEE MANY MORE MEN. SOME CARRY DOUBLE BALLS AND TRIPLE SCEPTERS—BANQUO'S SONS WILL RULE SCOTLAND AND MORE COUNTRIES BESIDES! HORRIBLE SIGHT! NOW I SEE IT IS TRUE: THESE MUST BE BANQUO'S DESCENDANTS, FOR HIS SMILING, BLOOD-CLOTTED GHOST IS POINTING AT THEM TO SHOW ME THEY ARE HIS.

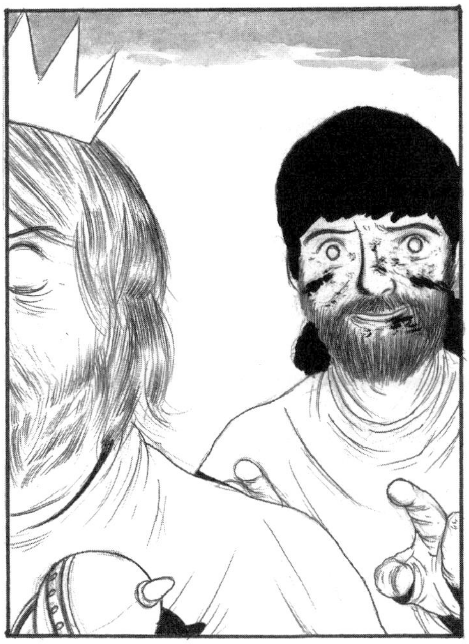

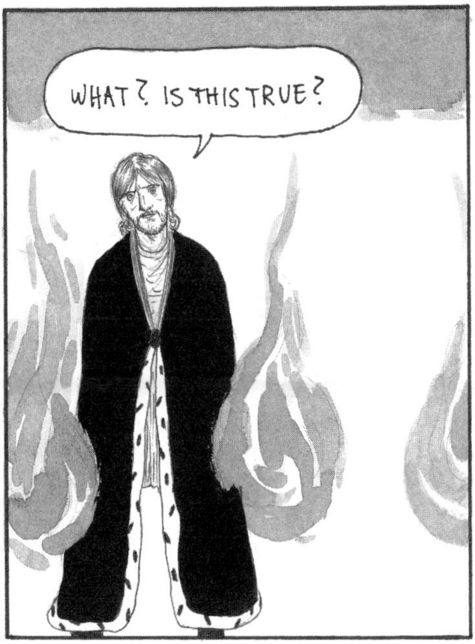
WHAT? IS THIS TRUE?

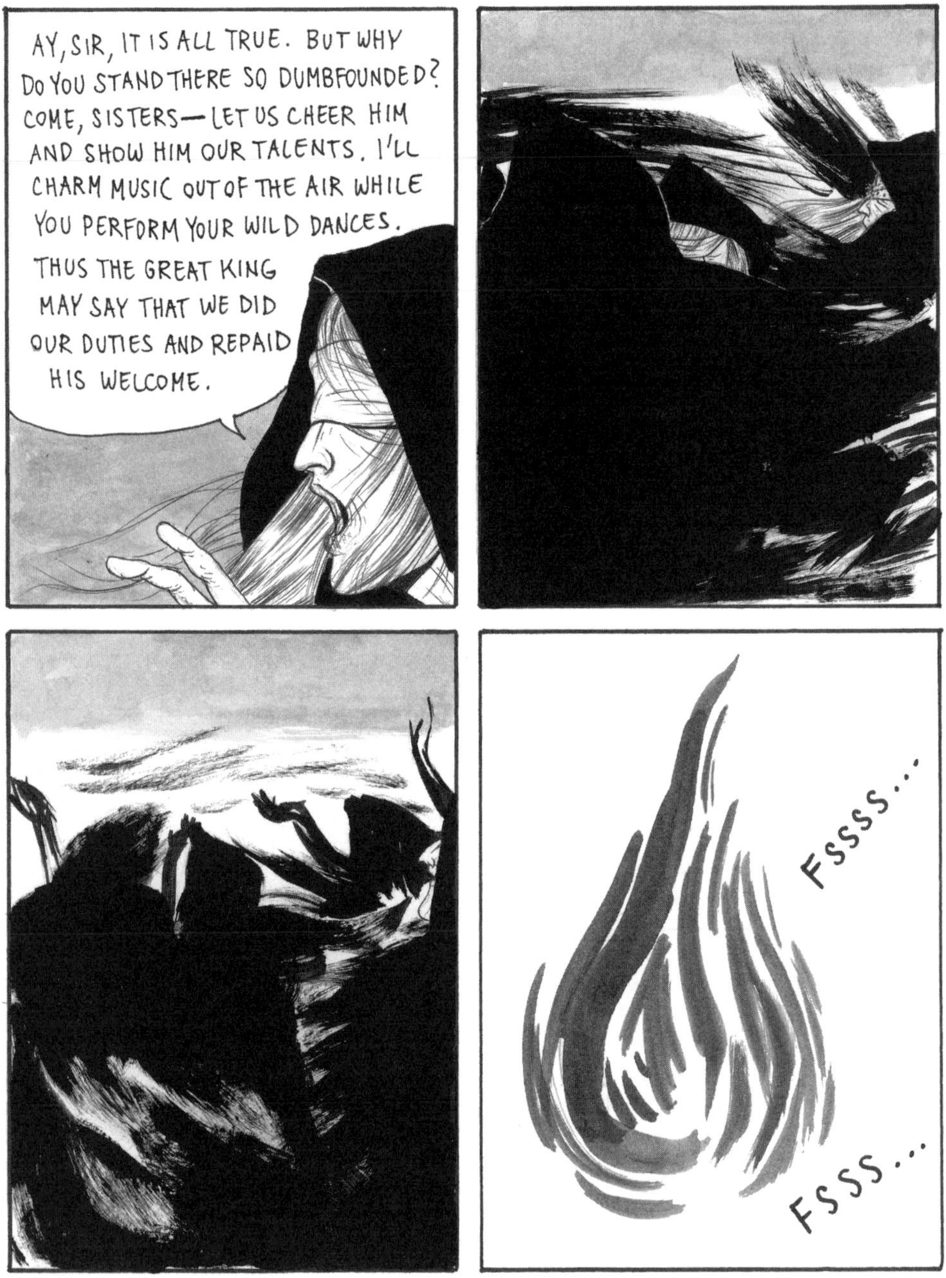
AY, SIR, IT IS ALL TRUE. BUT WHY DO YOU STAND THERE SO DUMBFOUNDED? COME, SISTERS—LET US CHEER HIM AND SHOW HIM OUR TALENTS. I'LL CHARM MUSIC OUT OF THE AIR WHILE YOU PERFORM YOUR WILD DANCES. THUS THE GREAT KING MAY SAY THAT WE DID OUR DUTIES AND REPAID HIS WELCOME.
FSSSS...
FSSS...

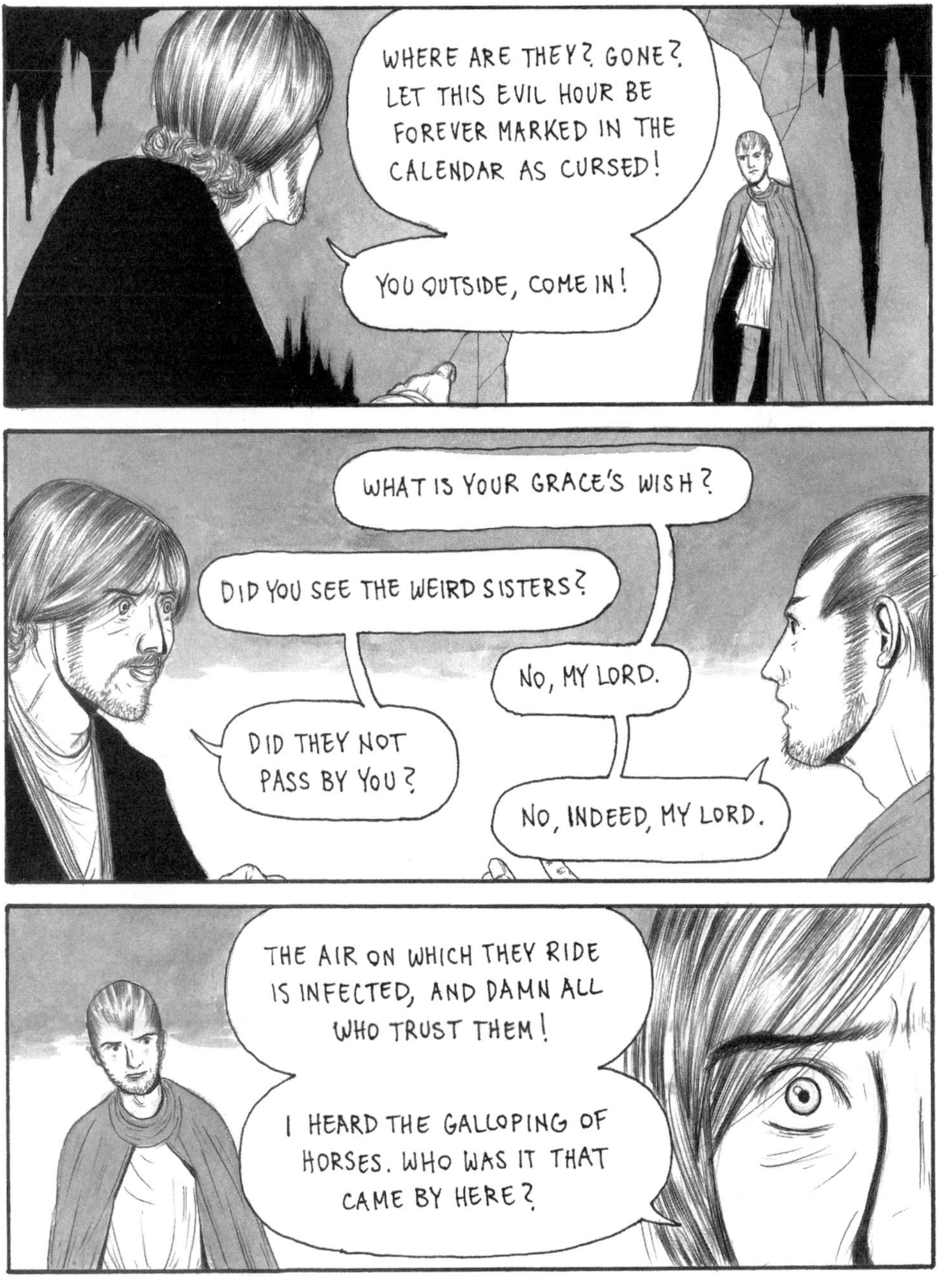
WHERE ARE THEY? GONE? LET THIS EVIL HOUR BE FOREVER MARKED IN THE CALENDAR AS CURSED!
YOU OUTSIDE, COME IN!
WHAT IS YOUR GRACE'S WISH?
DID YOU SEE THE WEIRD SISTERS?
NO, MY LORD.
DID THEY NOT PASS BY YOU?
NO, INDEED, MY LORD.
THE AIR ON WHICH THEY RIDE IS INFECTED, AND DAMN ALL WHO TRUST THEM!
I HEARD THE GALLOPING OF HORSES. WHO WAS IT THAT CAME BY HERE?

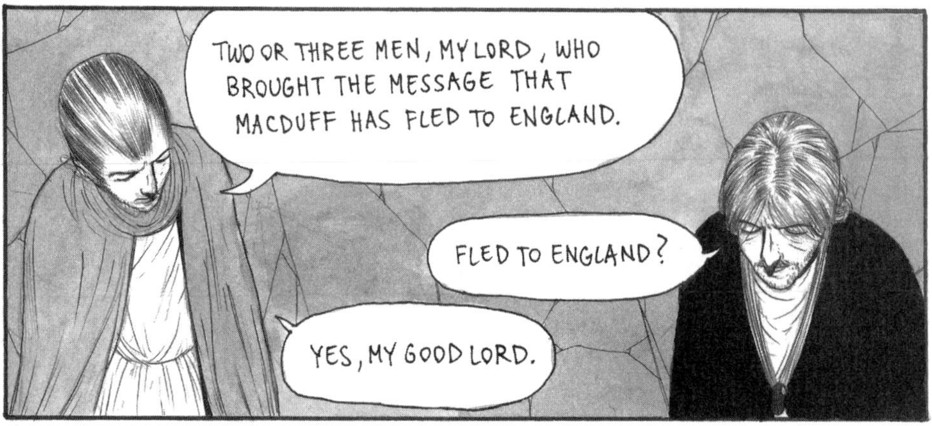
TWO OR THREE MEN, MY LORD, WHO BROUGHT THE MESSAGE THAT MACDUFF HAS FLED TO ENGLAND.
FLED TO ENGLAND?
YES, MY GOOD LORD.

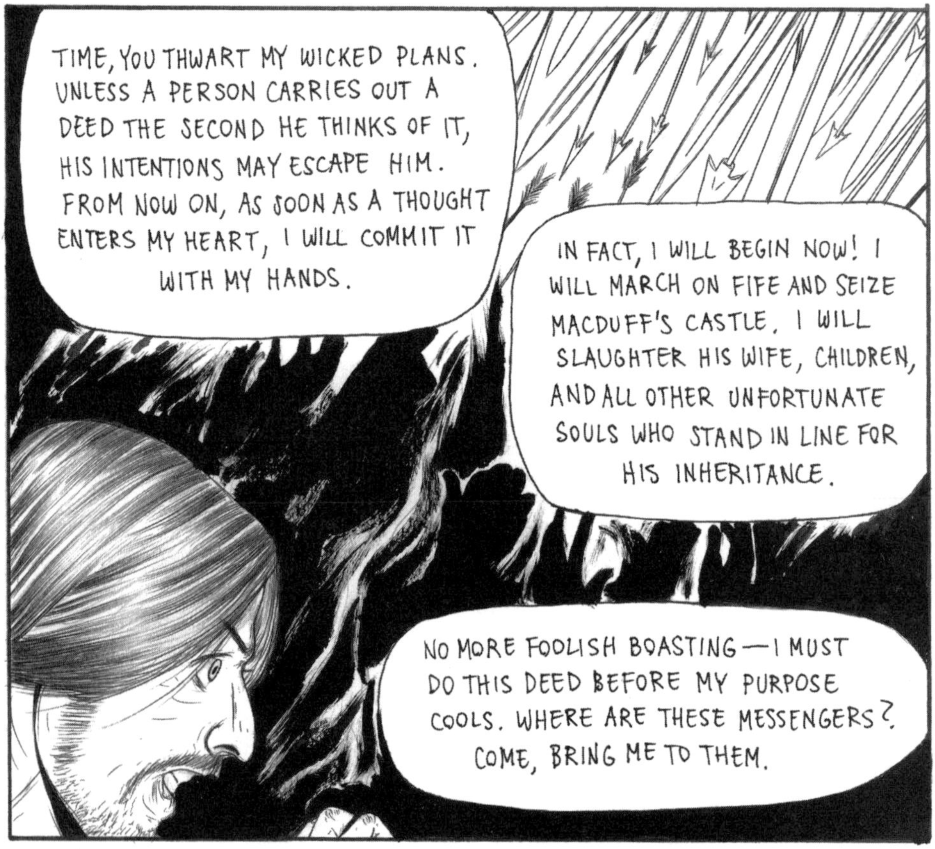
TIME, YOU THWART MY WICKED PLANS. UNLESS A PERSON CARRIES OUT A DEED THE SECOND HE THINKS OF IT, HIS INTENTIONS MAY ESCAPE HIM. FROM NOW ON, AS SOON AS A THOUGHT ENTERS MY HEART, I WILL COMMIT IT WITH MY HANDS.
IN FACT, I WILL BEGIN NOW! I WILL MARCH ON FIFE AND SEIZE MACDUFF'S CASTLE. I WILL SLAUGHTER HIS WIFE, CHILDREN, AND ALL OTHER UNFORTUNATE SOULS WHO STAND IN LINE FOR HIS INHERITANCE.
NO MORE FOOLISH BOASTING—I MUST DO THIS DEED BEFORE MY PURPOSE COOLS. WHERE ARE THESE MESSENGERS? COME, BRING ME TO THEM.

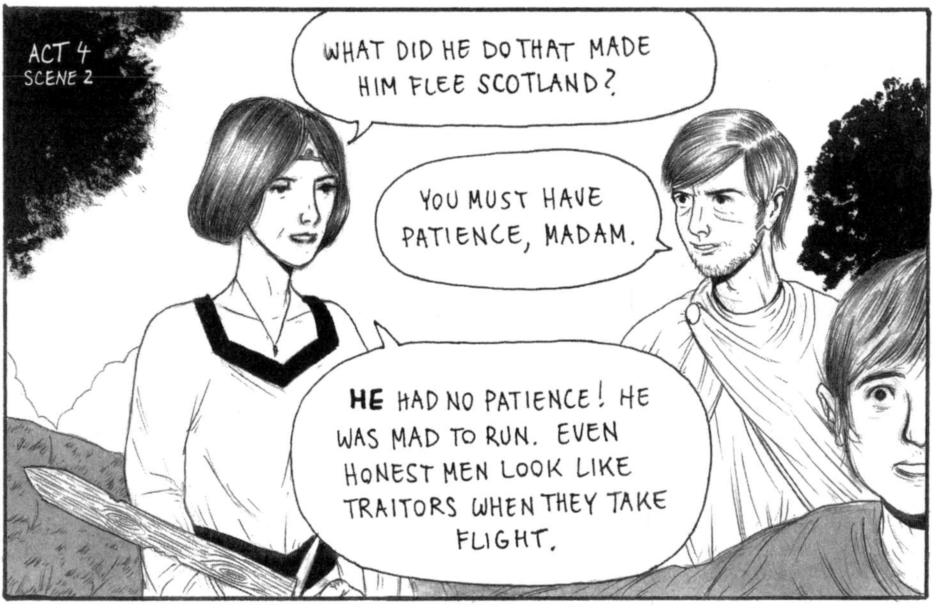
ACT 4
SCENE 2
WHAT DID HE DO THAT MADE HIM FLEE SCOTLAND?
YOU MUST HAVE PATIENCE, MADAM.
HE HAD NO PATIENCE! HE WAS MAD TO RUN. EVEN HONEST MEN LOOK LIKE TRAITORS WHEN THEY TAKE FLIGHT.

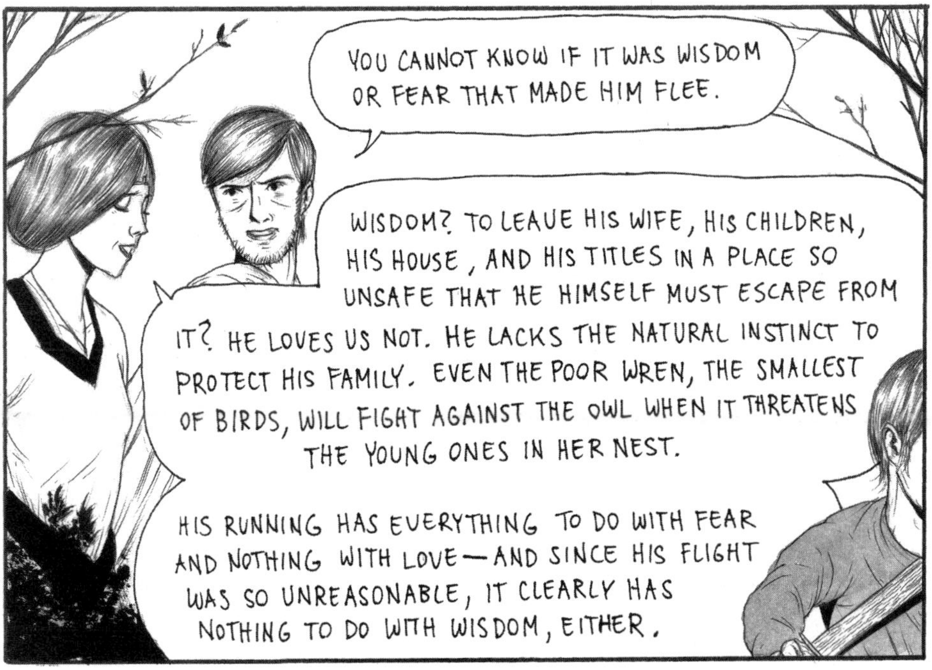
YOU CANNOT KNOW IF IT WAS WISDOM OR FEAR THAT MADE HIM FLEE.
WISDOM? TO LEAVE HIS WIFE, HIS CHILDREN, HIS HOUSE, AND HIS TITLES IN A PLACE SO UNSAFE THAT HE HIMSELF MUST ESCAPE FROM IT? HE LOVES US NOT. HE LACKS THE NATURAL INSTINCT TO PROTECT HIS FAMILY. EVEN THE POOR WREN, THE SMALLEST OF BIRDS, WILL FIGHT AGAINST THE OWL WHEN IT THREATENS THE YOUNG ONES IN HER NEST.
HIS RUNNING HAS EVERYTHING TO DO WITH FEAR AND NOTHING WITH LOVE—AND SINCE HIS FLIGHT WAS SO UNREASONABLE, IT CLEARLY HAS NOTHING TO DO WITH WISDOM, EITHER.

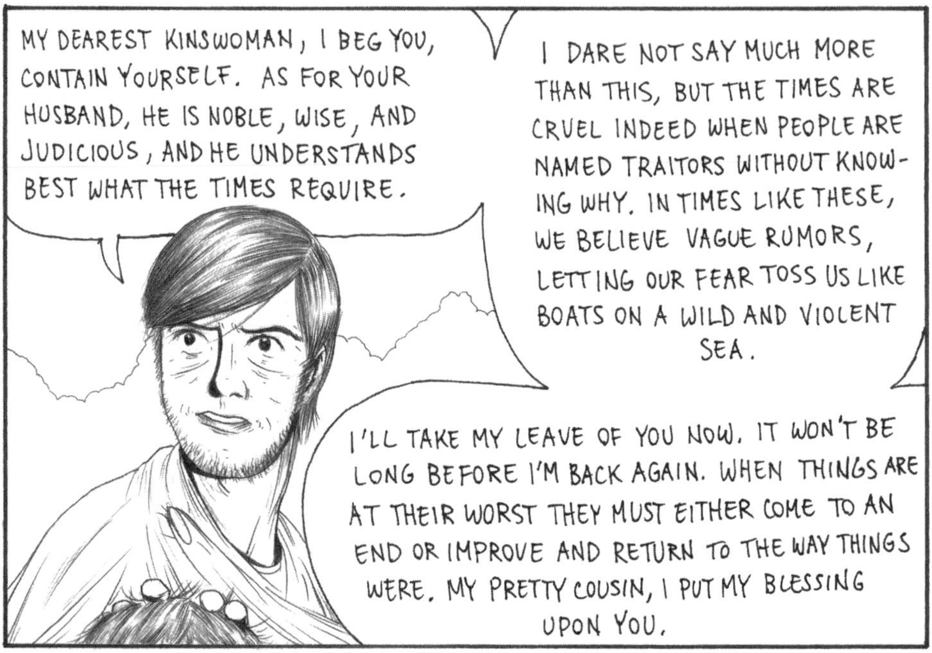
MY DEAREST KINSWOMAN, I BEG YOU, CONTAIN YOURSELF. AS FOR YOUR HUSBAND, HE IS NOBLE, WISE, AND JUDICIOUS, AND HE UNDERSTANDS BEST WHAT THE TIMES REQUIRE.
I DARE NOT SAY MUCH MORE THAN THIS, BUT THE TIMES ARE CRUEL INDEED WHEN PEOPLE ARE NAMED TRAITORS WITHOUT KNOWING WHY. IN TIMES LIKE THESE, WE BELIEVE VAGUE RUMORS, LETTING OUR FEAR TOSS US LIKE BOATS ON A WILD AND VIOLENT SEA.
I'LL TAKE MY LEAVE OF YOU NOW. IT WON'T BE LONG BEFORE I'M BACK AGAIN. WHEN THINGS ARE AT THEIR WORST THEY MUST EITHER COME TO AN END OR IMPROVE AND RETURN TO THE WAY THINGS WERE. MY PRETTY COUSIN, I PUT MY BLESSING UPON YOU.

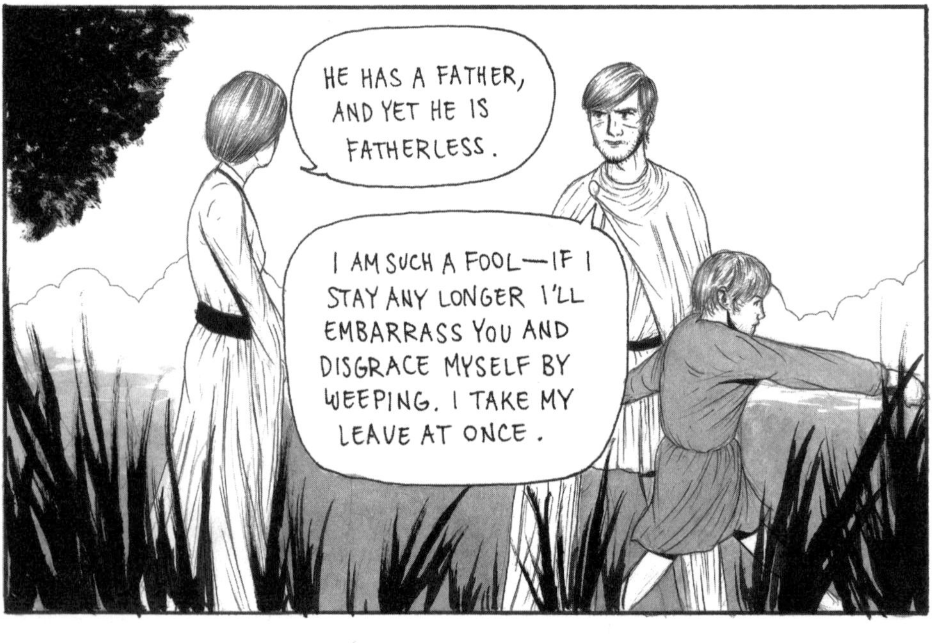
HE HAS A FATHER, AND YET HE IS FATHERLESS.
I AM SUCH A FOOL—IF I STAY ANY LONGER I'LL EMBARRASS YOU AND DISGRACE MYSELF BY WEEPING. I TAKE MY LEAVE AT ONCE.

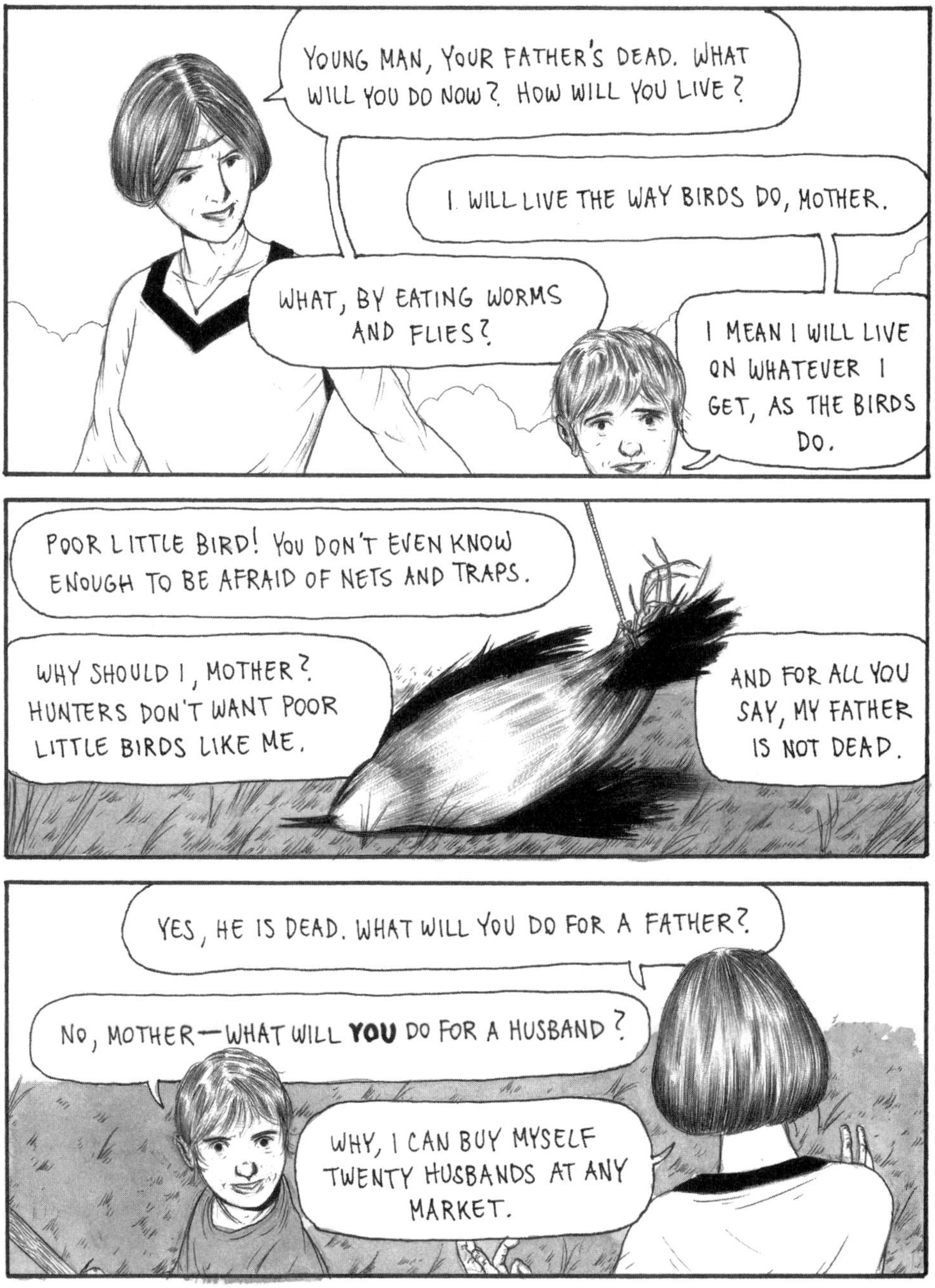
YOUNG MAN, YOUR FATHER'S DEAD. WHAT WILL YOU DO NOW? HOW WILL YOU LIVE?
I WILL LIVE THE WAY BIRDS DO, MOTHER.
WHAT, BY EATING WORMS AND FLIES?
I MEAN I WILL LIVE ON WHATEVER I GET, AS THE BIRDS DO.
POOR LITTLE BIRD! YOU DON'T EVEN KNOW ENOUGH TO BE AFRAID OF NETS AND TRAPS.
WHY SHOULD I, MOTHER? HUNTERS DON'T WANT POOR LITTLE BIRDS LIKE ME.
AND FOR ALL YOU SAY, MY FATHER IS NOT DEAD.
YES, HE IS DEAD. WHAT WILL YOU DO FOR A FATHER?
NO, MOTHER—WHAT WILL **YOU** DO FOR A HUSBAND?
WHY, I CAN BUY MYSELF TWENTY HUSBANDS AT ANY MARKET.

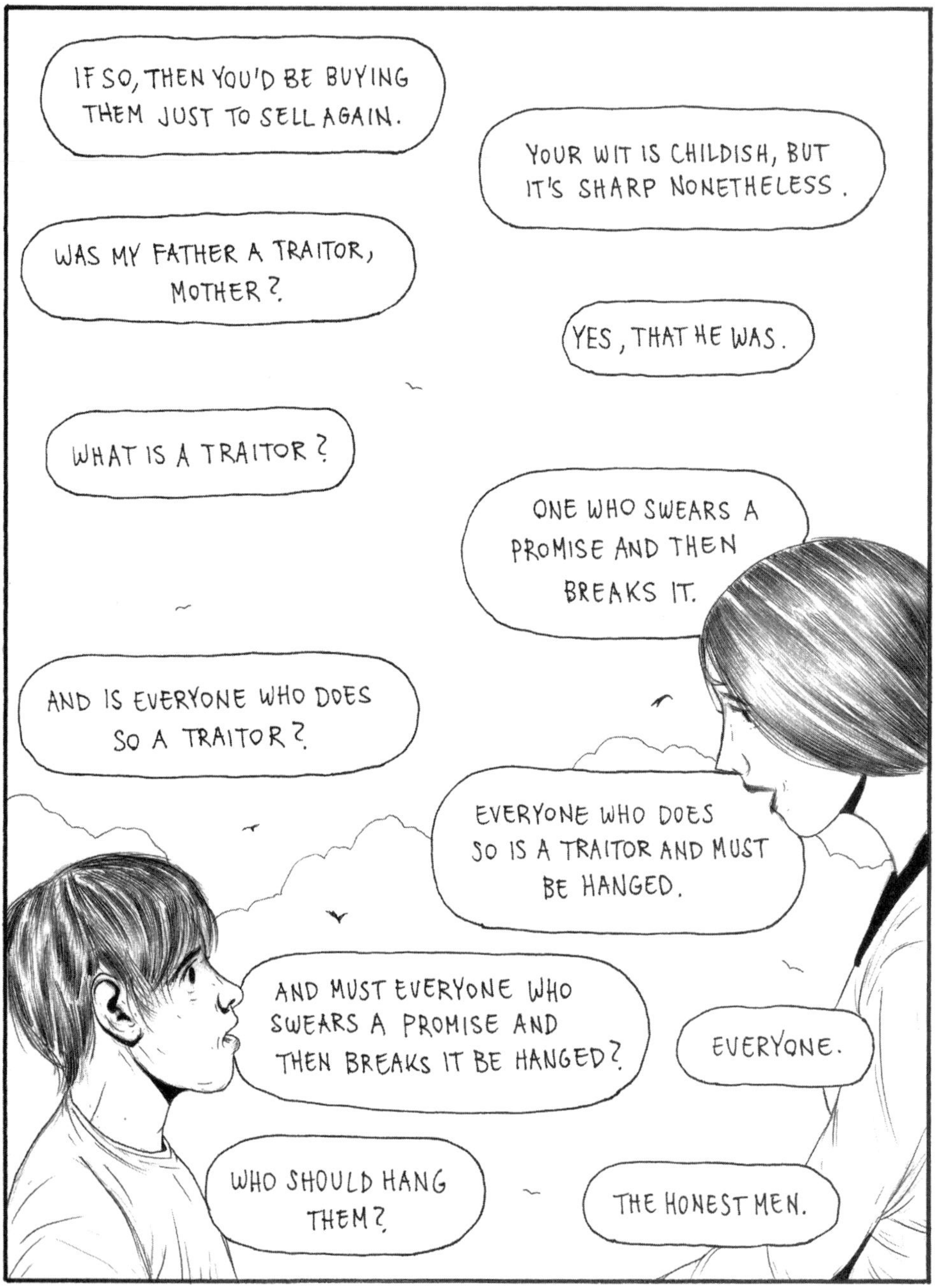
IF SO, THEN YOU'D BE BUYING THEM JUST TO SELL AGAIN.
YOUR WIT IS CHILDISH, BUT IT'S SHARP NONETHELESS.
WAS MY FATHER A TRAITOR, MOTHER?
YES, THAT HE WAS.
WHAT IS A TRAITOR?
ONE WHO SWEARS A PROMISE AND THEN BREAKS IT.
AND IS EVERYONE WHO DOES SO A TRAITOR?
EVERYONE WHO DOES SO IS A TRAITOR AND MUST BE HANGED.
AND MUST EVERYONE WHO SWEARS A PROMISE AND THEN BREAKS IT BE HANGED?
EVERYONE.
WHO SHOULD HANG THEM?
THE HONEST MEN.

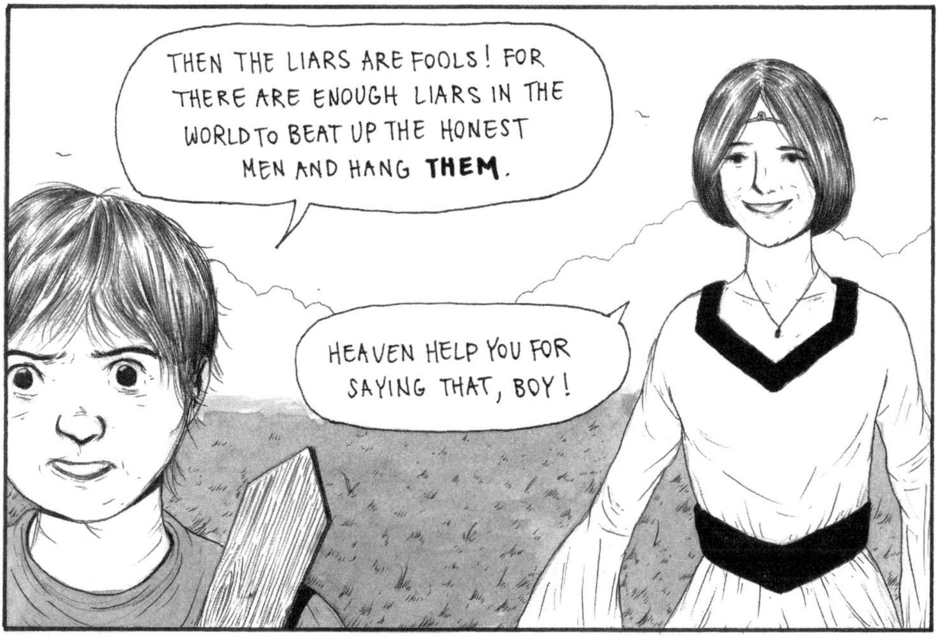
THEN THE LIARS ARE FOOLS! FOR THERE ARE ENOUGH LIARS IN THE WORLD TO BEAT UP THE HONEST MEN AND HANG **THEM**.
HEAVEN HELP YOU FOR SAYING THAT, BOY!

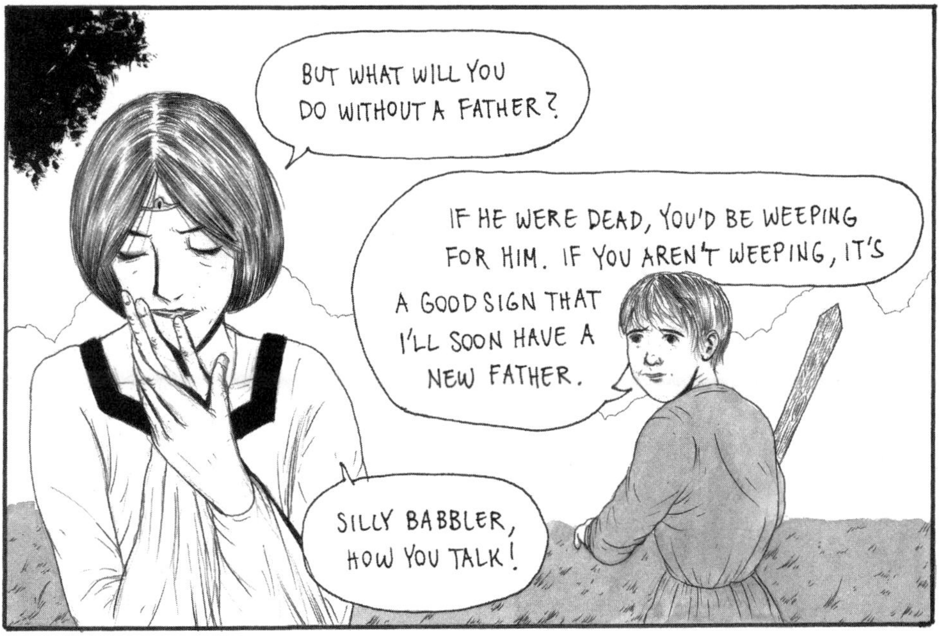
BUT WHAT WILL YOU DO WITHOUT A FATHER?
IF HE WERE DEAD, YOU'D BE WEEPING FOR HIM. IF YOU AREN'T WEEPING, IT'S A GOOD SIGN THAT I'LL SOON HAVE A NEW FATHER.
SILLY BABBLER, HOW YOU TALK!

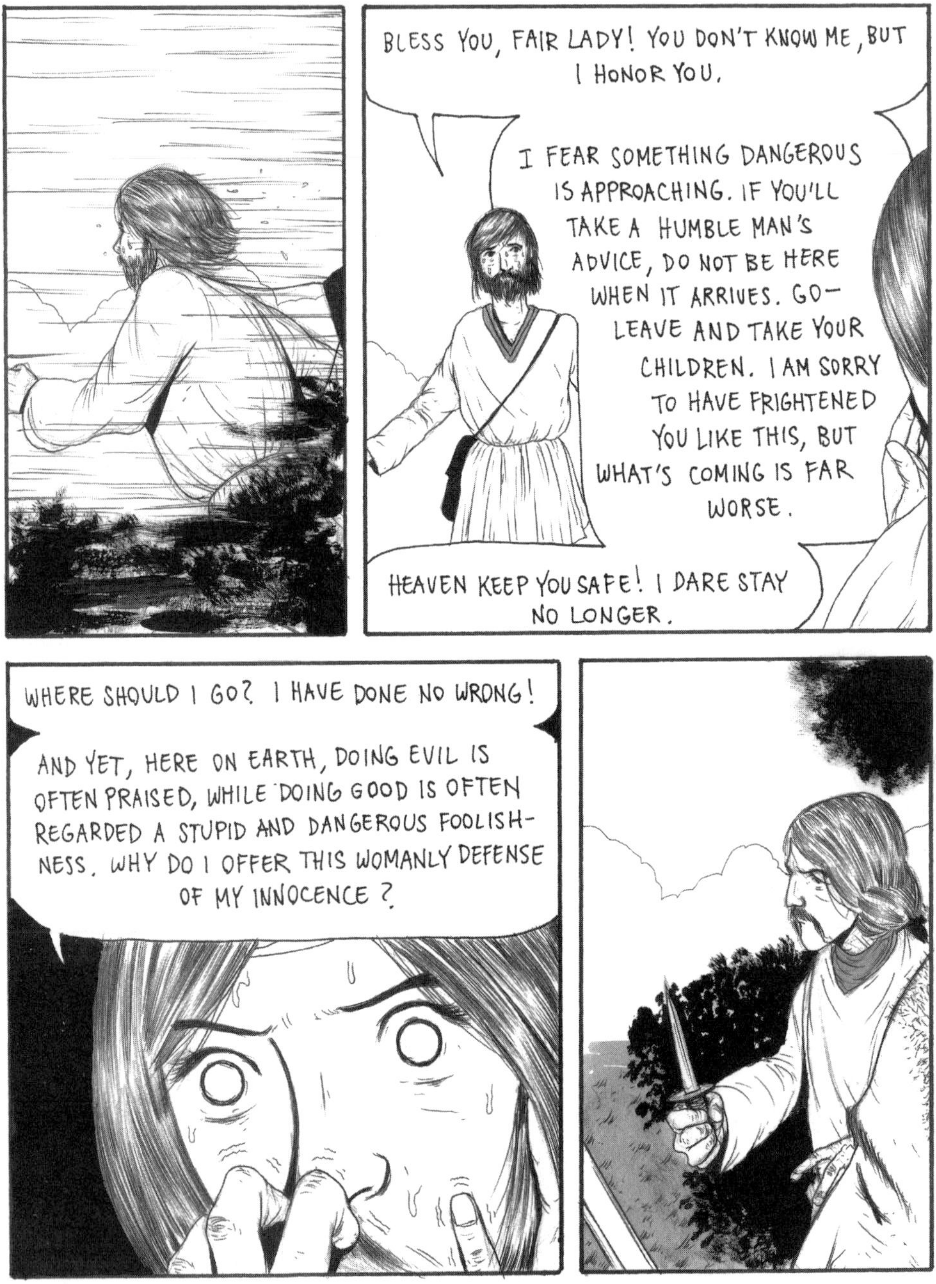
BLESS YOU, FAIR LADY! YOU DON'T KNOW ME, BUT I HONOR YOU.
I FEAR SOMETHING DANGEROUS IS APPROACHING. IF YOU'LL TAKE A HUMBLE MAN'S ADVICE, DO NOT BE HERE WHEN IT ARRIVES. GO—LEAVE AND TAKE YOUR CHILDREN. I AM SORRY TO HAVE FRIGHTENED YOU LIKE THIS, BUT WHAT'S COMING IS FAR WORSE.
HEAVEN KEEP YOU SAFE! I DARE STAY NO LONGER.
WHERE SHOULD I GO? I HAVE DONE NO WRONG!
AND YET, HERE ON EARTH, DOING EVIL IS OFTEN PRAISED, WHILE DOING GOOD IS OFTEN REGARDED A STUPID AND DANGEROUS FOOLISHNESS. WHY DO I OFFER THIS WOMANLY DEFENSE OF MY INNOCENCE?

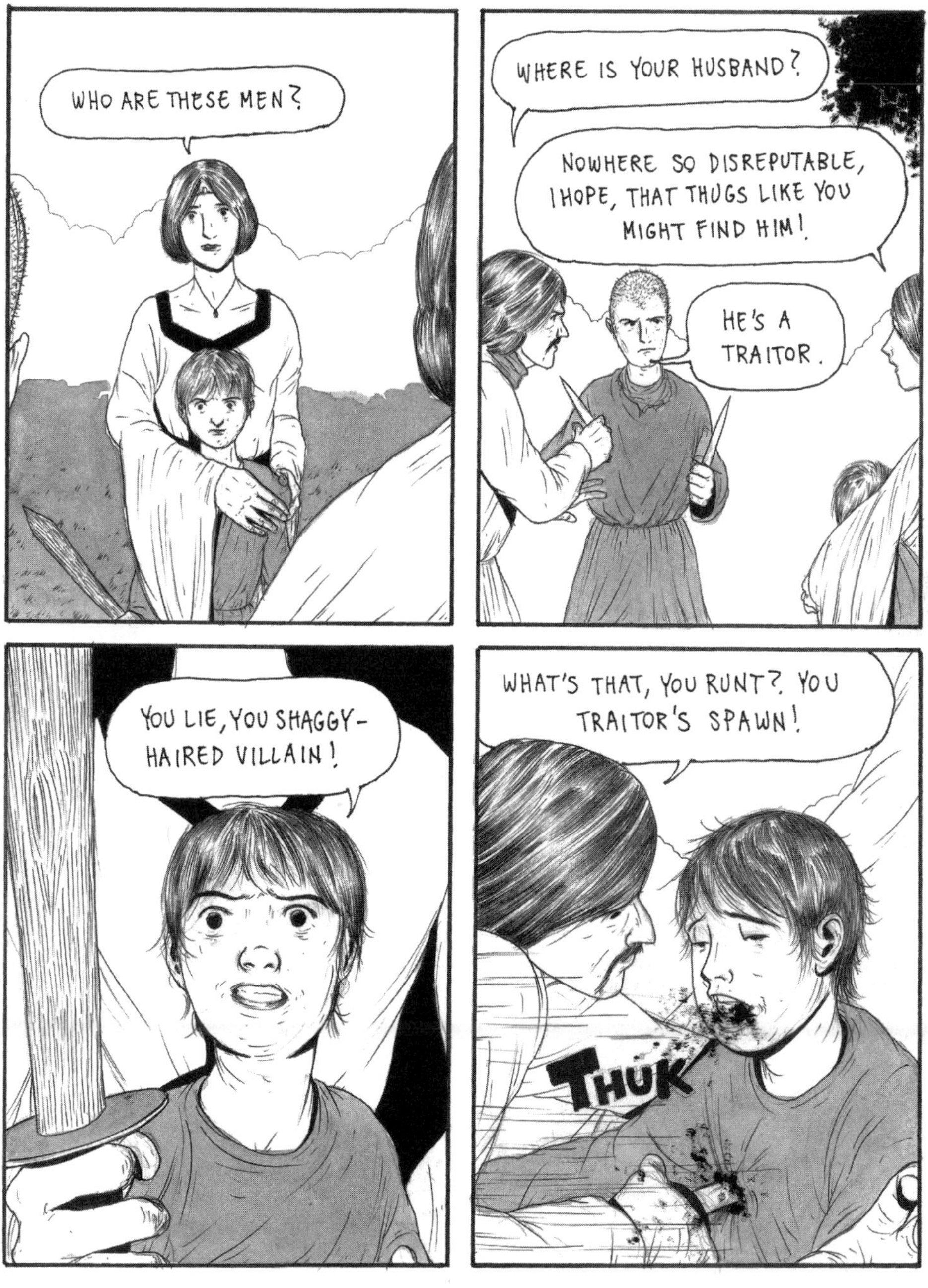
WHO ARE THESE MEN?
WHERE IS YOUR HUSBAND?
NOWHERE SO DISREPUTABLE, I HOPE, THAT THUGS LIKE YOU MIGHT FIND HIM!
HE'S A TRAITOR.
YOU LIE, YOU SHAGGY-HAIRED VILLAIN!
WHAT'S THAT, YOU RUNT? YOU TRAITOR'S SPAWN!
THUK

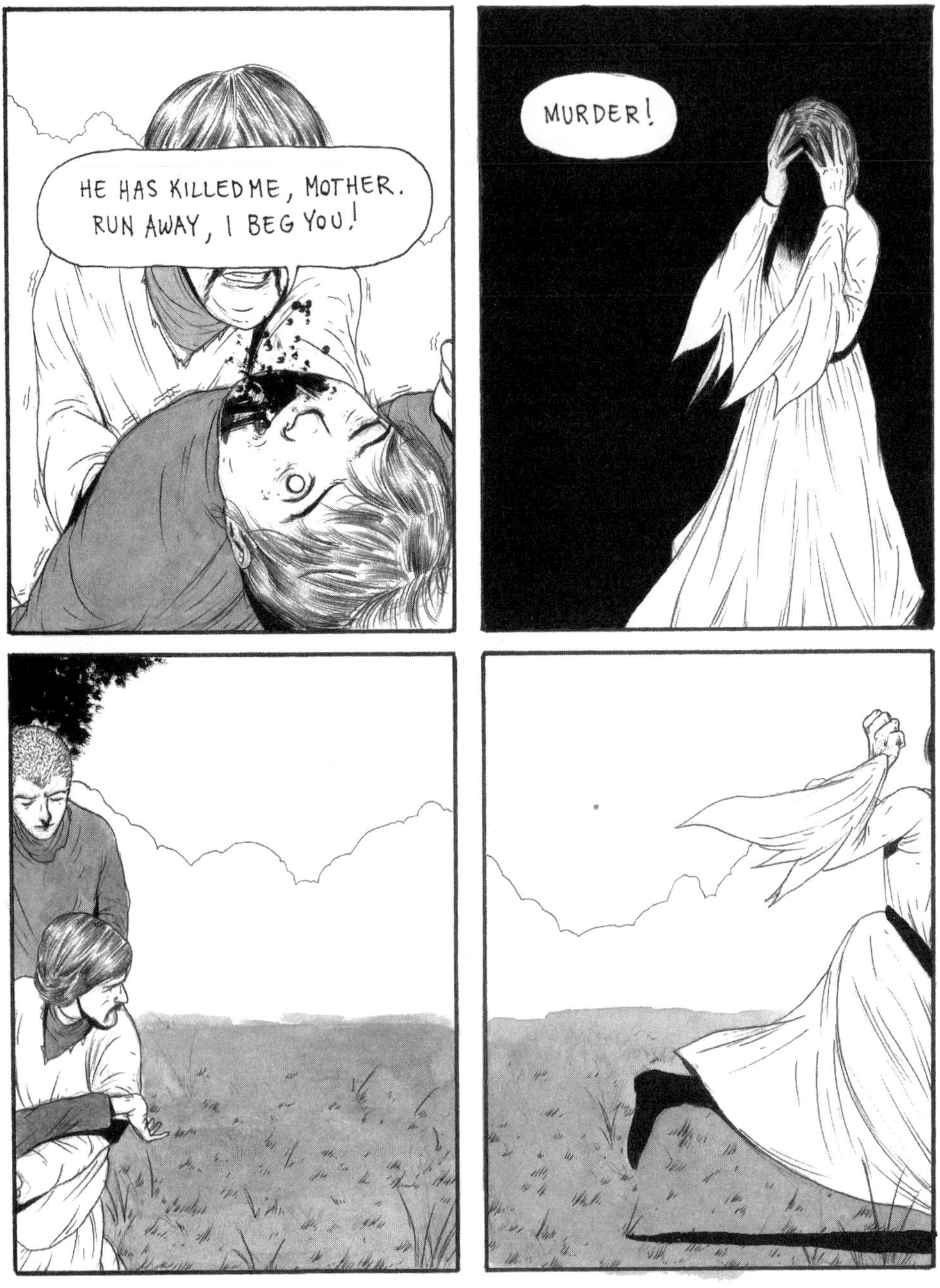
HE HAS KILLED ME, MOTHER. RUN AWAY, I BEG YOU!
MURDER!

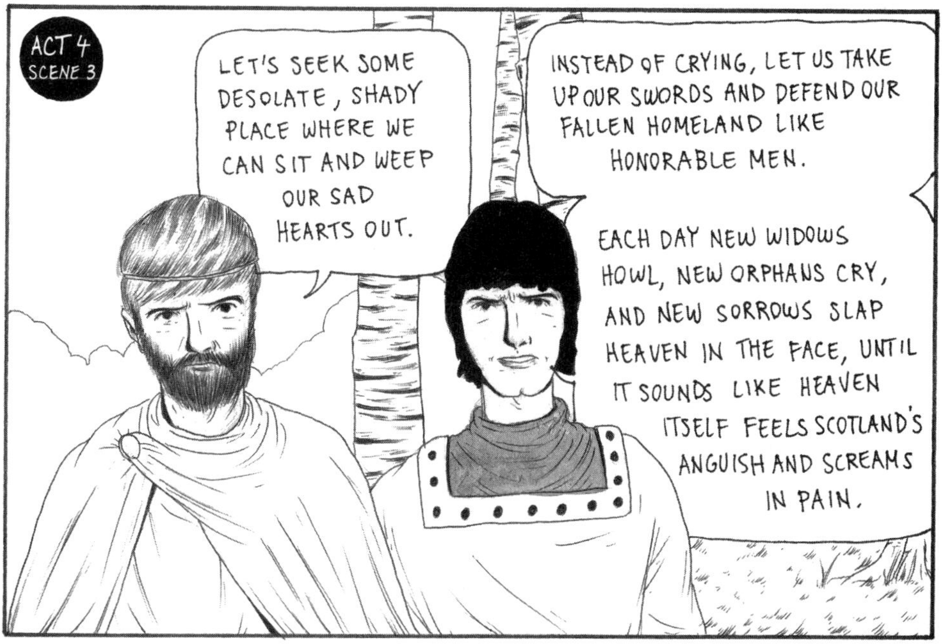
ACT 4
SCENE 3
LET'S SEEK SOME DESOLATE, SHADY PLACE WHERE WE CAN SIT AND WEEP OUR SAD HEARTS OUT.
INSTEAD OF CRYING, LET US TAKE UP OUR SWORDS AND DEFEND OUR FALLEN HOMELAND LIKE HONORABLE MEN.
EACH DAY NEW WIDOWS HOWL, NEW ORPHANS CRY, AND NEW SORROWS SLAP HEAVEN IN THE FACE, UNTIL IT SOUNDS LIKE HEAVEN ITSELF FEELS SCOTLAND'S ANGUISH AND SCREAMS IN PAIN.

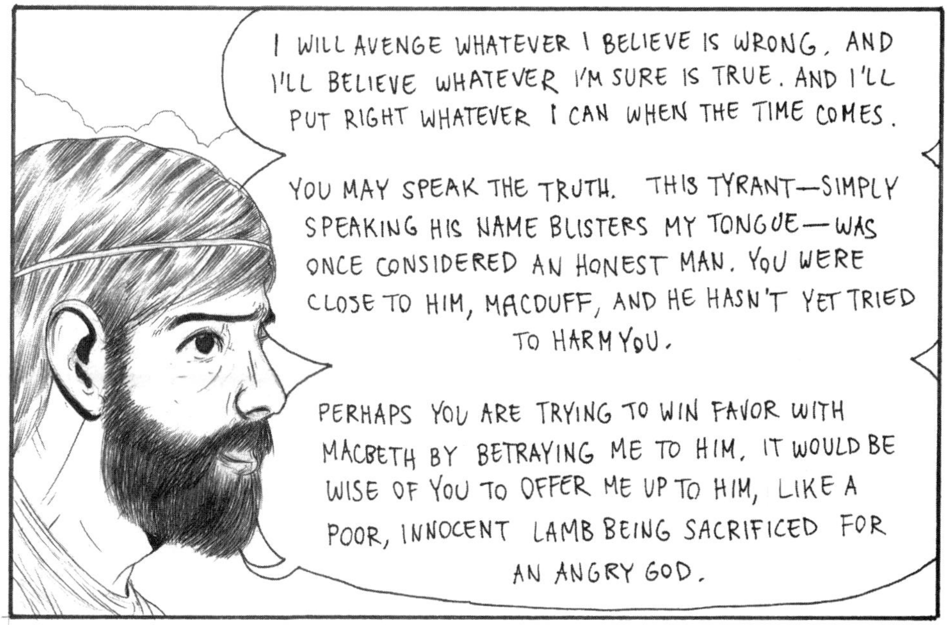
I WILL AVENGE WHATEVER I BELIEVE IS WRONG. AND I'LL BELIEVE WHATEVER I'M SURE IS TRUE. AND I'LL PUT RIGHT WHATEVER I CAN WHEN THE TIME COMES.
YOU MAY SPEAK THE TRUTH. THIS TYRANT—SIMPLY SPEAKING HIS NAME BLISTERS MY TONGUE—WAS ONCE CONSIDERED AN HONEST MAN. YOU WERE CLOSE TO HIM, MACDUFF, AND HE HASN'T YET TRIED TO HARM YOU.
PERHAPS YOU ARE TRYING TO WIN FAVOR WITH MACBETH BY BETRAYING ME TO HIM. IT WOULD BE WISE OF YOU TO OFFER ME UP TO HIM, LIKE A POOR, INNOCENT LAMB BEING SACRIFICED FOR AN ANGRY GOD.

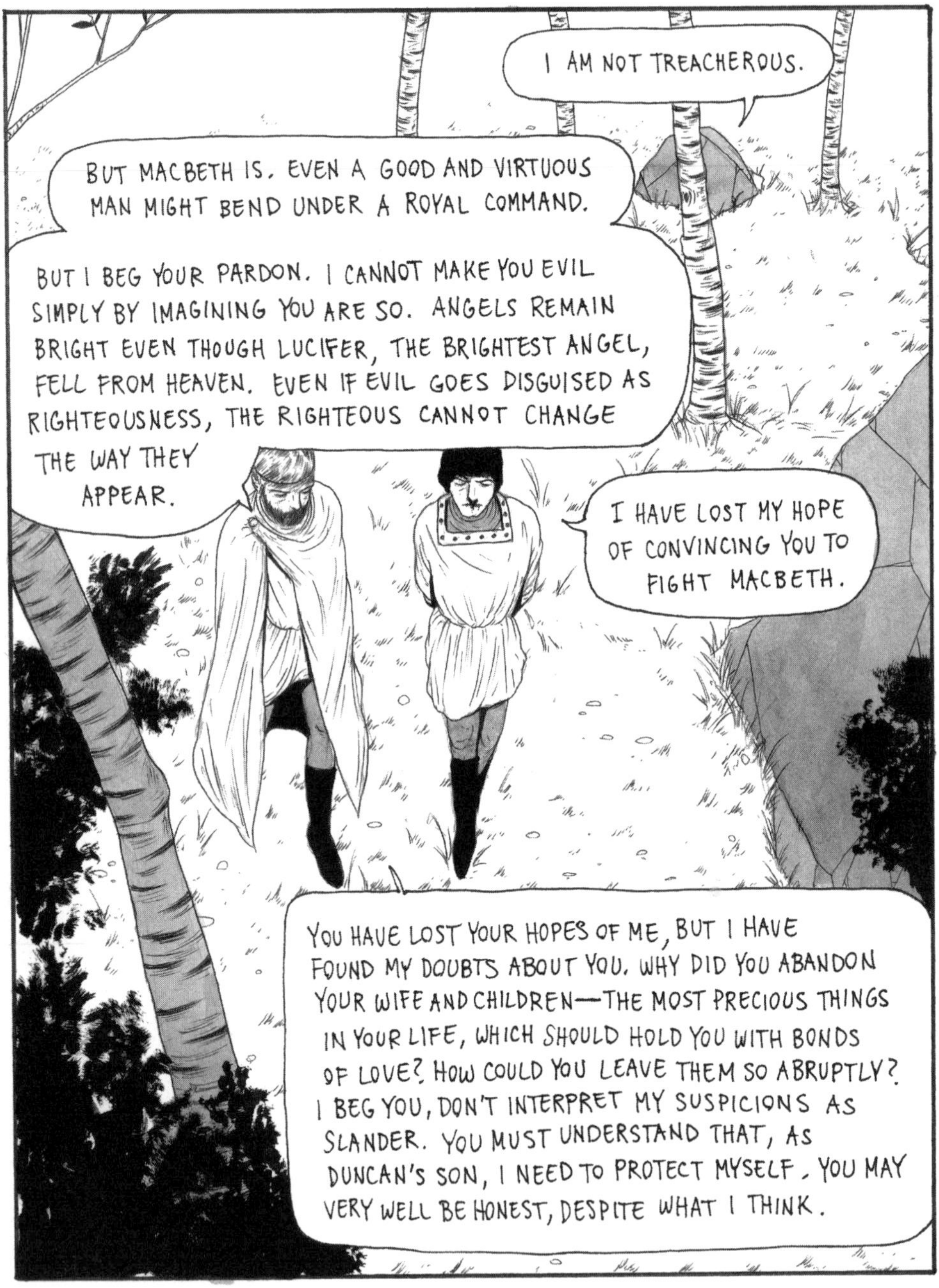
I AM NOT TREACHEROUS.
BUT MACBETH IS. EVEN A GOOD AND VIRTUOUS MAN MIGHT BEND UNDER A ROYAL COMMAND.
BUT I BEG YOUR PARDON. I CANNOT MAKE YOU EVIL SIMPLY BY IMAGINING YOU ARE SO. ANGELS REMAIN BRIGHT EVEN THOUGH LUCIFER, THE BRIGHTEST ANGEL, FELL FROM HEAVEN. EVEN IF EVIL GOES DISGUISED AS RIGHTEOUSNESS, THE RIGHTEOUS CANNOT CHANGE THE WAY THEY APPEAR.
I HAVE LOST MY HOPE OF CONVINCING YOU TO FIGHT MACBETH.
YOU HAVE LOST YOUR HOPES OF ME, BUT I HAVE FOUND MY DOUBTS ABOUT YOU. WHY DID YOU ABANDON YOUR WIFE AND CHILDREN—THE MOST PRECIOUS THINGS IN YOUR LIFE, WHICH SHOULD HOLD YOU WITH BONDS OF LOVE? HOW COULD YOU LEAVE THEM SO ABRUPTLY? I BEG YOU, DON'T INTERPRET MY SUSPICIONS AS SLANDER. YOU MUST UNDERSTAND THAT, AS DUNCAN'S SON, I NEED TO PROTECT MYSELF. YOU MAY VERY WELL BE HONEST, DESPITE WHAT I THINK.

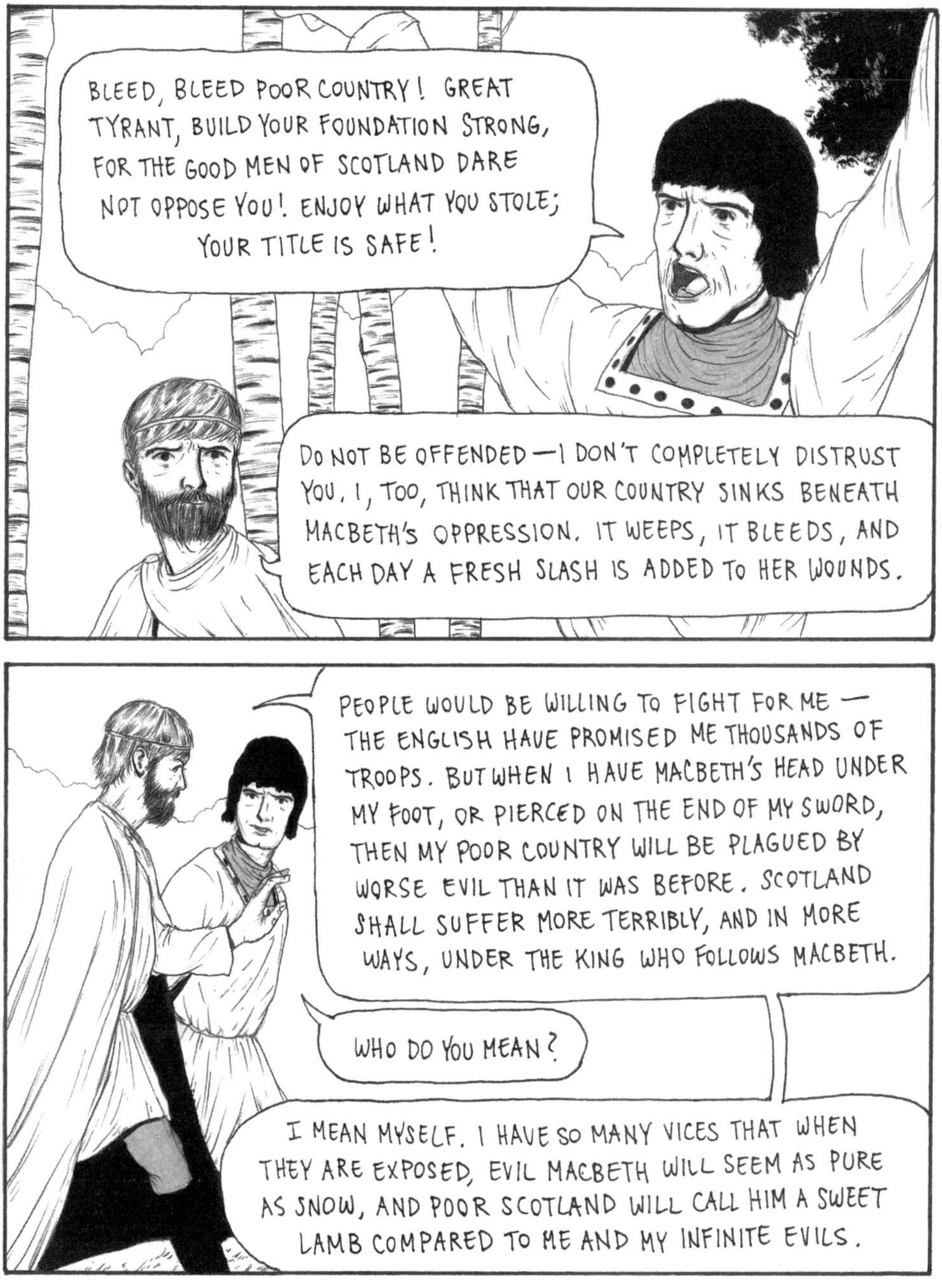
BLEED, BLEED POOR COUNTRY! GREAT TYRANT, BUILD YOUR FOUNDATION STRONG, FOR THE GOOD MEN OF SCOTLAND DARE NOT OPPOSE YOU! ENJOY WHAT YOU STOLE; YOUR TITLE IS SAFE!
DO NOT BE OFFENDED—I DON'T COMPLETELY DISTRUST YOU. I, TOO, THINK THAT OUR COUNTRY SINKS BENEATH MACBETH'S OPPRESSION. IT WEEPS, IT BLEEDS, AND EACH DAY A FRESH SLASH IS ADDED TO HER WOUNDS.
PEOPLE WOULD BE WILLING TO FIGHT FOR ME—THE ENGLISH HAVE PROMISED ME THOUSANDS OF TROOPS. BUT WHEN I HAVE MACBETH'S HEAD UNDER MY FOOT, OR PIERCED ON THE END OF MY SWORD, THEN MY POOR COUNTRY WILL BE PLAGUED BY WORSE EVIL THAN IT WAS BEFORE. SCOTLAND SHALL SUFFER MORE TERRIBLY, AND IN MORE WAYS, UNDER THE KING WHO FOLLOWS MACBETH.
WHO DO YOU MEAN?
I MEAN MYSELF. I HAVE SO MANY VICES THAT WHEN THEY ARE EXPOSED, EVIL MACBETH WILL SEEM AS PURE AS SNOW, AND POOR SCOTLAND WILL CALL HIM A SWEET LAMB COMPARED TO ME AND MY INFINITE EVILS.

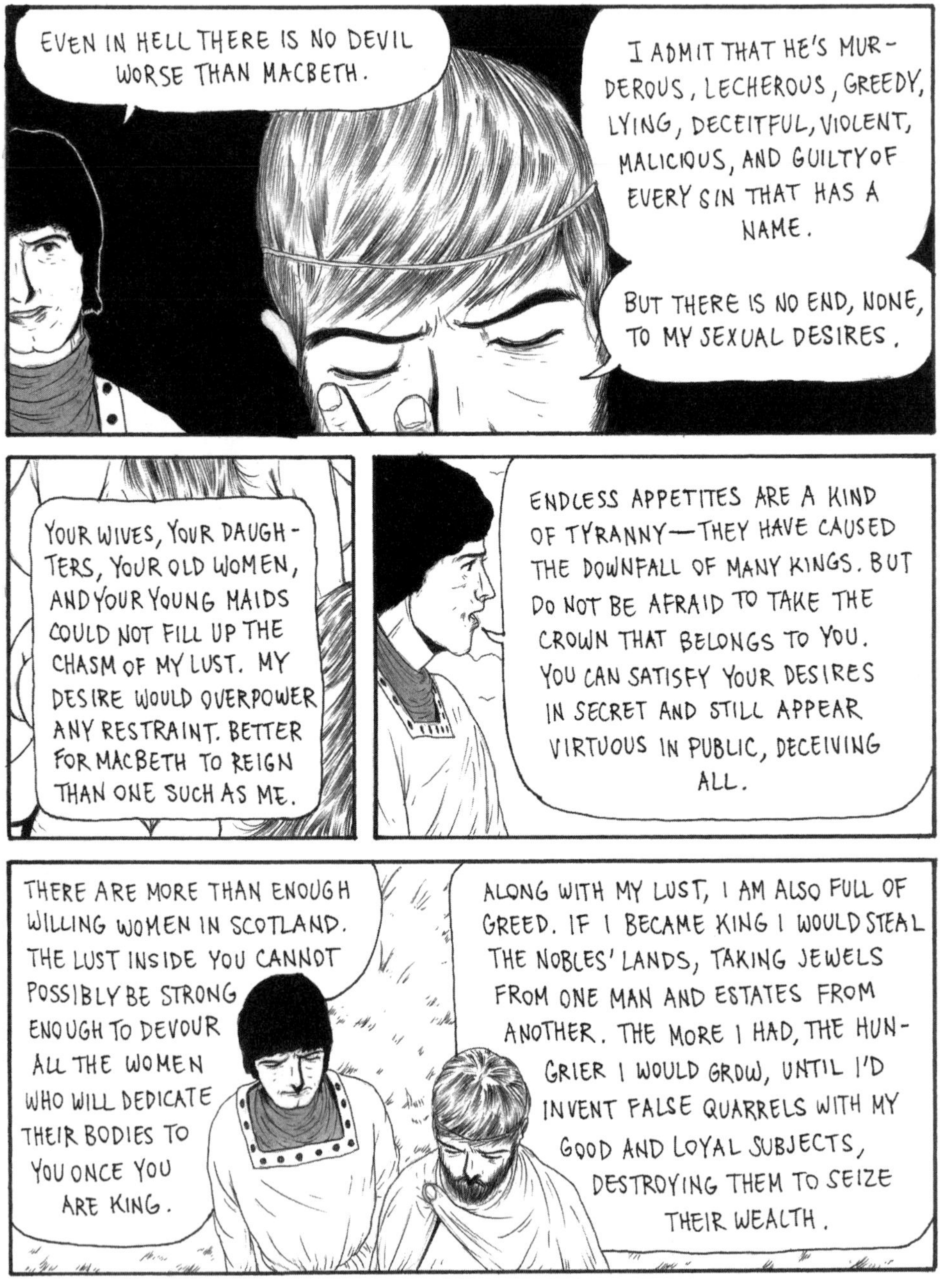
EVEN IN HELL THERE IS NO DEVIL WORSE THAN MACBETH.
I ADMIT THAT HE'S MURDEROUS, LECHEROUS, GREEDY, LYING, DECEITFUL, VIOLENT, MALICIOUS, AND GUILTY OF EVERY SIN THAT HAS A NAME.
BUT THERE IS NO END, NONE, TO MY SEXUAL DESIRES.
YOUR WIVES, YOUR DAUGHTERS, YOUR OLD WOMEN, AND YOUR YOUNG MAIDS COULD NOT FILL UP THE CHASM OF MY LUST. MY DESIRE WOULD OVERPOWER ANY RESTRAINT. BETTER FOR MACBETH TO REIGN THAN ONE SUCH AS ME.
ENDLESS APPETITES ARE A KIND OF TYRANNY—THEY HAVE CAUSED THE DOWNFALL OF MANY KINGS. BUT DO NOT BE AFRAID TO TAKE THE CROWN THAT BELONGS TO YOU. YOU CAN SATISFY YOUR DESIRES IN SECRET AND STILL APPEAR VIRTUOUS IN PUBLIC, DECEIVING ALL.
THERE ARE MORE THAN ENOUGH WILLING WOMEN IN SCOTLAND. THE LUST INSIDE YOU CANNOT POSSIBLY BE STRONG ENOUGH TO DEVOUR ALL THE WOMEN WHO WILL DEDICATE THEIR BODIES TO YOU ONCE YOU ARE KING.
ALONG WITH MY LUST, I AM ALSO FULL OF GREED. IF I BECAME KING I WOULD STEAL THE NOBLES' LANDS, TAKING JEWELS FROM ONE MAN AND ESTATES FROM ANOTHER. THE MORE I HAD, THE HUNGRIER I WOULD GROW, UNTIL I'D INVENT FALSE QUARRELS WITH MY GOOD AND LOYAL SUBJECTS, DESTROYING THEM TO SEIZE THEIR WEALTH.

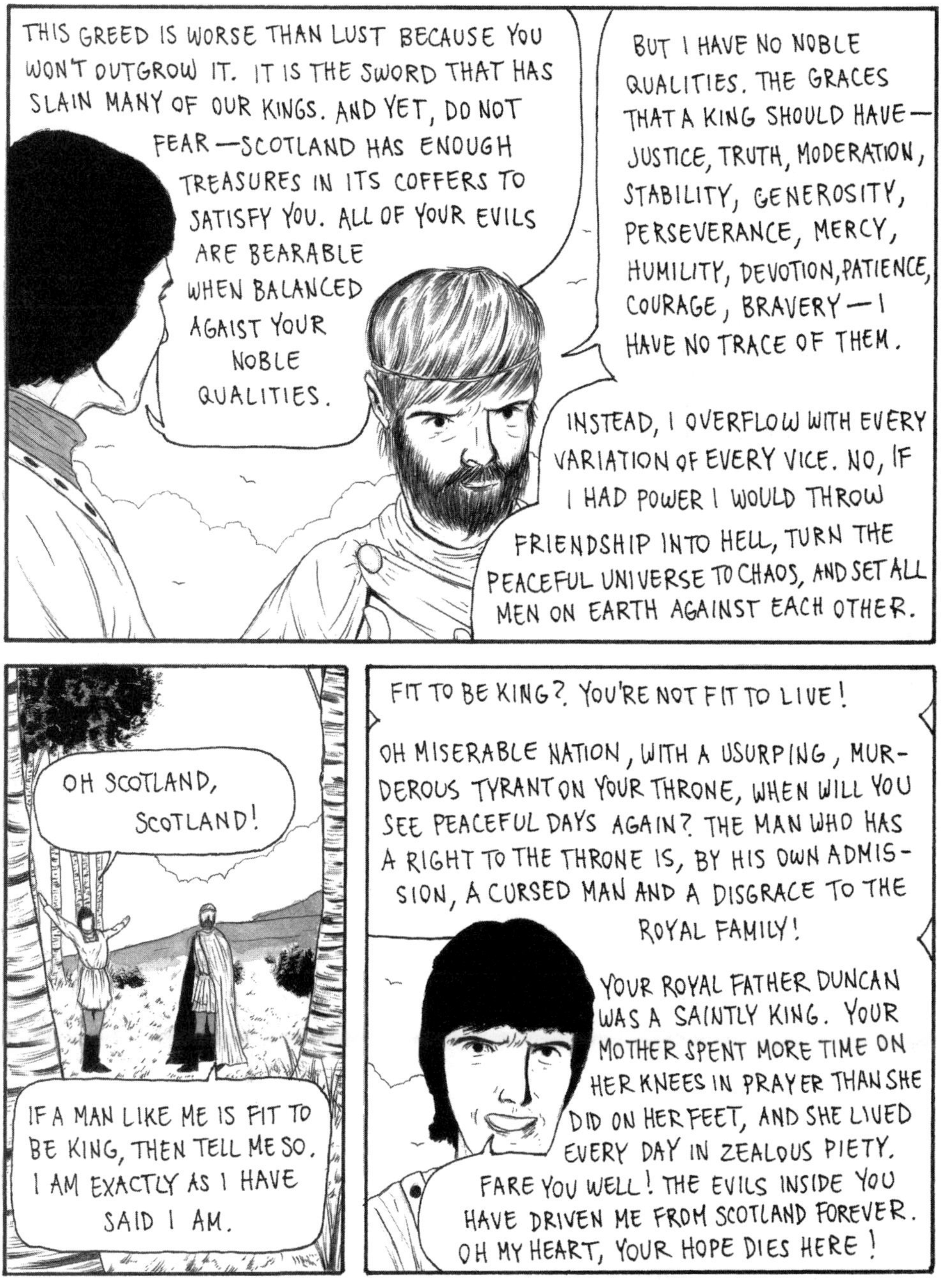
THIS GREED IS WORSE THAN LUST BECAUSE YOU WON'T OUTGROW IT. IT IS THE SWORD THAT HAS SLAIN MANY OF OUR KINGS. AND YET, DO NOT FEAR—SCOTLAND HAS ENOUGH TREASURES IN ITS COFFERS TO SATISFY YOU. ALL OF YOUR EVILS ARE BEARABLE WHEN BALANCED AGAIST YOUR NOBLE QUALITIES.
BUT I HAVE NO NOBLE QUALITIES. THE GRACES THAT A KING SHOULD HAVE—JUSTICE, TRUTH, MODERATION, STABILITY, GENEROSITY, PERSEVERANCE, MERCY, HUMILITY, DEVOTION, PATIENCE, COURAGE, BRAVERY—I HAVE NO TRACE OF THEM.
INSTEAD, I OVERFLOW WITH EVERY VARIATION OF EVERY VICE. NO, IF I HAD POWER I WOULD THROW FRIENDSHIP INTO HELL, TURN THE PEACEFUL UNIVERSE TO CHAOS, AND SET ALL MEN ON EARTH AGAINST EACH OTHER.
OH SCOTLAND, SCOTLAND!
IF A MAN LIKE ME IS FIT TO BE KING, THEN TELL ME SO. I AM EXACTLY AS I HAVE SAID I AM.
FIT TO BE KING? YOU'RE NOT FIT TO LIVE!
OH MISERABLE NATION, WITH A USURPING, MURDEROUS TYRANT ON YOUR THRONE, WHEN WILL YOU SEE PEACEFUL DAYS AGAIN? THE MAN WHO HAS A RIGHT TO THE THRONE IS, BY HIS OWN ADMISSION, A CURSED MAN AND A DISGRACE TO THE ROYAL FAMILY!
YOUR ROYAL FATHER DUNCAN WAS A SAINTLY KING. YOUR MOTHER SPENT MORE TIME ON HER KNEES IN PRAYER THAN SHE DID ON HER FEET, AND SHE LIVED EVERY DAY IN ZEALOUS PIETY.
FARE YOU WELL! THE EVILS INSIDE YOU HAVE DRIVEN ME FROM SCOTLAND FOREVER. OH MY HEART, YOUR HOPE DIES HERE!

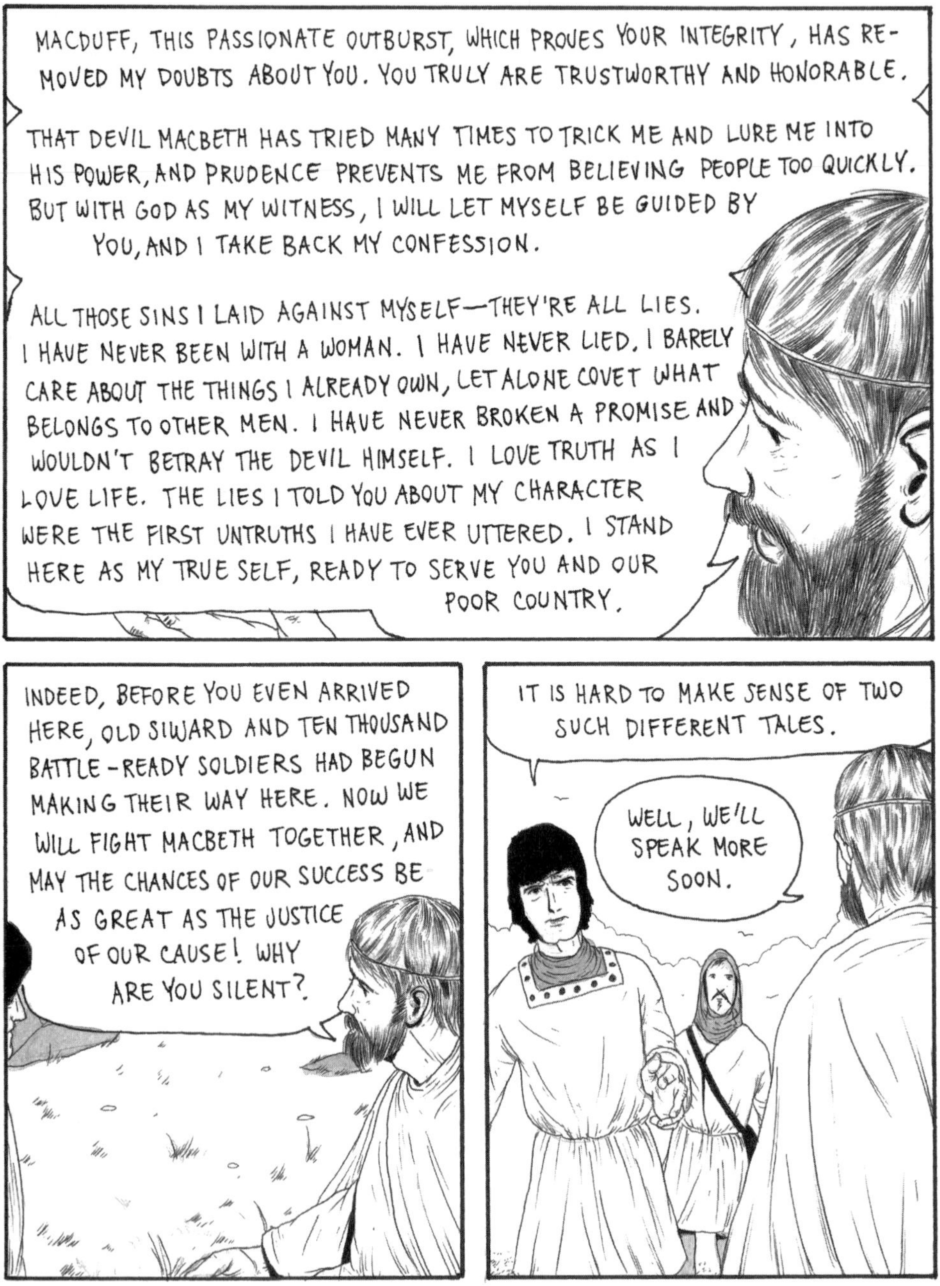
MACDUFF, THIS PASSIONATE OUTBURST, WHICH PROVES YOUR INTEGRITY, HAS REMOVED MY DOUBTS ABOUT YOU. YOU TRULY ARE TRUSTWORTHY AND HONORABLE.
THAT DEVIL MACBETH HAS TRIED MANY TIMES TO TRICK ME AND LURE ME INTO HIS POWER, AND PRUDENCE PREVENTS ME FROM BELIEVING PEOPLE TOO QUICKLY. BUT WITH GOD AS MY WITNESS, I WILL LET MYSELF BE GUIDED BY YOU, AND I TAKE BACK MY CONFESSION.
ALL THOSE SINS I LAID AGAINST MYSELF—THEY'RE ALL LIES. I HAVE NEVER BEEN WITH A WOMAN. I HAVE NEVER LIED. I BARELY CARE ABOUT THE THINGS I ALREADY OWN, LET ALONE COVET WHAT BELONGS TO OTHER MEN. I HAVE NEVER BROKEN A PROMISE AND WOULDN'T BETRAY THE DEVIL HIMSELF. I LOVE TRUTH AS I LOVE LIFE. THE LIES I TOLD YOU ABOUT MY CHARACTER WERE THE FIRST UNTRUTHS I HAVE EVER UTTERED. I STAND HERE AS MY TRUE SELF, READY TO SERVE YOU AND OUR POOR COUNTRY.
INDEED, BEFORE YOU EVEN ARRIVED HERE, OLD SIWARD AND TEN THOUSAND BATTLE-READY SOLDIERS HAD BEGUN MAKING THEIR WAY HERE. NOW WE WILL FIGHT MACBETH TOGETHER, AND MAY THE CHANCES OF OUR SUCCESS BE AS GREAT AS THE JUSTICE OF OUR CAUSE! WHY ARE YOU SILENT?
IT IS HARD TO MAKE SENSE OF TWO SUCH DIFFERENT TALES.
WELL, WE'LL SPEAK MORE SOON.

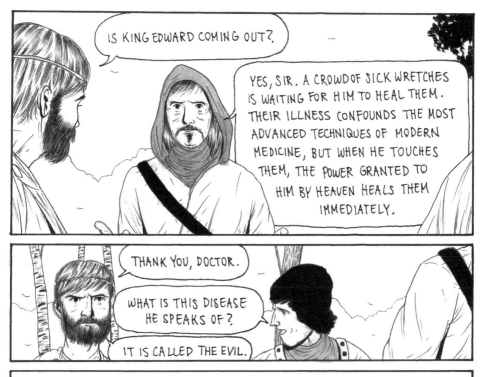

IS KING EDWARD COMING OUT?

YES, SIR. A CROWD OF SICK WRETCHES IS WAITING FOR HIM TO HEAL THEM. THEIR ILLNESS CONFOUNDS THE MOST ADVANCED TECHNIQUES OF MODERN MEDICINE, BUT WHEN HE TOUCHES THEM, THE POWER GRANTED TO HIM BY HEAVEN HEALS THEM IMMEDIATELY.

THANK YOU, DOCTOR.

WHAT IS THIS DISEASE HE SPEAKS OF?

IT IS CALLED THE EVIL.

EDWARD'S HEALING TOUCH IS A MIRACLE THAT I HAVE SEEN HIM PERFORM MANY TIMES DURING MY STAY IN ENGLAND. HOW HE RECEIVES THESE GIFTS FROM HEAVEN, ONLY HE CAN SAY. BUT HE CURES PEOPLE WITH STRANGE CONDITIONS—ALL SWOLLEN, PLAGUED BY ULCERS, AND PITIFUL TO LOOK AT, PATIENTS WHO ARE BEYOND HELP OF SURGERY— BY PLACING A GOLD COIN AROUND THEIR NECKS AND SAYING HOLY PRAYERS OVER THEM. THEY SAY THAT HE BEQUEATHS THIS ABILITY TO HEAL TO HIS ROYAL DESCENDANTS. ALONG WITH THIS STRANGE POWER, HE ALSO HAS THE GIFT OF PROPHECY, AS WELL AS OTHER BLESSINGS THAT MARK HIM AS A MAN GRACED BY GOD.

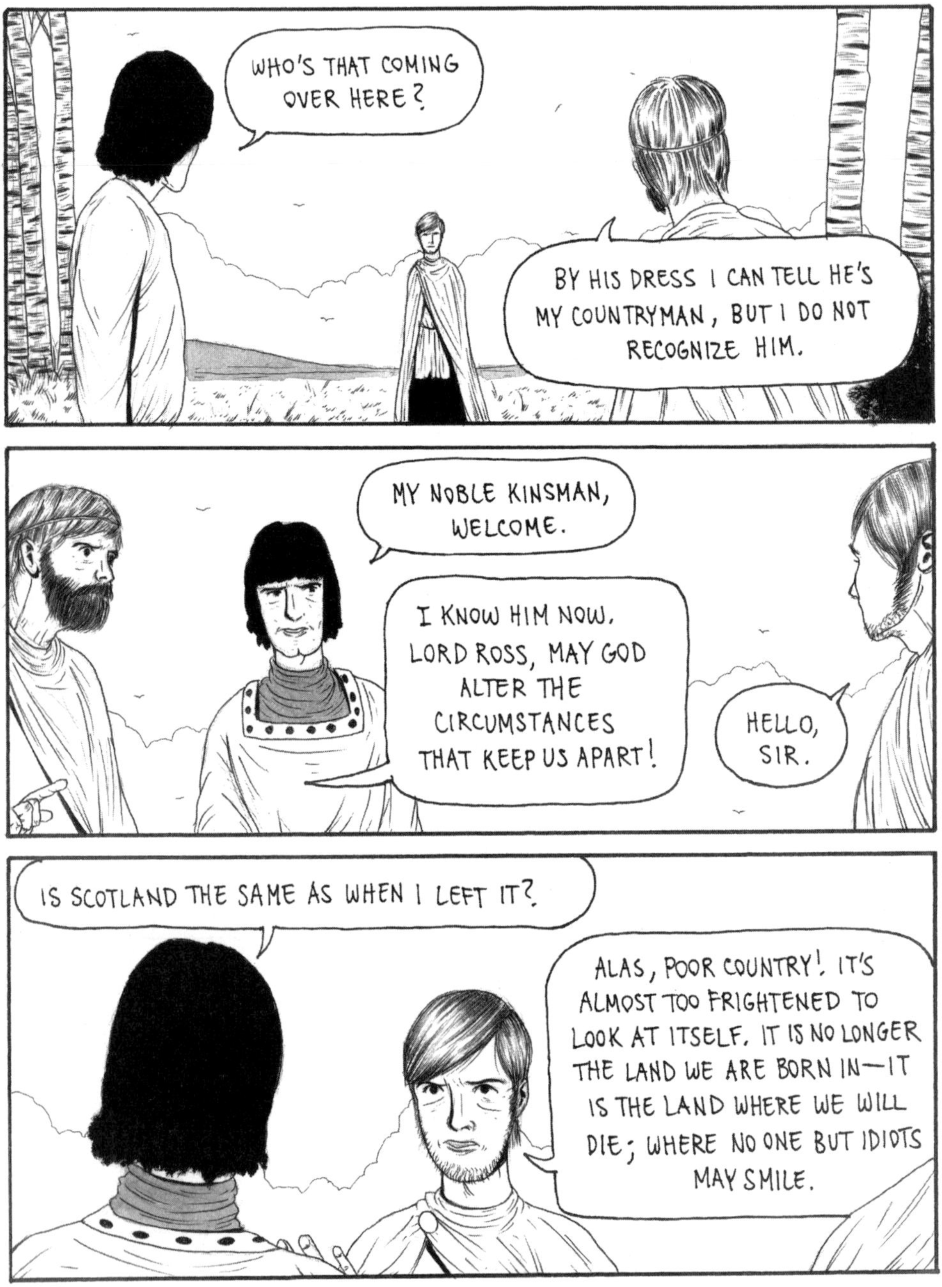
WHO'S THAT COMING OVER HERE?
BY HIS DRESS I CAN TELL HE'S MY COUNTRYMAN, BUT I DO NOT RECOGNIZE HIM.
MY NOBLE KINSMAN, WELCOME.
I KNOW HIM NOW. LORD ROSS, MAY GOD ALTER THE CIRCUMSTANCES THAT KEEP US APART!
HELLO, SIR.
IS SCOTLAND THE SAME AS WHEN I LEFT IT?
ALAS, POOR COUNTRY! IT'S ALMOST TOO FRIGHTENED TO LOOK AT ITSELF. IT IS NO LONGER THE LAND WE ARE BORN IN—IT IS THE LAND WHERE WE WILL DIE; WHERE NO ONE BUT IDIOTS MAY SMILE.

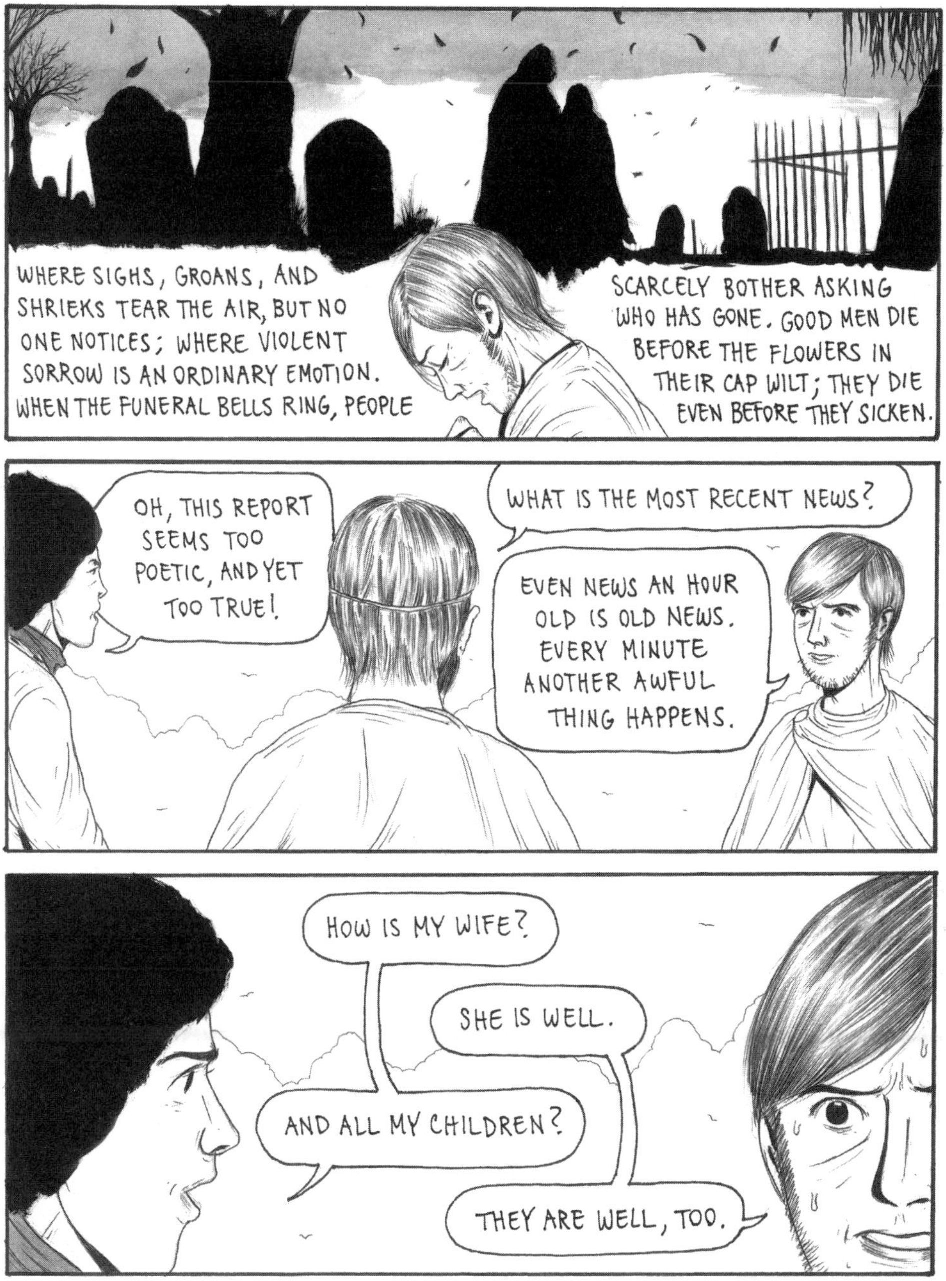
WHERE SIGHS, GROANS, AND SHRIEKS TEAR THE AIR, BUT NO ONE NOTICES; WHERE VIOLENT SORROW IS AN ORDINARY EMOTION. WHEN THE FUNERAL BELLS RING, PEOPLE
SCARCELY BOTHER ASKING WHO HAS GONE. GOOD MEN DIE BEFORE THE FLOWERS IN THEIR CAP WILT; THEY DIE EVEN BEFORE THEY SICKEN.
OH, THIS REPORT SEEMS TOO POETIC, AND YET TOO TRUE!
WHAT IS THE MOST RECENT NEWS?
EVEN NEWS AN HOUR OLD IS OLD NEWS. EVERY MINUTE ANOTHER AWFUL THING HAPPENS.
HOW IS MY WIFE?
SHE IS WELL.
AND ALL MY CHILDREN?
THEY ARE WELL, TOO.

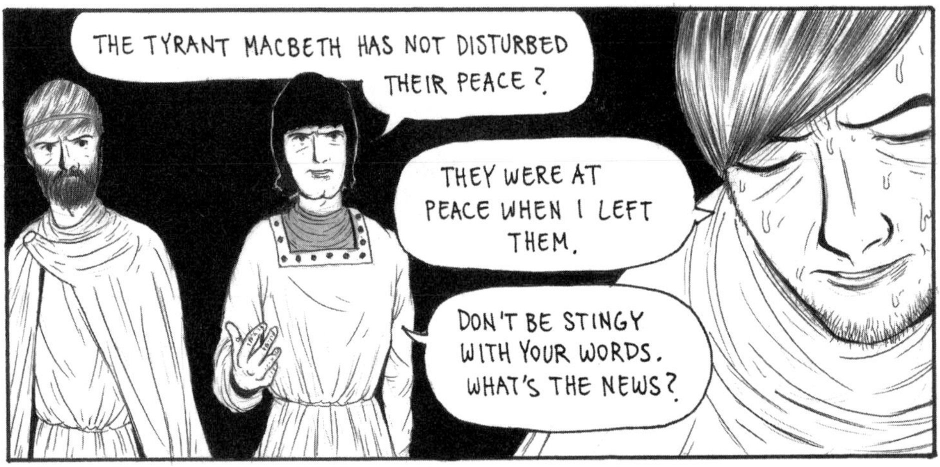
THE TYRANT MACBETH HAS NOT DISTURBED THEIR PEACE?
THEY WERE AT PEACE WHEN I LEFT THEM.
DON'T BE STINGY WITH YOUR WORDS. WHAT'S THE NEWS?

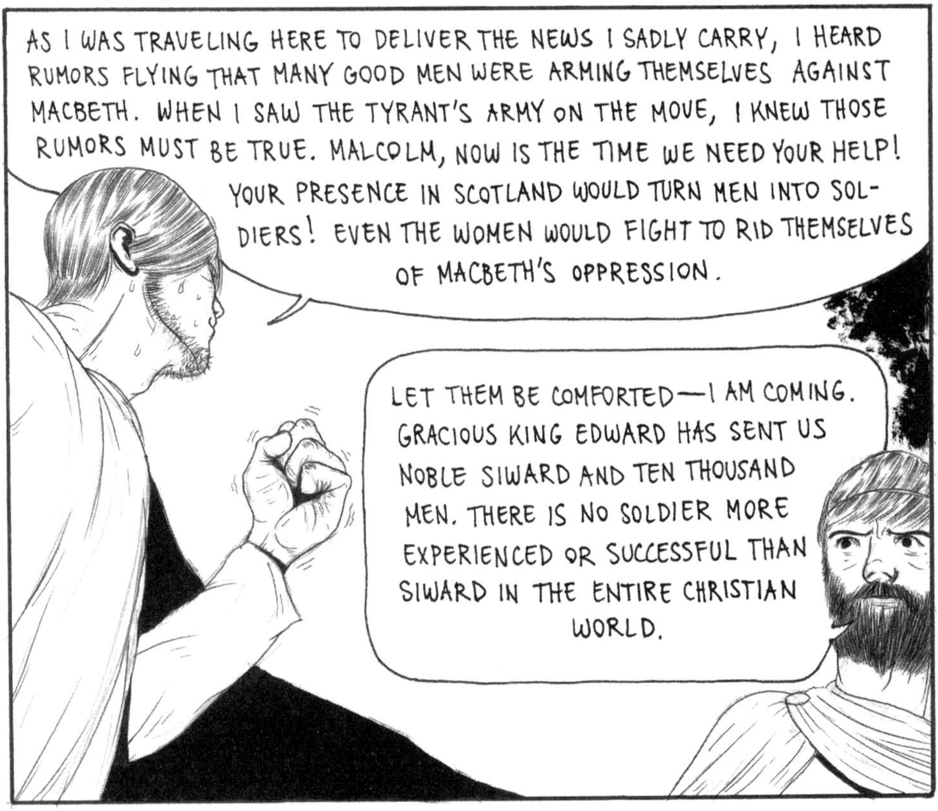
AS I WAS TRAVELING HERE TO DELIVER THE NEWS I SADLY CARRY, I HEARD RUMORS FLYING THAT MANY GOOD MEN WERE ARMING THEMSELVES AGAINST MACBETH. WHEN I SAW THE TYRANT'S ARMY ON THE MOVE, I KNEW THOSE RUMORS MUST BE TRUE. MALCOLM, NOW IS THE TIME WE NEED YOUR HELP! YOUR PRESENCE IN SCOTLAND WOULD TURN MEN INTO SOLDIERS! EVEN THE WOMEN WOULD FIGHT TO RID THEMSELVES OF MACBETH'S OPPRESSION.
LET THEM BE COMFORTED—I AM COMING. GRACIOUS KING EDWARD HAS SENT US NOBLE SIWARD AND TEN THOUSAND MEN. THERE IS NO SOLDIER MORE EXPERIENCED OR SUCCESSFUL THAN SIWARD IN THE ENTIRE CHRISTIAN WORLD.

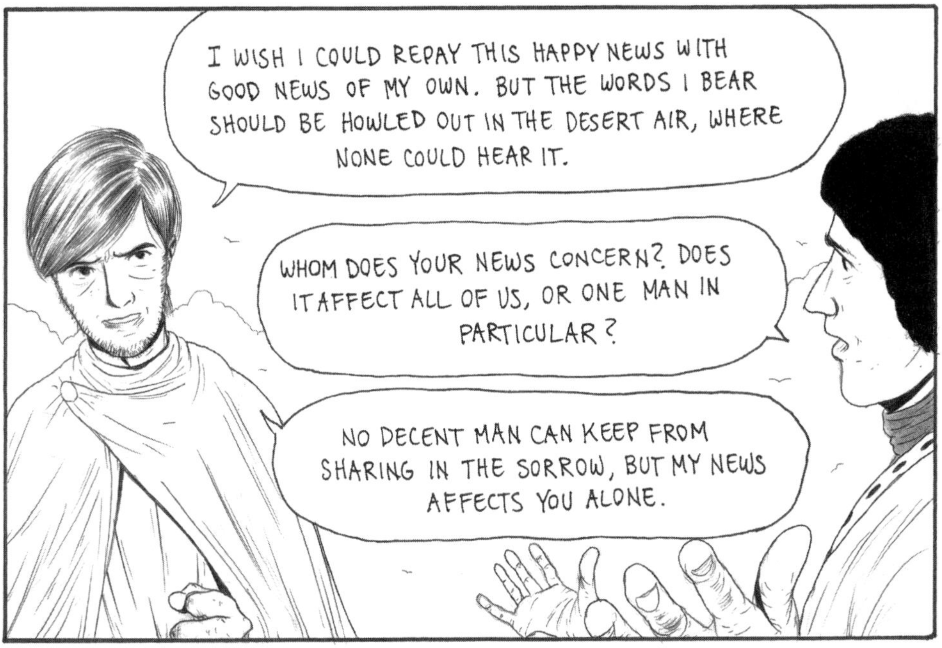
I WISH I COULD REPAY THIS HAPPY NEWS WITH GOOD NEWS OF MY OWN. BUT THE WORDS I BEAR SHOULD BE HOWLED OUT IN THE DESERT AIR, WHERE NONE COULD HEAR IT.
WHOM DOES YOUR NEWS CONCERN? DOES IT AFFECT ALL OF US, OR ONE MAN IN PARTICULAR?
NO DECENT MAN CAN KEEP FROM SHARING IN THE SORROW, BUT MY NEWS AFFECTS YOU ALONE.

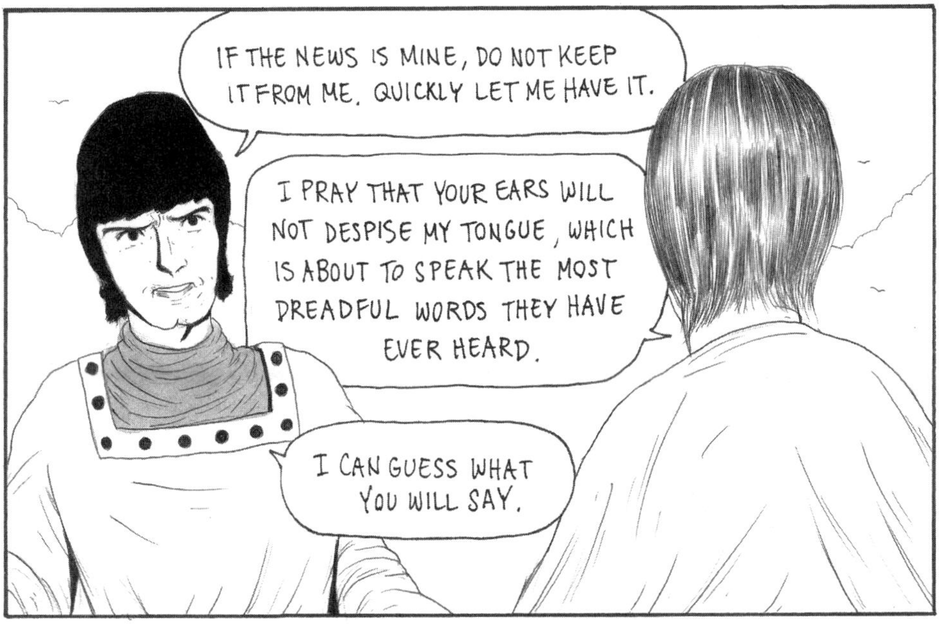
IF THE NEWS IS MINE, DO NOT KEEP IT FROM ME. QUICKLY LET ME HAVE IT.
I PRAY THAT YOUR EARS WILL NOT DESPISE MY TONGUE, WHICH IS ABOUT TO SPEAK THE MOST DREADFUL WORDS THEY HAVE EVER HEARD.
I CAN GUESS WHAT YOU WILL SAY.

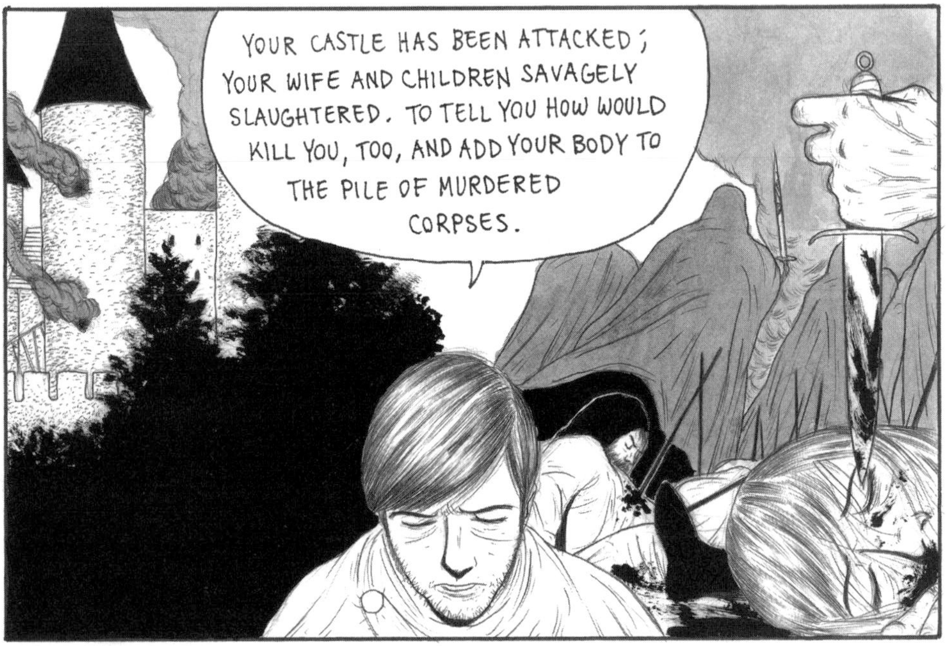
YOUR CASTLE HAS BEEN ATTACKED; YOUR WIFE AND CHILDREN SAVAGELY SLAUGHTERED. TO TELL YOU HOW WOULD KILL YOU, TOO, AND ADD YOUR BODY TO THE PILE OF MURDERED CORPSES.

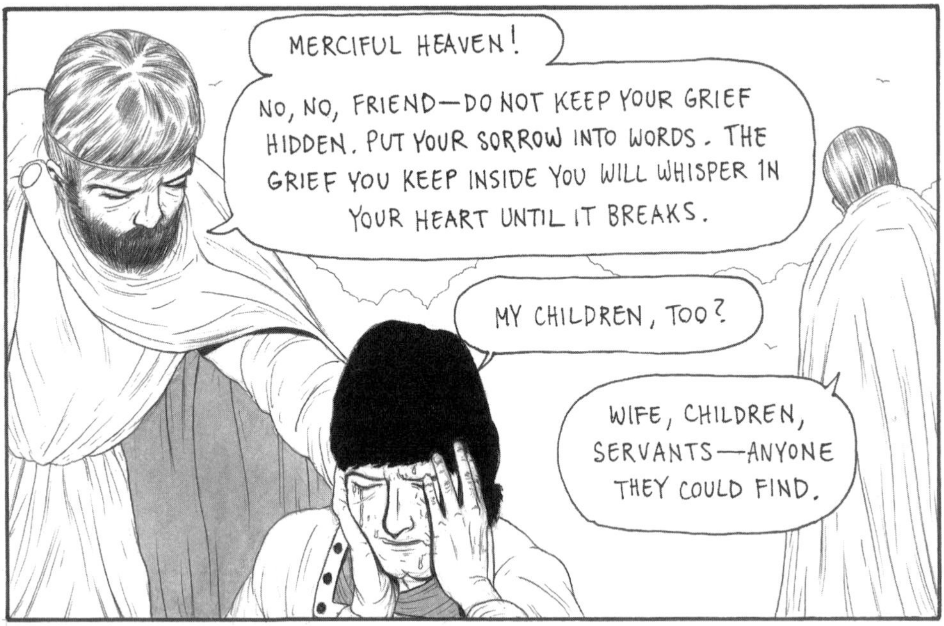
MERCIFUL HEAVEN!
NO, NO, FRIEND—DO NOT KEEP YOUR GRIEF HIDDEN. PUT YOUR SORROW INTO WORDS. THE GRIEF YOU KEEP INSIDE YOU WILL WHISPER IN YOUR HEART UNTIL IT BREAKS.
MY CHILDREN, TOO?
WIFE, CHILDREN, SERVANTS—ANYONE THEY COULD FIND.

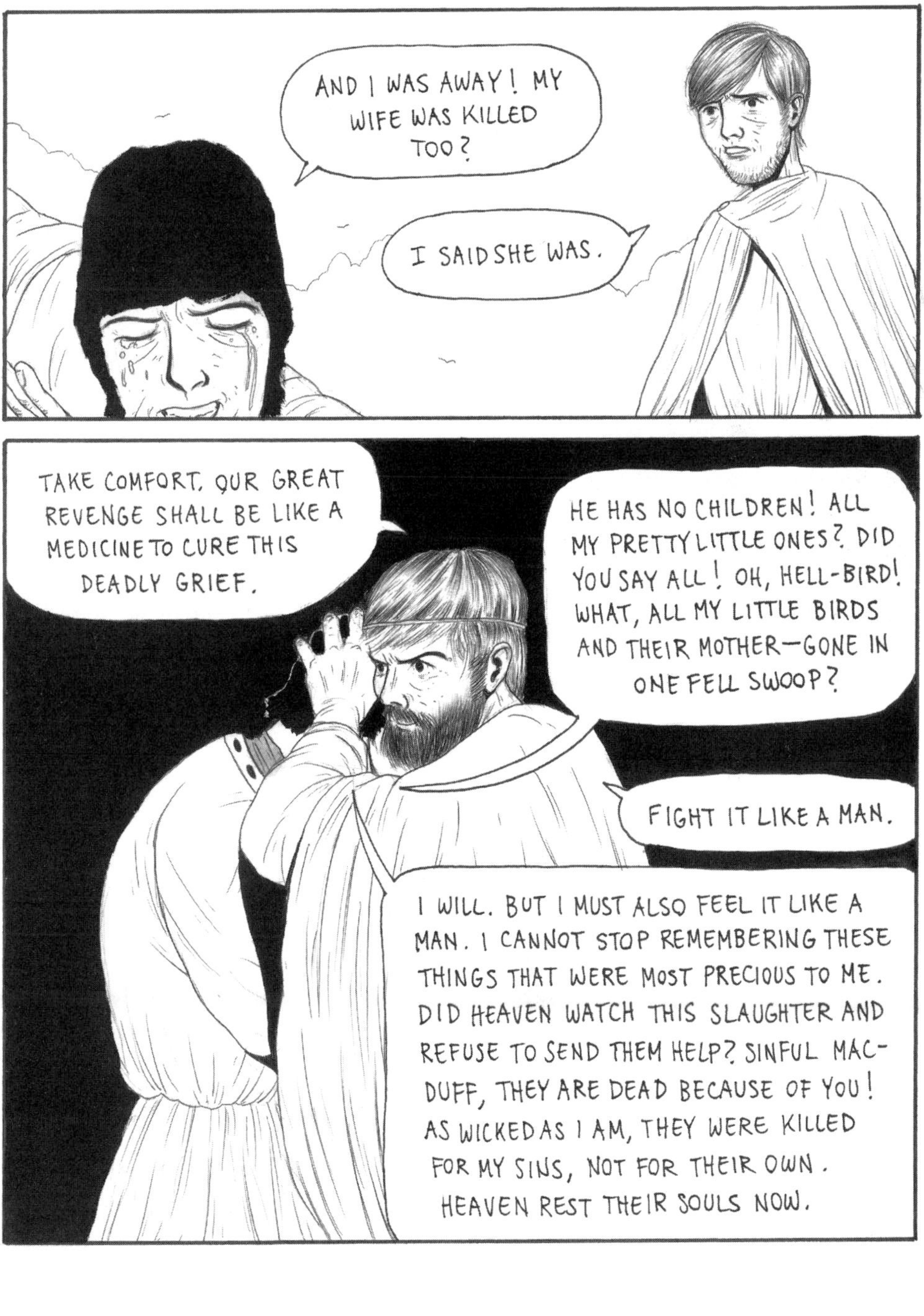
AND I WAS AWAY! MY WIFE WAS KILLED TOO?
I SAID SHE WAS.
TAKE COMFORT. OUR GREAT REVENGE SHALL BE LIKE A MEDICINE TO CURE THIS DEADLY GRIEF.
HE HAS NO CHILDREN! ALL MY PRETTY LITTLE ONES? DID YOU SAY ALL! OH, HELL-BIRD! WHAT, ALL MY LITTLE BIRDS AND THEIR MOTHER—GONE IN ONE FELL SWOOP?
FIGHT IT LIKE A MAN.
I WILL. BUT I MUST ALSO FEEL IT LIKE A MAN. I CANNOT STOP REMEMBERING THESE THINGS THAT WERE MOST PRECIOUS TO ME. DID HEAVEN WATCH THIS SLAUGHTER AND REFUSE TO SEND THEM HELP? SINFUL MACDUFF, THEY ARE DEAD BECAUSE OF YOU! AS WICKED AS I AM, THEY WERE KILLED FOR MY SINS, NOT FOR THEIR OWN. HEAVEN REST THEIR SOULS NOW.

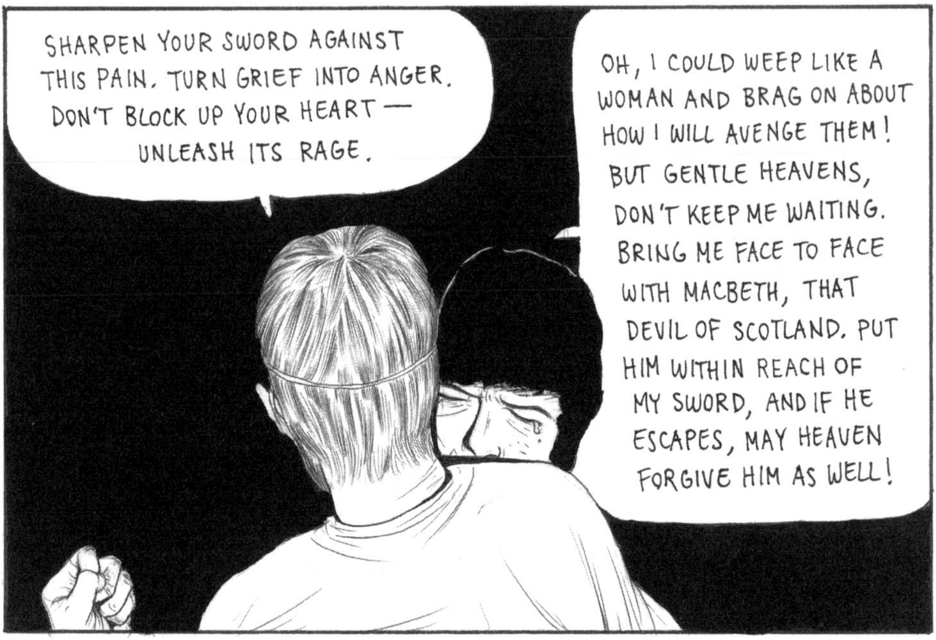
SHARPEN YOUR SWORD AGAINST THIS PAIN. TURN GRIEF INTO ANGER. DON'T BLOCK UP YOUR HEART — UNLEASH ITS RAGE.
OH, I COULD WEEP LIKE A WOMAN AND BRAG ON ABOUT HOW I WILL AVENGE THEM! BUT GENTLE HEAVENS, DON'T KEEP ME WAITING. BRING ME FACE TO FACE WITH MACBETH, THAT DEVIL OF SCOTLAND. PUT HIM WITHIN REACH OF MY SWORD, AND IF HE ESCAPES, MAY HEAVEN FORGIVE HIM AS WELL!

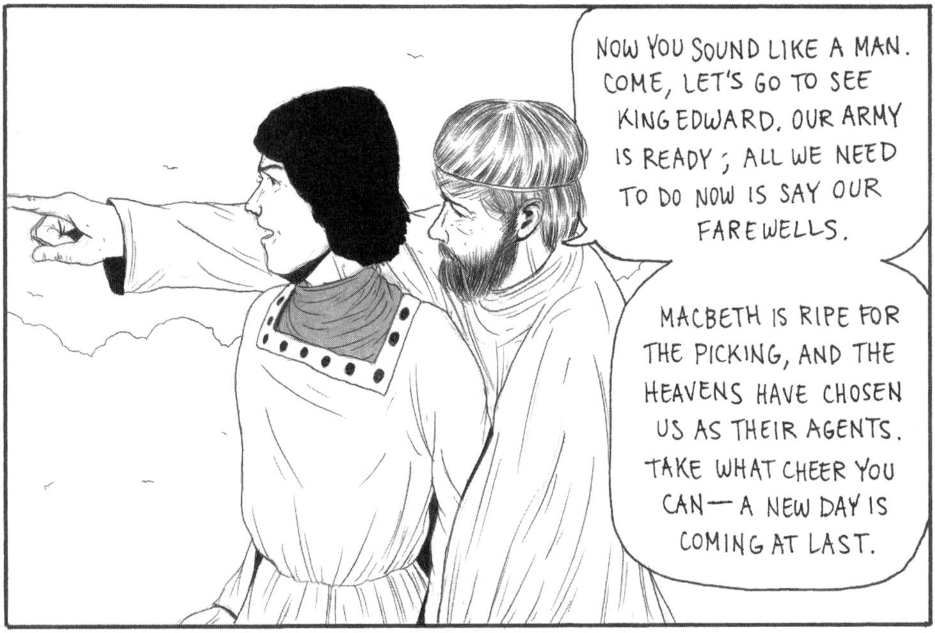
NOW YOU SOUND LIKE A MAN. COME, LET'S GO TO SEE KING EDWARD. OUR ARMY IS READY; ALL WE NEED TO DO NOW IS SAY OUR FAREWELLS.
MACBETH IS RIPE FOR THE PICKING, AND THE HEAVENS HAVE CHOSEN US AS THEIR AGENTS. TAKE WHAT CHEER YOU CAN — A NEW DAY IS COMING AT LAST.

ACT V

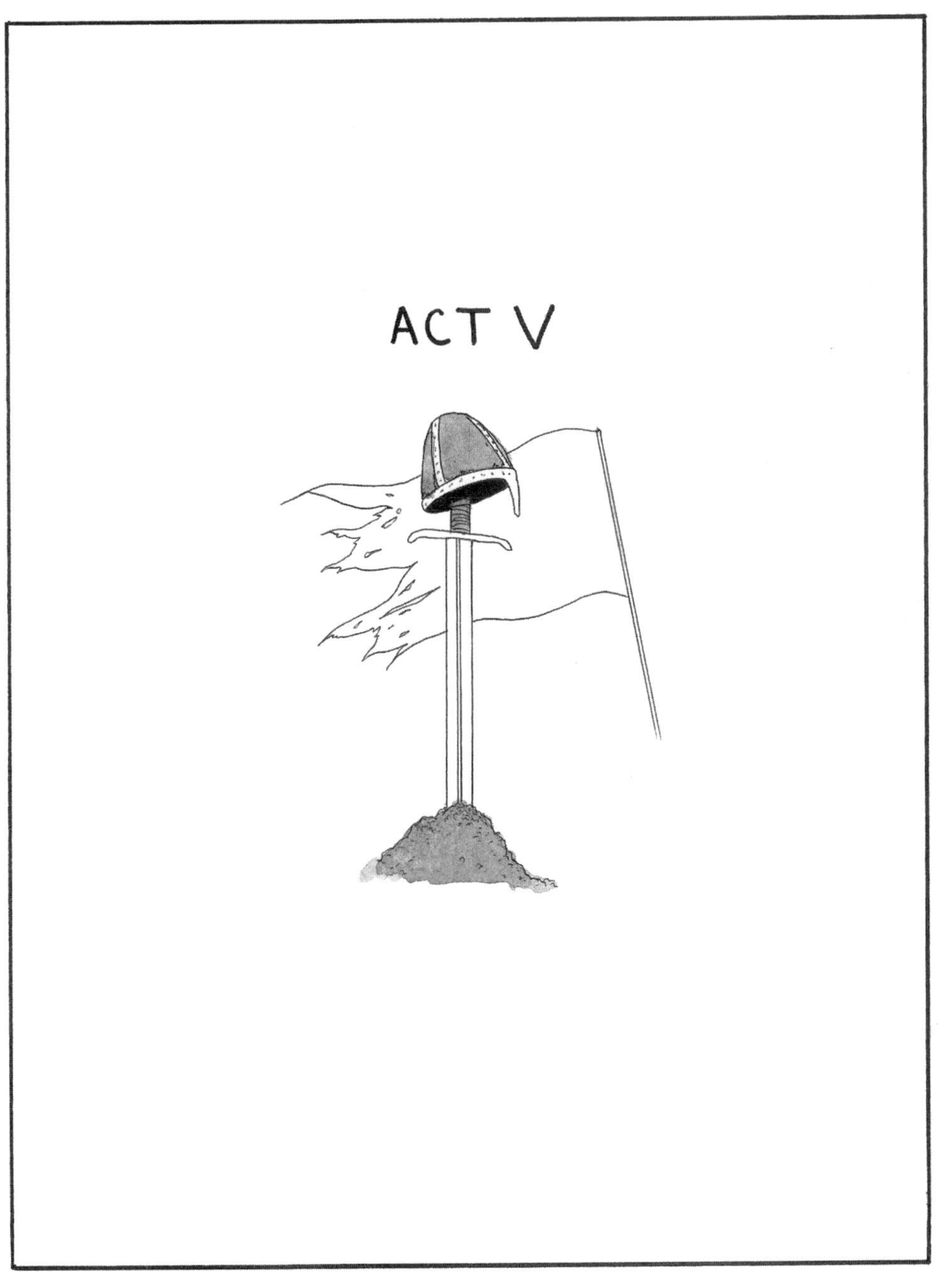

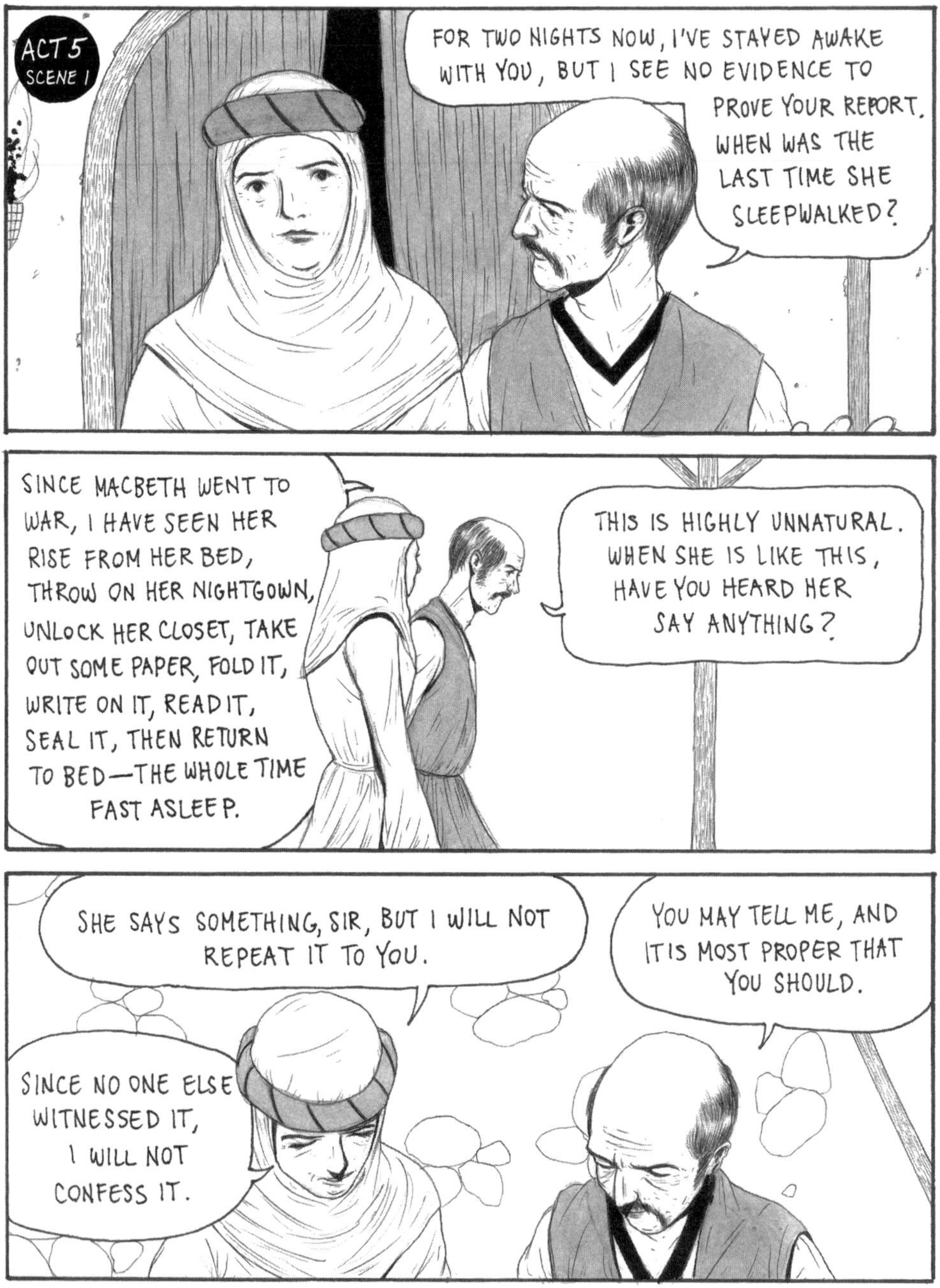
ACT 5 SCENE 1
FOR TWO NIGHTS NOW, I'VE STAYED AWAKE WITH YOU, BUT I SEE NO EVIDENCE TO PROVE YOUR REPORT. WHEN WAS THE LAST TIME SHE SLEEPWALKED?
SINCE MACBETH WENT TO WAR, I HAVE SEEN HER RISE FROM HER BED, THROW ON HER NIGHTGOWN, UNLOCK HER CLOSET, TAKE OUT SOME PAPER, FOLD IT, WRITE ON IT, READ IT, SEAL IT, THEN RETURN TO BED—THE WHOLE TIME FAST ASLEEP.
THIS IS HIGHLY UNNATURAL. WHEN SHE IS LIKE THIS, HAVE YOU HEARD HER SAY ANYTHING?
SHE SAYS SOMETHING, SIR, BUT I WILL NOT REPEAT IT TO YOU.
YOU MAY TELL ME, AND IT IS MOST PROPER THAT YOU SHOULD.
SINCE NO ONE ELSE WITNESSED IT, I WILL NOT CONFESS IT.

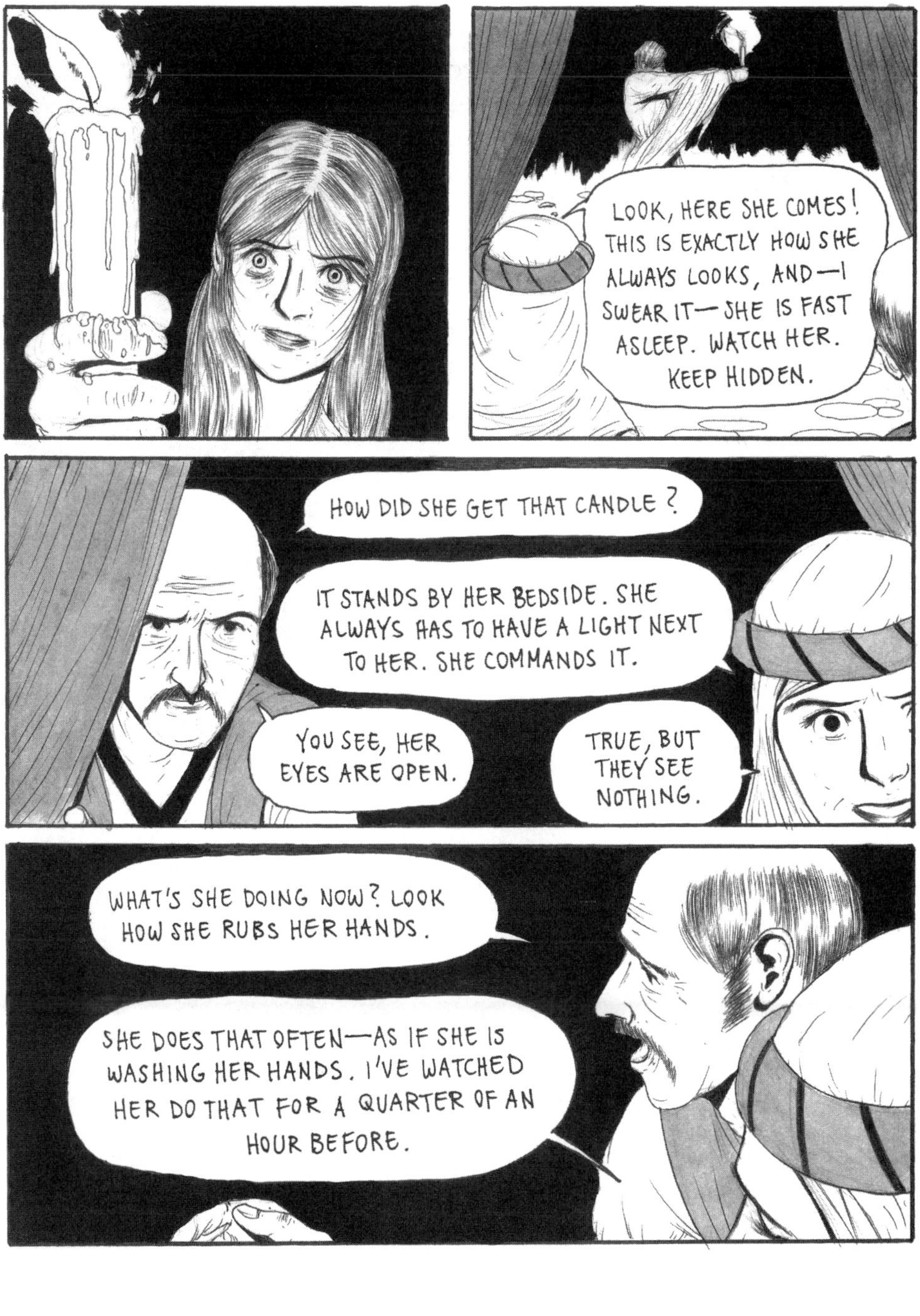
LOOK, HERE SHE COMES! THIS IS EXACTLY HOW SHE ALWAYS LOOKS, AND—I SWEAR IT—SHE IS FAST ASLEEP. WATCH HER. KEEP HIDDEN.
HOW DID SHE GET THAT CANDLE?
IT STANDS BY HER BEDSIDE. SHE ALWAYS HAS TO HAVE A LIGHT NEXT TO HER. SHE COMMANDS IT.
YOU SEE, HER EYES ARE OPEN.
TRUE, BUT THEY SEE NOTHING.
WHAT'S SHE DOING NOW? LOOK HOW SHE RUBS HER HANDS.
SHE DOES THAT OFTEN—AS IF SHE IS WASHING HER HANDS. I'VE WATCHED HER DO THAT FOR A QUARTER OF AN HOUR BEFORE.

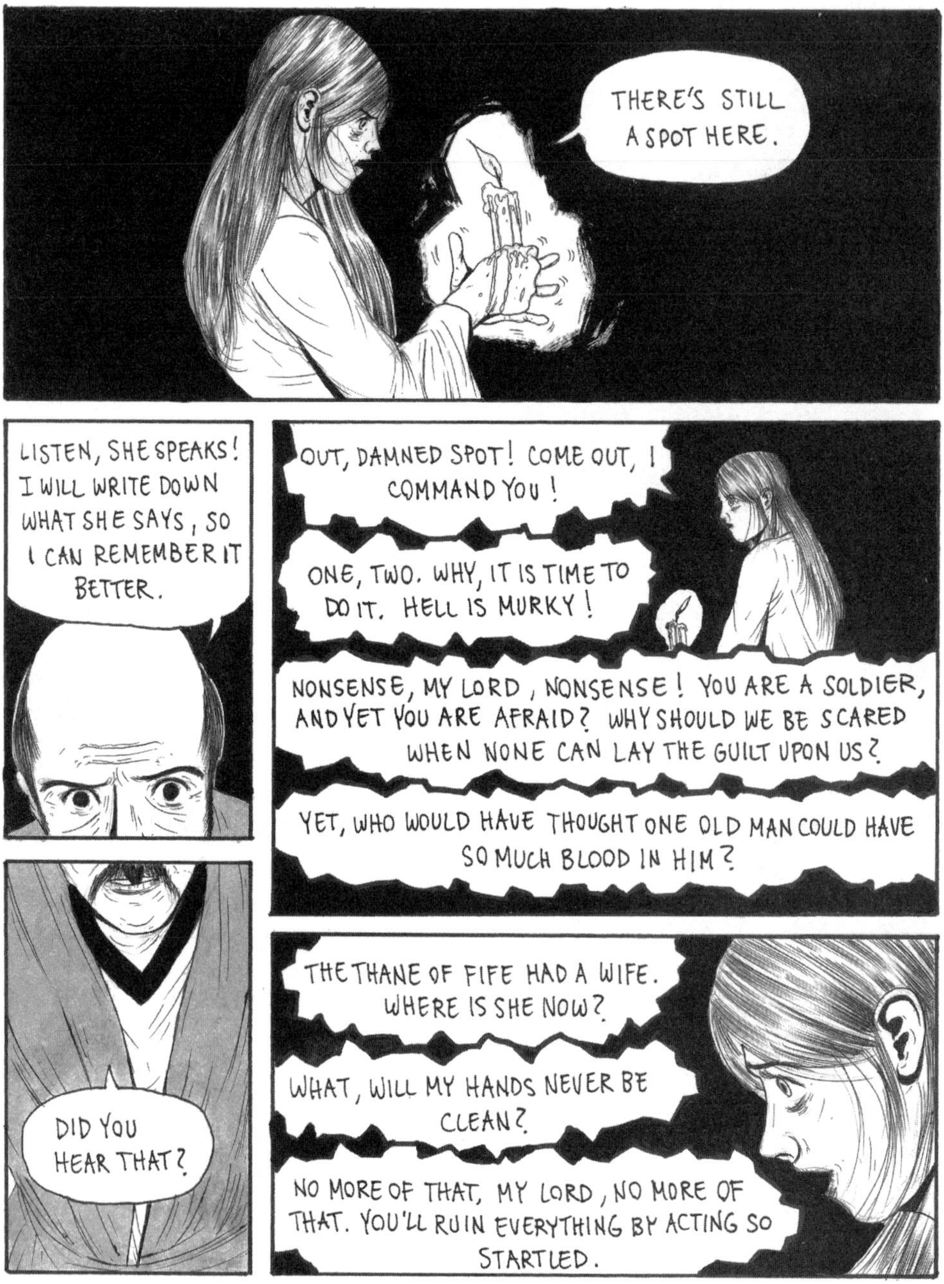
THERE'S STILL A SPOT HERE.
LISTEN, SHE SPEAKS! I WILL WRITE DOWN WHAT SHE SAYS, SO I CAN REMEMBER IT BETTER.
OUT, DAMNED SPOT! COME OUT, I COMMAND YOU!
ONE, TWO. WHY, IT IS TIME TO DO IT. HELL IS MURKY!
NONSENSE, MY LORD, NONSENSE! YOU ARE A SOLDIER, AND YET YOU ARE AFRAID? WHY SHOULD WE BE SCARED WHEN NONE CAN LAY THE GUILT UPON US?
YET, WHO WOULD HAVE THOUGHT ONE OLD MAN COULD HAVE SO MUCH BLOOD IN HIM?
DID YOU HEAR THAT?
THE THANE OF FIFE HAD A WIFE. WHERE IS SHE NOW?
WHAT, WILL MY HANDS NEVER BE CLEAN?
NO MORE OF THAT, MY LORD, NO MORE OF THAT. YOU'LL RUIN EVERYTHING BY ACTING SO STARTLED.

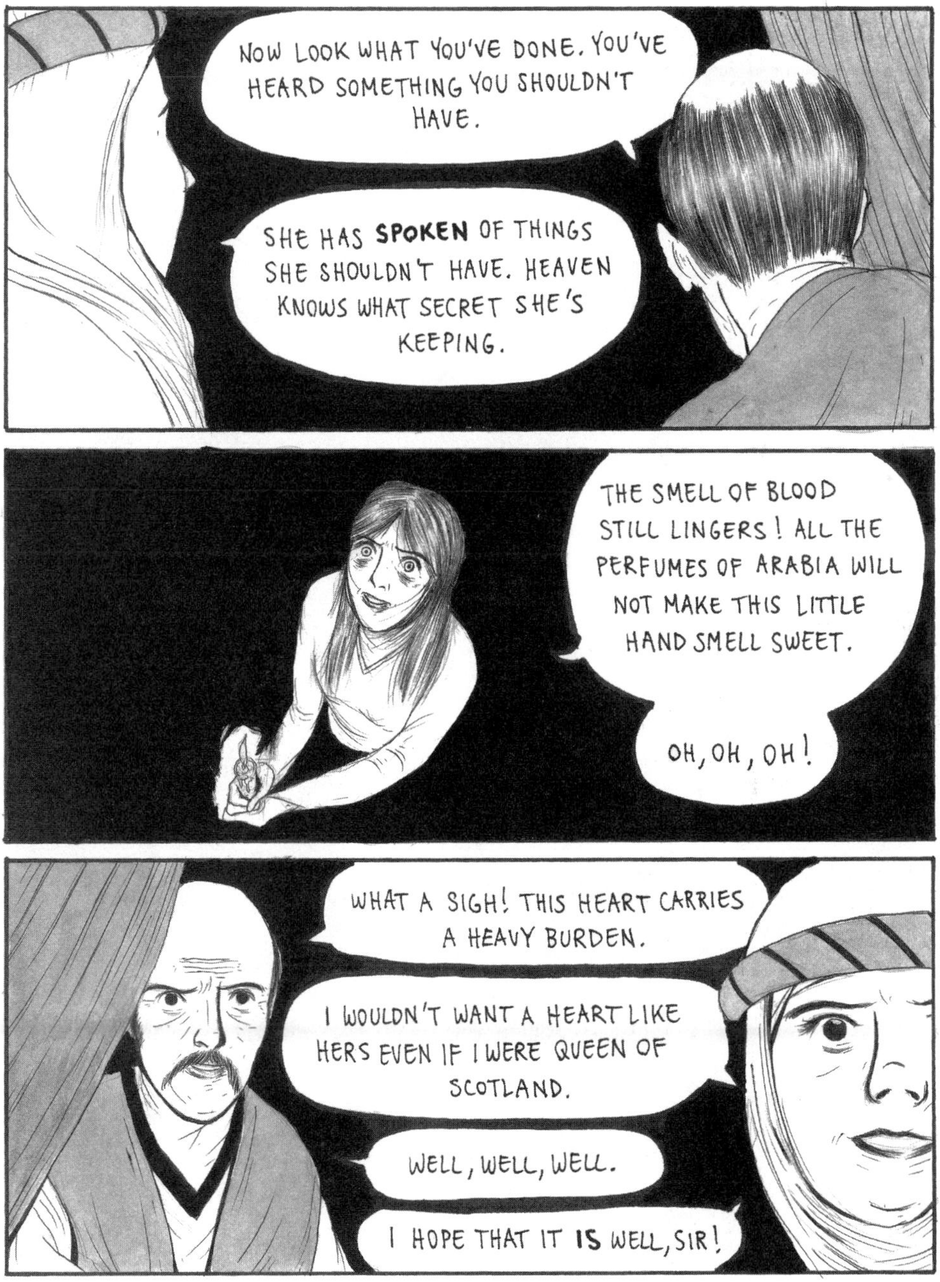
NOW LOOK WHAT YOU'VE DONE. YOU'VE HEARD SOMETHING YOU SHOULDN'T HAVE.
SHE HAS **SPOKEN** OF THINGS SHE SHOULDN'T HAVE. HEAVEN KNOWS WHAT SECRET SHE'S KEEPING.
THE SMELL OF BLOOD STILL LINGERS! ALL THE PERFUMES OF ARABIA WILL NOT MAKE THIS LITTLE HAND SMELL SWEET.
OH, OH, OH!
WHAT A SIGH! THIS HEART CARRIES A HEAVY BURDEN.
I WOULDN'T WANT A HEART LIKE HERS EVEN IF I WERE QUEEN OF SCOTLAND.
WELL, WELL, WELL.
I HOPE THAT IT **IS** WELL, SIR!

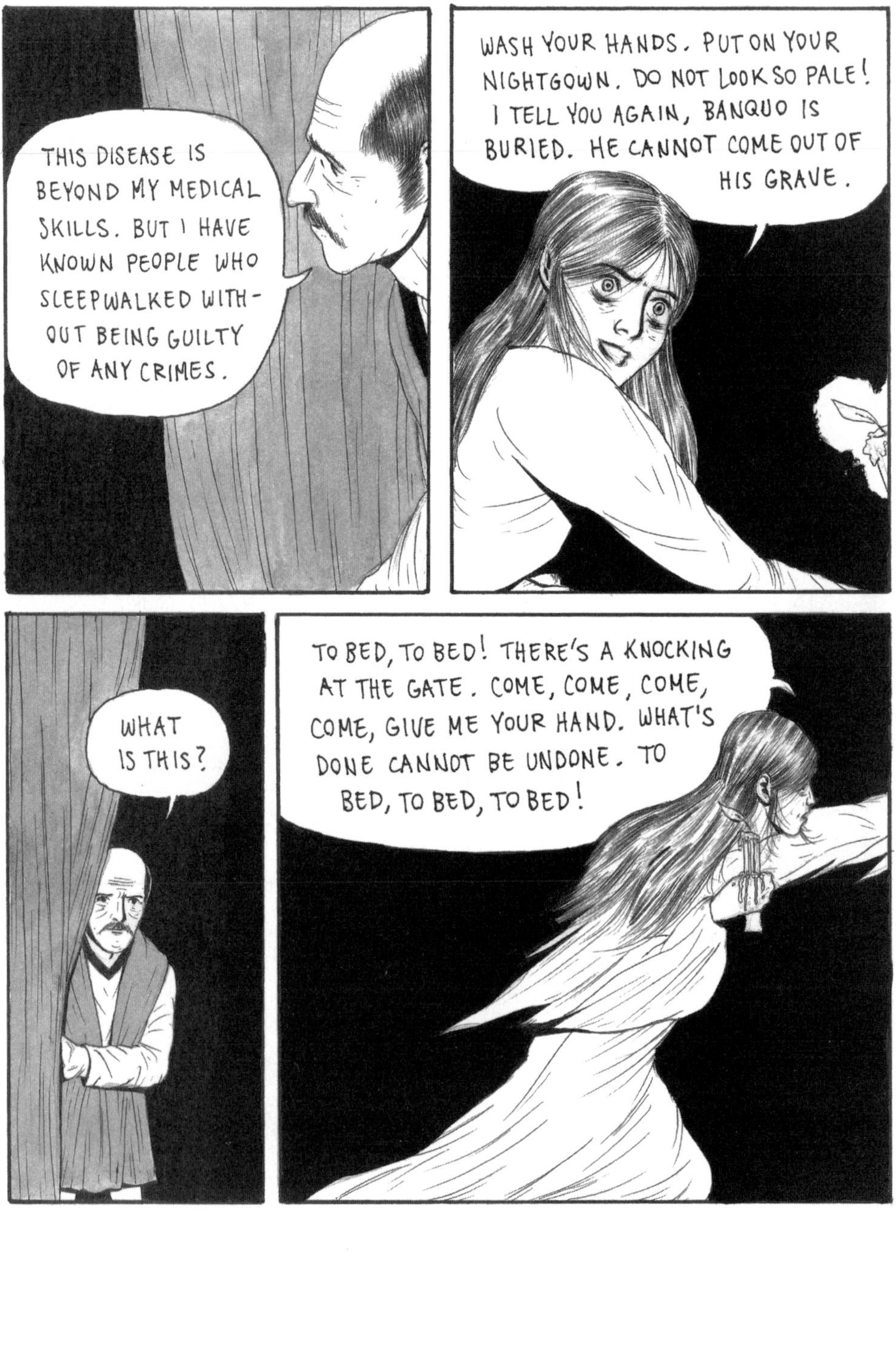
THIS DISEASE IS BEYOND MY MEDICAL SKILLS. BUT I HAVE KNOWN PEOPLE WHO SLEEPWALKED WITHOUT BEING GUILTY OF ANY CRIMES.
WASH YOUR HANDS. PUT ON YOUR NIGHTGOWN. DO NOT LOOK SO PALE! I TELL YOU AGAIN, BANQUO IS BURIED. HE CANNOT COME OUT OF HIS GRAVE.
WHAT IS THIS?
TO BED, TO BED! THERE'S A KNOCKING AT THE GATE. COME, COME, COME, COME, GIVE ME YOUR HAND. WHAT'S DONE CANNOT BE UNDONE. TO BED, TO BED, TO BED!

WILL SHE GO TO BED NOW?
YES, STRAIGHT THERE.
THERE ARE EVIL RUMORS GOING AROUND. UNNATURAL ACTS BRING UNNATURAL TROUBLES. THOSE WITH GUILTY AND DERANGED MINDS OFTEN CONFESS THEIR SECRETS TO THEIR PILLOWS AS THEY SLEEP. THE LADY NEEDS A PRIEST MORE THAN A PHYSICIAN. GOD FORGIVE US ALL!
LOOK AFTER HER; REMOVE ANYTHING THAT SHE MIGHT USE TO HARM HERSELF. WATCH HER CONSTANTLY. AND SO, GOOD NIGHT. SHE HAS BEWILDERED MY MIND AND AMAZED MY SIGHT. I DARE NOT SPEAK MY THOUGHTS ALOUD.
GOOD NIGHT, GOOD DOCTOR.

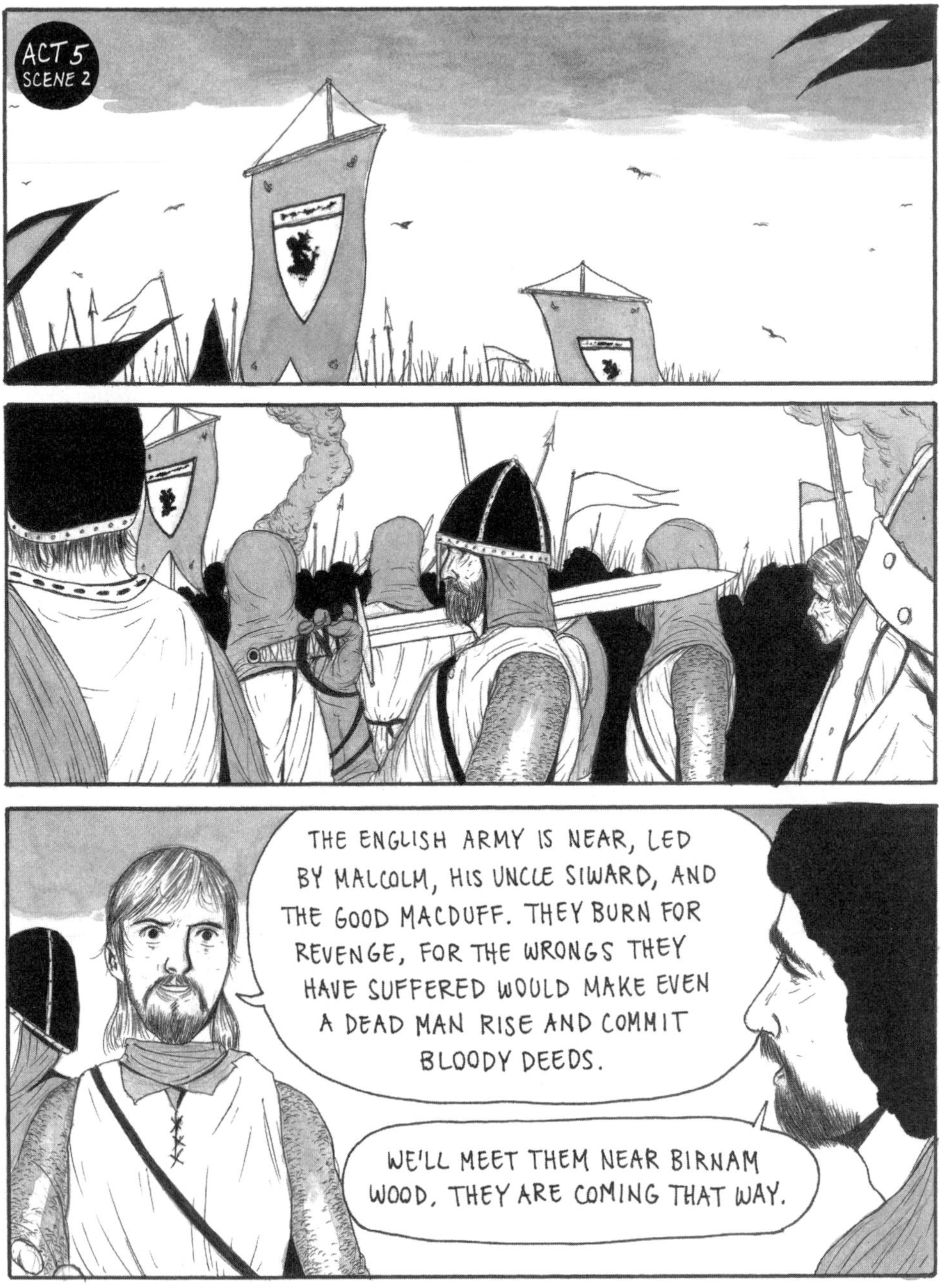
ACT 5
SCENE 2
THE ENGLISH ARMY IS NEAR, LED BY MALCOLM, HIS UNCLE SIWARD, AND THE GOOD MACDUFF. THEY BURN FOR REVENGE, FOR THE WRONGS THEY HAVE SUFFERED WOULD MAKE EVEN A DEAD MAN RISE AND COMMIT BLOODY DEEDS.
WE'LL MEET THEM NEAR BIRNAM WOOD. THEY ARE COMING THAT WAY.

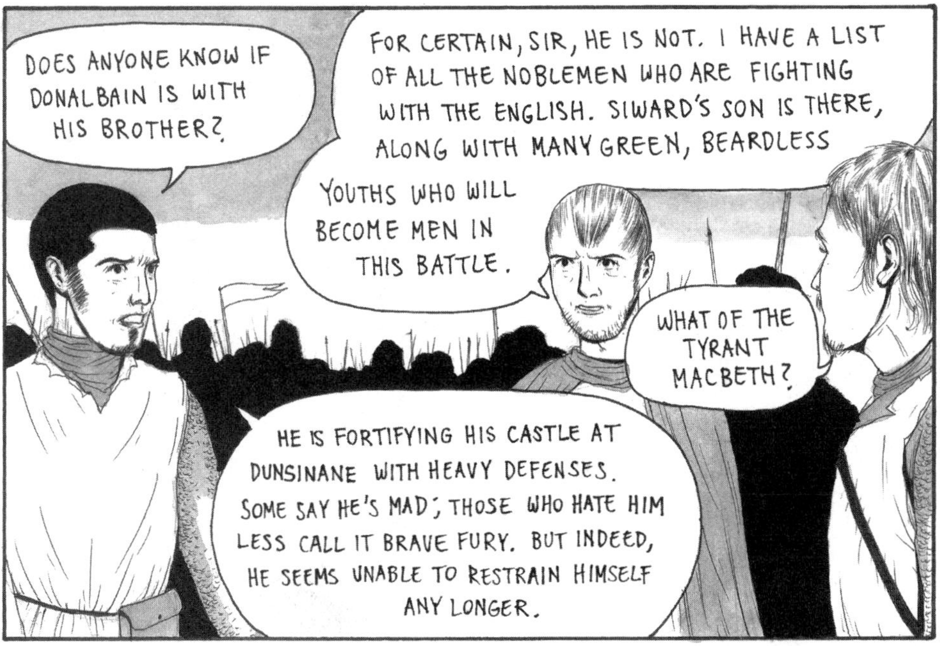
DOES ANYONE KNOW IF DONALBAIN IS WITH HIS BROTHER?
FOR CERTAIN, SIR, HE IS NOT. I HAVE A LIST OF ALL THE NOBLEMEN WHO ARE FIGHTING WITH THE ENGLISH. SIWARD'S SON IS THERE, ALONG WITH MANY GREEN, BEARDLESS
YOUTHS WHO WILL BECOME MEN IN THIS BATTLE.
WHAT OF THE TYRANT MACBETH?
HE IS FORTIFYING HIS CASTLE AT DUNSINANE WITH HEAVY DEFENSES. SOME SAY HE'S MAD; THOSE WHO HATE HIM LESS CALL IT BRAVE FURY. BUT INDEED, HE SEEMS UNABLE TO RESTRAIN HIMSELF ANY LONGER.

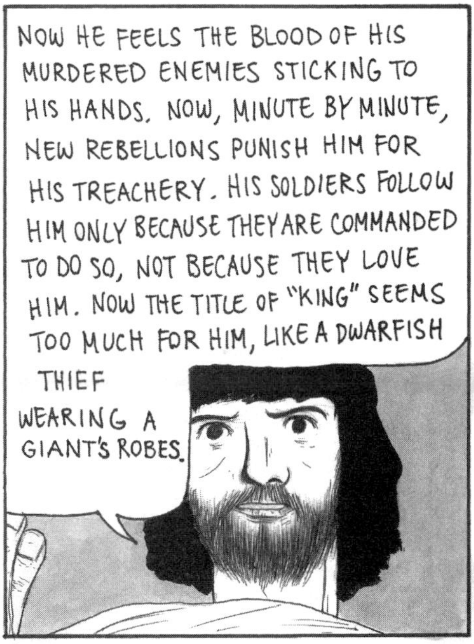
NOW HE FEELS THE BLOOD OF HIS MURDERED ENEMIES STICKING TO HIS HANDS. NOW, MINUTE BY MINUTE, NEW REBELLIONS PUNISH HIM FOR HIS TREACHERY. HIS SOLDIERS FOLLOW HIM ONLY BECAUSE THEY ARE COMMANDED TO DO SO, NOT BECAUSE THEY LOVE HIM. NOW THE TITLE OF "KING" SEEMS TOO MUCH FOR HIM, LIKE A DWARFISH THIEF
WEARING A GIANT'S ROBES.

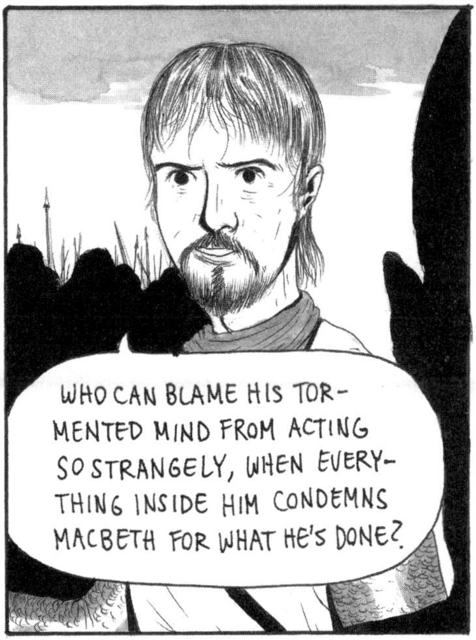
WHO CAN BLAME HIS TORMENTED MIND FROM ACTING SO STRANGELY, WHEN EVERYTHING INSIDE HIM CONDEMNS MACBETH FOR WHAT HE'S DONE?

WELL THEN, WE MARCH ON—TO GIVE OUR LOYALTY TO ONE WHO TRULY DESERVES IT. WE GO TO JOIN MALCOLM, THE MAN WHO WILL HEAL THIS DISEASED COUNTRY. EACH DROP OF OUR BLOOD WILL STRENGTHEN HIS MEDICINE.
WE'LL SHED AS MUCH BLOOD AS IS NEEDED TO WATER MALCOLM'S ROYAL FLOWER AND DROWN MACBETH'S USURPING WEEDS. WE MARCH TO BIRNAM!

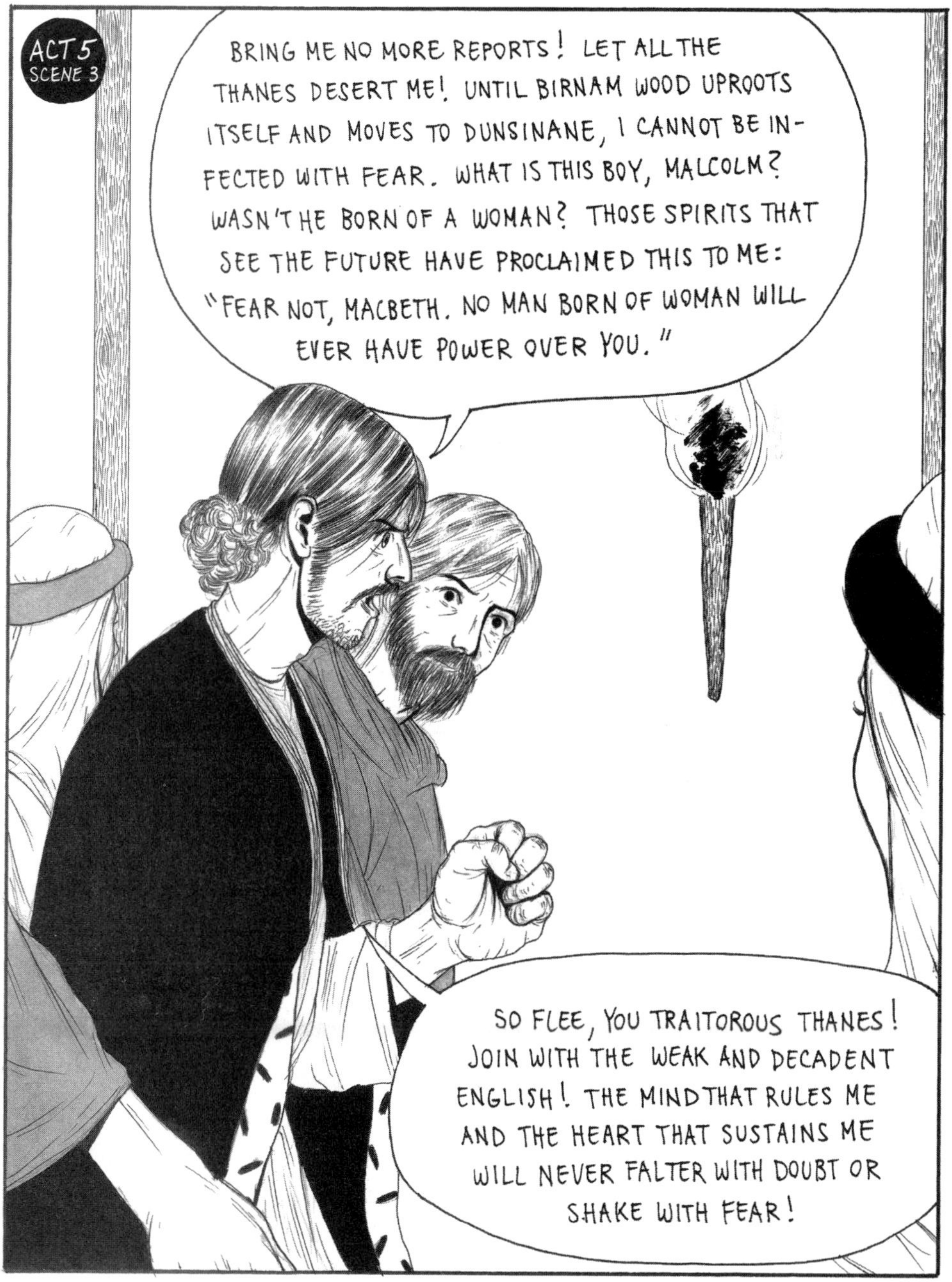
ACT 5 SCENE 3
BRING ME NO MORE REPORTS! LET ALL THE THANES DESERT ME! UNTIL BIRNAM WOOD UPROOTS ITSELF AND MOVES TO DUNSINANE, I CANNOT BE INFECTED WITH FEAR. WHAT IS THIS BOY, MALCOLM? WASN'T HE BORN OF A WOMAN? THOSE SPIRITS THAT SEE THE FUTURE HAVE PROCLAIMED THIS TO ME: "FEAR NOT, MACBETH. NO MAN BORN OF WOMAN WILL EVER HAVE POWER OVER YOU."
SO FLEE, YOU TRAITOROUS THANES! JOIN WITH THE WEAK AND DECADENT ENGLISH! THE MIND THAT RULES ME AND THE HEART THAT SUSTAINS ME WILL NEVER FALTER WITH DOUBT OR SHAKE WITH FEAR!

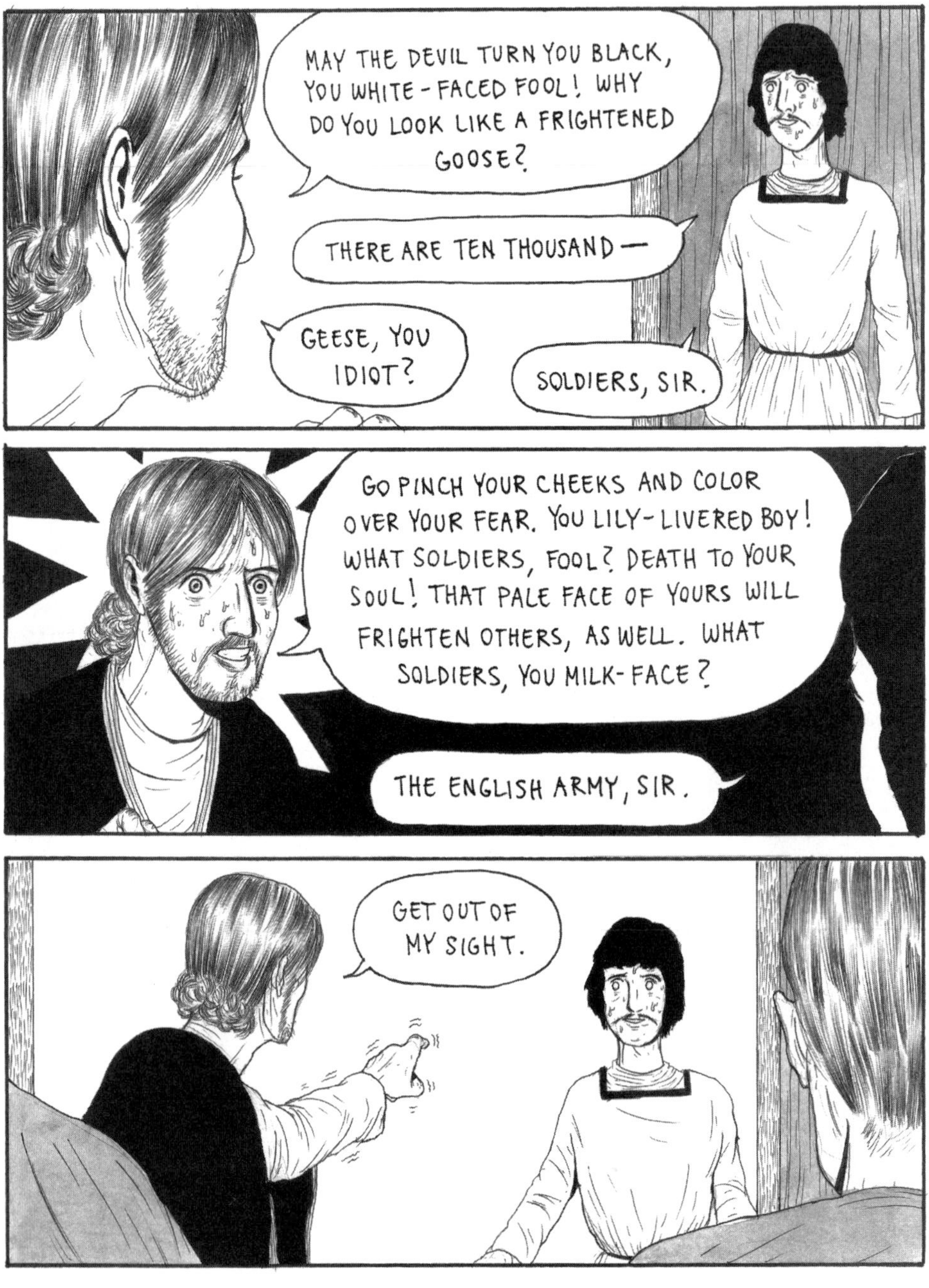
MAY THE DEVIL TURN YOU BLACK, YOU WHITE-FACED FOOL! WHY DO YOU LOOK LIKE A FRIGHTENED GOOSE?
THERE ARE TEN THOUSAND—
GEESE, YOU IDIOT?
SOLDIERS, SIR.
GO PINCH YOUR CHEEKS AND COLOR OVER YOUR FEAR. YOU LILY-LIVERED BOY! WHAT SOLDIERS, FOOL? DEATH TO YOUR SOUL! THAT PALE FACE OF YOURS WILL FRIGHTEN OTHERS, AS WELL. WHAT SOLDIERS, YOU MILK-FACE?
THE ENGLISH ARMY, SIR.
GET OUT OF MY SIGHT.

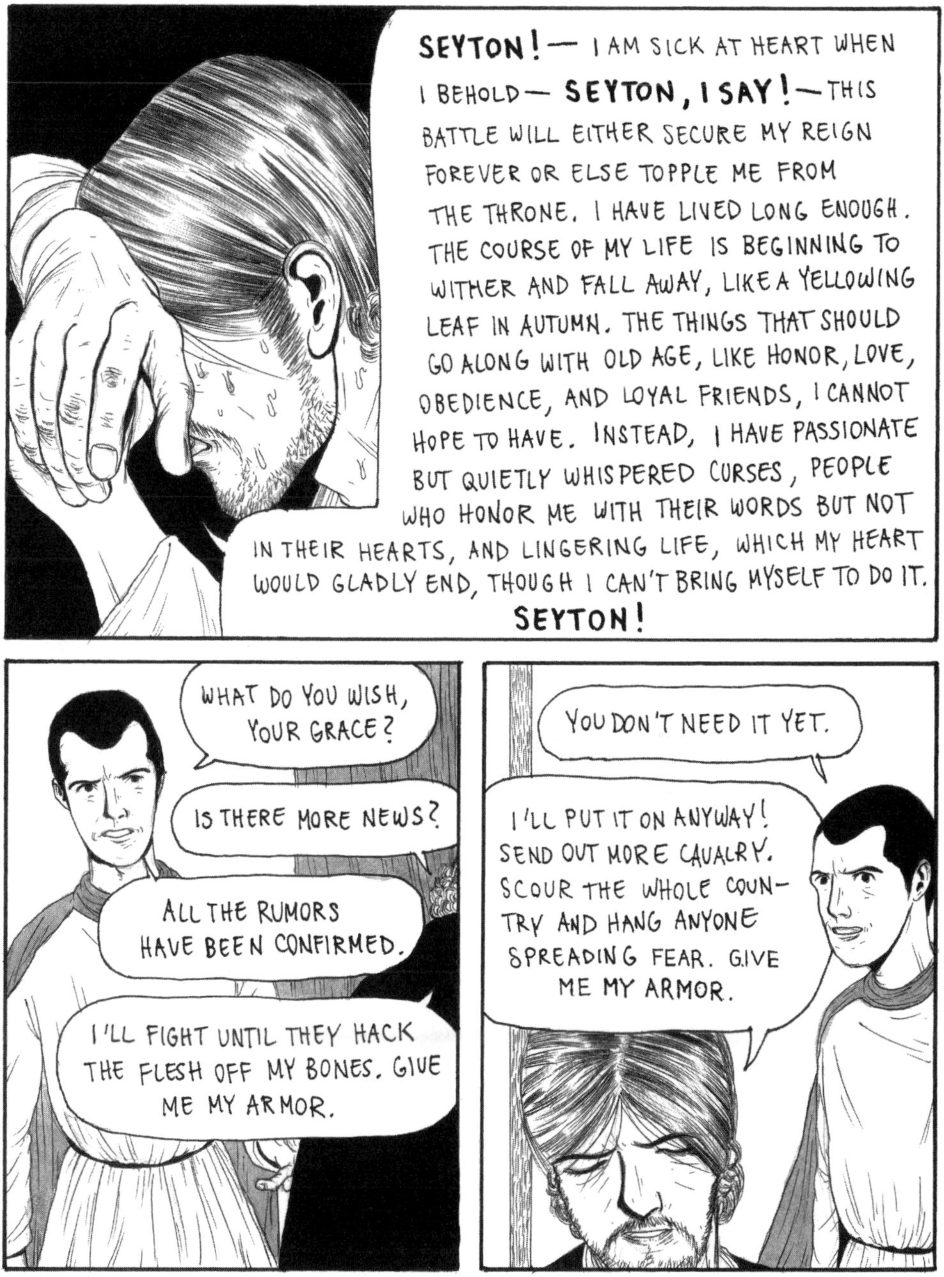
SEYTON!— I AM SICK AT HEART WHEN I BEHOLD— SEYTON, I SAY!—THIS BATTLE WILL EITHER SECURE MY REIGN FOREVER OR ELSE TOPPLE ME FROM THE THRONE. I HAVE LIVED LONG ENOUGH. THE COURSE OF MY LIFE IS BEGINNING TO WITHER AND FALL AWAY, LIKE A YELLOWING LEAF IN AUTUMN. THE THINGS THAT SHOULD GO ALONG WITH OLD AGE, LIKE HONOR, LOVE, OBEDIENCE, AND LOYAL FRIENDS, I CANNOT HOPE TO HAVE. INSTEAD, I HAVE PASSIONATE BUT QUIETLY WHISPERED CURSES, PEOPLE WHO HONOR ME WITH THEIR WORDS BUT NOT IN THEIR HEARTS, AND LINGERING LIFE, WHICH MY HEART WOULD GLADLY END, THOUGH I CAN'T BRING MYSELF TO DO IT. SEYTON!
WHAT DO YOU WISH, YOUR GRACE?
IS THERE MORE NEWS?
ALL THE RUMORS HAVE BEEN CONFIRMED.
I'LL FIGHT UNTIL THEY HACK THE FLESH OFF MY BONES. GIVE ME MY ARMOR.
YOU DON'T NEED IT YET.
I'LL PUT IT ON ANYWAY! SEND OUT MORE CAVALRY. SCOUR THE WHOLE COUNTRY AND HANG ANYONE SPREADING FEAR. GIVE ME MY ARMOR.

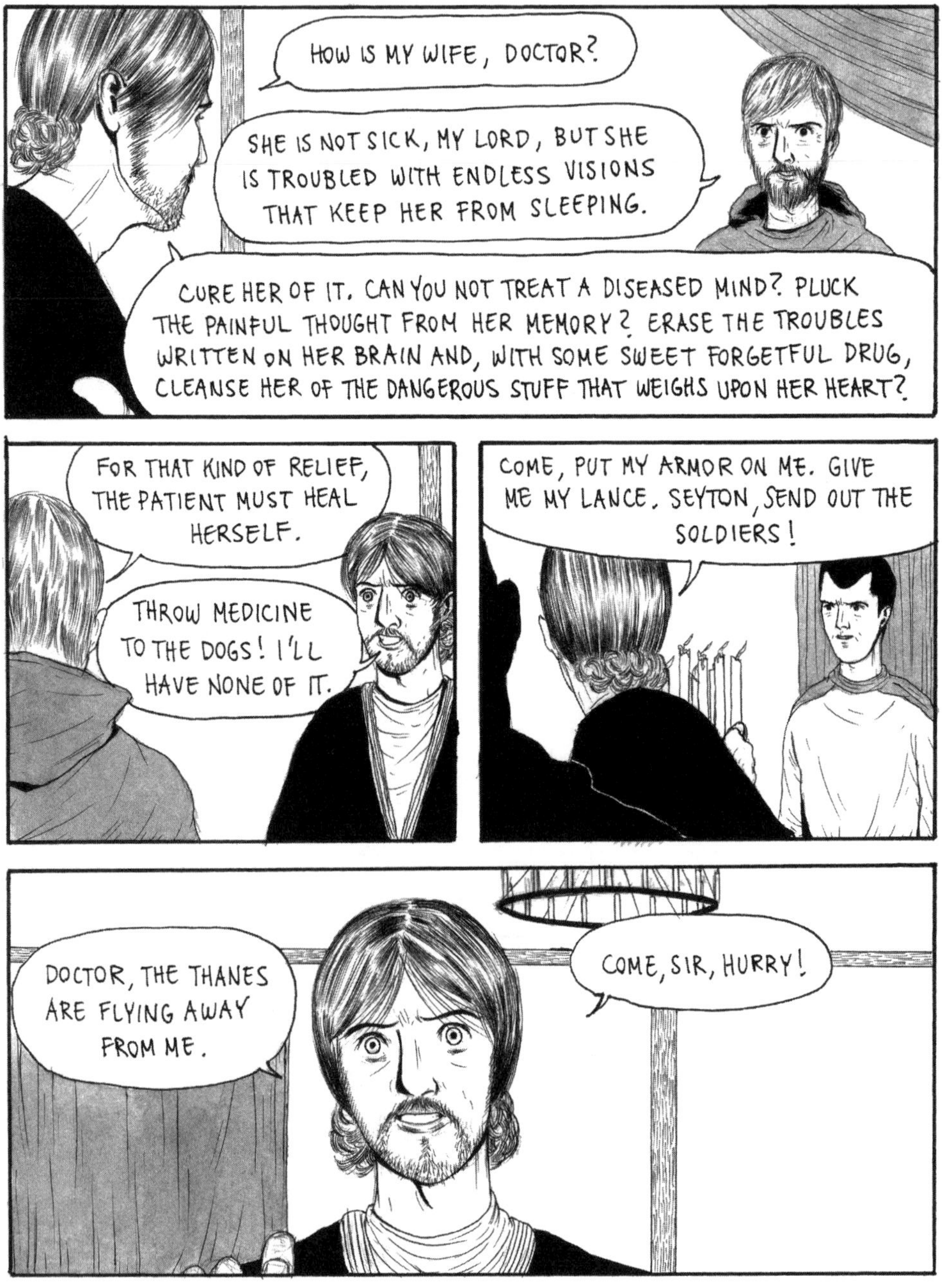
HOW IS MY WIFE, DOCTOR?
SHE IS NOT SICK, MY LORD, BUT SHE IS TROUBLED WITH ENDLESS VISIONS THAT KEEP HER FROM SLEEPING.
CURE HER OF IT. CAN YOU NOT TREAT A DISEASED MIND? PLUCK THE PAINFUL THOUGHT FROM HER MEMORY? ERASE THE TROUBLES WRITTEN ON HER BRAIN AND, WITH SOME SWEET FORGETFUL DRUG, CLEANSE HER OF THE DANGEROUS STUFF THAT WEIGHS UPON HER HEART?
FOR THAT KIND OF RELIEF, THE PATIENT MUST HEAL HERSELF.
THROW MEDICINE TO THE DOGS! I'LL HAVE NONE OF IT.
COME, PUT MY ARMOR ON ME. GIVE ME MY LANCE. SEYTON, SEND OUT THE SOLDIERS!
DOCTOR, THE THANES ARE FLYING AWAY FROM ME.
COME, SIR, HURRY!

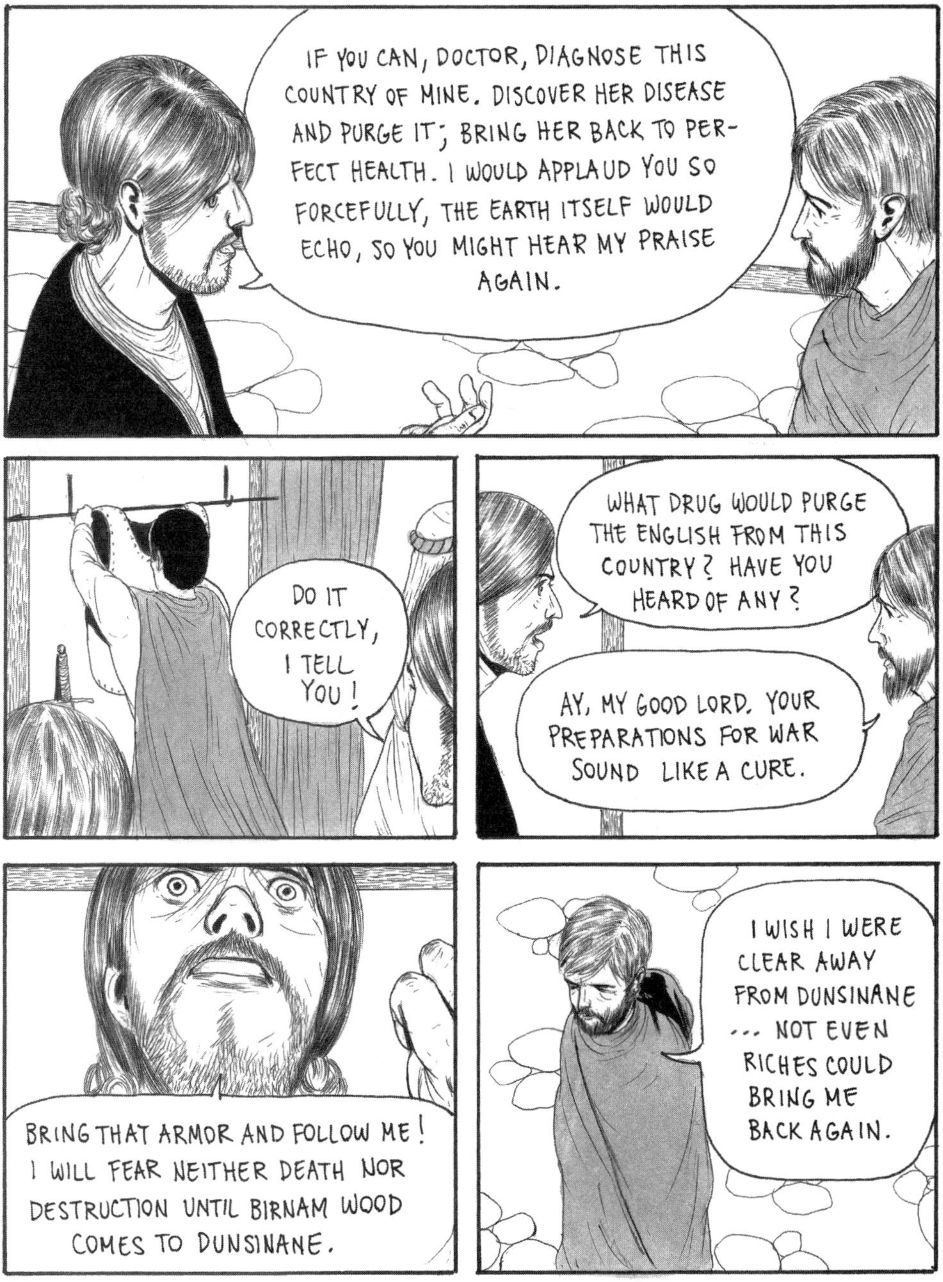
IF YOU CAN, DOCTOR, DIAGNOSE THIS COUNTRY OF MINE. DISCOVER HER DISEASE AND PURGE IT; BRING HER BACK TO PERFECT HEALTH. I WOULD APPLAUD YOU SO FORCEFULLY, THE EARTH ITSELF WOULD ECHO, SO YOU MIGHT HEAR MY PRAISE AGAIN.
DO IT CORRECTLY, I TELL YOU!
WHAT DRUG WOULD PURGE THE ENGLISH FROM THIS COUNTRY? HAVE YOU HEARD OF ANY?
AY, MY GOOD LORD. YOUR PREPARATIONS FOR WAR SOUND LIKE A CURE.
BRING THAT ARMOR AND FOLLOW ME! I WILL FEAR NEITHER DEATH NOR DESTRUCTION UNTIL BIRNAM WOOD COMES TO DUNSINANE.
I WISH I WERE CLEAR AWAY FROM DUNSINANE ... NOT EVEN RICHES COULD BRING ME BACK AGAIN.

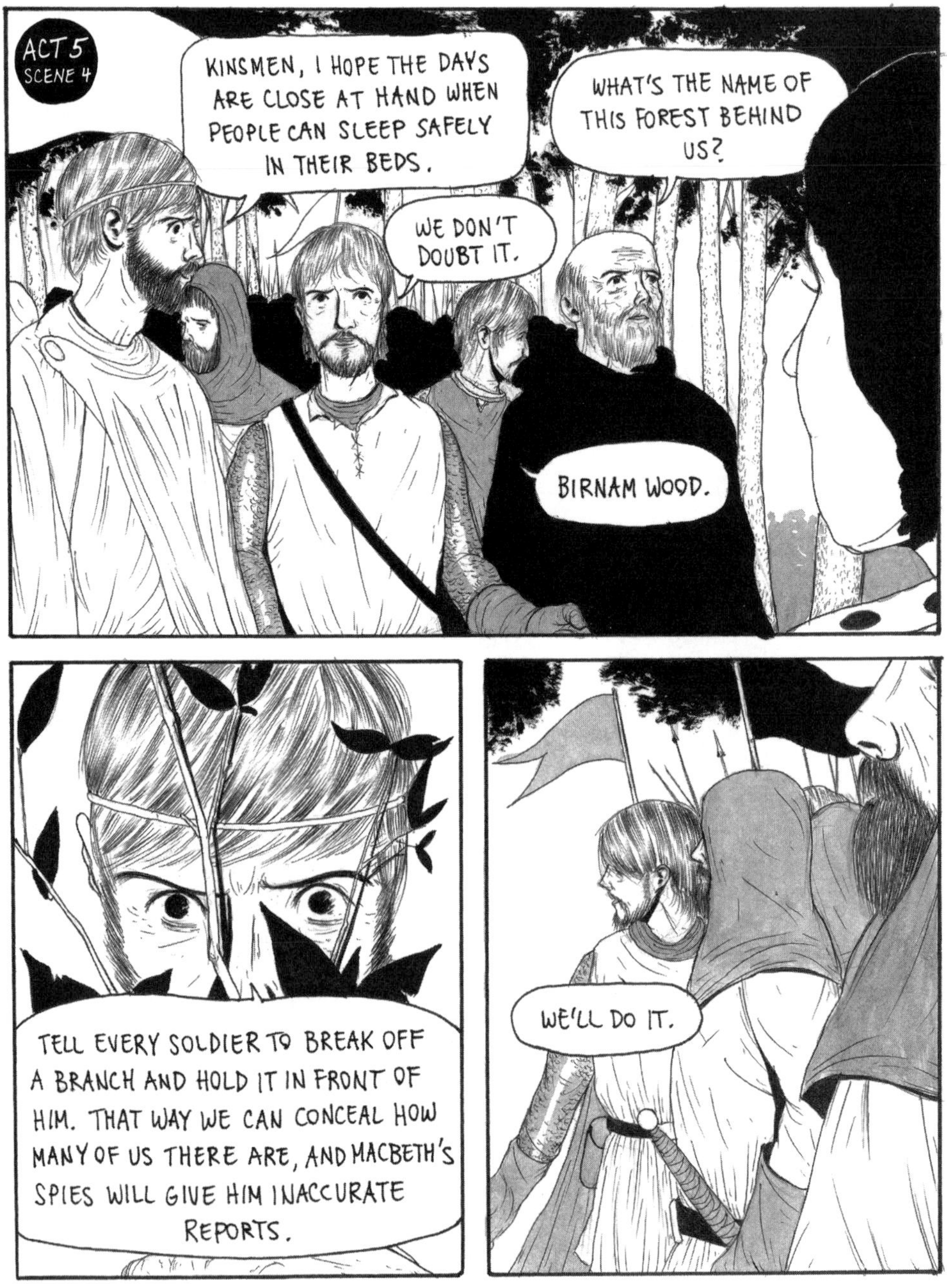
ACT 5
SCENE 4
KINSMEN, I HOPE THE DAYS ARE CLOSE AT HAND WHEN PEOPLE CAN SLEEP SAFELY IN THEIR BEDS.
WE DON'T DOUBT IT.
WHAT'S THE NAME OF THIS FOREST BEHIND US?
BIRNAM WOOD.
TELL EVERY SOLDIER TO BREAK OFF A BRANCH AND HOLD IT IN FRONT OF HIM. THAT WAY WE CAN CONCEAL HOW MANY OF US THERE ARE, AND MACBETH'S SPIES WILL GIVE HIM INACCURATE REPORTS.
WE'LL DO IT.

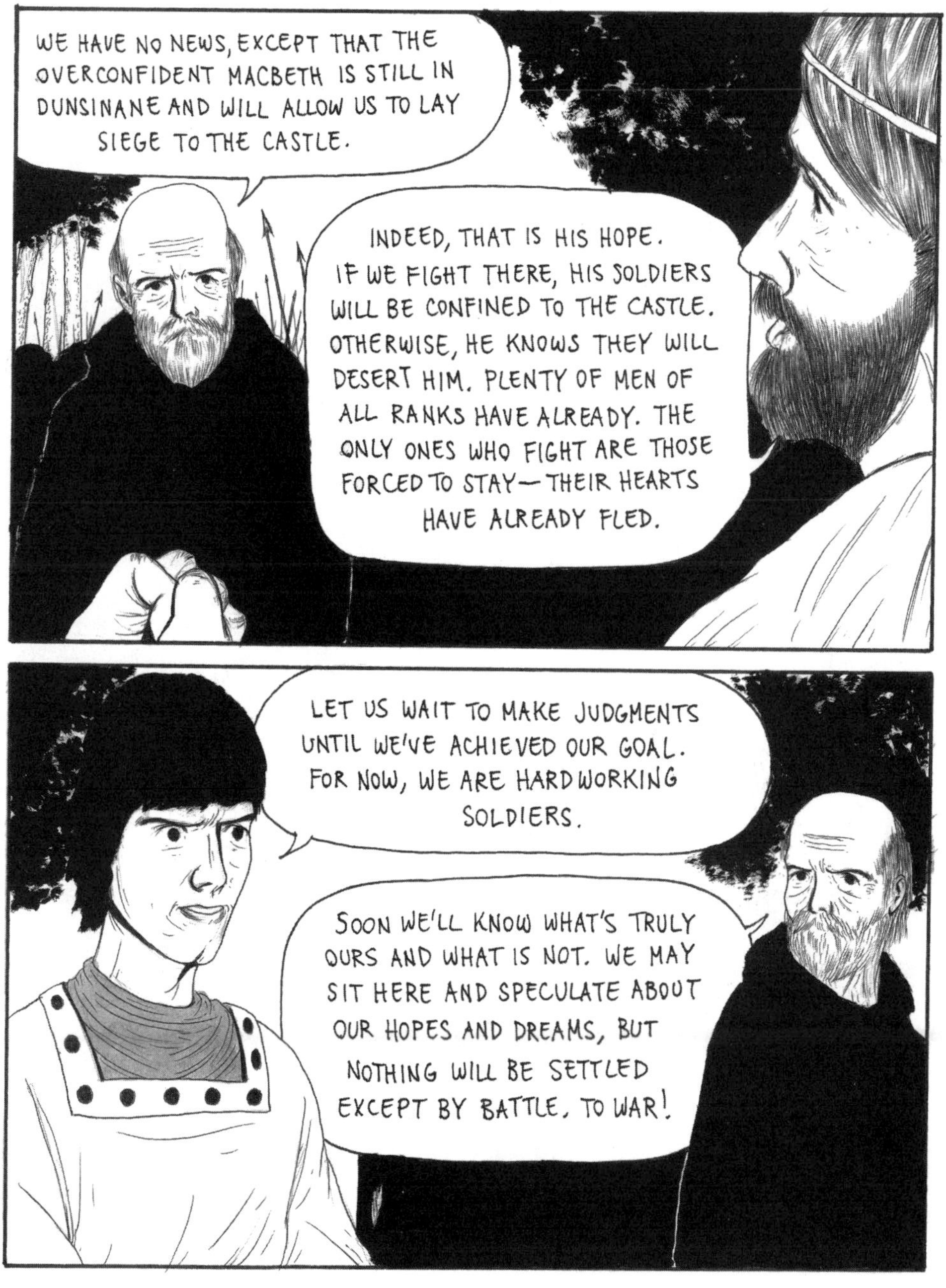
WE HAVE NO NEWS, EXCEPT THAT THE OVERCONFIDENT MACBETH IS STILL IN DUNSINANE AND WILL ALLOW US TO LAY SIEGE TO THE CASTLE.
INDEED, THAT IS HIS HOPE. IF WE FIGHT THERE, HIS SOLDIERS WILL BE CONFINED TO THE CASTLE. OTHERWISE, HE KNOWS THEY WILL DESERT HIM. PLENTY OF MEN OF ALL RANKS HAVE ALREADY. THE ONLY ONES WHO FIGHT ARE THOSE FORCED TO STAY—THEIR HEARTS HAVE ALREADY FLED.
LET US WAIT TO MAKE JUDGMENTS UNTIL WE'VE ACHIEVED OUR GOAL. FOR NOW, WE ARE HARDWORKING SOLDIERS.
SOON WE'LL KNOW WHAT'S TRULY OURS AND WHAT IS NOT. WE MAY SIT HERE AND SPECULATE ABOUT OUR HOPES AND DREAMS, BUT NOTHING WILL BE SETTLED EXCEPT BY BATTLE. TO WAR!

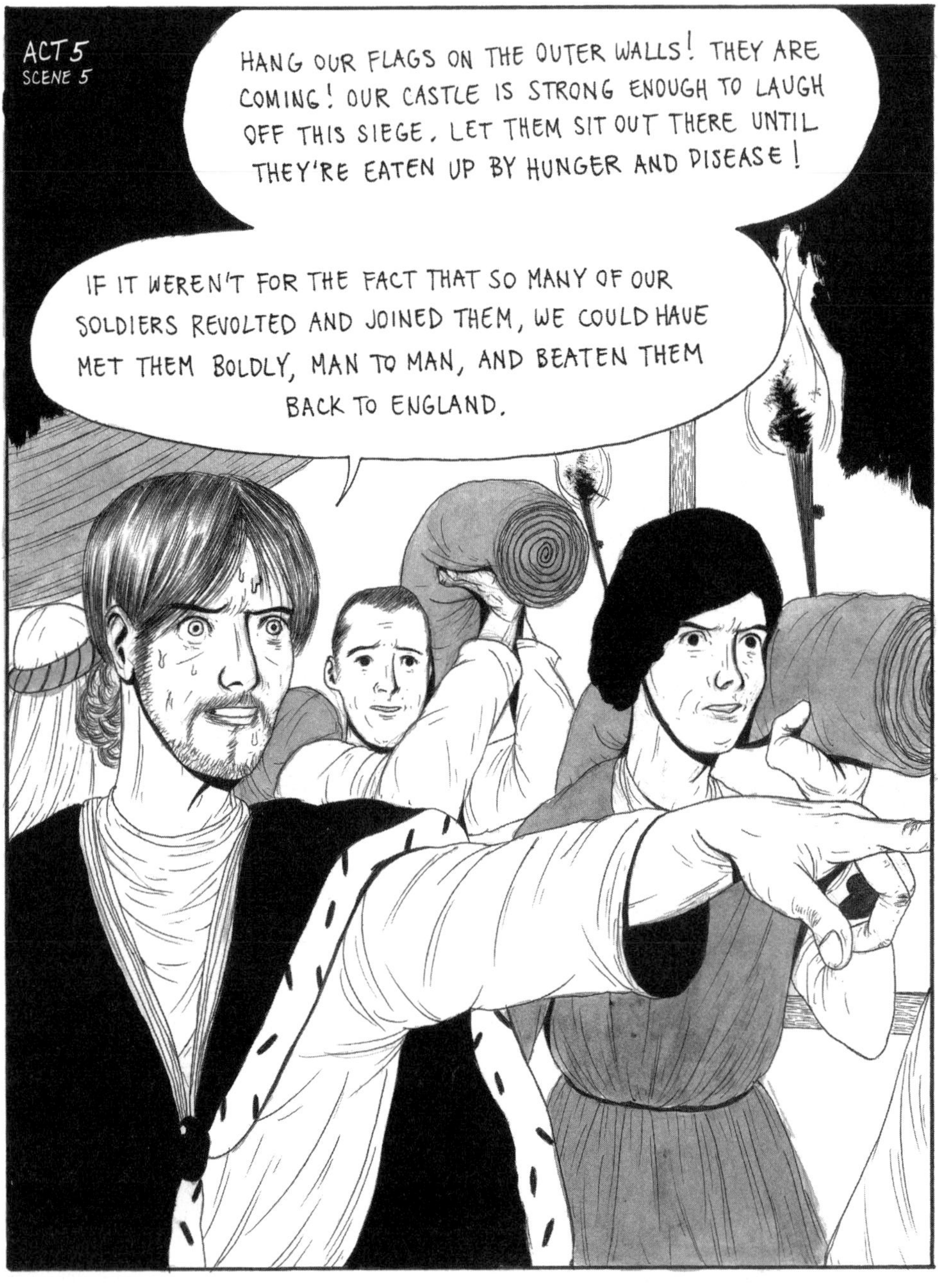
ACT 5
SCENE 5
HANG OUR FLAGS ON THE OUTER WALLS! THEY ARE COMING! OUR CASTLE IS STRONG ENOUGH TO LAUGH OFF THIS SIEGE. LET THEM SIT OUT THERE UNTIL THEY'RE EATEN UP BY HUNGER AND DISEASE!
IF IT WEREN'T FOR THE FACT THAT SO MANY OF OUR SOLDIERS REVOLTED AND JOINED THEM, WE COULD HAVE MET THEM BOLDLY, MAN TO MAN, AND BEATEN THEM BACK TO ENGLAND.

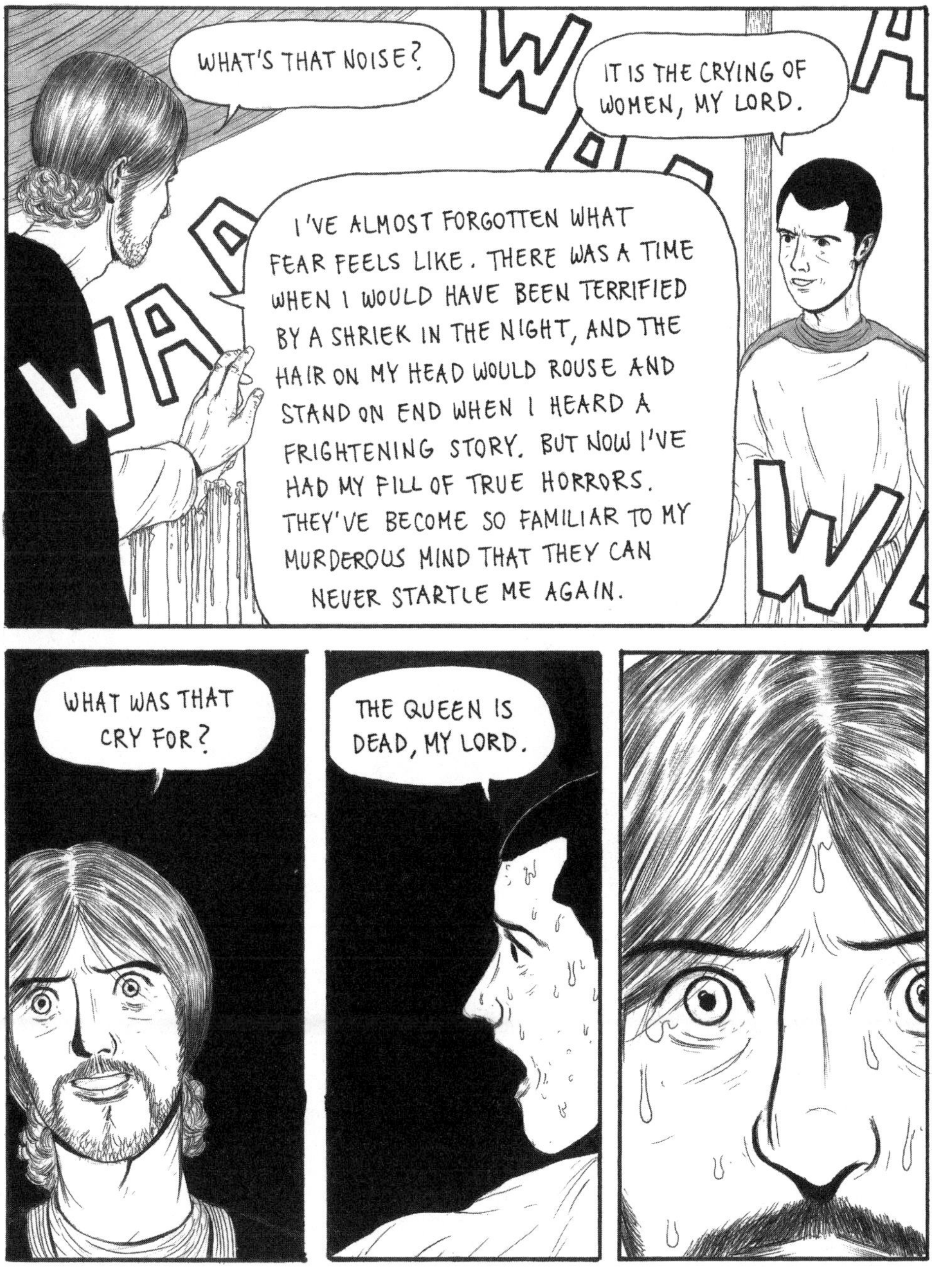
WHAT'S THAT NOISE?
IT IS THE CRYING OF WOMEN, MY LORD.
WA WA WA WA
I'VE ALMOST FORGOTTEN WHAT FEAR FEELS LIKE. THERE WAS A TIME WHEN I WOULD HAVE BEEN TERRIFIED BY A SHRIEK IN THE NIGHT, AND THE HAIR ON MY HEAD WOULD ROUSE AND STAND ON END WHEN I HEARD A FRIGHTENING STORY. BUT NOW I'VE HAD MY FILL OF TRUE HORRORS. THEY'VE BECOME SO FAMILIAR TO MY MURDEROUS MIND THAT THEY CAN NEVER STARTLE ME AGAIN.
WHAT WAS THAT CRY FOR?
THE QUEEN IS DEAD, MY LORD.

SHE SHOULDN'T HAVE DIED SO SOON — I SHOULD HAVE HEARD THIS NEWS SOME OTHER TIME! TOMORROW, AND TOMORROW, AND TOMORROW... OUR DAYS CREEP BY UNTIL THE END OF TIME, LIGHTING THE WAY TO DEATH LIKE CANDLES LEADING US TO BED.
OUT, OUT, BRIEF CANDLE! LIFE IS BUT A WALKING SHADOW, A POOR ACTOR THAT STRUTS AND WORRIES DURING HIS HOUR ON STAGE AND THEN IS NEVER HEARD FROM AGAIN. LIFE IS A TALE TOLD BY AN IDIOT, FULL OF NOISE AND CLAMOR BUT DEVOID OF MEANING.

YOU'VE COME TO TELL ME SOMETHING. TELL ME QUICKLY.
MY GRACIOUS LORD, I SHOULD TELL YOU WHAT I SAW, BUT I DON'T KNOW HOW TO SAY IT.
SAY IT, SIR.

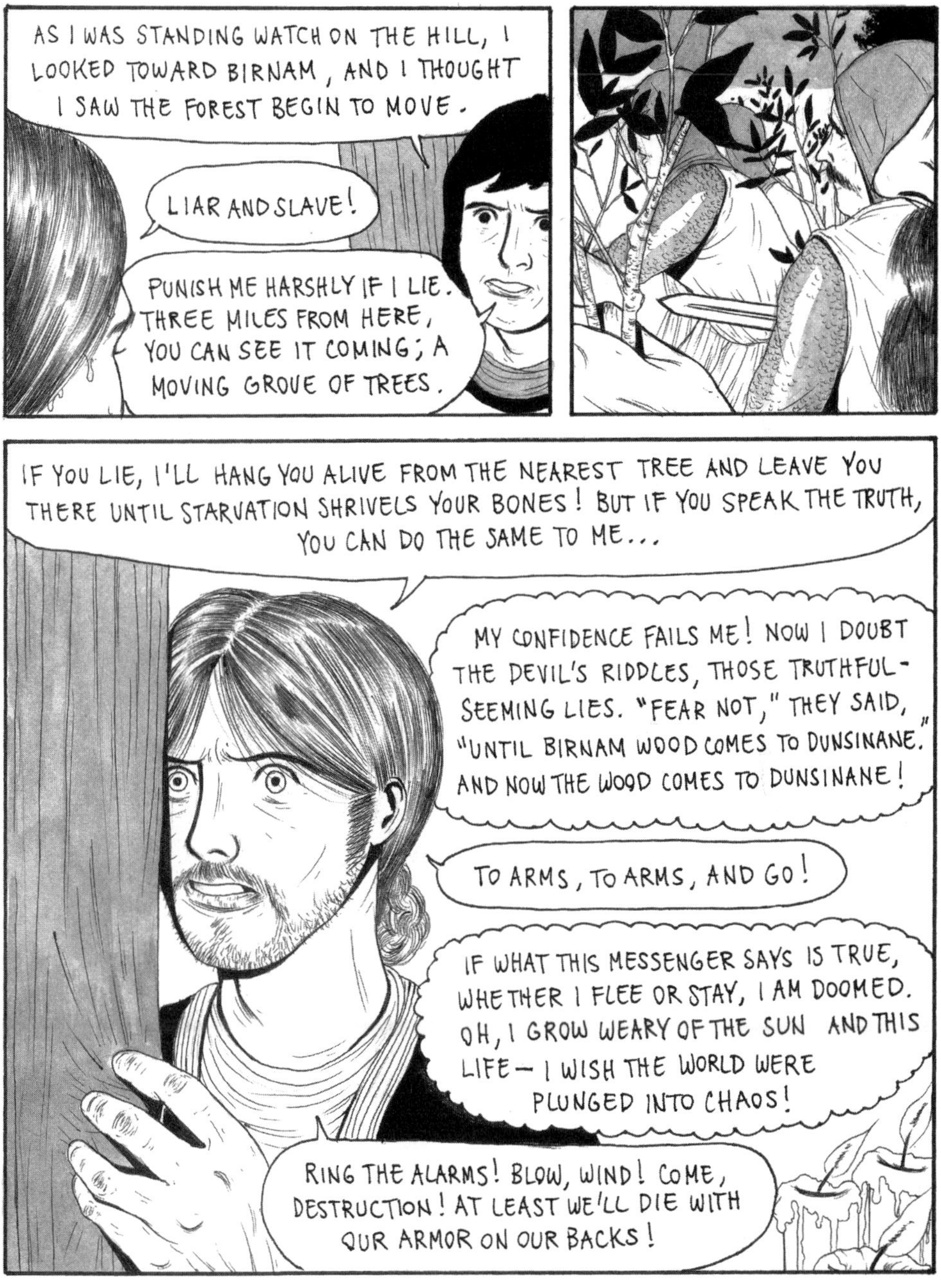
AS I WAS STANDING WATCH ON THE HILL, I LOOKED TOWARD BIRNAM, AND I THOUGHT I SAW THE FOREST BEGIN TO MOVE.
LIAR AND SLAVE!
PUNISH ME HARSHLY IF I LIE. THREE MILES FROM HERE, YOU CAN SEE IT COMING; A MOVING GROVE OF TREES.
IF YOU LIE, I'LL HANG YOU ALIVE FROM THE NEAREST TREE AND LEAVE YOU THERE UNTIL STARVATION SHRIVELS YOUR BONES! BUT IF YOU SPEAK THE TRUTH, YOU CAN DO THE SAME TO ME...
MY CONFIDENCE FAILS ME! NOW I DOUBT THE DEVIL'S RIDDLES, THOSE TRUTHFUL-SEEMING LIES. "FEAR NOT," THEY SAID, "UNTIL BIRNAM WOOD COMES TO DUNSINANE." AND NOW THE WOOD COMES TO DUNSINANE!
TO ARMS, TO ARMS, AND GO!
IF WHAT THIS MESSENGER SAYS IS TRUE, WHETHER I FLEE OR STAY, I AM DOOMED. OH, I GROW WEARY OF THE SUN AND THIS LIFE— I WISH THE WORLD WERE PLUNGED INTO CHAOS!
RING THE ALARMS! BLOW, WIND! COME, DESTRUCTION! AT LEAST WE'LL DIE WITH OUR ARMOR ON OUR BACKS!

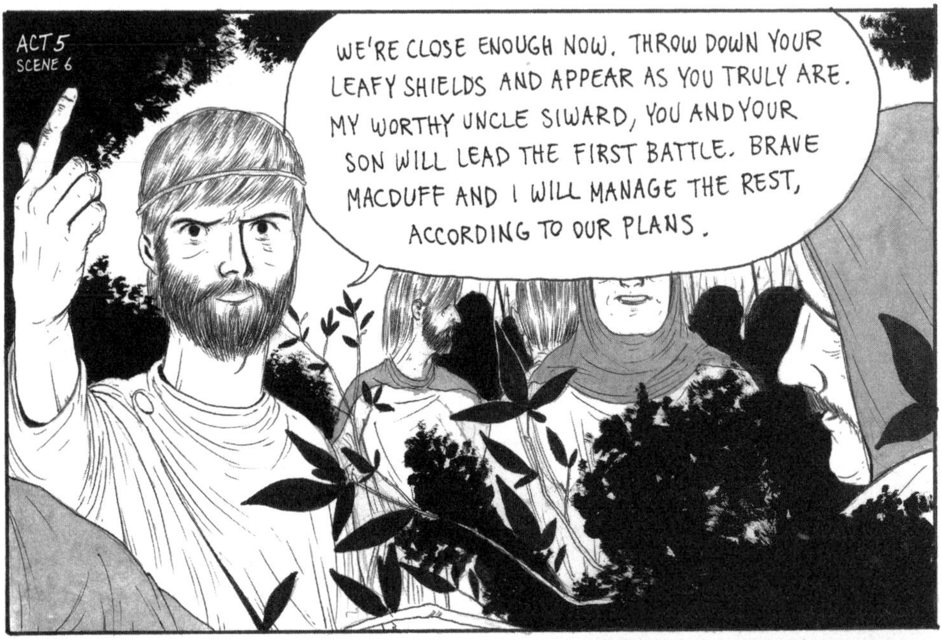
ACT 5
SCENE 6
WE'RE CLOSE ENOUGH NOW. THROW DOWN YOUR LEAFY SHIELDS AND APPEAR AS YOU TRULY ARE. MY WORTHY UNCLE SIWARD, YOU AND YOUR SON WILL LEAD THE FIRST BATTLE. BRAVE MACDUFF AND I WILL MANAGE THE REST, ACCORDING TO OUR PLANS.

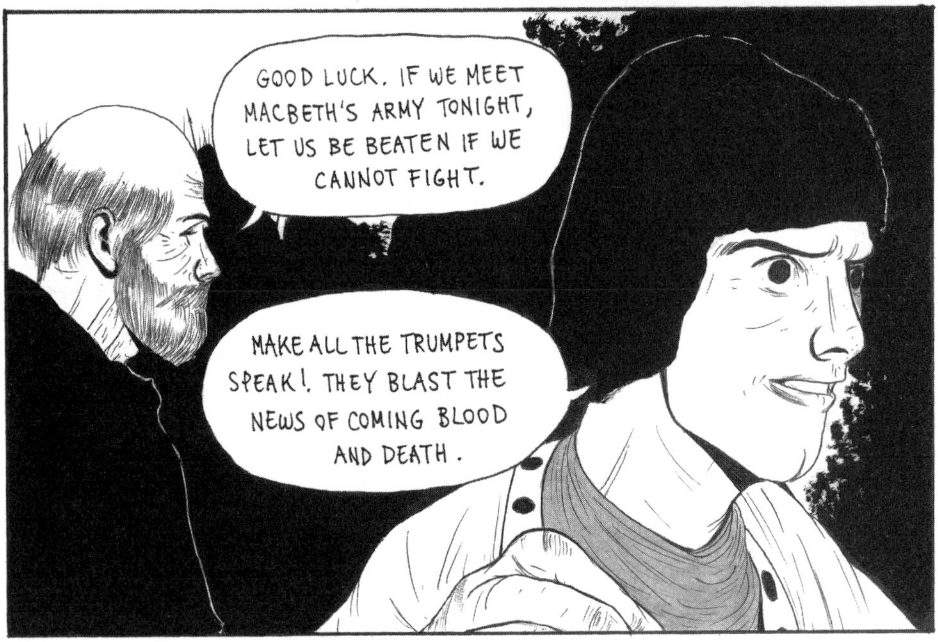
GOOD LUCK. IF WE MEET MACBETH'S ARMY TONIGHT, LET US BE BEATEN IF WE CANNOT FIGHT.
MAKE ALL THE TRUMPETS SPEAK! THEY BLAST THE NEWS OF COMING BLOOD AND DEATH.

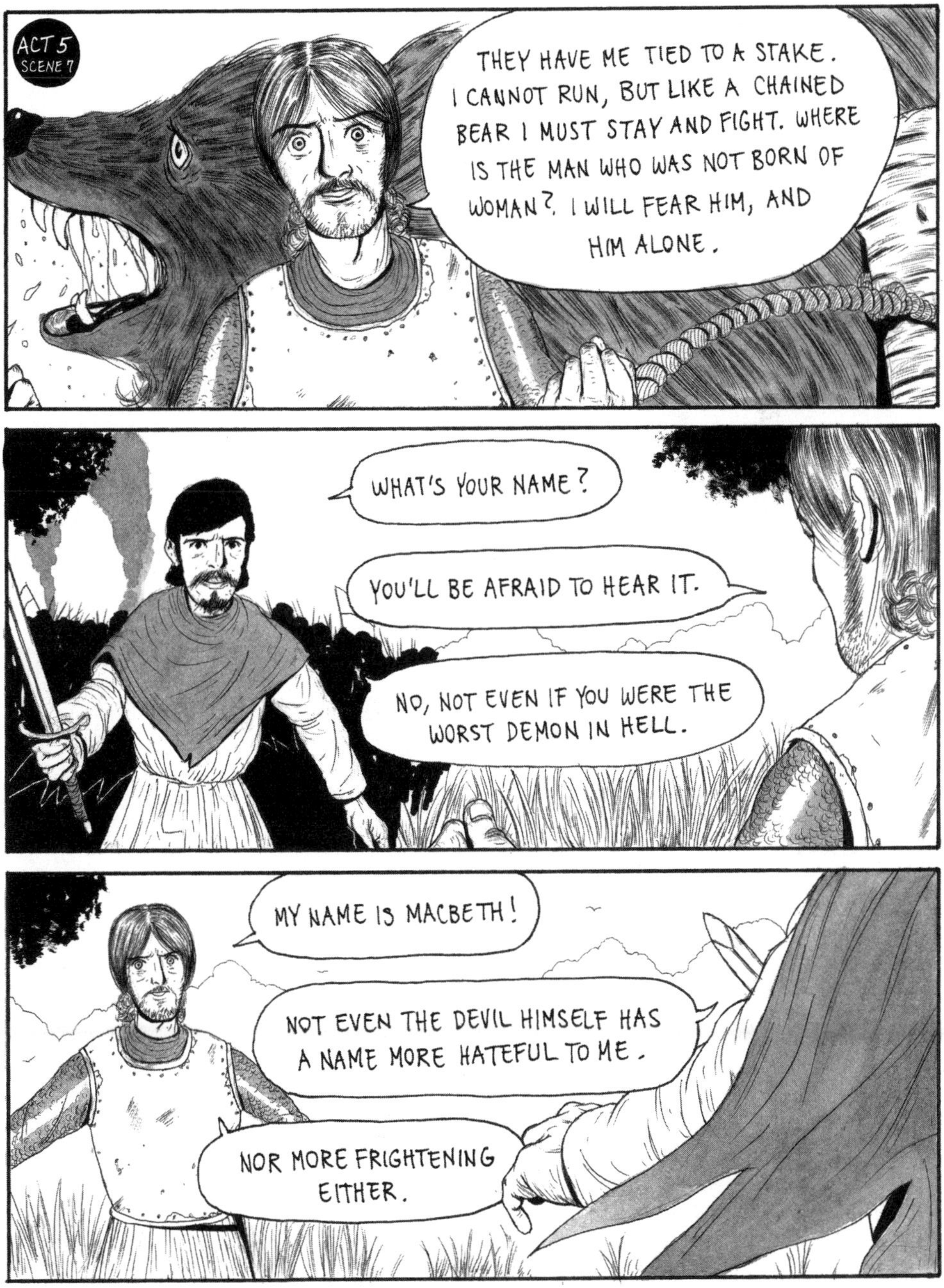
ACT 5 SCENE 7
THEY HAVE ME TIED TO A STAKE. I CANNOT RUN, BUT LIKE A CHAINED BEAR I MUST STAY AND FIGHT. WHERE IS THE MAN WHO WAS NOT BORN OF WOMAN? I WILL FEAR HIM, AND HIM ALONE.
WHAT'S YOUR NAME?
YOU'LL BE AFRAID TO HEAR IT.
NO, NOT EVEN IF YOU WERE THE WORST DEMON IN HELL.
MY NAME IS MACBETH!
NOT EVEN THE DEVIL HIMSELF HAS A NAME MORE HATEFUL TO ME.
NOR MORE FRIGHTENING EITHER.

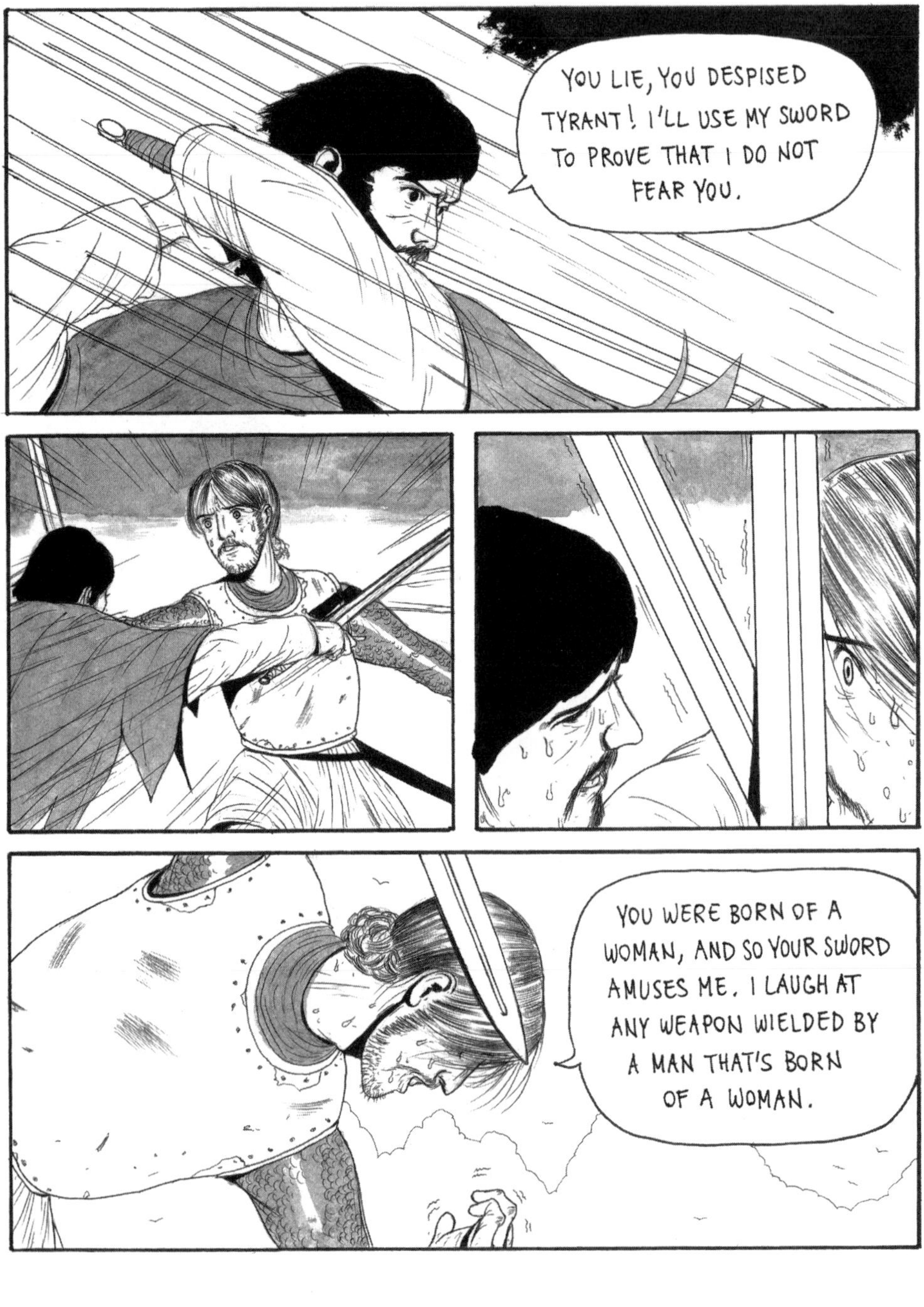
YOU LIE, YOU DESPISED TYRANT! I'LL USE MY SWORD TO PROVE THAT I DO NOT FEAR YOU.
YOU WERE BORN OF A WOMAN, AND SO YOUR SWORD AMUSES ME. I LAUGH AT ANY WEAPON WIELDED BY A MAN THAT'S BORN OF A WOMAN.

THE NOISE COMES FROM THAT DIRECTION. TYRANT, SHOW YOUR FACE! IF YOU ARE SLAIN BY ANOTHER MAN'S SWORD, AND NOT MY OWN, THE GHOSTS OF MY WIFE AND CHILDREN WILL HAUNT ME FOREVER. I CAN'T BE BOTHERED TO FIGHT THESE WRETCHED COMMONERS, WHO FIGHT FOR A SALARY. EITHER I'LL FIGHT YOU, MACBETH, OR ELSE I'LL SHEATHE THIS SWORD UNUSED.
YOU MUST BE OVER THERE — THIS GREAT CLATTER SEEMS TO ANNOUNCE THE ARRIVAL OF ONE OF THE HIGHEST-RANKING MEN. FORTUNE, LET ME FIND HIM AND I WILL BEG NOTHING MORE OF YOU!

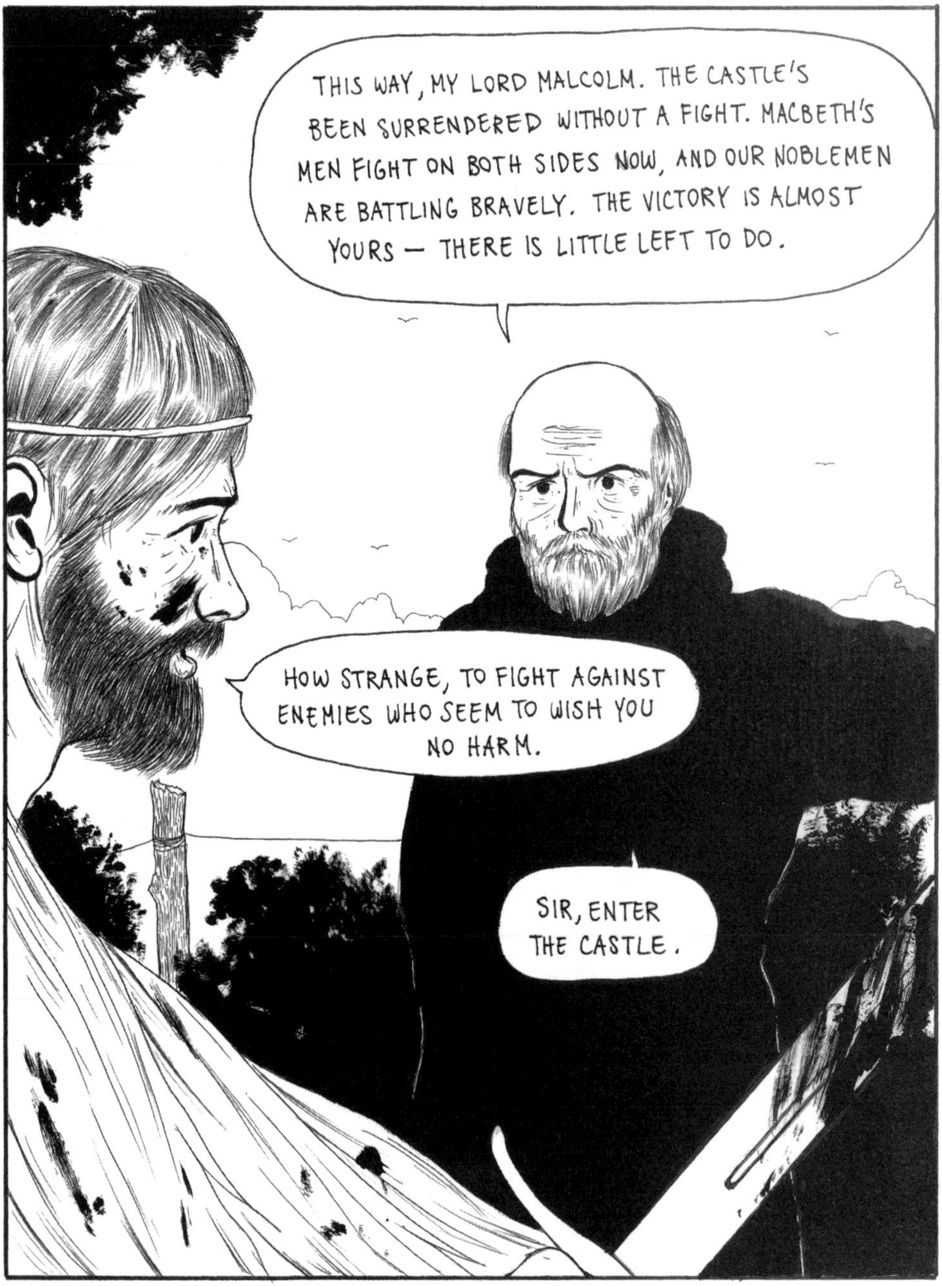
THIS WAY, MY LORD MALCOLM. THE CASTLE'S BEEN SURRENDERED WITHOUT A FIGHT. MACBETH'S MEN FIGHT ON BOTH SIDES NOW, AND OUR NOBLEMEN ARE BATTLING BRAVELY. THE VICTORY IS ALMOST YOURS — THERE IS LITTLE LEFT TO DO.
HOW STRANGE, TO FIGHT AGAINST ENEMIES WHO SEEM TO WISH YOU NO HARM.
SIR, ENTER THE CASTLE.

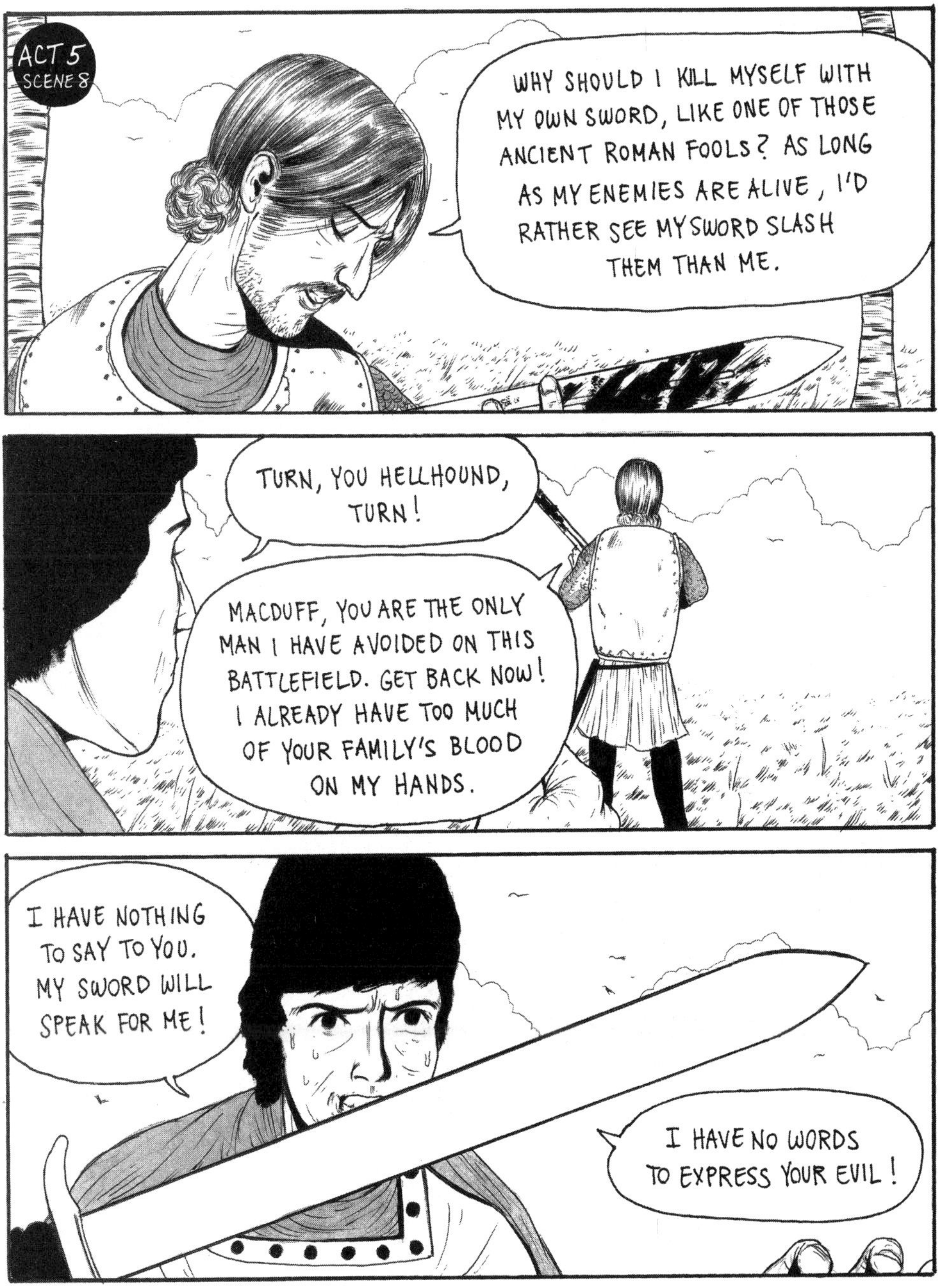
ACT 5
SCENE 8
WHY SHOULD I KILL MYSELF WITH MY OWN SWORD, LIKE ONE OF THOSE ANCIENT ROMAN FOOLS? AS LONG AS MY ENEMIES ARE ALIVE, I'D RATHER SEE MY SWORD SLASH THEM THAN ME.
TURN, YOU HELLHOUND, TURN!
MACDUFF, YOU ARE THE ONLY MAN I HAVE AVOIDED ON THIS BATTLEFIELD. GET BACK NOW! I ALREADY HAVE TOO MUCH OF YOUR FAMILY'S BLOOD ON MY HANDS.
I HAVE NOTHING TO SAY TO YOU. MY SWORD WILL SPEAK FOR ME!
I HAVE NO WORDS TO EXPRESS YOUR EVIL!

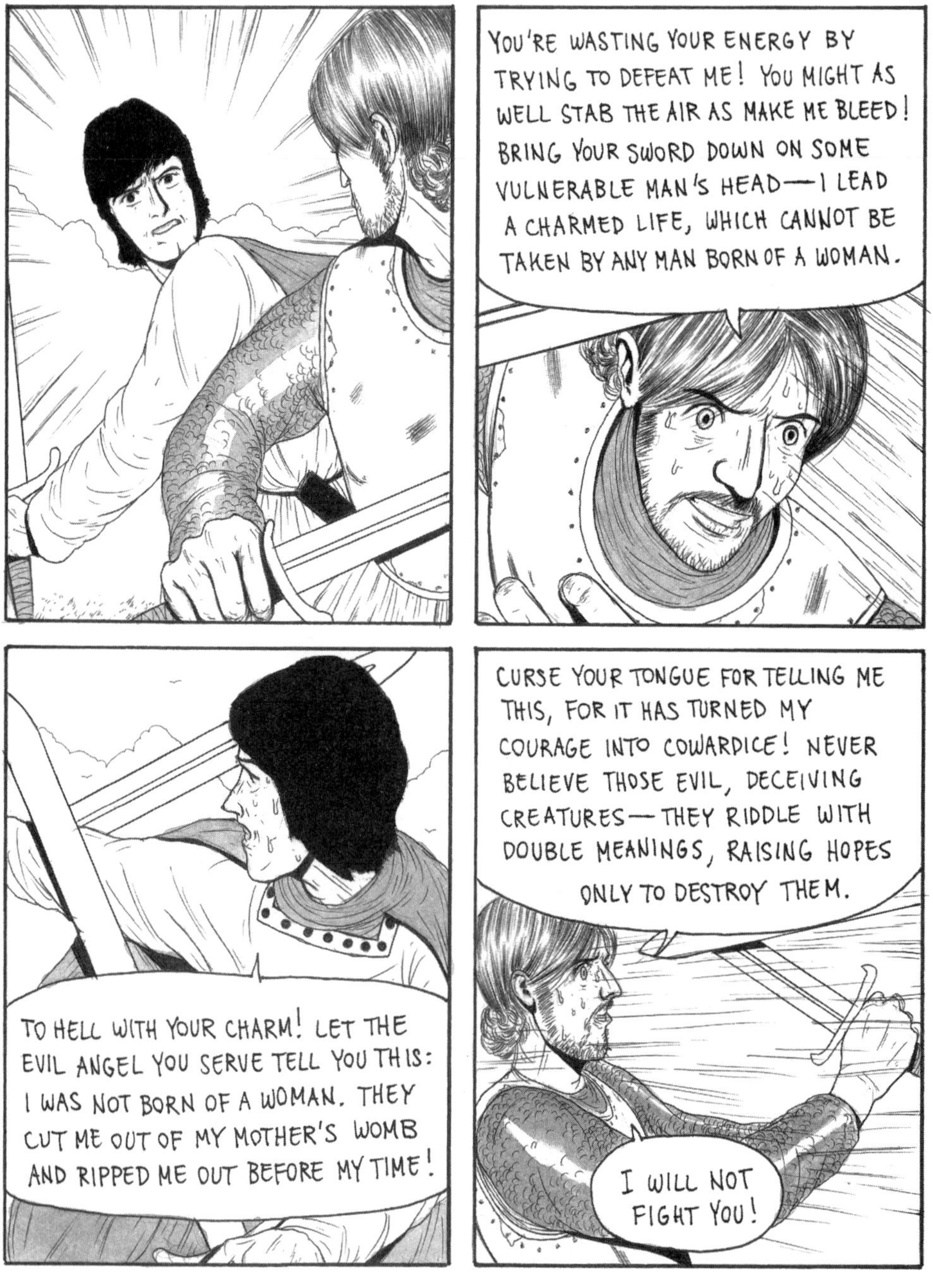
YOU'RE WASTING YOUR ENERGY BY TRYING TO DEFEAT ME! YOU MIGHT AS WELL STAB THE AIR AS MAKE ME BLEED! BRING YOUR SWORD DOWN ON SOME VULNERABLE MAN'S HEAD—I LEAD A CHARMED LIFE, WHICH CANNOT BE TAKEN BY ANY MAN BORN OF A WOMAN.
TO HELL WITH YOUR CHARM! LET THE EVIL ANGEL YOU SERVE TELL YOU THIS: I WAS NOT BORN OF A WOMAN. THEY CUT ME OUT OF MY MOTHER'S WOMB AND RIPPED ME OUT BEFORE MY TIME!
CURSE YOUR TONGUE FOR TELLING ME THIS, FOR IT HAS TURNED MY COURAGE INTO COWARDICE! NEVER BELIEVE THOSE EVIL, DECEIVING CREATURES—THEY RIDDLE WITH DOUBLE MEANINGS, RAISING HOPES ONLY TO DESTROY THEM.
I WILL NOT FIGHT YOU!

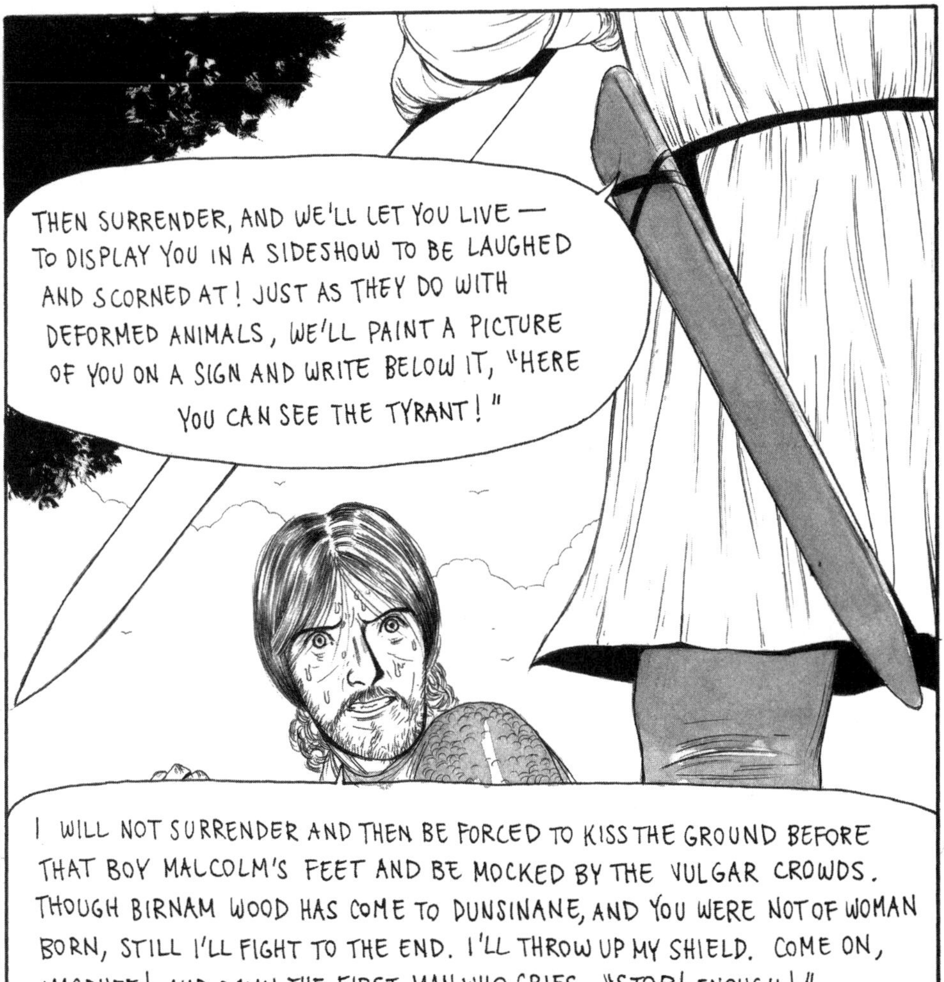
THEN SURRENDER, AND WE'LL LET YOU LIVE — TO DISPLAY YOU IN A SIDESHOW TO BE LAUGHED AND SCORNED AT! JUST AS THEY DO WITH DEFORMED ANIMALS, WE'LL PAINT A PICTURE OF YOU ON A SIGN AND WRITE BELOW IT, "HERE YOU CAN SEE THE TYRANT!"
I WILL NOT SURRENDER AND THEN BE FORCED TO KISS THE GROUND BEFORE THAT BOY MALCOLM'S FEET AND BE MOCKED BY THE VULGAR CROWDS. THOUGH BIRNAM WOOD HAS COME TO DUNSINANE, AND YOU WERE NOT OF WOMAN BORN, STILL I'LL FIGHT TO THE END. I'LL THROW UP MY SHIELD. COME ON, MACDUFF! AND DAMN THE FIRST MAN WHO CRIES, "STOP! ENOUGH!"

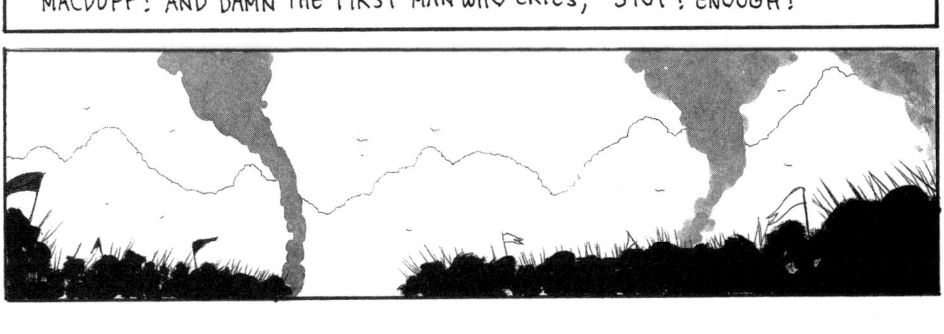

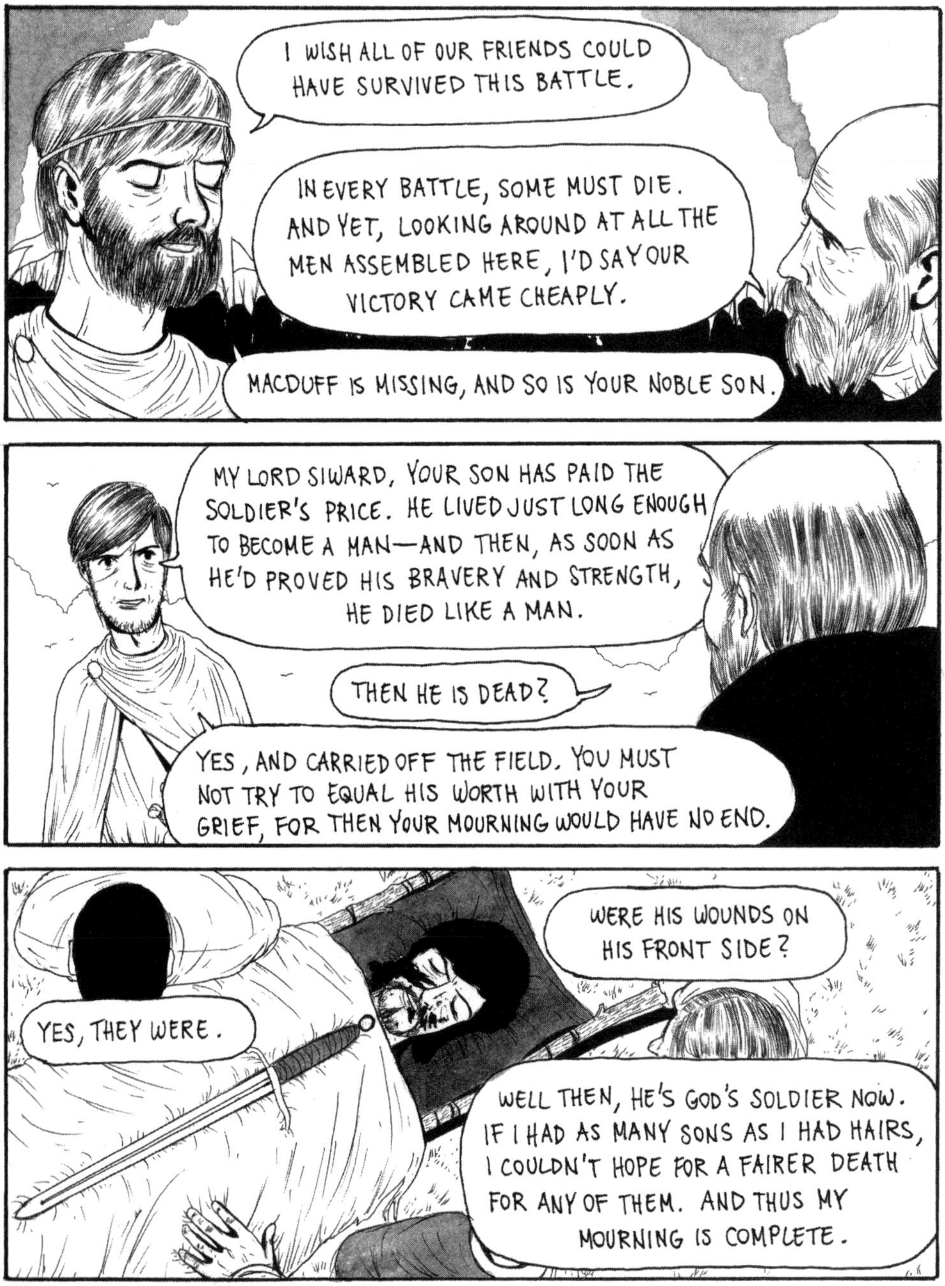
I WISH ALL OF OUR FRIENDS COULD HAVE SURVIVED THIS BATTLE.
IN EVERY BATTLE, SOME MUST DIE. AND YET, LOOKING AROUND AT ALL THE MEN ASSEMBLED HERE, I'D SAY OUR VICTORY CAME CHEAPLY.
MACDUFF IS MISSING, AND SO IS YOUR NOBLE SON.
MY LORD SIWARD, YOUR SON HAS PAID THE SOLDIER'S PRICE. HE LIVED JUST LONG ENOUGH TO BECOME A MAN—AND THEN, AS SOON AS HE'D PROVED HIS BRAVERY AND STRENGTH, HE DIED LIKE A MAN.
THEN HE IS DEAD?
YES, AND CARRIED OFF THE FIELD. YOU MUST NOT TRY TO EQUAL HIS WORTH WITH YOUR GRIEF, FOR THEN YOUR MOURNING WOULD HAVE NO END.
WERE HIS WOUNDS ON HIS FRONT SIDE?
YES, THEY WERE.
WELL THEN, HE'S GOD'S SOLDIER NOW. IF I HAD AS MANY SONS AS I HAD HAIRS, I COULDN'T HOPE FOR A FAIRER DEATH FOR ANY OF THEM. AND THUS MY MOURNING IS COMPLETE.

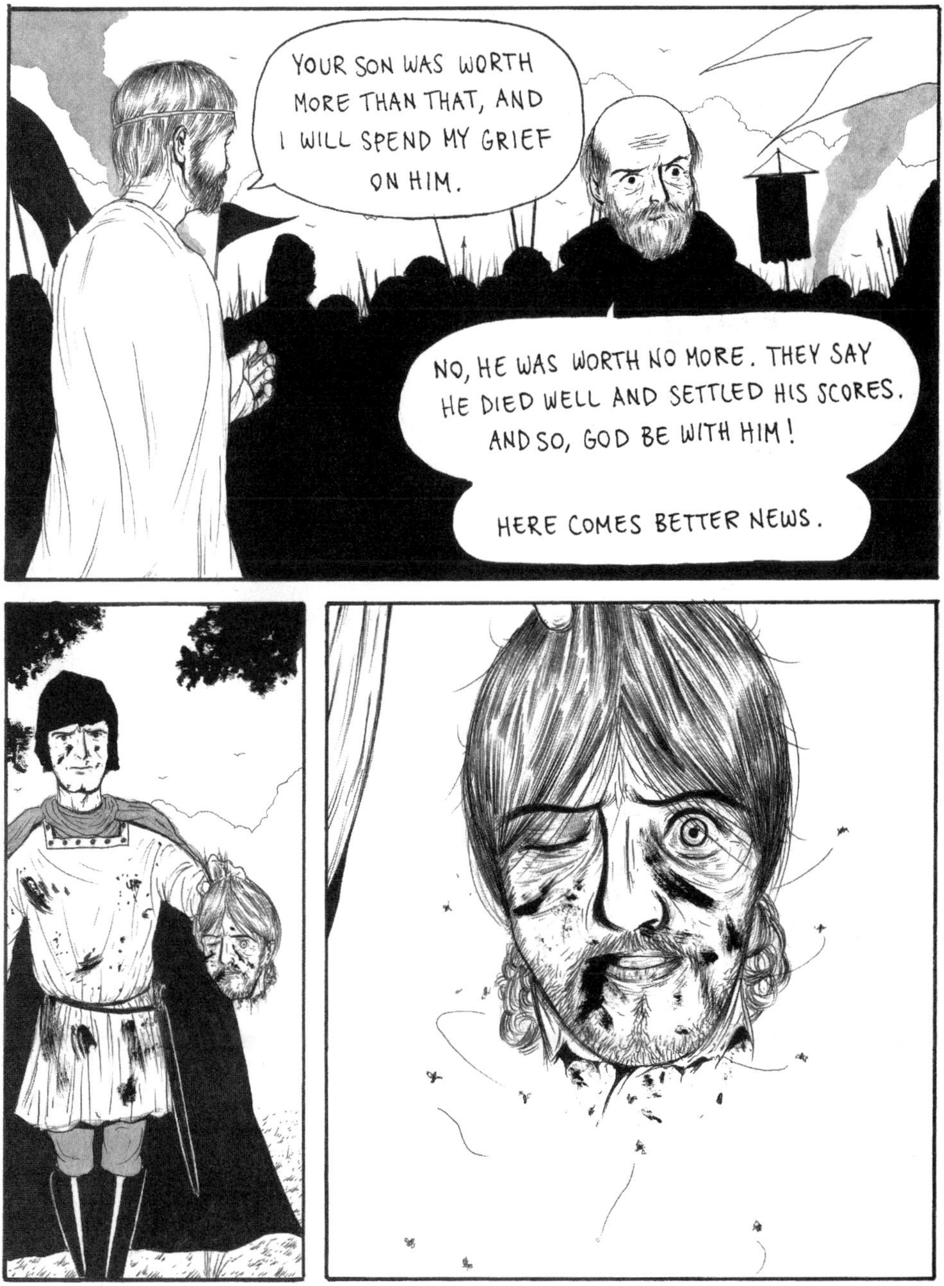
YOUR SON WAS WORTH MORE THAN THAT, AND I WILL SPEND MY GRIEF ON HIM.
NO, HE WAS WORTH NO MORE. THEY SAY HE DIED WELL AND SETTLED HIS SCORES. AND SO, GOD BE WITH HIM!
HERE COMES BETTER NEWS.

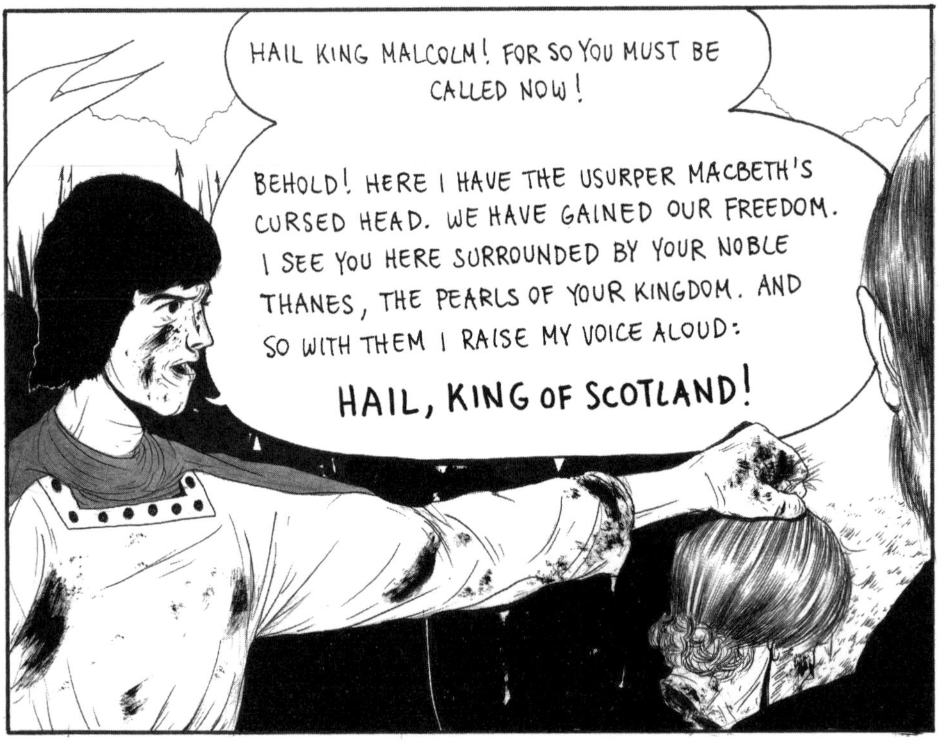
HAIL KING MALCOLM! FOR SO YOU MUST BE CALLED NOW!
BEHOLD! HERE I HAVE THE USURPER MACBETH'S CURSED HEAD. WE HAVE GAINED OUR FREEDOM. I SEE YOU HERE SURROUNDED BY YOUR NOBLE THANES, THE PEARLS OF YOUR KINGDOM. AND SO WITH THEM I RAISE MY VOICE ALOUD:
HAIL, KING OF SCOTLAND!

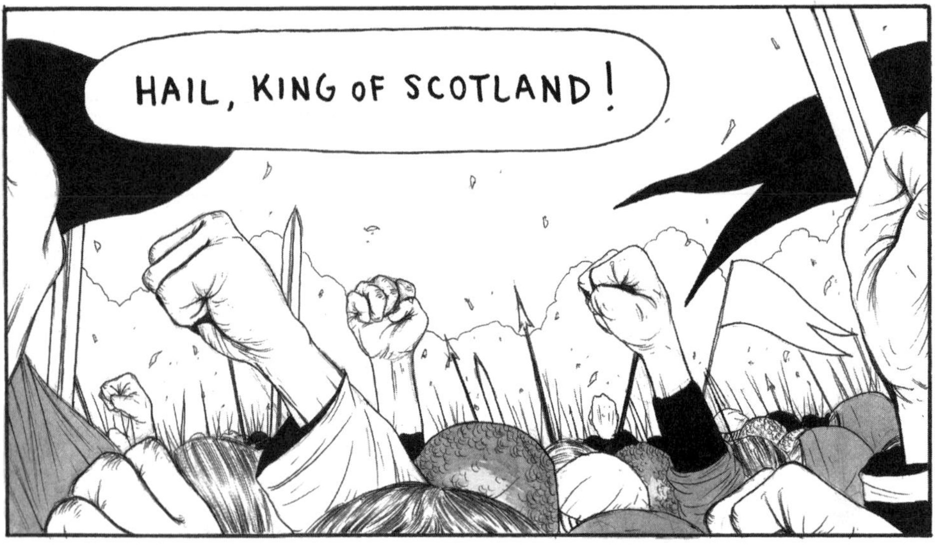
HAIL, KING OF SCOTLAND!

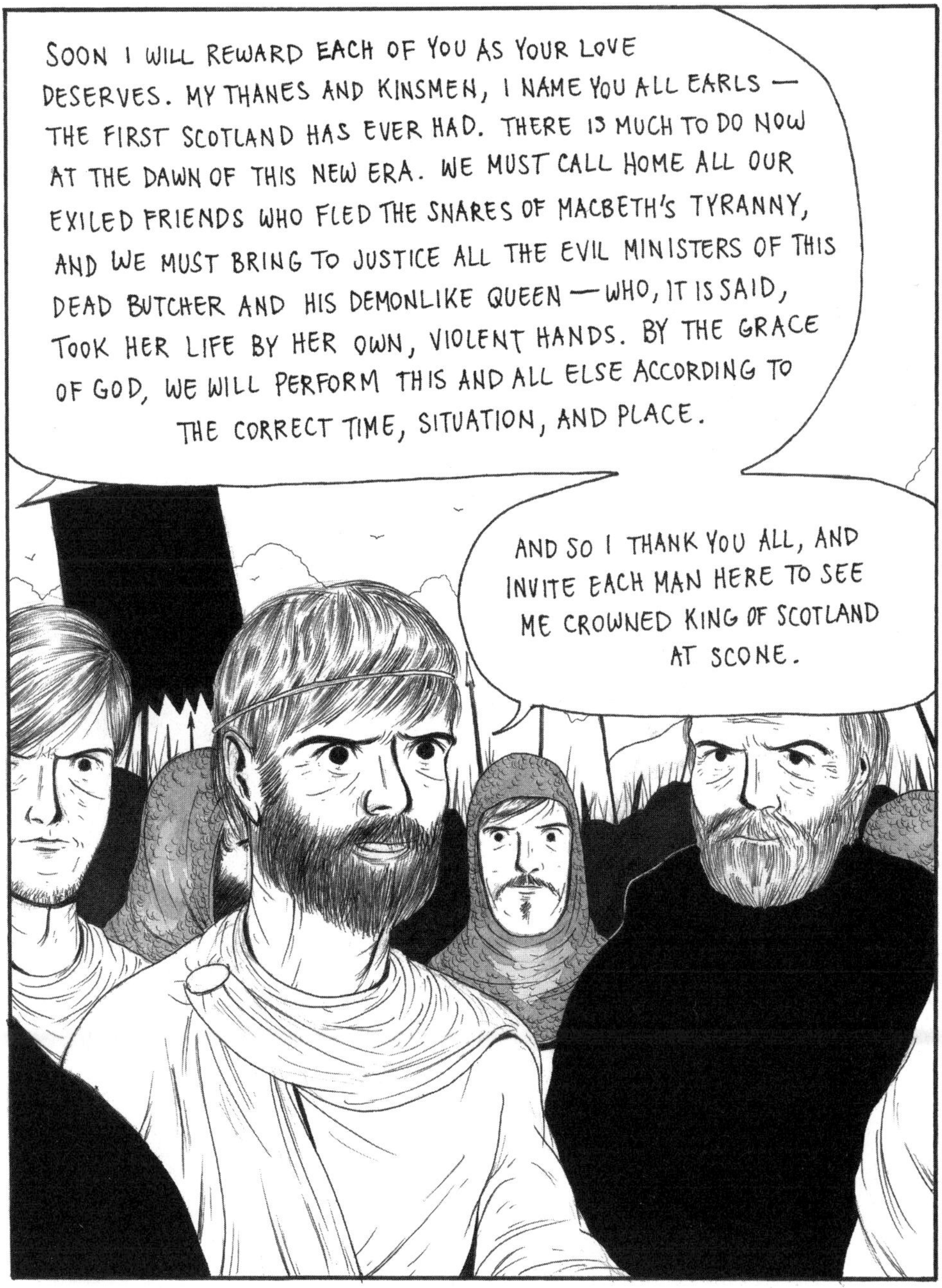
SOON I WILL REWARD EACH OF YOU AS YOUR LOVE DESERVES. MY THANES AND KINSMEN, I NAME YOU ALL EARLS — THE FIRST SCOTLAND HAS EVER HAD. THERE IS MUCH TO DO NOW AT THE DAWN OF THIS NEW ERA. WE MUST CALL HOME ALL OUR EXILED FRIENDS WHO FLED THE SNARES OF MACBETH'S TYRANNY, AND WE MUST BRING TO JUSTICE ALL THE EVIL MINISTERS OF THIS DEAD BUTCHER AND HIS DEMONLIKE QUEEN — WHO, IT IS SAID, TOOK HER LIFE BY HER OWN, VIOLENT HANDS. BY THE GRACE OF GOD, WE WILL PERFORM THIS AND ALL ELSE ACCORDING TO THE CORRECT TIME, SITUATION, AND PLACE.
AND SO I THANK YOU ALL, AND INVITE EACH MAN HERE TO SEE ME CROWNED KING OF SCOTLAND AT SCONE.

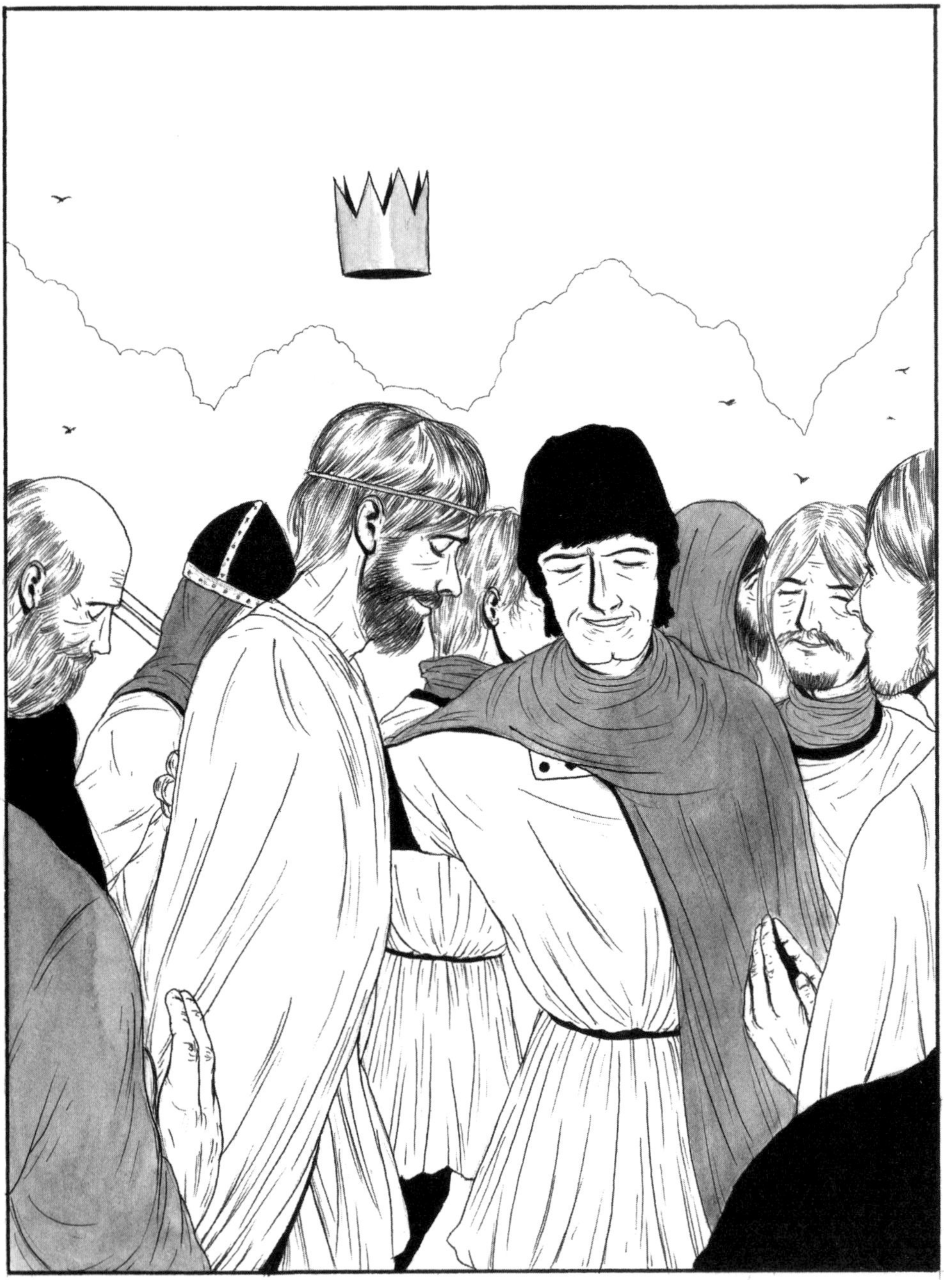

ABOUT THE ARTIST

KEN HOSHINE IS AN ARTIST LIVING AND WORKING IN NEW YORK CITY. THIS IS HIS FIRST MAJOR VENTURE INTO THE GRAPHIC NOVEL WORLD. WHEN HE'S NOT WORKING, HE ENJOYS LONG WINTERS, HOT BEVERAGES, AND BICYCLES.

"Shakespeare, Shakespeare, Shakespeare"

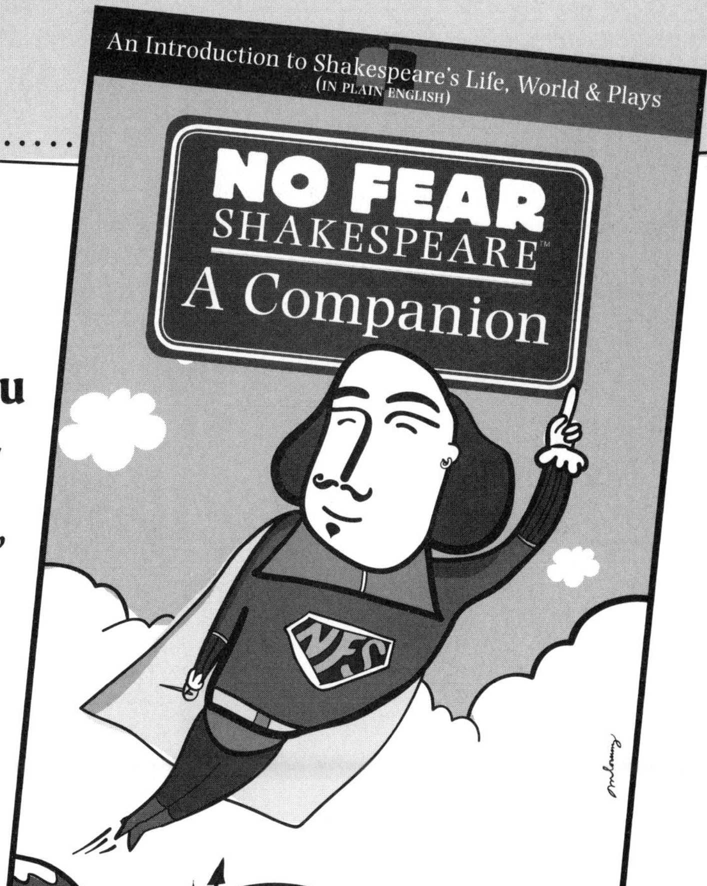
An Introduction to Shakespeare's Life, World & Plays
(IN PLAIN ENGLISH)
NO FEAR
SHAKESPEARE™
A Companion
NFS

Everything you need to know about the man, his work, and his world.

$9.95

No Fear Shakespeare: A Companion

ISBN-13: 978-1-4114-9746-7 ISBN-10: 1-4114-9746-5